Media for Your Life
A CONSUMER'S GUIDE TO EVERYTHING MEDIA

A Customized version of

Mass Communication: Producers and Consumers

Second Edition
by
Brent D. Ruben, Paul Reis, Barbara Iverson, Genelle I Belmas

Designed specifically for
Don Lowe
at the University of Kentucky

Kendall Hunt
publishing company

Cover image © Shutterstock, Inc.

Kendall Hunt
publishing company

www.kendallhunt.com
Send all inquiries to:
4050 Westmark Drive
Dubuque, IA 52004-1840

ᵈ in the United States of America

BRIEF CONTENTS

CONTENTS

x   CONTENTS

PREFACE

In the 50 years that introductory mass communication textbooks have been available, the definition of what constitutes mass communication has been expanding with each passing decade. Just a generation ago the study of mass communication was thought to encompass mainly the major news media: newspapers, magazines, radio, and television, along with books. Eventually the entertainment media—music and movies—were accorded space in textbooks. Then sections, and finally full chapters, were added to discuss advertising and public relations.

Today we need a still broader understanding of the concept of mass communication. First we must expand the catalog of mass communication instruments and institutions to include any carrier of information that goes "from one to many." The leaps and bounds that technology has made in the past several years changed the lives of people in countless ways and this will no doubt continue as technological advances further evolve.

The text is comprised of four parts:

Part 1: Understanding Mass Communication
Part 2: The Production of Information
Part 3: The Production of Information: Electronic Media
Part 4: Message Making

PART 1: UNDERSTANDING MASS COMMUNICATION

Chapter 1: Introduction

This chapter defines communication, mass communication, and mass media. It also presents an overview of the history of mass communication and identifies the components of a communication system. It explores the connection between media and culture and the significant changes taking place in mass communication and mass media.

Chapter 2: Mass Communication Effects

Researchers' ideas about the effects of mass media have evolved over time, and we review these as well as the theories of mass communication effects and the key issues in mass media research.

PART 2: THE PRODUCTION OF INFORMATION

Chapter 3: Books and Printing

The first methods used to create written documents, eventually making the modern book are explained in this chapter. Gutenberg's press and the print revolution transformed society, and the way books are made has changed and will continue to change as the book industry adapts to the digital age.

Chapter 4: Newspapers

This chapter outlines the historical development of newspapers in the United States as well as the evolution towards other news media, also identifying minority newspapers and explaining their purpose. It defines and distinguishes different forms of journalism such as jazz journalism and investigative journalism and identifies current trends in newspaper publication including online texts.

Chapter 5: Magazines

The magazine differentiated itself from books and newspapers and became a mass medium. Today's magazine industry moved from addressing a mass audience to addressing a specialized audience and digital media will also affect magazines, possibly to the point of them being available exclusively online.

PART 3: THE PRODUCTION OF INFORMATION: ELECTRONIC MEDIA

Chapter 6: Music Industry and a Shared Imagination

The invention of sound recording revolutionized music, and various recording formats are identified. Different kinds of music, such as rock and roll, have had a significant impact on American culture. Piracy and censorship are current controversies the music industry faces.

Chapter 7: Movies, Theater, Sports, and Evolving Forms of Entertaining

This chapter discusses how the entertainment industry performs many of the same roles as the news media. Technological changes are challenging the paradigm of the "blockbuster" mentality. Modern entertainment corporations apply synergy to their business deals. Mass entertainment has evolved since the 1970s, with increased popularity of theme parks, sports, and electronic games. The concept of an "attention economy" is also discussed.

Chapter 8: Radio

From the history of radio in its earliest days to the emergence of satellite radio, CPB stations, Internet radio and podcasts, this chapter explores radio growth and innovations.

The transition from military equipment to home entertainment device, the formation of networks, important figures in radio and news broadcasting, and talk radio are included in this chapter.

Chapter 9: Television, Cable and the Future

A description of how the television set and television broadcasting was developed, along with the different types of television programming and how the networks plan programming is explained. Cable television and future trends in the television industry are also discussed.

Chapter 10: The Internet

The concept of connecting computer networks and how the Internet began is a focus of this chapter. The people instrumental in creating the modern Internet and the challenges and opportunities the Internet introduced to traditional media outlets, as well as the difference between one-to-many and many-to-many media is discussed. Major concerns regarding the Internet and the role of social networking Web sites is explored.

PART 4: MESSAGE MAKING

Chapter 11: News

This chapter concentrates on identifying the characteristics that define newsworthiness and describes the concept of gatekeeping. It also identifies common criticisms of the news media and explains the effects of special interest groups and individual activists on news organizations. The seven adjectives that modern consumers look for in news are listed.

Chapter 12: Public Relations

The development of the public relations industry from inception to today is traced. Pioneering figures and their contributions, as well as the four public relations models and their major elements are outlined. The components involved in implementing a public relations plan and the varied roles and functions of public relations in the contemporary global marketplace are identified.

Chapter 13: Advertising

The evolution of the advertising industry as well as a description of how advertisements are used in mass media is a focus of this chapter. It also explains how advertisements benefit the consumer and media outlets and how the government regulates advertisers and how they regulate themselves. Future trends in the advertising industry are also listed.

Chapter 14: Law and Ethics

This chapter defines and distinguishes among law, policy, and ethics and explains the history, theories, and interpretations of free speech and free press in the United States. Legal, ownership, and regulatory issues faced by the mass media are identified and the ways in which ethics is relevant to individuals in the media, as well as to media organizations, is explored.

Chapter 15: Tomorrow's Media

Because the subject matter of this book in particular changes so rapidly, the last chapter is available via the Web so it can be updated frequently and remain current.

STUDENT ORIENTED PEDAGOGY

Because we recognize the importance of assessing student learning, we have included features that facilitate student learning and help instructors measure learning outcomes.

- Chapter Objectives preview the chapter content, focusing on the main points.
- Key Terms Lists/Running Glossary highlight the important terms in the chapter and provide clear definitions.
- Careers in the Field explore career potential and possible career growth areas.
- Discussion Questions encourage students to further explore the concepts they learned in the chapter.
- Glossary of Terms serves as a helpful reference tool at the end of the text.
- Web Material is integrated with the text to enrich student learning. The web access code is included on the inside front cover of the textbook. Look for the web icon in the text margins to direct you to various interactive tools.

ACKNOWLEDGMENTS

We gratefully acknowledge the constructive comments of the colleagues who provided reviews for individual chapters of this text. They include:

Ronald Allman
Indiana University Southeast

Maureen Asten
Worcester State College

Jeff Boone
Angelo State University

Douglas Campbell
Lock Haven University of Pennsylvania

Ginger Carter Miller
Georgia College & State University

Roger Desmond
University of Hartford

Bonnie Edwards
Mesabi Range Community & Technical College

William Florence
Chemeketa Community College

Cliff Fortenberry
Mississippi College

Barry Goldfarb
Monroe Community College

Neil Goldstein
Montgomery County Community College

Bonnie Gordon
Central Arizona College

Valerie Greenberg
University of the Incarnate Word

Edward Higgins
Montgomery County Community College

Anita Howard
Austin Community College

Matthew Killmeier
University of Southern Maine

Taehyun Kim
University of Louisiana at Monroe

Amy Lizie
Bridgewater State College

Christy McLean
Arizona Western College

Jad Menzie
Washburn University

Kathy Meyer
University of Wisconsin

Neil Nutter
Bloomfield College

Shirley Perry
Waynesburg College

Mark Phipps
Maryville University

Marilyn Ruengert
Pensacola Junior College

Carl Shriver
Ohio University

Rick Simmons
Western Illinois University

Susan Skotvold
University of South Dakota

Jacquelynn Smith
Wittenberg University

Matthew Snyder
University of Wisconsin

Melissa Stevens
Erie Community College

Gina Sylvester
Louisiana State University

Judith Tank
University of Wisconsin-Stout

Weiming Zarkin
Westminster College

UNDERSTANDING MASS COMMUNICATION

PART

1

INTRODUCTION

CHAPTER OBJECTIVES

- Define communication, mass communication, and mass media.
- Examine models of communication.
- Identify the basic components of the mass media industry including media conglomerates of today.
- Understand the depth of Americans' media consumption.

KEY TERMS

Communication
SMCR model of mass
  communication

Media conglomerate
sender, message, channel,
receiver

1

COMMUNICATION DEFINED

One of the oldest stories told about the differences in human perception comes to us from Ancient India. *The Blind Men and the Elephant* has been used to illustrate a range of truths and fallacies. In various versions of the tale, a group of blind men (or men in the dark) touch an elephant to learn what it is like. Each one feels a different part, but only one part, such as the side or the tusk. They then compare notes and learn that they are in complete disagreement. What we learn from this is that one's subjective experience can be true but that it does not account for other truths or totality of truth. This is the case for the task of defining communication. Many have their scientific perspective that clouds the overall definition, making one true definition nearly impossible to agree upon. With that said, we can then discuss a variety of offerings, combine them, and offer our own newly formed definition.

For decades, media scholars have offered their definitions of just what communication, that is, human communication, should be. Most vary in length and style but all share common roots, social scientific observation. Denis McQuail says, "there has never been an agreed definition of the central concept of 'communication'. The term can refer to very diverse things especially: the act or process of information transmission; the giving or taking of meaning; the sharing of ideas, information or emotion; . . ."[1]

There has, however, been one agreed upon basic model of the communication process. Sometimes known as a linear model of communication and sometimes referred to as the transmission or **SMCR** model. For our sake, we will use the latter. A basic **SMCR model of the communication process** includes four basic elements: the Sender→, the Message→, the Channel→, and the Receiver. Obviously, the *sender* is the source or origin of a message (in the case of mass media—the writer, director, producer, reporter, songwriter, rap artist, game developer, etc.), whereas the *message* is the information or emotion contained (in the case of mass media—the story, the photos, the advertisements with persuasive appeals, the newscasts, the songs, etc.) and the *channel* is the means through which you send the message (in the case of mass media—the book, magazine, newspaper, radio broadcast, film, television broadcast or cable program, and Internet web site) to an intended *receiver* (in the case of mass media—the reader, the audience, the viewer, the subscriber, and the listener) who receives and interprets the message.

From this, we can ascertain our modern definition as **Communication** occurs when human beings attempt to send one another messages using symbols across channels that naturally contain noise.

Mass Communication Defined

In order to define mass communication, we will use the traditional SMCR model of communication as it relates to mass media. We will look at basic areas including who (senders), what (messages), how (channels), and whom (receivers) as well as answer the questions how much (media consumption) and why (scientific method).

SENDERS

Who Owns the Media Business/Media Conglomerates?

So how does it all work? Who fits the bill? Why do we send so many messages across so many platforms so many times each day? The basic answer is simple—we have a few very large media conglomerates that make their money by sending messages through our various platforms. Before 1970, media outlets were primarily individually owned companies or small chains. Historically, most newspapers and radio stations were owned by members of the local community. Over time, this began to change. Changes in laws and regulations in the 1980s saw concentration of ownership move our system from hundreds of companies to just over 50 in 1983 and fewer than 29 by 1987.[2]

---

[1]Denis McQuail, *Mass Communication Theory: An Introduction* (London: Sage, 1987), pp. 52–53.

[2]*Hoover's Company Records—In Depth Records: Time Warner Inc.; Hooever's Company Records—In Depth Records: News Corporation.*

However, legislation passed by Congress in 1996 known as the Telecommunications Act dramatically changed the landscape of American media. This act relaxed most of the remaining rules that restricted the number of broadcast stations any one company could own.[3] Following this, a rapid turnover of properties and concentration of ownership occurred. The final product is today's **media conglomerate,** which is a very large corporation with large numbers of companies in various mass media platforms.

The five largest media conglomerates doing business in the United States are Time Warner, Disney, Viacom, Bertelsmann, and News Corporation.[4]

MESSAGES

What's in a Mass Media Message?

Mass media messages are as varied as the creators and distributors but essentially fall into only a few categories. While there are literally trillions or more messages sent daily by the thousands of mass media outlets, we can break those messages into smaller segments according to purpose. When we look at mass media messages in this way, we are left with only a few basic media messages or functions of the media, first brought forth by Howard Lasswell. They are providing *information* about the environment, which he termed surveillance; presenting options for *solving problems,* or correlation; and *socializing* and *education*, referred to as transmission. Charles Wright later added *entertainment* to Lasswell's list.[5]

Let us further examine these functions. To provide information, surveillance is primarily the function of news. Ideally, newspaper reporters and radio and television news personalities exist in order to provide our society (their readers and viewers) with the information that will keep them safe and bring order to their lives. In spite of how much we hate the local TV weatherman's interruptions of our favorite nightly programs, they are a necessary part of the function of the mass media. One, if not the most important function of the mass media, is to provide information that will keep the citizens in their audiences up to date on threatening situations in their environments, mainly weather related and other less immediate concerns such as the rise of illegal drug use or dangerous weapons as well.

Today, we say Google it. The idea of searching the Internet for information has been so dominated by one company that it has become a verb, Google. We often say I Googled it or Google it, when confronted with retrieving information necessary

---

[3]Brooks Boliek, "FCC Finally Kills off Fairness Doctrine," Politico, August 22, 2011. www.politico.com/news/stories/0811/61851.html;Dylan Matthews, "Everything You Need to Know about the Fairness Doctrine in One Post," Washington Post, August 23, 2011. www.washingtonpost.com/blogs/ezra-klein/post/everything-you-need-to-know-about-the-fairness-doctrine-in-one-post/2011/08/23/glQAN8CXZJ_blog.html.

[4]Ben H. Bagdikian, *The New Media Monopoly* (Boston: Beacon Press, 2004).http://budgeting.thenest.com/much-money-average-american-spend-entertainment-year-26018.html

[5]Lasswell, Harold. "The Structure and Function of Communication in Society." In *The Communication of Ideas.* Edited by Lyman Bryson. New York: Institute for Religious and Social Studies, 1948, pp. 37–51.

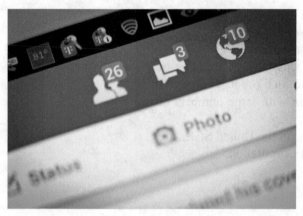

Message photo
© JaysonPhotography, 2014, Used under license from
Shutterstock, Inc.

for solving problems. Remember, Lasswell theorized that a function of mass media was to present options for solving problems. While Googling something has become synonymous with "researching" a subject, advertising has long since been the purveyor of this area. Since Colonial times, entrepreneurs have used mass media advertising to promote their business or service. From the local farmer selling apples in the monthly newspaper to Microsoft selling the latest iPhone app via push notification to your phone, advertising has been offering consumers options for solving problems for centuries (sometimes offering solutions to problems we didn't even know we had such as new Tide detergent to get our whites even whiter).

These advertisements often come sandwiched in between news and entertainment programs. Remember Wright added entertainment as a function of mass media (we can also use Lasswell's transmission here as entertainment media is often used to transmit culture from one generation to the next). Entertainment is where most of us live with mass media. We believe mass media messages to be ways to escape or avoid our realities—ways to relax and unwind—ways to get our minds off our problems. It's no wonder then that the vast majority of mass media messages are of the entertainment variety. Each year, the major media companies release hundreds of new songs, movies, books, magazines, TV shows, video games, web sites, and more. There are even magazines such as *Entertainment Weekly* and web sites such as E! online to help us navigate our way through all the choices. And then there's sports. Sports entertainment media continues to grow and include more and more sports (and even games such as poker tournaments on ESPN). We now have, in addition to magazines and web sites devoted to individual sports, cable TV channels that feature 24 hr of specific sports such as the Tennis Channel and the Golf Channel and even specific collegiate conferences such as the Big Ten Network and the SEC Network.

The sheer amount of mass media messages is often overwhelming to comprehend. Can we ever ascertain the exact number of mass media messages sent in a day? An hour? A minute? And do we really need to know the amount? Or do we simply need to understand the reasoning behind the messages being sent in the first place? These questions will continue to drive researchers for decades to come.

CHANNELS
What Is Mass Media?

We can now move forward and add the term mass media to our discussion. Platforms such as books, magazines, newspapers, radio, film, television, and the Internet, including messages that inform, persuade, or entertain—or a combination thereof, are the main channels known as mass media. While mass communication is about the message being conveyed, **mass media** is the channel or means through which we send the messages. There are thousands and thousands of mass media outlets around the world.

According to recent reports, in the United States alone, there are approximately 39,000 movie screens, 7 major motion picture studios, 1,400 daily newspapers, 6,700 weekly newspapers, 20,700 magazines, 1,937 broadcast television stations, 9,520 cable systems, over 330 cable networks, and thousands of book publishers.[6] Add to that hundreds of millions of web sites worldwide (some estimates go as high as 1 billion web sites) and don't forget the hundreds of new video games and smart phone apps that are consumed across new and diverse platforms such as smart phones, laptops, tablets, personal computers, and, of course, in their original forms.

RECEIVERS
Who Is the "Mass" in Mass Communication?

When we add the word mass to our description of communication, we complicate our definition immensely. To begin, how on Earth are we to define the word Mass? In media terms, mass has always been rather vague. What constitutes a mass is almost certainly going to differ from scholar to scholar as well as from school of thought to school of thought. Let's see what our scholars have to say once again.

Dennis McQuail says, "Mass communication is a network that connects very many receivers to one source . . . which can reach and involve all citizens to varying degrees . . . and can be seen as one of several community wide sources of communication."[7]

McQuail's thoughts are often reflected in traditional definitions of mass communication. Stephen W. Littlejohn says, "Mass Communication is the process whereby media organizations produce and transmit messages to large publics."[8]

While purposefully vague, from these definitions, we can suppose that the word mass can mean anything from one person to billions of people. Each day, media outlets around the world set new

Girl on ground with tablet
© Rasstock, 2014, Used under license from Shutterstock, Inc.

---

[6]Potter, Media Literacy: Newspaper Association of America, "Trends and Numbers," www.naa.org/ TrendsandNumbers.aspx; American Society of Magazine Editors, "Magazine Media Factbook 2011/2012." www.magazine.org/asme/editorial_trends/index.aspx; National Association of Theater Owners, "Number of U.S. Movie Screens," www.natoonline.org/statisticsscreens.htm.

[7]Denis McQuail, *Mass Communication Theory: An Introduction* (London: Sage, 1987), pp. deleted??

[8]Stephen W. Littlejohn, *Theories of Human Communication* (Belmont, CA: Wadsworth Publishing Company, 1999), p. 327.

viewership/readership records. The 2014 Super Bowl, according to CBS, had over 110,000,000 viewers in spite of the fact that the game wasn't very competitive.[9] The widely popular Summer Olympic Games exceeded 4.5 billion viewers (of at least some portion of the 2-week programming) for each of the last two competitions—that number is nearly 70% of the world's population. Popular online web sites such as Google can receive upward of 5 billion visits in a single day while Facebook has fewer users with more visits for a whopping 2 billion.[10]

CONSUMPTION OF MEDIA

Thus far, we have the *what* (our definition of mass communication), the *how* (our model of mass communication), and the *who* (the big media conglomerates); now we must turn our attention to *how* much mass communication we consume and then attempt to explain *why* we consume as much as we do.

Last year, the average American spent over $2,500 on media products.[11] These products included new apps for smart phones, games for portable devices, e-titles for book readers and tablets, music and podcast downloads, satellite radio services and more traditionally, cable TV and home Internet services, movie tickets, magazine and newspaper subscriptions, DVDs, compact disks, and the list goes on.

Buy box of media
© Max Griboedov, 2014, Used under license from Shutterstock, Inc.

We don't just use mass media, we live with it. Recent statistics state that we use some form of media, on average, 8 hr each day.[12] Television viewing is still the owner of the largest percentage of our time coming in at around 3 hr per day per person (statistics vary greatly by age with children and retired persons viewing more than the average working adult). We spend, on average, around 2 hr online each day in our leisure time. This, of course, does not count going online for work purposes. We still read outside the Internet at the rate of about 1 hr each day and we spend around ½ hr using social media.[13]

However, our time spent participating in more than one mass media activity has been greatly increased by the advent of social media web sites and more and more portable devices. For instance, we don't just watch TV anymore, we watch TV and while doing so, we socialize by text, check Facebook, Tweet, post pictures to Instragram, pin items to our Pinterest boards, and more. We even work as we pay bills, look for solutions to problems, shop our favorite stores, do homework, all while laughing

[9]http://www.cbsnews.com/news/super-bowl-2014-ratings-set-new-record/

[10]http://www.statisticbrain.com/google-searches/

[11]http://budgeting.thenest.com/much-money-average-american-spend-entertainment-year-26018.html

[12]http://www.bls.gov/news/release/pdf/atus.pdf

[13]http://www.bls.gov/news/release/pdf/atus.pdf

at the latest antics of Sheldon on the Big Bang Theory (currently running for hours nightly on TBS).

If you take a quick look at a 24-hr day, it shows that we will spend one-third of our lives consuming media.

This exposes us to over 4,000 advertisements each day resulting in a startling 100,000,000 plus ads in the average American lifetime of 72 years.[14]

Social media
© Quka, 2014, Used under license from Shutterstock, Inc.

So, this is how we answer the question, why study mass media? To say that mass media is an essential part of our lives is quite the understatement. In my courses, students are often asked "Could you go an entire day without using/accessing any mass media?" and, of course, their responses are adamant Nos! Just the mere thought of "doing without" threatens their views of what is a normal day. Mass media usage is so engrained in our culture that when faced with the proposition of failing this course, students were prepared to drop the course while some said that they would change their major to avoid the assignment stating it would violate their rights to spend their leisure time as they please.

Heard enough? How much money and time we spend and the growing number of media outlets are figures that are obviously fairly easy to come by. Marketing firms provide the data to advertisers on a daily basis. The numbers are, have been, and will continue to rise and our technology seems to have no end in sight and neither does our appetite for new media.

Why Do We Consume So Much Mass Media?

But why? Why do we spend so much time on our tablets, phones, laptops, etc. and instead spend what seems like less time actually interacting with the people right next to us? Social scientists have been dedicating their professional lives to the pursuit of such questions.

In the United States, we have studied mass communication from a wide variety of perspectives. Many studies have been conducted in attempts to explain, understand, and erase the fear we have of mass media. Toward the end of the 1800s, people were starting to become wary of the media. They had just seen a massive shift in our basic fiber—our society, thanks to the Industrial Revolution, had quickly gone from primarily self-sufficient rural townships to large urban areas where people worked for wages, had leisure time, and expendable income. People began to fear that the mass media, largely blamed as being responsible for most of this shift in lifestyle, were replacing the church, family, and community in shaping public opinion. Around 1920, researchers began using social scientific research methods to study mass media and its effects on audiences (Chapter Two is devoted to this pursuit). This field of study has continued to grow and encompass more

---

[14]http://www.youtube.com/watch?v=ZWNXg7Vt-ig

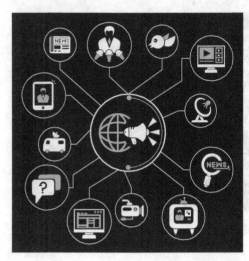

Vector
© phipatbig, 2014, Used under license from
Shutterstock, Inc.

and more areas of concern as we add more media platforms and messages at an alarmingly fast rate. Why do we flock to mass media many times a day in habitual ways? Social scientists are only beginning to understand this phenomenon. In addition, also of great concern is the issue of what effects are the users exposed to? Again, more on these engaging topics is coming up in Chapter Two.

CONCLUSION

It is at this point that many students start to become alarmed about their interactions with mass media. They have, by reading this opening chapter, been exposed to information and theories they have never before considered. Armed with huge numbers and newly formed fears, they begin to distrust all things related to mass media. This is not the attempt of this textbook or this course. This textbook is merely a means to an end. In the chapters that follow, we will give you (1) an overview of the history of American mass media, (2) an overview of the results of social scientific research in regard to mass media consumption and its effects on consumers, and (3) a discussion of issues that cross all media platforms including advertising, media law, and media ethics. The attempt of this textbook and course is to give you, the student reader, the necessary information to become a better consumer of mass media.

Finally, to complete our understanding of just what is and how we define mass communication, let us offer this modern definition: **Mass communication** occurs when professionals create messages for large audiences in attempts to inform, persuade, or entertain.

SUMMARY

- Communication occurs when human beings attempt to send one another messages using symbols across channels that naturally contain noise.
- Mass media is the channel or means through which we send the messages.
- Media conglomerates are very large corporations with large numbers of companies in various mass media platforms.
- The five largest media conglomerates doing business in the United States currently are Time Warner, Disney, Viacom, Bertelsmann, and News Corporation.
- Americans consume mass media on average for 8 hr each day and spend over $2,500 monthly on media products.
- Mass communication occurs when professionals create messages for large audiences in attempts to inform, persuade, or entertain.

DISCUSSION QUESTIONS

1. How would you feel if you were forced to do without any contact with any form of mass media for a 24-hr period? Could you do it? Would it be easy for you? Difficult for you? Explain.
2. Discuss the dangers of only five media conglomerates controlling the majority of mass media messages in this country. What can be done to protect freedom of information?
3. Why, in your opinion, do Americans spend so much time using mass media? Is that a problem? Why or why not?
4. If you had the opportunity, what would you change about the way the United States runs mass media corporations?
5. What do you see as the future of mass media? More messages? More platforms? One unified platform? Discuss.

SUPPLEMENTAL WEB SITES

Media Timeline
https://elearning.uky.edu/webapps/portal/frameset.jsp?tab_tab_group_id=_22_1
    &url=%2Fwebapps%2Fblackboard%2Fexecute%2Flauncher%3Ftype%3D
    Course%26id%3D_97473_1%26url%3D

SUPPLEMENTAL READINGS

SUPPLEMENTAL VIDEOS

Media in Everyday Life
http://www.youtube.com/watch?v=ZWNXg7Vt-ig
Media Consumption in the United States
http://www.youtube.com/watch?v=nCzOGAIJIpU

MEDIA EFFECTS

CHAPTER OBJECTIVES

- Understand the basic evolution of mass media research.
- Review and understand the basic mass media effects theories.

KEY TERMS

EPS Cycle Merrill and Lowenstein
Direct Effects Model (Uniform Effects)
Magic Bullet
Payne Fund Study
People's Choice Study
Opinion leader, Two-Step Flow
Indirect Effects Model (Selective Effects)

Four classes of indirect effects
Behavioral, Attitudinal, Cognitive, and Psychological

Theories of Indirect Effects

Functional Approach	Spiral of Silence Theory
Agenda Setting Theory	Cultivation Analysis
Uses and Gratifications Theory	Technological Determinism
Social Learning Theory	Diffusion of Innovations

2

HISTORY OF MEDIA EFFECTS RESEARCH

In this chapter, we briefly examine the historical foundations of mass media effects research and overview the basic mass media theories used as foundations today. To begin such an endeavor, one must first examine the climate that produced the need for such inquiries. In the late 1800s, the United States saw enormous growth in population and literacy rates, migration to larger cities, and joining of the workforce—like no other period in its history. As immigrants came flooding through the northeast sea ports, the rise in manufactured goods simply skyrocketed. We went from a self-sustaining rurally dominated culture to one in which our citizens worked for wages and began careers. With these wages, they

Vector mass media jumble
© topform, 2014, Used under license from Shutterstock, Inc.

could purchase their own goods and services and, therefore, had more free time and expendable income. Enter the mass media, the earliest and still most powerful way for manufacturers to reach consumers with news of their latest products and services. The media have ever since been linked to big business and mass consumption of goods. This made even the most trusting of individuals take notice. Why? The move from rural to urban from self-sustaining to purchasing basic necessities such as food and clothing was not an easy one. Admittedly, for some, it was an exciting new proposition full of adventure and new ways of life to explore, but for most, it was the tearing away of the way of life they had known for generations. This sudden shift was unsettling and made people question the motives of those who were promoting the changes. In addition, motion pictures were, at first at least, a frightening proposition for most people had barely gotten used to the idea of seeing themselves in still photographs and now large objects such as boats and trains and horses were moving about on the walls. All of this and the World Wars would make for what seems to be an unending distrust of big business and mass media.

DIRECT EFFECTS MODEL

Magic Bullet Theory

When media studies began, people were, as mentioned earlier, quite cynical of mass media outlets. So much of what was studied, theorized, and published in those early days were often overgeneralized and reductive ideas to say the least. One such theory was the magic bullet theory (often referred to as the theory of uniform effects), which was the crudest form of a theoretical effects model.[1] Basically, the theory says that everyone exposed to a media message would react in the same manner. Harold Lasswell suggested the hypodermic needle metaphor of media after World War I (Lasswell, 1927, 1935).[2] Assumption was that viewers exposed to media messages would be helpless against bringing out their worst behaviors and thoughts.

Many critics of media at the time pointed toward motion pictures and theorized that viewers, especially young children, would be so impacted by viewing images on the big screens that they would not be able to control their urges to emulate the behaviors portrayed by Hollywood movie stars. The assumption was that if an actor on screen was smoking cigarettes and he was the hero of the film, young boys then would seek out cigarette smoking as a way to become heroes.

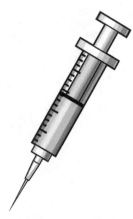

Hypodermic needle
© Tribalium, 2014, Used under license from Shutterstock, Inc.

---

[1] Richard Jackson Harris, *A Cognitive Psychology of Mass Communication,* 3rd ed., Lawrence Erlbaum Associates, Publishers, Mahwah, New Jersey, 1999, p. 17.

[2] Ibid.

Did some boys see actors smoking in films and take up the habit? Absolutely. Did *all* boys who saw actors smoking in films take up the habit? Of course not. We see this clearly today but remember, we are discussing a period in time nearly 100 years ago. Research was only beginning. We had many lessons to learn.

PAYNE FUND STUDY

One lesson to learn came from the Payne Fund Study. The overall impact of the Payne Fund Study was positive but some of the methods and reported results were a source of controversy.[3] As stated earlier, many were concerned with the mere exposure to motion pictures unlike printed materials before it that appealed to only one of the senses, many believed seeing motion pictures to be a multisensory experience. This, along with their growing popularity, caused certain questions to be raised about the influence that motion pictures were having on the audiences. The Motion Picture Research Council began efforts to study these concerns. The Payne Fund Study was one of the first large-scale attempts at measuring the impact of motion pictures on their audiences. It was one of the first times researchers considered a link between mass media and juvenile delinquency. A total of 13 reports were published in the 10-year research period from 1920 to 1930 and most of what was reported confirmed critics charges and parental fears. This is where the controversy occurred. The study revealed that 40 million minors in a year including almost half under 14 went to the movies on a weekly basis. While the findings did show that children who saw motion pictures on a regular basis were also likely to exhibit declining morals, delinquent behaviors, lower intelligence, and a number of other factors, the researchers were unable to show causality. That is, they concluded that there is no simple cause-and-effect relationship between motion picture attendance and juvenile delinquency. But instead, the relationship was more likely one of reciprocity, meaning children who saw violent movies were more likely to participate in juvenile delinquency and aggressive behavior before seeking out motion pictures with that content.[4] So allowing people to interpret the findings as generalizable to all children was somewhat unethical. This study would be a barometer for future research.

PEOPLE'S CHOICE STUDY

A more successful, more ethical study was the People's Choice Study of 1940, conducted by Paul Lazarsfeld during the 1940 Presidential Election in Eerie County Ohio, between Democratic President Franklin D. Roosevelt and Republican Wendell Wilkie. Often referred to as the Lazarsfeld Study, researchers

---

[3]Shearon Lowery, Melvin Lawrence DeFleur, *Milestones in Mass Communication Research: Media Effects*, Longman Publishers, USA, 1995.

[4]Ibid.

examined the correlation between exposure to mass media coverage of the campaign and voter behavior. In results still being used today, Lazarsfeld reported three major patterns in voter behavior and discovered the Opinion Leader as essential in a two-step flow process of mass media and interpersonal communication. First, voters who begin with strong opinions are unlikely to change those opinions regardless of campaign-related media messages. Second, voters who pay the most attention to media messages about a campaign are those with the strongest political views and are unlikely to change those views. Third, the most persuadable voters are those who are least informed and are not likely to pay attention to campaign-related media messages and are, therefore, not strongly influenced by those messages.[5]

Finally, Lazarsfeld suggested that information flows from media to opinion leaders and then to the general public, a two-step flow, and that instead of direct influence from mass media messages, voters are more likely to be influenced by people they know, respect, and interact with on a regular basis.[6] In other words, voters are more likely to change their voting behavior on the basis of information obtained through interpersonal communication with individuals whose opinions they respect than they would be from exposure to mass media messages alone.

This study helps move us from a rigid, somewhat unforgiving, model of media effects to the more modern, more scientifically sound, indirect effects model.

Indirect Effects Model

When defining an indirect effects model of mass media, Harris (p. 18), says, "We still believe that media can have substantial effects, but often they occur only under certain conditions. This is a model of selective effects based on individual differences."[7] Harris continues to say that people perceive the same message differently and respond to it in varied forms. We can see this in many forms in our society today. Are you a fan of the horror film franchise Saw? They have many sequels and much violence is portrayed in some of the most graphic scenes ever filmed. Many flock to the theater to get a front row seat; others shutter at the thought and won't even watch the trailers.

These selective effects must be measurable.[8] According to Harris, there are four general classes of measurable effects: behavioral, attitudinal, cognitive, and physiological. Asa Berger also discusses psychological effects.[9]

---

[5]Paul Lazarsfeld, Bernard Berelson, and Hazel Gaudet, *The People's Choice,* 3rd ed. Columbia University Press, 1968.

[6]Ibid.

[7]Richard Jackson Harris, *A Cognitive Psychology of Mass Communication,* 3rd ed., Lawrence Erlbaum Associates, Publishers, Mahwah, New Jersey, 1999, p. 18

[8]Ibid, p. 18.

[9]Arthur Asa Berger, *Media Analysis Techniques,* 3rd ed. Sage Publications, Thousand Oaks, California, 2005.

Behavioral Effects

Perhaps the most feared and yet the most difficult effect to achieve is that of behavioral change. We recall that the first to ponder the effects of mass media were afraid that watching violent movies would jump start the viewer to commit acts of violence of their own based solely on their media exposure. This is the emphasis among proponents of social learning theory, which is discussed later in this chapter. Although behavior may conceptually be the most obvious type effect, it is often very difficult to measure and even harder to definitively attribute a causal role to the media.[10] Examples of behavioral effects range from voting for a candidate, imitating a dance move seen on a Disney Channel show, clipping coupons, visiting a web site, and the list goes on and on. Behavioral effects, as stated earlier, are often what most people think of when they discuss mass media messages. While many fear the power of mass media messages, social scientists continue to struggle to find the appropriate structure to affect behavioral change through mass media. It is one of the most perplexing theories we examine in this text.

Attitudinal Effects

Less feared and less difficult to achieve would be the change related to attitudinal effects. The way we feel about something, someone, and some idea can be greatly influenced by media messages, but as stated earlier, making the change in attitude will not necessarily translate to behavioral change. Often cigarette smokers will tell you that they need to quit. Their attitude has been changed by exposure to information about the ills of smoking or firsthand observations of others or even their own poor health. Yet they continue to smoke cigarette after cigarette, day after day, with no real end in sight. The same can be said for those who are considered obese. They are often found saying that they need to lose weight and they know how to accomplish this feat—diet and exercise, proven entities in the war against obesity. Yet, they continue to overeat and under exercise, day after day, with no real end in sight.

Cognitive Effects

Simply put, this area of effects is about learning new information. Whether we intend to or not, through our exposure to mass media messages, we usually learn something. This learning takes place on a variety of levels. We may tune in to programs such as Myth Busters or cable channels such as Discovery or National Geographic feeling we are seeking knowledge. We learned from Myth Busters that we will have a worse hangover from drinking beer alone than if we drink liquor and beer, a myth busted for most will tell you it's the other way around. We may also view competition reality shows believing that we are just looking for entertainment but we learn something anyway. We certainly didn't know what

---

[10]Richard Jackson Harris, *A Cognitive Psychology of Mass Communication,* 3rd ed., Lawrence Erlbaum Associates, Publishers, Mahwah, New Jersey, 1999, p. 18

smizing (smiling with your eyes, a phrase coined by show producer Tyra Banks) was before America's next top model and we probably never heard people say to singers "it's a bit pitchy dog" before Randy Jackson popularized the phrase on American Idol.

A final note on cognitive effects, Political scientist Doris Graber found that people who want to be able to talk intelligently with others about media content (news, sports, or entertainment) learn much more from the media than people who are simply seeking entertainment. So, in short, cognitive effects depend greatly on the motivation level of the consumer.[11]

Physiological Effects

Probably, the least often measured but increasingly used are the physiological changes in our bodies resulting from exposure to the media.[12] Very similar to cognitive effects in that our motivations are often unclear, physiological effects are at least, in part, responsible for our choice of mass media messages. Scary movies have been documented to increase heart rate and induce rapid breathing. Pornography is a source of sexual arousal with many physiological effects. There are many medical studies that examine the impact of exposure to mass media messages. It is only recently that social scientists have employed techniques to measure physiological responses are part of the communication process. This area of research is in its infancy.

Psychological Effects

Exposure to mass media messages often results in a variety of feelings. People often seek emotional release from everyday stress and strain by listening to music, viewing a film, watching television, or browsing the Internet.[13] Fans of horror films tell you that they liked to be scared while fans of Nicholas Sparks novels say that they feel happiness during and after reading his stories. In short, media content can inspire fear, joy, revulsion, happiness, and amusement, among other feelings.[14]

THEORIES OF MASS COMMUNICATION

Functional Approach

As discussed in Chapter One, Lasswell put forth the idea of a functional analysis of mass media. In other words, what does mass media do? He stated three basic functions: they are providing *information* about the environment, which he termed

---

[11]Doris A. Graber, *Processing the News: How People Tame the Information Tide,* 2nd ed., Longman, New York, 1988.

[12]Richard Jackson Harris, *A Cognitive Psychology of Mass Communication,* 3rd ed., Lawrence Erlbaum Associates, Publishers, Mahwah, New Jersey, 1999, p. 20.

[13]Arthur Asa Berger, *Media Analysis Techniques*, 3rd ed. Sage Publications, Thousand Oaks, California, 2005

[14]Ibid.

surveillance; presenting options for *solving problems,* or correlation; and *socializing* and *education,* referred to as transmission. Charles Wright later added *entertainment* to Lasswell's list.[15]

Let us further examine these functions. To provide information, surveillance, is primarily the function of news. One, if not the most important function of the mass media, is to provide information that will keep the citizens in their audiences up to date on threatening situations in their environments, such as weather events posing immediate dangers and less threatening but equally dangerous wrongdoings or corruption of the government.

Surveillance camera
© martin33, 2014, Used under license from Shutterstock, Inc.

A second function Lasswell theorized was to present options for solving problems. While Googling something has become synonymous with "researching" a subject, we have many means to gain information so that we may weigh our options and make sound decisions. This is also true of advertising. Advertisers have long been comparing their products to their competitors giving us the reasons their offering is superior in categories that range from cost to environmental concerns. We learn that you can save 15% or more in just 15 min with a certain lizard-friendly company.

These advertisements often appear before, during, and after news and entertainment programs. Remember Wright added entertainment as a function of mass media (we can also use Lasswell's transmission here as entertainment media is often used to transmit culture from one generation to the next). Entertainment is the largest function of mass media for most of us. We spend tremendous amounts of time (remember our statistics about mass media consumption from Chapter One) daily with all things related to mass media from social media web sites to hours of TV watching to listening to music while we study and workout. It seems that we are never really without media as we want it to both entertain and keep us company.

Agenda Setting Theory

In addition to the People's Choice Study, another political campaign study adds to the literature of mass media effects theory. The agenda setting theory is attributed to Donald Shaw and Maxwell McCombs who write, "Considerable evidence has accumulated that editors and broadcasters play an important part in shaping our social reality as they go about their day to day task of choosing and displaying news. . . . This impact of the mass media—the ability to effect cognitive change among individuals, to structure their thinking—has been labeled the agenda setting function of mass communication. Here may lie the most important effect of

[15]Harold Lasswell, "The Structure and Function of Communication in Society." In *The Communication of Ideas*. Edited by Lyman Bryson. New York: Institute for Religious and Social Studies, 1948, pp. 37–51.

Phone and tablet used
© bloomua, 2014, Used under license from Shutterstock, Inc.

mass communication, its ability to mentally order and organize our world for us. In short, the mass media may not be successful in telling us what to think, but they are stunningly successful in telling us what to think about."[16]

McCombs and Shaw based their theory on results from a study conducted during the 1968 presidential election in Chapel Hill, North Carolina. Essentially, they found a strong correlation between the content of the press and the attitudes of voters. While they found no correlation between media messages and voting behaviors, there was evidence to support that issues featured in the press were issues that voters felt important.[17]

Uses and Gratifications Theory ⚹

This theory takes a much more modern, realistic view of the interaction between users and mass media as it places much emphasis on the active role of the audience in making choices and being goal directed in their media use behavior.[18] The experience and effects of media depend in part on the uses one is putting those media to and the gratifications one is receiving from them. Uses and gratifications theory is based on assumptions that include (1) audience members have wants and needs and make decisions about mass media usage based on those wants and needs, (2) mass media competes with other sources of gratifications, (3) audience members are aware of the choices they make, and (4) our value of the media usage comes from the audience members' perspectives.[19]

In today's society with DVRs and On-Demand TV services, audiences are more active than ever. No longer do we rush home in time to watch a basketball game, movie, or our favorite crime drama. We have so many options as to when and how we view television. This is in part, at least, a response to the user-driven Internet. Television founds itself being outdated by strict schedules and thus reluctant media corporations jumped on the new, more user friendly television viewing schema.

In short, the audience was found to be active and not passive in selecting media content for personal uses and gratifications. Choices are made on the basis

---

[16]Donald L. Shaw and Maxwell E. McCombs, *The Emergence of American Political Issues,* West, St. Paul, Minnesota, 1977.

[17]Shearon Lowery, Melvin Lawrence DeFleur, *Milestones in Mass Communication Research: Media Effects*, Longman Publishers, USA, 1995.

[18]Richard Jackson Harris, *A Cognitive Psychology of Mass Communication,* 3rd ed., Lawrence Erlbaum Associates, Publishers, Mahwah, New Jersey, 1999, p. 23

[19]Elihu Katz, Jay G. Blumler, and Michael Gurevitch, "Utilization of Mass Communication by the Individual" in *The Uses of Mass Communications: Current Perspectives on Gratifications Research* , Sage Publications, Beverly Hills, 1974.

of individual needs, interests, and values based on all aspects of socialization. Socialization will predispose the person to select certain media that they will use for diversion or entertainment or problem solving.[20]

Social Learning Theory ✯

Perhaps the most widely known social science experiment of all time is that of Albert Bandura's now legendary Bobo Doll Experiment. Essentially, Bandura exposed a series of children to behaviors in a playroom and then sent those children into the same playroom and observed their reactions. One group of children was shown only "normal" playful behaviors and did not involve any acts of violence. Those children, as expected, played quietly and did not engage in any form of violent behavior during their play times. A second group of children were shown playful behaviors in which the adult models repeatedly punched and hit a blow up Bobo Doll. Those children not only mimicked the adult's violent behaviors, they also created new ways to violently abuse the Bobo Doll including using toy guns to shoot it and a baby doll to strike it.

From these experiments, Bandura says, "humans go through steps to engage in social learning: (1) through observation they extract important information, (2) they create rules about how the world operates from those observations, and (3) they use these rules to guide their own behavior and predict the behavior of others."[21]

Bandura writes, "If knowledge and skills could be acquired only by direct experience, the process of human development would be greatly retarded, not to mention exceedingly tedious and hazardous."[22]

Spiral of Silence Theory ✯

Many times, we fear speaking out for fear of social ridicule or even punishment or retribution. Why is this such a common occurrence? Why do we, mostly bright, mostly educated, mostly current on the issues, people suddenly clam up when our opinion may not be received with praise? One theorist's explanation is called the spiral of silence theory. Elisabeth Noelle-Neumann demonstrated how interpersonal communication and media operate together in the development of public opinion.

The spiral of silence occurs when individuals who perceive their opinion is popular express it, whereas those who do not think their opinion is popular remain quiet. This process occurs in a spiral, so that one side of an issue ends up with much publicity and the other side with little.[23]

The spiral of silence, then, is a phenomenon involving personal and media channels of communication. The media publicize public opinion, making evident

---

[20]Stan Le Roy Wilson, *Mass Media/Mass Culture: An Introduction*. New York: McGraw Hill, 1994, pp. 3–21.

[21]Albert Bandura, "Social Cognitive Theory of Mass Communication," in *Media Effects: Advances in Theory and Research*, Lawrence Erlbaum and Associates, Hillsdale, NJ, 1994.

[22]Ibid.

[23]Elisabeth Noelle-Neumann *The Spiral of Silence: Public Opinion—Our Social Skin*, University of Chicago Press, Chicago, 1984.

which opinions predominate. Individuals express their opinions or not depending on the predominant points of view; the media, in turn, attend to the expressed opinion, and the spiral continues.[24]

Cultivation Analysis

Expanding on the idea that exposure over time truly does make a stronger, more lasting impact on the user of mass media than does one limited exposure, George Gerbner, put forth the theory of cultivation analysis. Primarily concerned with television, Gerbner believed that because it is the great common experience of almost everyone, it has the effects of providing a shared way of viewing the world. He writes, "Television is a centralized system of storytelling. It is part and parcel of our daily lives. Its drama, commercials, news, and other programs bring a relatively coherent world of common images and messages into every home. Television cultivates from infancy the very predispositions and preferences that used to be acquired from other primary sources. Transcending historic barriers of literacy and mobility, television has become the primary common source of socialization and everyday information (mostly in the form of entertainment) of an otherwise heterogeneous population. The repetitive pattern of television's mass produced messages and images forms the mainstream of a common symbolic environment."[25]

Because the idea of cultivation, especially in the context of television, is so prevalent among media scholars, a more popular subtheory if you will has evolved out of Gerbner's findings. It is a subtheory that often overshadows cultivation analysis; it is known as mean world syndrome.

Heavy television viewing cultivates a response Gerbner calls the Mean World Syndrome. He stated, "The most general and prevalent association with television viewing is a heightened sense of living in a "mean world" of violence and danger. Fearful people are more easily manipulated and controlled, more susceptible to deceptively simple, strong, tough measures and hardline postures. . . . They may accept and even welcome oppression if it promises to relieve their insecurities. That is the deeper problem of violence-laden television."[26]

Further Gerbner believed that heavy viewers of televised violence are more likely to (1) overestimate their chances of experiencing violence, (2) believe that their neighborhood is unsafe, (3) believe that crime is a serious personal problem, and (4) assume that the crime rate is rising.[27]

Little girl TV violence
© Alexandra Thompson, 2014, Used under license from Shutterstock, Inc.

---

[24]Ibid.

[25]George Gerbner, Larry Gross, Michael Morgan, and Nancy Signorielli, "Living with Television" in *Perspectives on Media Effects*, Erlbaum, Hillsdale, N.J., 1986.

[26]Wilson Biographies, "Gerbner, George," Wilson Web, hwwilsonweb.com.

[27]Gerbner et al., "Growing up with Television."

Technological Determinism

Canadian scholar Marshall McLuhan famously stated "the medium is the message." He wrote, "For the past 3,500 years of the Western world, the effects of media—whether it's speech, writing, printing, photography, radio or television—have been systematically overlooked by social observers. Even in today's revolutionary electronic age, scholars evidence few signs of modifying this traditional stance of ostrichlike disregard."[28] McLuhan held that inventions in technology invariably cause cultural change.[29]

Consider the idea that each time a new medium is created, our society reacts, adopts, and changes because of that creation. Now imagine we take away all media (remember from Chapter One my students' reluctance to do so) and where are we as a society? Thankfully, we will never have to experience this.

So, we can agree with McCluhan and say with some certainty that each new medium has changed the way we live. Think about your life before you got a cell phone—how dramatically has the way you send and receive messages both interpersonally and from the mass media changed? What about life before the Internet? Get the picture? Thought so.

Diffusion of Innovations

How long does it take for you to get a new cell phone? Do you envy those with the latest updated technology while you anxiously wait for your contract to expire so you can run to nearest phone dealer to upgrade? Or are you content with the model cell phone you've had for several years? The diffusion of innovations theory, by Everett M. Rogers, says that the way we adopt new technology or innovations.[30] The diffusion of information is one of the most significant outcomes of communication. Often distributed information promotes the adoption of innovation.[31] The diffusion of an innovation occurs when an idea spreads from a point of origin to surrounding geographic areas or from person to person within a single area. Rogers relates dissemination to the process of social change, which consists of invention, diffusion (or communication), and consequences.[32]

Diffusion
© T. L. Furrer, 2014, Used under license from Shutterstock, Inc.

28"Playboy Interview: Marshall McLuhan," *Playboy*, March 1969, p. 54.

29Ibid.

30Everett M. Rogers, *Diffusion of Innovations*, 4th ed. Free Press, New York, 1995.

31Ibid.

32Ibid.

So, we adopt certain technologies and even behaviors through the process of diffusion (communication), and this adoption may take many years or may occur quite suddenly. Therefore, people are more apt to adopt earlier than others for a variety of individual differences but the essence of diffusion is that we teach others, inform each other, and persuade each other to adopt new technologies and often new behaviors through this process.

EPS CYCLE

Formulated by John Merrill and Ralph Lowenstein in 1971, the EPS cycle of media adoption is a very useful tool in examining the relationship between society and mass media. The three-stage cycle is (1) elite—a small number of people usually wealthy and powerful, (2) popular—the majority of the population is exposed to the same message, and (3) specialized—the population is segmented into small groups usually by interest levels and each group has a specialized message.[33] Essentially, Merrill and Lowenstein theorized that as we adopt new media, each society will likely be exposed to that new media in a very deliberate process. Usually, new media is expensive as well as complex to the novice consumer and the ability to use it generates at least a small amount of power over those who have not yet mastered the use. Take books and the written word, for example. When language became something that could be mass produced, it was rare. Very few could read and write so books were only for the elites, the religious leaders, and the monarchies. As time went on and inventions made printing faster and less expensive, more books were printed, and therefore, more people began to read. In its early stages, the public stage of book adoption was wildly popular. Books moved into a part of mostly everyone's lives (in developed countries of course) and everyone read generally the same books. In today's society, books are definitely in the specialized stage with so many titles available for mostly any taste. Books come in so many categories it would be difficult to attempt to name them all here.

CONCLUSION

So now we can see that there is, to say the least, a very vast body of knowledge that has been gained through social science's examination of mass media. In this chapter, we have only begun to cover this fascinating and perplexing series of questions. What we have seen and social scientists have experienced is an evolution from a direct effects model (uniform effects) in which we believed everyone exposes to a media message would be impacted in the exact same way to a more modern workable model, indirect effects model (selective effects). In this model, we believe that everyone exposed to a media message is impacted differently and

---

[33]Stan Le Roy Wilson, *Mass Media/Mass Culture: An Introduction*. New York: McGraw Hill, 1994, pp. 3–21.

responds differently based on individual differences. Finally, today, we understand that the audience is found to be active and not passive in selecting media content for personal uses and gratifications. Choices are made on the basis of individual needs, interests, and values based on all aspects of socialization. Socialization will predispose the person to select certain media they will use for diversion or entertainment or problem solving.

We have a long way to go and much more to discover about mass media messages and their impacts on consumers. We have moved from a fearful place to a place of guarded optimism that instead of being powerless over large media corporations and their strong messages that we, the consumer, are becoming more media literate and, therefore, better media consumers with each passing day.

SUMMARY

- Mass media effects researched evolved from a rigid view of uniform direct effects model to a variable-based view of selective indirect effects model.
- Early media hypotheses and studies such as magic bullet theory and the Payne Fund studies helped researchers understand the fallacies of overgeneralization and the dangers of rushing to report results.
- Media effects research generally looks for effects in general classes: behavioral, attitudinal, cognitive, physiological, and psychological.
- Media is often adopted using and EPS cycle featuring elite, popular, and specialized stages.
- Lazarsfeld discovered the opinion leader as an important part of a two-step flow of communication from mass media message to individuals.
- The basic theories of mass communication include but are not limited to

Functional Approach	Spiral of Silence Theory
Agenda Setting Theory	Cultivation Analysis
Uses and Gratifications Theory	Technological Determinism
Social Learning Theory	Diffusion of Innovations

DISCUSSION QUESTIONS

1. Do you think people are afraid of mass media? Why or why not?
2. Which of the four classes of mass media effects do you think affects you most on an individual level? Why?
3. Pick one of the theories of mass media and relate it to a modern medium, that is, TV show, film, web site, video game, and song. How can you support the theory with your example medium?
4. Is the world a threatening, violent place to live? Why or why not?
5. Which of the theories of mass media do you believe to be the most relevant to our everyday lives? Why?

SUPPLEMENTAL WEB SITES

SUPPLEMENTAL READINGS

SUPPLEMENTAL VIDEOS

Bandura Bobo Doll
http://www.youtube.com/watch?v=Z0iWpSNu3NU
Gerbner Cultivation Analysis/Mean World Syndrome
http://www.youtube.com/watch?v=ylhqasb1chI

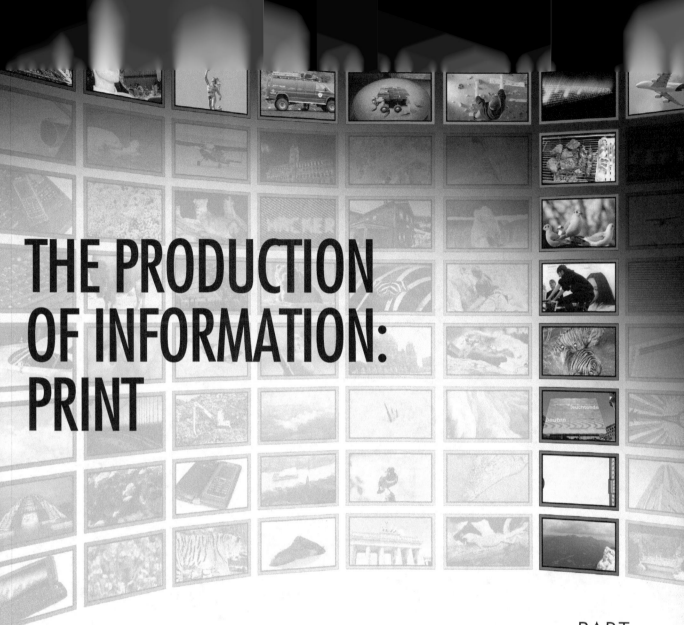

THE PRODUCTION OF INFORMATION: PRINT

PART

2

BOOKS AND PRINTING

CHAPTER OBJECTIVES

- Understand the first methods used to create written documents and how those methods evolved into the modern book
- Describe the print revolution and why Gutenberg's press had a major affect on society
- Explain why paperbacks were introduced and the purpose that they serve
- Name and explain the different categories of books
- Name two changes the book industry will need to make as the world adapts to the digital age

KEY TERMS

block printing
codex
copyright
dime novels
incunabula
International Standard
    Book Number (ISBN)
moveable type

papyrus
parchment
print-on-demand
pulp fiction
scriptoria
vanity presses
vellum
vernacular languages

INTRODUCTION

What comes to mind when you think of books? As a student, the image of a tall stack of textbooks may appear in your mind or perhaps dusty reference books on a library shelf. In this age of DVR, text messaging, and the Internet, it is easy to forget that the book is a major form of mass media. While many Americans may look to more high-tech forms of media for information or entertainment, books are far from being a dying industry. According to the Association of American Publishers, book sales topped $25 billion in 2007. More than $3.7 billion of that total revenue came from higher education books, such as this textbook. Overall the book industry has seen a compound growth rate of 2.5% each year since 2002, showing the largest growth in the adult hardbound (3.4%) and religious (7.1%) books. These promising numbers show that the book industry is vibrant and thriving and shows little sign of slowing down, even in the digital age.

To better understand how the book industry has stayed relevant for thousands of years, let's look at the early stages of books and printing.

BOOKS IN THEIR EARLIEST FORM

The production of books would, of course, not be possible without writing. Mesopotamian legend states that a high priest of the ancient city of Uruk invented writing by pressing symbols into wet clay. Current research suggests that writing may have begun as early as 7000 BC. Some archaeologists now maintain that small clay tokens found in Iraq, Syria, and Iran, which were once thought to be ancient games, were actually used to count goods. Upon further investigation, they found that the symbols on those tokens represented trade items such as grain.[1] A few thousand years later these symbols were put together to record information and tell stories in a primitive form of the book.

Many believe the earliest form of the book was created in 3500 BC by the Sumerians in Mesopotamia. Sumerians pressed symbols into clay with a triangular stylus, or writing utensil. The clay was then cut into tablets and dried or fired for longevity. One of the oldest surviving books was inscribed on a clay tablet around 4000 BC. The writing on the tablet told a Chaldean story of a great flood that engulfed the earth. By 2000 BC, the ancient cultures of Egypt, Rome, and Greece used scrolls to record information. Unlike clay tablets, scrolls could be rolled up and easily stored. The first scrolls were made of **papyrus**, from which the word *paper* is derived. They were created by mashing papyrus plants into a watery pulp and then pressing the pulp into long rolls. The rolls were then dried and inscribed with handwritten symbols. Many historical documents such as the *Book of the Dead* and the Bible were created on papyrus scrolls.[2]

For many cultures, scrolls or other writing materials were made of items that were abundant in the region: the Chinese wrote on tablets made of bamboo, Indians used birch bark and palm leaves, and Middle Eastern societies used leather. Around 200 BC, Middle Eastern societies replaced leather with

papyrus
a plant that is mashed into a watery pulp and then pressed into long rolls for use as a material on which to be written

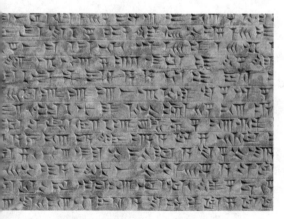

Many believe that clay tablets were the earliest form of the book.
© Kmiragaya/Shutterstock

---

[1]Andrew Lawler, "Writing Gets a Rewrite," *Science*, 29 June 2001, Volume 292, Number 5526, pp. 2418–2420.

[2]Philip G. Altbach, Edith S. Hoshino, *International Book Publishing*, Garland Publishing, Inc. New York 1995.

parchment, a thin material made from calfskin, goatskin, or sheepskin.[3] Unlike leather, parchment was not stretched, tanned, or treated in any other way, leaving it as a stiff, yellowish or translucent material. Parchment is also sometimes referred to as **vellum**, a finer quality of parchment.

Books began to take a modern form around 100 BC when the scroll was replaced with the Roman codex. In the **codex**, sheets of papyrus are folded to make pages, and then the pages are covered with waxed wooden tablets and bound together by string. The codex had several advantages: sections of text could be easily accessed, both side of the leaf could carry writings, and longer text could be bound together in one volume.[4] Vellum eventually replaced papyrus in the codex. This form of book was used for several centuries until the Chinese introduced paper.

The first paper was made of hemp, bark, and used fish nets. Chinese records state that papermaking was invented in 105 by Ts'ai Lun; however researchers believe that paper had been made for at least two hundred years before that date. Still, paper did not reach Europe until nearly the thirteenth century.[5]

parchment
a thin material made from calfskin, goatskin, or sheepskin that is untreated and used as a material on which to be written

vellum
a finer quality of parchment

codex
a method of book making in which sheets of papyrus are folded to make pages, and then the pages are covered with waxed wooden tablets and bound together by string

The Royal Alexandria Library

In 295 BC, King Ptolemy I Soter of Egypt enlisted the services of Demetrios Phalereus, a former governor of Athens, and asked that he collect, or try to collect, every book in the world. Ptolemy and Demetrios envisioned creating the world's largest library in the Egyptian city of Alexandria. To aid Demetrios in this monstrous task, the king sent letters to all known sovereigns and governors throughout the world and requested all works by poets, rhetoricians, doctors, historians, and law makers. Several scouts were sent to cities in Asia, Europe, and North Africa to purchase scrolls and manuscripts. The Library of Alexandria flourished under the control of Ptolemy's son Philadelphus, and then his grandson Euergetes, but many works were acquired through unscrupulous methods. All foreign ships that entered Alexandria were searched for written works. The transcripts of confiscated documents were eventually released to owners, but the originals were kept in the library. Euergetes also convinced the people of Athens to let him borrow the original manuscripts of great Greek poets such as Sophocles, Aeschylus, and Euripides on the promise that they would be safely returned after they were copied, but instead Euergetes kept them and placed the documents in the library. Eventually the library became so large that it needed to expand. A second library was created at the temple of the god Serapis, called the Serapeum. From what historians know, almost a half a million books were housed in the Library of Alexandria

---

[3]Ibid.

[4]book. *Encyclopedia Britannica* at http://www.britannica.com/EBchecked/topic/73295/book. Accessed November 25, 2008.

[5]Book History Timetable, Resources for the History of Books and Printing, University of Pennsylvania. Retrieved from http://www.xs4all.nl/~knops/timetab.html.

and the Serapeum, making it the largest library of the ancient world.[6] Unfortunately, the Library of Alexandria was damaged by fire in the year 47 when Julius Caesar's troops overwhelmed the city. The majority of the works were destroyed. More damage was inflicted in the late 200s AD during a civil war, and by 400, there was nothing left. In 2003, the Library of Alexandria was re-inaugurated with a replica of the library's Great Hall. The architectural details of the building are based on scholarly evidence.[7]

scriptorium
a room in a monastery used for writing

block printing
a printing technique that used pieces of paper applied to a block of inked wood

moveable type
a printing technique in which individual characters were created and put together to create a full text

Books Become a Mass Medium

During the early stages of bookmaking, access to books was limited, even for members of royalty and the upper class, due to the fact that most works only had one copy. During the Middle Ages, early Christian monks laboriously copied manuscripts by hand in their **scriptoria**, rooms in monasteries for writing. Such duplication was time-intensive, making books scarce and expensive during this period. These manuscripts were the models for the first printed books. Actual printed books appeared in Asia with the invention of **block printing**. The printing technique used pieces of paper applied to a block of inked wood. The entire text was carved in reverse onto a block of wood, making the duplication process fairly easy. The earliest carved printing block was found in Korea and dates from 750 to 751 AD. The oldest printed book, *Diamond Sutra* by Wang Chieh, was produced with block printing in China in 868.[8] The technique was unique to Asia for more than 500 years. Italian explorer Marco Polo discovered block printing during an expedition to the Far East and brought the technique to Europe.

While the introduction of block printing greatly increased the number of printed works, it was the advent of movable type that set the book on the path to becoming a mass medium. With **movable type**, instead of entire pages carved into one block of wood, individual characters were created, first in clay and later in wood and metal. Moveable type had many advantages, the most obvious being the ability to move around and reuse letters. Any letters that were lost or worn could be replaced at little cost, as letters were made with a mold which made them cheap to produce. Movable type also made it easier for the reader. The individual blocks created a standardized size and shape to each letter, which resulted in a uniform, easy to comprehend text.[9] One of the earliest metal movable types was invented in Korea in 1234.

With moveable type, individual characters are created so letters can be moved around and re-used.
© Dariusz Sas/Shutterstock

[6]Kelly Trumble, The Library of Alexandria, Clarion Books, New York 2003.

[7]SIS Publications, Perspectives, *Egypt Magazine*, Winter 2003. Retrieved from http://www.sis.gov.eg/En/Pub/magazin/winter2003/110225000000000007.htm.

[8]Sacred Text: Diamond Sutra, British Library. Retrieved from http://www.british-library.uk/onlinegallery/sacredtexts/diamondsutra.html.

[9]Thomas Kingston Derry, Trevor I. Williams, *A Short History of Technology*, Courier Dover Publications Mineola, New York 1993.

The Gutenberg Revolution

Johannes Gutenberg, a German goldsmith, is associated with the "invention" of printing because he brought various printing technologies together in a way that made quality reproduction of books and pamphlets possible with greater speed and lower cost. While Gutenberg did not invent movable type, he revolutionized its use with the invention of the first printing press. In his shop in Mainz, Germany, Gutenberg adapted a wine press, which had a giant screw that could be tightened and gradually move down against a flat surface, into a device that could be used for printing. Instead of pressing grapes into wine, he pressed sheets of paper against ranks of raised movable type arranged in words and locked into a flatbed form.

Gutenberg's printing press used a giant screw to press paper against movable type.
© *Crixtina/Shutterstock*

While the time saved over manual duplication was tremendous, Gutenberg's press was still labor-intensive. Each page's type had to be hand-set and each sheet of paper pressed individually. The finished product was not cheap either. His two-volume Bible sold for 300 florins in 1455, the equivalent of a year's salary for an upper-level civil servant, three years' salary for a clerk. This version became known as the Gutenberg Bible. The number of original copies is unknown, but a few are preserved in history museums around the world.[10] Gutenberg's printing technique prevailed for centuries. Even after the evolution of high-speed rotary presses and, still later, electronic photo-offset and desktop publishing techniques that rendered raised metal printing obsolete, Gutenberg's basic concepts survived. Today, some specialized printing is still performed on flatbed presses modeled after Gutenberg's original press.

While Gutenberg's name became known throughout the world, Gutenberg died a personal failure. His son-in-law, Johann Fust, actually carried out the printing operations that made Gutenberg famous. That printing operation ignited the imagination of others, who set up similar presses and gave birth to the craft of printing in Europe. Guilds of craftsmen became invested in production during the mid-fifteenth century, as printed materials were in high demand. Printed works from this period were known as **incunabula**, and are an important part of the printing revolution.

incunabula
printed materials from the fifteenth century

Why was it a revolution? Revolutions occur when basic functions of society are changed radically, such as an overthrow of government—or, for our purposes, when innovation explodes, captures the attention of the masses, and reworks the fundamental ways that a society receives, distributes, and processes information. The printing press made a true mass medium possible for the first time. Through that medium, regular people were able to get information in numbers never before realized, injecting the concept of thought and scholarship into society.

The introduction of printing started many cultural changes. By the beginning of the sixteenth century, books printed in **vernacular languages**, non-Latin languages such as German and Italian, were available throughout Europe. Literate people, whose numbers were growing, could read materials that were not regulated

vernacular languages
non-Latin languages

---

[10]Gutenberg Bible. *Encyclopedia Britannica* at http://www.britannica.com/EBchecked/topic/249893/Gutenberg-Bible. Accessed November 25, 2008.

by the state or church and were limited to the highly educated. The ability to read independently, instead of being informed by priests, academics, or lords allowed individuals to create interpretations and raise questions on their own.

BOOKS IN AMERICA

As the book developed into a mass medium, it took on many roles. The book became a device used to inform, educate, and entertain the masses. It also became a device used to exercise the freedom of expression as the book industry developed in America.

Currently, the United Nations Educational, Scientific, and Cultural Organization (UNESCO) defines a book as a "non-periodical printed publication of at least 49 pages excluding covers." However, this definition is simply for statistical purposes. There is no strict definition of a book that satisfactorily covers the variety of publications that have been found throughout history.

Establishing an Industry

An Englishman named William Caxton set up his country's first printing press in 1476 and, in turn, was credited with printing the first books in English. With this newfound mass medium came governmental regulation: English governments licensed these presses, and censorship was common. Henry VIII had time between his many courtships to ban the publication of books not on an approved list, including most foreign titles. It was not until a general revolution broke out in 1640 that publishers routinely begin to defy the ever-changing laws regulating written expression.

It did not take long for the first American colonists, landing at Plymouth Colony in 1620, to start their own publishing enterprises. In 1638, former locksmith turned printer Stephen Day (sometimes spelled Daye) set up the first printing press in Cambridge, Massachusetts. Day was contracted by Reverend Jose Glover, a wealthy clergyman, to print religious texts for settlers. The *Freeman's Oath* and *The Whole Booke of Psalmes*, now known as the Bay Psalm Book, were among the first titles published in America. Day's press eventually became the forerunner for the Harvard University Press.[11] While printed books were available in the colonies, they were still expensive and difficult to distribute.

To solve this problem, shorter publications that were neither newspapers nor magazines, yet hardly substantial enough to put between hard covers, were created and fed colonist's appetite for information. The most celebrated of these publications was *Poor Richard's Almanac*, a compendium of planting information, proverbs, quips, commonsense health tips, tide tables, and comments on manners and morals. Poor Richard was a fictional character created by Benjamin Franklin. Franklin painted Poor Richard as a homespun philosopher from the country who

---

[11]Stephen Day. *Encyclopedia Britannica* at http://www.britannica.com/EBchecked/topic/153062/Stephen-Day. Retrieved November 26, 2008.

knows the value of hard work and honesty. Many of his practical proverbs such as "Early to bed, early to rise, makes a man healthy, wealthy, and wise" and "God helps those who help themselves" are still used today. Franklin edited the annual almanac from 1732 to 1757.[12] Today the approach of including short snippets of information is again popular, with the opening pages of such sites as Yahoo and AOL offering tidbits to readers.

Franklin opened the first lending library in 1731. As America grew, education was put at a premium, and the new school systems created new readers. Cities began to provide more services for their citizens, including free libraries. Book reading and publishing began to surge. By the 1850s, book prices dropped dramatically as machine-made paper replaced expensive hand-made paper and steam-powered printing machines produced books in mass quantities. Cloth and paper covers replaced leather covers, creating paperback titles that were accessible and affordable. Among the most popular paperbacks were the **dime novels**, books which literally sold for 10 cents, a few hours' pay for a laborer. These works were also called pulp novels or **pulp fiction** because of the cheap pulp paper used in their production.

By 1885, nearly one-third of all books sold were paperbacks or dime novels.[13] The "Luck and Pluck" series written by Horatio Alger, Jr. in the 1870s, similar to his earlier "Ragged Dick" and "Tattered Tom" series, appealed to recent immigrants who longed to pull themselves up by their bootstraps in the land of opportunity. Alger and other popular authors extolled the virtues of hard work, honesty, and willingness to try again in the face of adversity. Also during this period the American novel came into its own with the publication of such classics as *The Scarlet Letter* by Nathaniel Hawthorne and *Moby Dick* by Herman Melville, ending a dependence on Europe for quality fiction.

The almanac approach of including short snippets of information is popular even today.
© *Kenneth V. Pilon/Shutterstock*

dime novels
paperback books which literally sold for 10 cents

pulp fiction
paperback books made out of cheap pulp material

The Literate Society

In early colonial days, literacy was limited to aristocrats. But in the 1700s, literacy grew in colonial America, and unlike in Europe, reading was not an activity limited to the few. Tom Paine's *Common Sense*, published in 1776, is estimated to have sold 300,000 copies at a time when the country's population was only three million people, which would mean one in 10 colonists owned this particular title.[14]

The literacy rate in the United States reached 90% by the beginning of the twentieth century, and soon it began to seem as if writing the "great American

---

[12]Poor Richard. *Encyclopedia Britannica* at http://www.britannica.com/EBchecked/topic/469948/Poor-Richard. Retrieved November 26, 2008.

[13]Cynthia J. Davis, Kathryn West, *Women Writers in the United States*, Oxford University Press, New York 1996.

[14]Daniel J. Boorstin, *The Americans: The Colonial Experience* (New York: Vintage Books, 1958), p. 22.

novel" had become the goal of every college-educated American who was exposed to the writings of Dos Passos, Faulkner, Hemingway, and Steinbeck. Publishing and reading fiction would remain popular until television wrought its change on the American use of leisure time.

In 1939, publishing company Simon & Schuster's Pocket Books division introduced the mass market paperback format. Popular in the 1940s, 25-cent paperbacks, or pocket books were sold on newsstands and at train and bus stations, as well as in bookstores. During World War II the government urged publishers to issue slimmed-down versions of books for the troops to carry with them. Literary agent Richard Curtis calls paperbacks "the tail that wags the dog" of the publishing industry.[15] By the 1950s, the boom in paperback sales continued, and today they make up the majority of books sold in the United States. In 2007, consumers spent over $6 billion on paperbacks.[16] By the 1970s, paperback reprints of the previous year's best-selling novels were setting publishing records, with titles like *Jaws*, *Shogun*, and *The Godfather* selling as many as ten million copies—unheard of for a hardcover edition.

According to some analysts, however, paperbacks are not carrying as much weight in the publishing business as they once did. Despite strong sales, the format has seen sales decrease 2.5% percent over the last five years.[17] In 2005, in response to what it perceived to be an aging reading population, Simon & Schuster increased the height of some of its mass market paperbacks by three-quarters of an inch, to 7½ inches. This format allows larger type and additional space between rows of type—a move intended to aid those aging baby boomers. However, as we will discuss in the next section, "original paperbacks" have made an entrance into the publishing world and are continuing to increase in number.

Today's bookstores have grown to meet the needs of diverse consumers.
© Lucian Coman/Shutterstock

THE BOOK INDUSTRY

Like most major industries, the book industry must adjust to changing trends. Books, along with other forms of print media, have become specialized. One customer enters a bookstore and goes directly to the Health and Fitness section. Another is interested in a genre such as romance, gothic, or horror fiction. Today's bookstore is as complex as a major department store, thanks in part to the proliferation of the paperback—and easier to browse from the comfort of a home, an office or even a laptop in the park. We can find books we never knew existed and that it's likely that we'll like. And today's books are more likely to be read from a computer screen or cell phone, or listened to on an MP3 player, than ever before.

---

[15]http://www.bksp.org/secondarypages/articles/agentseditors/RCurtis2.htm.

[16]Industry Statistics 2007, The Association of American Publishers, March 31, 2008. Retrieved from http://www.publishers.org/main/IndustryStats/indStats_02.htm.

[17]Ibid.

The AAP's List

The Association of American Publishers (AAP), the main trade organization for the publishing industry, divides books into the follow broad categories, which can be further subdivided by genre:

- **Trade:** Subdivided into hardcover and paperback for both juveniles and adults; these are books distributed to the general public through booksellers.
- **Book clubs and mail order:** Titles that are delivered to niche markets.
- **Mass-market paperback:** Books often sold at magazine racks, newsstands, and supermarkets as well as traditional bookstores and book clubs.
- **Audiobooks:** Titles read or performed on cassette tapes, CDs, or MP3 files.
- **Religious:** Classic and modern religious works including scripture, hymns, and spiritually-based fiction and non-fiction.
- **E-books:** Books produced for use on an electronic reader. These are often sold online.
- **Professional:** Information particular to a specific field of business or trade, and directories or handbooks necessary for conduct of business. These often are sold through professional associations or by direct mail, as well as in retail outlets.
- **El-Hi (K-12 education):** Books published for the educational markets—primary and secondary.
- **Higher Education:** Textbooks or manuals used at the collegiate level.

Growing Markets

Between 2002 and 2007 the largest percent increases for traditional books were seen in the juvenile hardbound and religious categories. The sixth book in the blockbuster Harry Potter series of children's books, *Harry Potter and the Half-Blood Prince*, was released in July 2005 and sold 11 million copies in its first nine weeks. The seventh and final book, *Harry Potter and the Deathly Hollows*, sold more than 8 million copies in the first 24 hours of its July 2007 release.[18] J.K. Rowling's best-selling series of a teenage wizard and his exploits accounts for much of the increase in the juvenile market. Now that final edition of the series is released publishers hope other juvenile fantasy books such as *Twilight* and other works in the vampire series by Stephanie Meyer will create a similar jolt in juvenile sales.

The Harry Potter series was a blockbuster in the juvenile book market.
© *Walter Weissman/Corbis*

Similarly, religious book sales got a boost from *The Purpose-Driven Life* by California pastor Rick Warren, which sold about 2.5 million copies in 2005 and Joel Osteen's *Live Your Best Life Now*, which sold 3 million copies in 2007. The Book Industry Study Group suggests that the increase in the religious book market was due to increased sales in mainstream retailers and expects the genre to continue to do well in the next several years as well.[19]

---

[18]Steven Zeitchik, "Deathly Hallows' Sells 8.3 million" *Variety*, July 22, 2007. Retrieved from http://www .variety.com/article/VR1117968991.html?categoryid=21&cs=1.

[19]http://www.bisg.org/news/press.php?pressid=27.

The Oprah Effect

When Oprah speaks, America listens—or at least reads. Talk show host and media giant Oprah Winfrey started the Oprah Book Club in 1996 as a way to introduce her viewers to books she enjoyed, many not from the bestseller lists. However, her choices make bestsellers: When Winfrey chooses a book for her book club, it is almost a guaranteed bestseller. Known as "The Oprah Effect," her choice can propel an author from unknown to breakfast-table conversation in weeks. An example: Robert Morgan, an English professor whose book *Gap Creek* was chosen by Winfrey in 2000, reports that the book sold 650,000 copies within a month. Book club books tend to be primarily about women struggling against adversity. Jonathan Karp, editor-in-chief at Random House, notes, "If she gets behind a book, it's an avalanche. She has a massive audience that actually listens to her. . . No one compares to her." If a book is selected, publishers have a week to print and distribute up to a million copies with the Oprah Book Club seal on them. As every single Book Club choice has become a bestseller, they are happy to comply.[20]

The Industry's Cornerstone

Textbooks and educational materials for K-12 and college levels account for almost 40% of the 2007 revenue of the publishing industry—a percentage greater than either trade books or professional books. Consider, too, that the category of professional books enumerated by the AAP includes volumes needed for higher education. This fact further proves that textbooks are a major category of book publishing.

Because textbooks are such an important source of revenue for publishers, they must protect their **copyright**, or exclusive legal rights to reproduce, publish, sell, or distribute matter. A 1991 decision against Kinko's Copy Center for violating the Copyright Act encouraged an industry-wide clamp down on wholesale photocopying of protected materials. Book publishers, responding to the need for custom texts, have set up computerized operations that allow individual instructors to select from materials in a large database to request textbooks that reflect the material taught in their courses.[21] For example, custom publishing company XanEdu.com will work with a professor to develop a coursepack that is available either in printed or online versions and that is copyright-compliant. Despite the passing of the baby boom that populated the school systems in the 1970s and 1980s, the textbook market is expected to continue as a major sector of American book publishing.

copyright
exclusive legal rights to reproduce, publish, sell, or distribute matter

---

[20]Caitlin Kelly, "The Oprah Effect," *Broadcasting & Cable Magazine*, January 24, 2005.

[21]Robert E. Baensch, "Wither Custom Textbook Publishing?" *Publishers Weekly*, June 21, 1991, p. 27.

A Changing Market

Perhaps one of the most interesting changes in the book industry is the whopping 55.7% compound growth rate of *e-books*, or electronic books over the last five years. These books, either digital versions of traditional books or exclusively digital works, account for the lowest number of sales in the market, but have the most potential for growth. The public's familiarity with handheld electronic devices such as cell phones, personal digital assistants (PDAs), and digital music players, may eventually make consumers more comfortable with the idea of using an electronic book reader to virtually flip through the pages of their favorite book.

First-generation e-book reading devices, such as the Rocket eBook, were expensive and clumsy, and their manufacturers quit producing them in the early 2000s. Newer versions such as the Amazon's Kindle and the Barnes & Noble Nook have perfected the e-book technology so works can be read from a screen with the same comfort as from a page. E-book devises can cost $300 to $500, but e-books titles are usually half the cost of a traditional hardcover book and can instantly be downloaded and stored in one convenient device.

Audiobooks also account for a small section of overall industry sales, but like e-books, audiobooks have potential to grow with new technology. Audiobooks are audio versions of books that consumers can listen to rather than read, using a CD player or other personal audio device such as an MP3 player. The Audio Publishers Association estimates the size of the 2007 audiobook market over $1 billion, with downloadable sales showing the most growth, increasing by 50 percent a year since 2001. Nearly one in four adults listened to an audiobook in 2007. Audiobooks are not just one person reading into a microphone anymore—the award-winning book *Hitchhiker's Guide to the Galaxy* is a fully acted play, with actors and sound effects. You can also learn languages or take a class using audiobooks. The "Modern Scholar" series is available, with lectures from top professors from universities around the world. Audiobooks are available through many online bookstores, as well as through audiobook-only stores like Audible.com.

E-books provide the most potential for growth in the book industry.
© *Photosani/Shutterstock*

Today's Book Market: A Long Tail?

Specialization has become a trend in the book publishing industry, as it has in most other mass media. In his book *The Long Tail*, author Chris Anderson suggests that today's consumer is going "deep" rather than "wide" for his/her entertainment needs. The term long tail is derived from a statistical distribution pattern where a high population is clustered at one end and gradually trails off, and the aggregate of the long tail entries might overpower the obvious high population. In other words, if a consumer liked a certain book, that consumer is likely to look for similar books.

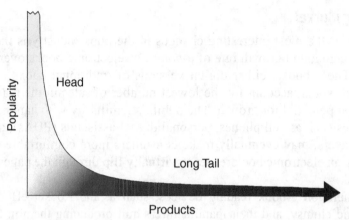

FIGURE 3.1 The new marketplace

Anderson provides the example of the sudden upsurge in sales of a 1988 book, *Touching the Void*, which was a story of survival in the Peruvian Andes, after the success of the 1997 book *Into Thin Air*, a story of surviving a Mount Everest climb. He attributes this phenomenon to Amazon.com's recommendations feature, where customers can see what others who liked a particular book also purchased. Publishers' backlists, books that have been in print for a year or more, have traditionally accounted for most of their sales. Under the long-tail scenario, they become even more important because customers want more of what they know they like.

Anderson suggests that the future of entertainment is selling more of less. In other words, breaking away from the blockbuster mentality that currently rules many entertainment business decisions and focusing instead on smaller runs of more specialized products. He quotes Amazon.com as saying, "We sold more books today that didn't sell at all yesterday than we sold today of all the books that did sell yesterday."[22] The trend may be hard to follow, but it is certainly heading towards the path of higher sales for the publishing industry.

A New Marketplace

As you probably realize, many books are purchased without the customer setting foot into a traditional brick and mortar bookstore like Borders, Barnes & Noble, or locally owned shops. Amazon.com, recognizing that books were one commodity a consumer did not need to try on or hold to purchase, hit the book-selling market in 1995. While not an immediate success story (the company did not turn an annual profit until 2004), Amazon.com became the harbinger of a new way to purchase books, CDs, DVDs, and other products like them. Traditional bookstores felt the heat: Amazon.com sold $2.8 billion in books, music, and DVDs in 2007.

---

[22]Chris Anderson, "The Long Tail" *Wired* October 2004. Retrieved from http://www.wired.com/wired/archive/12.10/tail.html.

Amazon.com provides many services a traditional bookstore cannot. As noted, consumers can get recommendations based on what they have already purchased. Other consumers can post lists on any topics they wish, to be viewed by any visitor to the site. A consumer can put items into a "wish list" for others to view and purchase as gifts. Amazon.com can remember what you purchased the last time and make suggestions on what you might be interested in today—a service sometimes rendered by a friendly clerk but reliant on memory and availability. Its innovative "one-click shopping" button permits a customer to immediately purchase a product without going through usual check-out procedures. Small publishers like Amazon.com because it gives their books a global reach, whereas traditional local bookstores have a far more limited audience.

Amazon.com does not provide the tactile sensation of feeling a book's heft or paging leisurely through it with a cup of coffee at your local bookstore (although you can see table of contents and sample pages), but its ability to connect consumers with other products and to make the online buying process relatively painless and seamless has made it an industry leader. In the spirit of "if you can't beat 'em, join 'em," Barnes & Noble opened its own virtual bookstore, barnesandnoble.com. Other traditional bookstores followed. Now most bookstores, whether national chains like Borders or local chains such as Powell's in Portland, Ore., have a web presence. Powell's, in fact, claims to have sold its first book online in 1993, "when Amazon was just a river."[23]

Online Personal Book Shoppers

No, these are not actual people who are paid to purchase books for very busy intellectuals. The term **online personal shoppers** refers to software programs that use very complex algorithm systems to try to "guess" what kind of products an online shopper might be interested in purchasing next.

If you have ever bought a book through Amazon.com or BarnesandNoble.com, chances are you have experienced these programs—even without being aware of them. Online personal book shoppers will make suggestions and create lists of books (or music or DVDs) each time you buy a book, and remind you of what were the books you purchased or browsed during your last visit. If they're doing their job right, online personal shoppers will actually generate new business for the web site, steering consumers to products they might actually be interested in purchasing and weren't aware of.

[23]http://www.powells.com/info/details.html.

What advantages does a tangible book have?
© Steven Belanger/Shutterstock

A Reusable Resource

The wonderful thing about a tangible book is that it is reusable. It doesn't dissolve after it is read once or have any digital sharing restrictions; it can be passed on to a string of new readers. Consumers spent $2.2 billion and 8.4 percent of total book spending on used books, buying over 111 million copies, according to the most recent report from the Book Industry Study Group.[24] Students, for example, spend 74% of their used-book dollars on books that were available new.

Much of this growth is attributed to the availability of used books on online bookselling venues, such as eBay's Half.com, Amazon.com used books, and online textbook stores like Ecampus.com. Abebooks.com, which proclaims 80 million used, new, and rare books, has a very active online community forum where participants can interact in an online book club and talk about everything related to books.

If you have a book you don't want anymore but don't want to throw out, share it with the world. BookCrossing.com allows users to print a registration label for any used book, register it on the web site and then release it into the world for another person to enjoy. For example, you can leave the used book with its respective label at a hotel, for the next guest to enjoy, and the label will allow the new owner to go back to the web site and "track" where the book has been and where it is going next. This social networking element allows BookCrossing members get the pleasure of watching a book be enjoyed by others and passed on.

Self-Publishing

vanity presses
printing houses that publish works at the author's expense

print-on-demand
a publishing method that prints manuscripts as they are needed

International Standard Book Number (ISBN)
an identification number that can be entered into an international book database

Vanity presses, or printing houses that publish works at the author's expense, have been around for over 50 years. Traditionally the last hope for a rejected book to get published, authors paid a vanity press to publish their works, instead of a publishing house paying the author for the privilege of selling his/her book. Today, vanity presses have been replaced by publishers specializing in **print-on-demand**. For a few hundred dollars, a print-on-demand company will take an author's manuscript and turn it into a paperback, complete with custom cover and an **International Standard Book Number (ISBN)**, an identification number that can be entered into an international book database. Then, when an order is placed for the book, the book is printed and delivered to the consumer. Print-on-demand is beneficial for both the author and the printer because it does not require a large investment in pre-printed documents.

Much of the stigma of paying your own way as an author is being eliminated by print-on-demand companies. The three large companies iUniverse in Lincoln, Nebraska, AuthorHouse in Bloomington, Indiana, and Xlibris in Philadelphia use digital printing rather than expensive offset presses to keep production costs low. Traditional vanity presses charge in the thousands or tens of thousands of dollars to print limited runs of books using traditional offset technology.

---

[24]*Used-Book Sales: A Study of the Behavior, Structure, Size and Growth of the U.S. Used-Book Market,* Book Industry Study Group.

Self-published books can be marketed like traditional books and made available on online bookstores like Amazon.com and barnesandnoble.com. In addition, even established authors who want to break out of their genres are turning to print-on-demand when their publishers don't want them to change. For example, Piers Anthony, an author known for fantasy and science fiction titles, has published more than 15 books with Xlibris that are not in his typical genres; he wanted to publish his serious historical fiction and make his out-of-print books available.[25] Even Amazon.com is getting into the print-on-demand business, acquiring BookSurge, based in Charleston, South Carolina, in 2005.

NEW TRENDS
Straight to Paperback

Hardcover is normally the first "format" for most books. Hardcover books are more expensive to produce and purchase than their paperback cousins, and when a publishing house releases a hardcover book, they are implicitly telling the world that they believe in that book's quality and potential for success. If a hardcover book sells well, paperback and later, mass paperback versions will follow.

However, hardcover books are no longer necessarily the mark of ultimate success in the publishing world. Many hardcover books are returned to the publishers, unsold. This has given rise to a new publishing trend, adopted by publishers from the very small to the very large–paperback originals of literary fiction. Rather than publishing even major literary books in hardcover, many publishers are revamping their paperback offerings to have hardcover touches like ragged edges on the pages and flaps on the covers, indicating a higher-quality book, but for a price lower than a hardcover.

Although authors and publishers make more money on hardcover sales, paperbacks are less likely to be returned by bookstores and more likely to go to the cash register. One concern of publishers was getting paperback originals reviewed by top reviewers like *The New York Times Book Review*. But several publishers say that tradition has changed, citing the watershed Feb. 6, 2005 review of "Death of An Ordinary Man," by Glen Duncan, a paperback original book published by Grove/Atlantic's Black Cat imprint, featured on the front page of *The New York Times Book Review*.[26] As Jane von Mehren, publisher of trade paperbacks at Random House puts it, "Getting somebody to spend $22 on a book by an author who they've never heard of is hard, but getting them to spend $13.95 on a paperback is much easier."

Google Books

Imagine sitting down at your computer, typing a term into a search engine, and pulling up books that contain that term. That's what Google Book Search does by creating a comprehensive, full-text searchable database of many of the world's books. Typing a search term into http://books.google.com results in a list of books

[25]Sarah Glazer, "How to Be Your Own Publisher," *New York Times*, April 24, 2005, Sect. 7, p. 10.
[26]Edward Wyatt, "Literary Novels Going Straight To Paperback," New York Times, March 22, 2006.

that contain that term, and in some cases you can download the full text of that book. In 2004, Google partnered with Stanford University to digitize all nine million of its books, and since then five other universities have signed on in some capacity to share their libraries with Google.

However, the ambitious project has hit some legal snags. In September 2005, the Authors Guild and five major publishers sued Google to prevent the company from going forth with the book scanning project. They were concerned about copyright infringement. It was questioned whether scanning books that are under copyright protection and making them searchable, even if searchers cannot download the entire book, is a legal use of the book. Since Google makes only snippets of the books available for examination its scanning process has not been stopped. However, if the wholesale, unlicensed scans of university library collections are made available, Google could be in trouble. Google argues that making copyrighted books searchable is a "transformative use" permitted under copyright law.[27] Google's Book Search is also useful for searching the full text of books that are not copyrighted or whose copyrights have expired.

PATRIOT Act Section 215

In the wake of the September 11, 2001 terrorist attacks on the World Trade Center, the Pentagon, and Flight 93, Congress passed the PATRIOT Act to enhance the government's surveillance efforts to aid the fight against terrorism. Section 215 of that act permits the Federal Bureau of Investigation (FBI) to order any person or entity to turn over "any tangible things," so long as the FBI specifies that the order is "for an authorized investigation . . . to protect against international terrorism or clandestine intelligence activities." Librarians and booksellers are particularly worried about this section, as it permits the FBI to search their records of books lent and sold to their patrons, and the librarians and booksellers are not permitted to tell their patrons that their records have been searched. The idea behind this section of the law is that those book records could provide clues into a potential terrorist's intentions or frame of mind.

Parts of the PATRIOT Act were reauthorized in 2006, and some changes were made. Librarians and booksellers can now consult attorneys, challenge search orders in court, and contest gag orders that forbid the revealing of the searches to the patrons, which are lifted after one year. Search requests must be approved by one of three top FBI officials, and the FBI must publicly report the number of bookstore and library searches every year. Activist groups such as the American Booksellers Foundation for Free Expression and the Campaign for Reader Privacy continue to work to protect reader rights post-9/11.

---

[27]Bob Thompson, "Search Me?; Google Wants to Digitize Every Book. Publishers Say Read the Fine Print First," Washington Post, August 13, 2006, p. D01.

The Fight for Literacy

Believing literacy to be universal in the United States, publishers hardly expected to lose potential readership to the problem of illiteracy. But in urban America today, the school dropout problem and increasing immigration have resulted in an alarming increase in non-readers. Yet according to the latest study conducted by the National Institute for Literacy, about four million adults were non-literate in English and another seven million had below basic literacy. About 80 million adults could not understand enough English to properly fill out a basic form with an address and zip code. Publishers are among many organizations striving to combat the problem through programs in schools and through community groups. In fact, materials to help tutor the illiterate or non-English readers are a new field of specialized publishing.

In 1991, President George H.W. Bush signed into law a measure that earmarked more than $1 billion to be spent over four years to fund anti-illiteracy programs. In 2002, President George W. Bush signed the "No Child Left Behind Act," which established "Reading First," a program that provides assistance to establish reading programs for kindergarteners through third graders. The ultimate purpose is to ensure that children read at grade level by grade three, and $900 million was pledged in state grants. "No Child Left Behind" has been controversial, as it permits states to set their own standards, and some have called for changes in how success is measured and how teachers are compensated and tenured based on students' test results. The act was renewed and slightly altered in January 2007.

BOOK PUBLISHING: THE FUTURE

Book publishers have come a long way since Gutenberg first printed his famous Bible in 1455. Today's book publishing industry is more than printing presses and "brick and mortar" bookstores. Traditional books with paper pages are giving way to different forms of content delivery. The electronic innovations that have changed the ways in which media are distributed and consumed have had a powerful impact on the book publishing industry as well. Books are marketed in innovative ways unimagined even 25 years ago. The book publishing industry has had to adapt to an audience that increasingly expects flexibility and choice.

Still, there is an allure to conventional books that keep them marketable. For generations of Americans, a rainy day is best spent sitting near a roaring fire with a cup of hot coffee and a good book. As an author and Librarian of Congress Daniel J. Boorstin said, "A wonderful thing about a book, in contrast to a computer screen, is that you can take it to bed with you." Despite the technological advances that have consumed mass media production and consumption, traditional paper-and-ink books are still popular and profitable. Still, just as they have for the last 9000 years, books will evolve with new technology.

Even with all the technological advances, reading a real book still appeals to many.
© HamsterMan/Shutterstock

The Cutting Edge: Electronic Paper Displays

Early e-book readers, as noted earlier, suffered from short battery lives, hard-to-read screens, and general consumer dislike. But the technology is improving. E Ink, founded in 1997 based on Massachusetts Institute of Technology (MIT) media lab research, markets itself as "the leading provider of electronic paper display (EPD) technologies".[28] E Ink is made up of microcapsules that appear as either black or white depending on a positive or negative charge determined by the content. The E Ink displays can be read in direct sunlight and from any angle, like a sheet of paper. E Ink can be used in other applications as well, including outdoor signs.

"The Sony Reader, released in 2006, the Amazon Kindle, released in 2008, and the Barnes & Noble Nook, released in 2009, use E Ink technology." This new wave of electronic reading devices can hold hundreds of books, and more with additional memory cards. They boast near-paper quality and do not use a backlight, so readers will not experience the fatigue as they do reading computer screens. The text is clear and legible–a large improvement over first-generation e-book readers. E Ink is also experimenting with very thin flexible displays—essentially reusable paper.

CAREERS IN THE FIELD

If you love books and like to be a part of a creative process, book publishing could be a great industry in which to start your career. Perhaps you might like to write a best selling novel, or perhaps you want to be one of the people that helps turn manuscripts into books that can be bought and sold. The book publishing industry enlists the help of many talented individuals to bring quality works to the book shelves. Large publishing houses will typically have several divisions including acquisitions and development; editing, design, and production; and marketing and sales. The first person in line in the process is the acquisitions editor. This person works as a scout in search of authors. Once an acquisition editor finds an author, the two parties establish a contract that outlines the author's subsidiary right. Typically authors will be given a signing bonus and then between five and fifteen percent of the book's cover price.

Next, an acquisition editor may work with a developmental editor to flesh out any problems or issues with a manuscript. Developmental editors are typically used to fill in blanks of a rough manuscript. Once the content of a manuscript is complete, the text moves to copyedit. A copyeditor looks for specific problems with grammar or length and creates a clean manuscript. Then, the design and production departments work on the aesthetics of the book, making sure the layout, type set, and artwork are correct. Once the text is reviewed multiple times, it is sent to press.

Even before the pages are printed and the book is bound, individuals who work in a marketing department of a publishing house are at work finding new and inventive ways to make the public aware of the book. Marketers may send advanced copies to various magazines in hope that the book will receive a

[28]eink.com.

good review. Once the marketing department gets bookstores to stock the title, the sales team works to distribute the correct quantities of the text. This job is important because an overstock of books can be sent back at the publisher's expense and an inadequate supply of books can result in lost sales.

Perhaps one of these roles is right for you. Whether you like to be on the creative or strategic side of business, the book publishing industry can offer plenty of opportunities.

SUMMARY

- Clay tablets and scrolls were replaced by parchment codex to create the first modern book.
- Gutenberg's press ignited the print revolution in which printed materials were readily available to the masses.
- Paperback books were introduced as a way to feed the public's desire for reading materials, but at a lower cost.
- Book sales are tracked in several categories, educational materials such as textbooks account for nearly 40% of the sales in the industry.
- Digital readers and scanned books will become increasingly popular in the future, forcing publishing houses to offer most of their titles in digital form.

DISCUSSION QUESTIONS

1. What advantages did the codex have over the scroll?
2. What role did Gutenberg's printing press play in the print revolution?
3. Why are educational materials so important to the book industry? How have textbooks changed over the course of your education?
4. What affect have online book stores had on the book industry?
5. What changes do you expect to see in the book industry in the next five years? Ten years? Twenty years?

SUPPLEMENTAL WEB SITES

SUPPLEMENTAL READING

The Long Tail: Why the Future of Business is Selling Less of More by Chris Anderson.

NEWSPAPERS

CHAPTER OBJECTIVES

- Understand the historical development of newspapers in the United States as well as the evolution towards other news media
- Identify minority newspapers and understand their purpose
- Define and distinguish different forms of journalism such as jazz journalism and investigative journalism
- Identify current trends in newspaper publication including online texts

KEY TERMS

abolitionists	muckraking
Associated Press	partisan
broadsheets	penny press
calamity	public affairs reporting
entrepreneurs	rotary press
flatbed press	RSS feeds
halftone engravings	tabloids
inverted pyramid	underground press
investigative journalism	wire service
jazz journalism	woodcuts
joint operating agreements	yellow journalism

INTRODUCTION

While sipping coffee in the local cafe, you are fairly likely nowadays to see the people around you staring at a computer screen. They're scrolling through pictures with a click of the mouse or

Even in today's technological world, people still read newspapers.
© Stephen Coburn/Shutterstock

responding to an email from a friend. It's even expected that some of them will be reading the news. But what are the chances that you see someone sitting next to you, coffee in one hand, and a newspaper in the other?

According to the Project for Excellence in Journalism, 48 million people on average still buy a newspaper, and 65 million visit a newspaper web site each month.[1] To paraphrase Mark Twain, the report of newspapers' death is an exaggeration. Yet it is probably not news to the majority of people that newspaper readership is in decline. In 2009, according to the same report, circulation fell 4.6 percent for daily newspapers and 4.8 percent for Sunday editions for the six months ending in September compared to that period a year earlier.

But there are bright spots for newspapers. Online readership continues to grow. It was 65 million in the third quarter of 2008 over a year earlier, according to measurements by Nielsen Online, and newspapers are continuing to take advantage of the Internet's content delivery opportunities to provide timely and complete coverage.

Consumers are the newspaper's final editors, whether online or offline. They select what interests or affects them. Most newspaper readers have definite personal agendas that cause them to jump from department to department. They are able to do this because of the way the modern newspaper is organized. The investor moves quickly to the stock market listings, and then checks out stories that tell what companies are introducing new products or considering merger offers. The sports fan can't be bothered with anything else until the scores and plays of last night's games have been absorbed. This is true online as well. Many newspaper websites allow the reader to personalize the newspaper reading experience and can deliver content that interests each reader in the ways that reader wants, via email, a website, or both.

But newspapers had a long and rich history before they ever hit the Internet. From the earliest news sheets to today's newspaper websites with audio and video content, newspapers continue to deliver the news with the same mission they have always had—to provide important information to interested individuals.

THE EVOLUTION OF THE AMERICAN NEWSPAPER

Newspapers began as a mere "sideline" enterprise for printers and gradually developed into the main source of a fresh commodity called news. They now contain news that is a notice of current events in local areas as well as far-flung places. The news is of interest to readers not only for its usefulness but also for its unusualness. For well over a century the print medium enjoyed this exclusive role until the age of electronic media changed the way people receive news.

---

[1]"The State of the News Media," Retrieved from http://www.stateofthemedia.org/2009/narrative_newspapers_audience.php?media=4&cat=2#111.

Broadsheets: A Profitable Sideline

Until the early 1700s, few printers gave any thought to being the purveyors of the tidbits of trivia and gossip and happenings about town. These forms of communication were usually passed throughout the community by word of mouth. Printing was a slow and laborious process that did not lend itself to speedy distribution of the latest talk. Also, governments did not look with favor on those who disseminated frivolous information that they had not approved.

Yet when a technology is available, **entrepreneurs** will think of ways to use it to cater to the public. As a society forms, expands, and has more time and money to spend, a market develops for new products. In colonial America, these conditions occurred in the early 1700s. Previously, the presses worked hard until books and government publications had been printed and then stood quiet. Eventually, printers realized they had a salable commodity in the letters they received from Europe. This was particularly true when the communications dealt with **calamity**, changes in government, or rumors about people remembered from "the old country." Excerpts from these European letters were a staple of a new kind of publication, the earliest form of newspaper. These printings were called **broadsheets**, so named because they were single-page impressions made from the full width of the printer's press.

Other broadsheets arrived from England, and printers on this side of the Atlantic quickly combed them, as well as other periodicals, for tidbits of information that would interest colonial readers. The concept of "reporters" was to come much later. Printers merely relied on what they could crib from other sources or what walked in their door in the form of gossip from friends and employees. This information was set in columns of type, without illustration, graphic devices, or anything but the most rudimentary headlines. The broadsheets were printed in quick impressions on the single page, or, at most, four pages when a single sheet was folded. These papers were sold at the printer's counter or hawked outside in the street by an apprentice or a child. Because broadsheets were printed only on one side of the paper people often wrote the latest news on the reverse side before passing the text onto their neighbors.

entrepreneurs
the person who organizes, manages, and assumes the risks of a business or enterprise

calamity
great misfortune or disaster

broadsheets
an early newspaper consisting of single-page impressions made from the full width of the printer's press

Early Colonial Newspapers

The publication usually acknowledged as the first newspaper in the colonies was *Publick Occurrences Both Foreign and Domestick,* published in Boston in 1690 by Benjamin Harris. In form, it was a newspaper. The content, however, was offensive to the government because of its disrespect for the established order. It never had a chance to become a periodical because it was banned instantly by the governor.

True newspapers, appearing with regularity, can be traced to the introduction of the *Boston News-Letter* in 1704. The publisher, John Campbell, was the postmaster; thus, he not only had government approval, but he could also distribute his publication through mail. Early in its publication, the *Boston News-Letter* consisted mostly of news from England and stories about British politics. Campbell's paper was technically government "approved," however, its content

The earliest newspapers were called broadsheets.
© *Kenneth V. Pilon/ Shutterstock*

was of little interest to the people. Consequently, it never achieved the success of later endeavors such as the *Boston Gazette*, introduced in 1719. That paper was printed by Benjamin Franklin's older brother James on behalf of Campbell's successor as postmaster, William Brooker.

When James Franklin decided to publish the *New-England Courant* on his own in 1721, newspapers were beginning to play a larger role in the community. They mixed information from the town and neighboring villages with essays, opinion pieces, columns, and even "exposés." Both of the Franklin brothers were men who were not afraid to take risks. Benjamin willingly operated the irreverent paper on the occasions when James found himself in jail for an indiscretion.

Eventually Ben Franklin left Boston, finding Philadelphia more to his liking. There he took over the *Pennsylvania Gazette* and molded it into a lively, entertaining, literate, and provocative flagship paper for a chain of small local newspapers in eastern Pennsylvania. Newspapers were springing up and dying quickly, but Franklin showed that the medium could survive and become dependable as a conduit for information and ideas. Under Franklin's command, the *Pennsylvania Gazette* was the most successful paper in the colonies. Part of the success can be attributed to the inclusion of political cartoons, many of which Franklin himself created. One such cartoon, *Join, or Die*, shows a snake divided into eight pieces, each depicting one of the colonies. This cartoon was Franklin's way of telling his readers that they must be united.

Benjamin franklin's cartoon told his readers that they must be united. *Courtesy of Library of Congress*

Probably the greatest contribution of the colonial newspapers was the forum they provided for discussion of the important issues that seeded the revolution. The *Federalist Papers*, written by John Jay, Alexander Hamilton, and James Madison, saw light of day in various newspapers to which they were distributed by the authors. These 85 essays called for the *ratification* of the United States *Constitution*, a topic that was under much debate across the country. The authors explained how the new government would operate, thus showing the people why ratification was beneficial and necessary. For example, Federalist No. 84 opposed the Bill of Rights. In it Hamilton states his fears that it would be considered a list of the only rights Americans had, therefore limiting their power and freedom. The *Federalist Papers* originally appeared in three New York newspapers. They were later additionally distributed in other states, though publication outside New York was irregular. It would be misleading to call the colonial newspapers a true mass medium because they circulated primarily to the literate populace who had both leisure time and money to spend on publications. It was several decades after the American Revolution and the founding of the new republic before cheap newspapers were read by the average citizen and were considered a necessity for keeping in touch with the world.

partisan
a firm adherent to a party, faction, cause, or person

Early American newspapers were highly **partisan**; that is, they followed political party lines and published vitriolic critiques of other perspectives. The Republican viewpoint was highlighted by Philip Freneau's *National Gazette* and Benjamin Franklin Bache's *Aurora* (published by Benjamin Franklin's grandson). The editors of these publications were critical of the presidency of John Adams. Isaiah Thomas' *Massachusetts Spy* and Noah Webster's *American Minerva* (later *The Commercial Advertiser*) supported Federalist political positions.

The 1800s: Development of the Popular Press

The introduction of the **rotary press**, with its revolving cylinders printing at many times the speed of the **flatbed press**, made possible the cheap mass production of newspapers. In 1833, Benjamin Day founded the daily *New York Sun*, and within a few years he was using the new technology to produce 30,000 copies each day. The paper sold for a mere penny (in relative value, about the equivalent of what we spend for a daily newspaper today). Thus began the era of the **penny press**, the first truly popular newspapers. By 1835 there were 1,200 newspapers in the United States.

Just two years after Day founded the *Sun*, James Gordon Bennett introduced the *New York World* and combined the technology used by Day with a new technique called reporting. He sent people out on the streets to visit the police halls, to observe comings and goings at the piers, and to chronicle the daily occurrences of a busy commercial city. With the New York dailies providing a model, daily newspapers sprang up in major cities around the country in the mid-1800s.

Bennett's success with the *Herald* led to competition. Horace Greeley founded the *New York Tribune* in 1841, hiring the legendary managing editor Charles A. Dana to oversee the news-gathering operation while Greeley concentrated on developing the editorial page's interpretative function. A decade later, in 1851, Henry J. Raymond founded *The New York Times* and emulated *The Times* of London in offering foreign coverage, in-depth reporting, and serious-minded editorials. *The New York Times* is recognized today as a paper that sets an example for completeness in **public affairs reporting**.

After the rotary press, other new technologies wrought similar changes to the newspaper industry, resulting in circulation increases for ever-improving products. One was the **wire service**, which brought stories from afar by telegraph to

Flatbed press. © *Bettmann/CORBIS*

rotary press
a *printing press* in which the images to be printed are curved around a cylinder

flatbed press
a printing press that uses a flat surface for the type against which paper is pressed, either by another flat surface acting against it or by a cylinder rolling over it

penny press
cheap, *tabloid*-style papers produced in the middle of the 19th century.

public affairs reporting
journalism that informs readers, listeners and viewers about ongoing events and activities

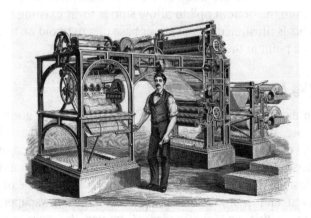

Rotary press. © *Bettmann/CORBIS*

newspapers that shared the costs. The first, the **Associated Press** (AP), was formed in 1848 by six New York newspapers as a way to reduce the expenses caused by duplicated efforts to obtain news from afar. Duplication of effort on local stories was viewed as useful because each paper was competing for an exclusive report on events that directly affected its readers. The formation of the AP also served to widen the horizons of smaller papers that could not afford their own correspondents around the country and abroad.

Wars speed the development and use of technology. The value of the telegraphic wire services in speeding news from the Civil War battlefronts to the big-city newspapers was a spur to readership and circulation. Faster printing methods were developed that enabled papers to increase daily circulation and offer large Sunday editions with preprinted feature sections. Newspapers in the South and the Midwest grew and improved as they fed the readers' appetite for information about the war. Following the war, westward expansion led to growth of newspapers in the mountain and Pacific states. By the 1870s the New York newspapers were rivaled in quality by important regional papers such as Joseph Pulitzer's *St. Louis Dispatch*, the *Chicago Tribune* edited by Joseph Medill, William Allen White's *Emporia Gazette* in Kansas, the *Courier-Journal* in Louisville, and the Portland *Oregonian*.

wire service
an organization of *journalists* established to supply *news* reports to organizations in the *news trade*: *newspapers, magazines,* and *radio* and *television* broadcasters

Associated Press
a cooperative news agency in the United States

The Inverted Pyramid

With the invention of the telegraph in 1845 came a new kind of reporting. Previously a newspaper article might not get to the actual news until the very end of the writing. The background would come first and lead to the real noteworthy information. The telegraph, when it was first used, was considered expensive. During the Civil War, newspapers were shelling out high costs to get the latest news via telegraph. This caused a shift in writing known today as the **inverted pyramid**.

inverted pyramid
journalistic style of writing where an article begins with the most important information

abolitionists
people who believed in getting rid of slavery

The inverted pyramid style of writing begins an article with the most important information. Everything you need to know about the story comes in the first paragraph of the article. The details come after in the body and conclusion, permitting easier editing "from the bottom up" to allow stories to fit existing "news holes." This is illustrated by the larger base of a pyramid on top, narrowing to a point at the bottom.

The Abolitionist Press

In the years leading up to the Civil War, a robust **abolitionist** press arose, dedicated to fighting slavery and supporting efforts to free slaves. The abolitionists were social radicals and used their newspapers to create a network for advocacy, information, and support. In Boston, William Lloyd Garrison's *Liberator* was one of the longest-lived and best-known of the abolitionist newspapers. Garrison, provocative and fiery, wanted immediate emancipation of the

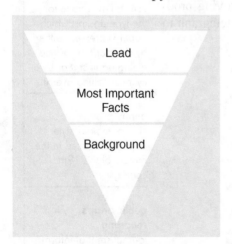

Lead

Most Important Facts

Background

FIGURE 4.1 The inverted pyramid style of writing begins an article with the most important information.

slaves. His incendiary articles provoked both the northern states that wanted a compromise solution to the slavery issues, and the southern states that the status quo benefited.

Garrison's colleague was Frederick Douglass, an escaped slave whose master's wife had broken the law by teaching him to read. Douglass gave speeches about his experience as a slave and published several autobiographies. His newspaper, *The North Star*, had as its motto "Right is of no Sex—Truth is of no Color—God is the Father of us all, and we are all brethren." Differences in opinion about the anti-slavery movement and particularly about the U.S. Constitution caused a split between Douglass and Garrison, resulting in Garrison believing *The North Star* to be a competitor to his *Liberator*. After the Emancipation Proclamation abolished slavery in 1862, Douglass went on to help with Southern reconstruction. Sadly, when Douglass' home in Rochester, New York burned in 1872 (a suspected arson), an entire run of *The North Star* burned with it.

Frederick Douglass gave speeches about his experience as a slave and published several autobiographies, as well as the newspaper *The North Star*. © *Bettmann/CORBIS*

The abolitionist press was not without its enemies. In 1837, Elijah Lovejoy, publisher of the abolitionist newspaper *Alton Observer* in Alton, Ill., was shot to death in his publishing warehouse by an angry mob. His printing press was destroyed and thrown into the river—the fourth press for the *Observer* to have met such a fate. The *Alton Observer* was the third of Lovejoy's newspapers to be shut down. He had written in the *Observer*, "We distinctly avow it to be our settled purpose, never, while life lasts, to yield to this new system of attempting to destroy, by means of mob violence, the right of conscience, the freedom of opinion, and of the press."

Early Minority Papers

The earliest African-American owned and operated newspaper in the United States was *Freedom's Journal*, published in New York by John Russwurm and Samuel Cornish from 1827 to 1829. An abolitionist paper, it published calls for an end to slavery, as well as served as a newspaper of record for the New York black community. Events such as lynchings as well as more positive news like births and marriages in the African-American community were reported. *Freedom's Journal* circulated in 11 states, the District of Columbia, Haiti, Canada, and some European countries. By the start of World War I, there was another newspaper written particularly to address African-American issues, the *Chicago Defender*. During the war, the paper used its influence to encourage African Americans in the United States to move north. Editorials, articles, and cartoons showed the benefits of a move while the paper included train schedules and job listings. Today there are multiple African-American newspapers including *New York Amsterdam News, St. Louis Sentinel,* and *Omaha Star*.

The *Cherokee Phoenix* was published from 1828 to 1835 and was the first Native American newspaper. Its purpose was to publish both

Courtesy of Library of Congress

The cherokee phoenix published laws of the cherokee nation as well as news.
Courtesy of Library of Congress

laws and documents of the Cherokee nation as well as to print news. Published by Elias Boudinot, the newspaper changed its name to *The Cherokee Phoenix and Indian Advocate* in 1829 to reflect the need to be more inclusive of other tribes. Started in New Echota, Georgia, the capital of the Cherokee Nation, a newspaper of the same name is now published in Tahlequah, Okla. Independent American Indian newspapers today include *News from Indian Country* published since 1986 in Hayward, Wis., and *Indian Country Today*, from Canastota, NY.

Serving the early Hispanic immigrant population in New York were *El Mercurio de Nueva York* (1829–1830) and *El Mensagero Semanal de Nueva York* (1828–1831). According to one researcher, from the 1850s through the 1870s, San Francisco supported the longest running and most financially successful Spanish-language newspapers in the United States. These papers helped new immigrants adjust to their new homes and covered news from home. Other large-city daily Hispanic newspapers included two Los Angeles papers, *La Opinión* (founded in 1926) and *El Heraldo de México* (1915); San Antonio's *La Prensa* (1913); and New York City's *La Prensa* (1913). In Tampa, Fla., Cuban tobacco workers started a labor newspaper, *La Federación*, in 1899.[2]

Underground Press in the United States

underground press
independent publications that focus on unpopular themes, or counterculture issues

In many countries, the term **underground press** is used in reference to publications that are illegal. Governments in other countries have been known to forbid the printing of newspapers and magazines that they feel are inappropriate. In the U.S., this is not the case. Because of the First Amendment, there are very few reasons the government can shut down a publication.

In the U.S. the term underground press typically refers to an independent publication, such as a newspaper, mostly those that focus on unpopular themes, or counterculture issues.

Possibly one of the best known underground newspapers is the *Village Voice* of New York. The paper was started by Dan Wolf, Ed Fancher and Norman Mailer in October of 1955. It was then, and still is today, known for its no-holds-barred reporting. It has published news about New York politics, the writings of authors such as Allen Ginsberg, and even has a section with advice on sex and a list of "adult services." Other underground publications in the United States include the *Boston Phoenix*, *Chicago Reader*, *Seattle Gay News*, *The Black Panther*, *New Age*, and *Bay Guardian*.

<hr />

[2]Nicolás Kanellos, "Recovering and Re-constructing Early Twentieth-Century Hispanic Immigrant Print Culture in the US," *American Literary History* 2007, 19(2):438–455.

Photography Illustrates the Stories

Before and during the Civil War, sketches made by artists and reproduced through **woodcuts** generally served as pictorial representation of the events reporters wrote about. An artist would draw an image in reverse on a wooden block, and engravers would cut out the design, which could then be inked and pressed. Thus, the scenes from the battlefields existed for most Americans as a result of pen and ink work.

Sketches served as pictorial representations of the Civil War battlefield scenes. © Bettmann/CORBIS

Newspapers were limited to publishing duplications of these woodcuts, but readers were unsatisfied. They increasingly wanted more realistic visuals of the battles going on throughout the country. Photo documentation of the epic struggle between the Union and the Confederacy by the renowned Mathew Brady, as well as other artists, was widely exhibited after the war. This helped spur interest in the use of the photograph to capture true images of important events.

In the 1870s the first use of photographs by newspapers heralded the day when totally realistic representation became a basic part of visual news coverage. By the 1890s, the techniques had been developed for **halftone engravings**—the system for translating photos into small "dots"—and photos began to appear regularly in the New York newspapers. Efficient production of newspapers with photographs came when the printing press was able to reproduce halftone images at the same rate as pages without images. The real ability for speed and efficiency, however, came with wire transmission of photography. Wire transmission was not possible until 1924, and it was 1935 before AP established a regular Wire photo network to supply pictures to its members.

woodcuts
an artistic technique in *printmaking* in which an image is carved into the surface of a block of wood

halftone engravings
an *engraving* used to reproduce an illustration, created by a series of dots

Yellow Journalism

By the end of the nineteenth century, a distinct pattern emerged among major city newspapers: strong-headed owners built booming businesses out of newspapers by sensationalizing stories concerning crime, abnormal behavior, and government wrongdoing. These newspapers complemented their coverage of human behavior with an eagerness to crusade against wrongs in government, while lauding the spirit of the common working person who plunked down a penny or two for a copy.

The era provides us a term still used to describe journalistic excesses. **Yellow journalism** is any sensational attempt at selling newspapers by depicting the seamier side of life, such as prying into the lives of celebrities or sex scandals involving government officials. The term comes from a comic strip, "Hogan's Alley," which featured the "Yellow Kid," a child dressed in a yellow gown who mocked upper-class customs and rituals. The strip was originally popularized in Joseph Pulitzer's *New York World*. The Yellow Kid was so popular that his face graced every kind of item from cookie tins to soap to cigarette packs. Among the

yellow journalism
a type of *journalism* that downplays legitimate news in favor of eye-catching headlines that sell more newspapers

stunts and gimmicks favored by Pulitzer to sell papers was the sponsorship of Nellie Bly's around-the-world trip in quest of the fictional 80-day record popularized by Jules Verne in his book *Around the World in Eighty Days.*

William Randolph Hearst is the publisher most often associated with this period of the first press barons. His *New York Journal* attempted to outdo Joseph Pulitzer's *World.* He even hired the "Yellow Kid" cartoonist, R.F. Outcault. Legends abound of the lengths to which Hearst went to buy, plant, or control a story. His competition with Pulitzer to dramatize and place blame for the sinking of the battleship *Maine* in Havana Harbor in 1898 fed the flames of nationalism that led to involvement in the Spanish-American war. Hearst is reputed to have told his photographer covering the rumored conflict, "You supply the pictures, I'll supply the war." Elected to Congress in 1902, Hearst lusted for higher power—perhaps even the presidency of the United States—but his romantic life, personal spending, and ruthless control of his enterprises worked against his ambitions. Orson Welles's classic film *Citizen Kane* is a barely fictionalized account of the excesses of Hearst.

During the yellow journalism era, banner headlines, the comics, puzzles, sports sections and other innovations were developed to please the consumer.

NEWSPAPERS IN THE TWENTIETH CENTURY

While newspapers peaked as a mass medium about 1900, yellow journalism has never entirely gone away. As long as there were three or more competing newspapers in the big cities, at least one stayed with the tradition of printing sensational headlines and pictures of bathing beauties.

When magazines developed the exposé story—*McClure's* ran a critical look at Standard Oil by Ida Tarbell in 1902 followed by Lincoln Steffen's series, "Shame of the Cities" (1903–1905)—newspapers followed suit with articles that exposed wrongdoing and corruption. An angry President Theodore Roosevelt labeled the practice **muckraking**. Other famous muckrakers include Nellie Bly, who wrote "Ten Days in a Mad-House," chronicling an 1887 stay at Blackwell's Island, an asylum for the insane in New York, and Upton Sinclair, whose 1906 book *The Jungle*, written about Chicago meat-processing plants, caused public outrage that resulted in the passage of the Meat Inspection Act and the Pure Food and Drug Act of 1906.

One of the resurgences of yellow journalism came in the 1920s, when several new **tabloids** were published in New York City, each trying to outdo the other with crime stories, lurid photographs, coverage of scandals involving the rich and famous, and sex escapades. The period came to be known as the era of **jazz journalism** because it seemed in tune with the raucous music of the time. Muckraking became more sophisticated and eventually gained a more respectable label: **investigative journalism**.

The economic woes brought on by the Great Depression cut heavily into newspaper profits and effectively ended the last major wave of yellow journalism's popularity. Nevertheless, as recently as the 1970s, Australian publisher Rupert Murdoch was buying tabloids and injecting them with new doses of yellow

muckraking
a term associated with a group of American *investigative reporters*, novelists, and critics from the late 1800s to early 1900s, who investigated and exposed societal issues such as conditions in slums and *prisons*, *factories*, insane *asylums*, *sweatshops*, *mines*, *child labor* and *unsanitary* conditions in food processing plants

tabloids
newspapers that tends to emphasize sensational stories and *gossip columns*

jazz journalism
the *journalism* style of the roaring twenties, named after its energetic fashion and well illustrated tabloid layout

investigative journalism
a type of reporting in which reporters deeply investigate a topic of interest, often involving crime, *political corruption*, or some other *scandal*

Women Journalists in the Twentieth Century

Ida Tarbell and Nellie Bly both made names for themselves as journalists in the twentieth century. Their fame, however, did not come easily. They are just two examples of women who were able to succeed in a world that was dominated by men.

Ida Tarbell never chose to write about the challenges of becoming a professional woman. That does not refute the fact that she constantly found out the troubles of being a woman during this time period. When she went away to Allegheny College, she was surrounded by men. She was the only female student in her class, all of her professors were male, and there were no dormitories for female students.

During this time period, women were expected to marry and take care of a family. Those that did manage to get through school and have a career faced many challenges. Female journalists were expected to write about being a homemaker. Both Ida Tarbell and Nellie Bly refused to abide by this ideal. For example, Ida Tarbell wrote about corruption in the oil industry. Also, in 1911, Nellie Bly became the first woman to cover the Eastern Front in WWI.

Nellie Bly was one of the first women journalists.
© Bettmann/CORBIS

journalism—stories about the "killer bees" advancing on the United States from South America, for example—in an attempt to hold readers lured away by television and other entertainment media.

Supermarket checkout "newspapers" such as *The Star* and *The National Enquirer* use modern-day yellow journalism with their headlines proclaiming "Elvis Is Living with Martians" and "Baby Kicks Twin out of Womb." Even though the sensational tabloids aren't really newspapers at all in the traditional sense, as they do not focus on conventional news coverage, some researchers suggest that while the headlines of many tabloid stories are sensational, the content is often presented rationally. For example, a story headlined "Woman Pregnant for Twelve Years" described a woman who carried a dead fetus for 12 years.[3] One company, American Media, owns 65 percent of supermarket tabloid titles, including the *National Enquirer*, the *Globe*, the *National Examiner*, the *Sun*, the *Star*, and *Weekly World News*. The company also owns health and fitness magazines *Shape* and *Men's Fitness*.

Newspapers of Record

The New York Times became the nation's "newspaper of record." © Bettmann/CORBIS

Beginning in 1896, under the leadership of Adolph Ochs, *The New York Times* started to carve out a niche for itself as the "newspaper of record," first for its city, and then for the entire nation. Increasingly, newspaper publishers saw that they could ensure profitability by offering readers a responsible information package based on reporting of public affairs in the circulation area, along with a mix of national and international news, sports, entertainment features, social news, and coverage of local business.

The "newspaper of record" plays the role of an agenda-setter, helping decide which issues will move to the forefront of national debate. In addition to *The New York Times*, newspapers that have attracted national audiences include the *Washington Post*, *The Wall Street Journal*, the *Los Angeles Times*, and the *Christian Science Monitor*. Many newspapers grew into roles as leading voices in their state or region: the *Atlanta Constitution*, the *Chicago Tribune*, the *Des Moines Register*, and the *Miami Herald* are examples.

The Opinion Function

In the nineteenth century, flamboyant editors used their news columns to wage political battles and attempt to influence national debate. Increasingly in the twentieth century, the opinions of the publisher, editors, columnists, and letter-writers were reserved for the editorial page. Editorials will often be followed by Letters to the Editor, where readers can respond to the opinions as well as the actual news presented by the newspaper. Expanded space was made available for exchanges of views in the "op-ed" (opposite editorial) page and even in entire opinion sections, especially in Sunday newspapers. Herbert Baynard Swope of *The New York Evening World* is said to have created the first modern op-ed page in 1921. The National Conference of Editorial Writers (NCEW) was founded in 1946 to foster appreciation of the role of editorial pages among both journalists and readers.

Journalism as a Profession

Movies and plays in the 1920s and 1930s portrayed newspaper editors and reporters as chain-smoking, hard-drinking, coarse, street-wise individuals driven by an obsession to yell "Stop the presses . . . I've got a scoop!" While the portrait

---

[3] Andrea Parrot; Joan Ormondroyd, "Can a Woman Really Be Pregnant for Twelve Years? Or Is Scholarly Learning Possible from Reading the Tabloids?" *Teaching Sociology*, Vol. 20, No. 2. (Apr., 1992), pp. 158–164.

offered by the classic farce *The Front Page* was not entirely fictional, the reality was that newspaper editors and reporters in the twentieth century were beginning to view themselves as professionals rather than craftsmen. Far from the "ink-stained wretches" of the nineteenth century, journalists in the twentieth century adhered to a model of social responsibility—turning to professional education and codes of ethics to improve their images. Rather than looking for the sensational angle, the social responsibility model encouraged the press to provide truth and accuracy to the public it serves.

The American Newspaper Publishers Association (ANPA), formed at the end of the nineteenth century as a trade association, emerged in the twentieth century as an organization dedicated to improving newspapers through its research institute, regular publications focusing on business practices and law, and an information service for the profession. In 1909, Sigma Delta Chi was formed as a secret fraternity on the DePauw University campus in Greencastle, Ind., only to emerge as an association serving the needs and interests of working journalists. Now known as the Society of Professional Journalists (SPJ), it holds an annual convention, publishes a monthly professional magazine, and lobbies for freedom of the press. Student chapters exist all over the country to support student press efforts. Interestingly, the organization voted to admit women sixty years after its creation, in 1969.

Both SPJ and the American Society of Newspaper Editors (ASNE), formed in 1922, have a code of ethics governing behavior by journalists. The ASNE's Canons of Journalism, issued a year after formation of the organization, is a code of conduct for journalists and a ringing statement of principles that include protection of the freedom of the press and the people's right to know. The ASNE has a number of standing committees that monitor journalistic practices, issue publications, and work for professional standards.

The Newspaper Guild, the journalists' trade union, also is concerned with improving the profession. Tired of working long and odd hours for little pay, journalists formed the guild in the 1930s. Today, however, only some 32,000 of the nearly half-million employees of newspapers are guild members, and in the days of automation and computers, the union poses virtually no strike threat to publishers. Wage increases accepted by the union in the 1980s actually lagged behind gains made by other professional workers.

While membership in all these journalism organizations is voluntary, they speak for the field, advance its welfare, and have enhanced its respect.

USA TODAY: The First Truly National Newspaper

Until Gannett Co., Inc. introduced *USA TODAY* in the fall of 1982, newspapers were the only non-national medium in the United States. Also, the United States was one of the few countries in the world without a national newspaper. *The Wall Street Journal* and *The New York Times* have editions that circulate throughout the country, but it can be argued that both are specialized papers appealing to a specialized audience rather than true national newspapers aiming at the widest number of potential readers.

USA TODAY, while it circulates throughout the nation, does not function as a strong editorial voice in the nation's political and social arena. What it does well, however, is to provide capsulated information that can be digested quickly by busy consumers with an interest in national trends. The paper is as much a "databank" as a news vehicle. Easy-to-understand color graphics put statistics and facts in a form that can be read quickly. Printed as a newspaper, *USA TODAY* has much in common with the online databases that busy executives use to keep abreast of the latest trends and developments.

Detractors have called it "McPaper" because while it is cheap, convenient, and easy to find in any urban area. Initially, advertisers warmed slowly to the new medium, not sure exactly what it was and how it served its audience. Other newspapers, were quick to imitate the colorful graphics and quick-reading charts, starting with the giant multicolored weather map.

Not content with merely inventing a new national medium, Al Neuharth, who shepherded the project from drawing board to financial success, said he envisions an information network that includes television, radio, computer databases, and virtually any other medium into which information gathered by the Gannett system can be channeled. More than any other publisher, he appears to have realized that the newspaper in the twenty-first century will be just part of a complex information system. The headline in *Advertising Age* on *USA TODAY's* fifth anniversary offered a prognosis for the new style of newspaper: "Here to Stay."

USA TODAY's short stories, informational graphics, and approach to news heralded the new age of newspapers—one that is built on adapting to fast-changing media preferences and savvy media consumers.

USA TODAY Celebrates Its Silver Anniversary

On September 15, 2007, *USA TODAY* celebrated its 25th anniversary. Revolutionary in its birth, with short articles and an emphasis on fast information delivery, *USA TODAY* is now solidly entrenched as a national newspaper. With four consistent sections—News, Money, Sports and Life—*USA TODAY* has become a staple in hotels, airports, and other places where the public gathers.

Pollster Lou Harris suggested to Al Neuharth, the founder of *USA TODAY,* the basic premise of the paper. He showed Neuharth the *New York Times* and *Wall Street Journal* and said, "Here I've got two that are very dull and very grey and very good . . . But if you want to grab the television generation you've got to transfer from the tube to print a lot of the stuff that the TV generation likes on the tube. It's pretty simple."

The newspaper is in many ways a reflection of its creator. Neuharth's premise of a "journalism of hope," an emphasis on good news, is still the premise today, although perhaps not quite as unabashedly. So is Neuharth's mandate that women and minorities should appear on the front page above the fold every day. Perhaps the most notable impact USA TODAY has had is that over half the newspapers in the United States have been redesigned to imitate its use of full-color photographs and lavish "spot color" graphics around boxes and charts.

According to one commentator, USA TODAY is better poised than its national competitors to go digital. Because of how users read Web pages, moving around quickly from link to link and story to story, and because of how they tend to skim rather than read entire long stories, USA TODAY's small-bite formula suits a digital platform better than a lengthy New York Times article. The paper's come a long way from punsters' jokes that it would win prizes for "Best Investigatory Paragraph."[4]

Newspaper Ownership and Circulation

Until recently newspapers were predominantly an independent medium in terms of ownership. Many were still the property of the heirs of their founders—family-run papers as small as the smallest weeklies and dailies and as large as *The New York Times*. Most chains had no more than a dozen small- or medium-sized papers and were regionally concentrated.

That pattern has changed. In the United States, Gannett Co., Inc. owns 85 daily newspapers, including *USA TODAY,* and nearly 1,000 non-daily publications, with a combined daily paid circulation of approximately 7.2 million. *USA TODAY's* circulation alone is approximately 2.3 million. The company is the largest newspaper publisher in the United States. Knight-Ridder, the second-largest publisher with 32 daily newspapers, was purchased by the McClatchy Company in 2006, which then sold about half of the papers to other buyers. McClatchy also sold its largest remaining newspaper, the *Minneapolis Star Tribune,* in 2007.

Concern about Gannett's dominance of such a large segment of the newspaper market, especially when the circulation of *USA TODAY* is included, has been voiced by many critics of American journalism. To date, however, admiration for Gannett's ability to run papers profitably has far overshadowed serious concern about any desire to control the market.

---

[4]*Edmonton Journal* (Alberta), "Revolutionary *USA Today* turns 25; Rivals mocked, then copied easy-to-read newspaper for the TV generation," September 14, 2007, pg. E6; John K. Hartman, "Assessing *USA TODAY* As a 25th Anniversary Approaches," *Editor & Publisher*, September 6, 2007. Retrieved from http://www.mediainfo .com/eandp/news/article_display.jsp?vnu_content_id=1003635101.

How has rupert murdoch influenced the american newspaper industry?
© Peter Foley/epa/CORBIS

joint operating agreements
permitting two newspapers, one considered to be "failing," to share business and operating costs

Criticism of another ownership trend has been much louder: the purchase of newspapers by owners who appear merely to want to squeeze profits out of them, with little concern for quality or the integrity of the product. The acquisition of papers across America, including the floundering *New York Post,* by Rupert Murdoch was viewed with alarm by many journalists who decried his formula of crime coverage, sensational reporting, and gossip as news. Many advertisers were wary of the lowest-common-denominator audiences attracted by such newspapers. Similar cries were heard when Murdoch acquired the *Wall Street Journal* in late 2007—an acquisition whose outcome and effects have yet to be seen. But at the beginning of the 1990s, critics grudgingly conceded that Murdoch and deceased British "press lord" Robert Maxwell saved many newspapers that might otherwise have died.

The phenomenon of newspapers being sold to other newspapers is viewed as a consolidation of power within the industry. Of even greater concern to some is the sale of newspapers to broadcast media companies that want to diversify, and to non-information producers who buy into the information business. The president of the Newspaper Guild, the union for reporters and lower-level editors, warned of the dangers of "an industry dominated by bankers and big investors" as well as the threat of concentrated media power being used for "political propaganda purposes."

In 1970, newspaper publishers convinced Congress to pass the Newspaper Preservation Act. This enabled them to cut costs—and save failing newspapers by merging business and printing operations (but not news and editorial operations) in cities where newspaper competition still existed. Both small and large papers have taken advantage of the law. In 2007, there were twelve **joint operating agreements** in effect, permitting two newspapers, one considered to be "failing," to share business and operating costs—an exception to usual antitrust laws. Early in 1990, Detroit's two 650,000-circulation papers, the *Free Press* and the *News,* finally got the go-ahead to join business operations. This came only after a lengthy legal battle. As the nation's ninth- and tenth-largest newspapers by circulation, both Gannett's *News* and the then-Knight-Ridder's *Free Press* were losing money for the parent companies. The joint operating decision did not solve the papers' problems. Advertisers rebelled against sharply increased advertising rates. Subscribers complained about a joint Sunday edition that combined sections and features from each of the papers. All factions could agree that the merger had one benefit: 2,000 jobs were saved because neither of the papers had to fold.

Regardless of ownership, newspapers are largely declining in circulation. As seen in Table 4.1, circulation of daily newspapers declined by an average of 2.6 percent between 2006 and 2007. Sunday circulations dropped an average of 3.5 percent. However, the Audit Bureau of Circulations, recognizing that its circulation measurement tools penalized the newspaper business, piloted a new method of determining circulation that takes into account more than just paper pages delivered.

TABLE 4.1	Top 25 Daily Newspapers by Circulation, September 2007[5]		
Newspaper	**Sep. 30, 2007**	**Sep. 30, 2006**	**% Change**
USA TODAY	2,293,137	2,269,509	(+1.04%)
The Wall Street Journal	2,011,882	2,043,235	(−1.53%)
The New York Times	1,037,828	1,086,797	I(−4.51%)
Los Angeles Times	779,682	775,765	(+0.50%)
Daily News, New York	681,415	693,423	(−1.73%)
New York Post	667,119	704,011	(−5.24%)
The Washington Post	635,087	656,298	(−3.23%)
Chicago Tribune	559,404	576,131	(−2.90%)
Houston Chronicle	507,437	508,091	(−0.13%)
Newsday	387,503	410,578	(−5.62%)
The Arizona Republic	382,414	397,295	(−3.75%)
The Dallas Morning News	373,586	404,652	(−7.68%)
San Francisco Chronicle	365,234	373,805	(−2.29%)
Boston Globe	360,695	386,417	(−6.66%)
The Star-Ledger, Newark, N.J.	353,003	363,100	(−2.78%)
The Philadelphia Inquirer	338,260	330,622	(+2.31%)
Star Tribune, Minneapolis	335,443	358,887	(−6.53%)
The Plain Dealer, Cleveland	334,195	336,940	(−0.81%)
Detroit Free Press	320,125	328,719	(−2.61%)
The Atlanta Journal-Constitution	318,350	350,159	(−9.08%)
The Oregonian, Portland	309,467	310,805	(−0.43%)
St. Petersburg (Fla.) Times	288,807	288,679	0.04%
The Orange County Register	278,507	287,204	(−3.03%)
San Diego Union-Tribune	278,379	304,334	(−8.53%)
St. Louis Post-Dispatch	265,111	276,677	(−4.18%)

A Truer Method of Assessing Newspaper "Reach"

In late 2007, after releasing circulation data for newspapers that showed another significant decline, the Audit Bureau of Circulations announced changes in the assessment of newspaper circulation. The new scheme will permit newspapers, over the next three years, to be considered paid regardless of the price paid for them; "other paid" copies, like those purchased by sponsors or provided to schools, will become known as verified (nonpaid); and there will be a new paid-circulation category for hotel and employee copies. For most of its existence, the ABC focused just on paid circulation,

---

[5]*Editor and Publisher*, November 5, 2007, from Audit Bureau of Circulations data.

the distribution of paid physical copies. Circulation is crucial because it is a primary concern for advertisers, and advertising revenues (more so than the sale of papers) are critical to economic well-being.

The ABC also released Audience-FAX, a new section to its FAS-FAX circulation reports, which accounts for both print and online readership, unduplicated combined readership and monthly unique users. According to the ABC, "Audience-FAX is the latest step in a multilevel industry initiative to answer advertisers' needs for measurement data that fully reflects newspapers' full reach and audience. The combination of readership and online audience data reflects a more complete picture of a newspaper's total audience and enables advertisers to truly gauge the impact of a newspaper in the community it serves."

Participation in Audience-FAX is voluntary, and currently about 30 percent of daily newspapers who participated in FAS-FAX are trying out the new metric. Audience-FAX is a combined effort of the ABC, Scarborough Research and the Newspaper Association of America. The companies say the metric is still a work in progress but believe that it more accurately reflects the "full reach" of newspapers instead of merely limiting circulation counts to paid physical copies.

NEWSPAPERS TODAY: "INNOVATE OR DIE"

The message is clear, say many media watchers. If newspapers cling to antiquated notions of what news is, how to design it, and how to deliver it, they will perish. Yet in some ways the notion of what has to be done is startlingly similar to what has always been done. As *Atlanta Journal-Constitution* editor Julia Wallace said in a posting to a media blog: "We have four clear jobs: Grow digital. Reinvent print. Create more regular local enterprise (distinctive content) that readers cannot get elsewhere. Improve our news and information gathering."[6] Most reporters would tell you that they are always looking for new ways to localize news stories and improve their information-gathering techniques. Most of what has changed, then, is digital. But that is a lot of change.

In his book *Faster: The Acceleration of Just About Everything,* James Gleick writes, "We believe that we possess too little time: that is a myth we now live by. What is true is that we are awash in things, in information, in news, in the old rubble and shiny new toys of our complex civilization, and—strange, perhaps—stuff means speed." The challenge for newspapers, and in fact every form of mass media, is to get useful information to its users quickly and efficiently.

Early personal delivery technology included attempts by some newspapers to fax abridged copies of their papers to consumers as early as 1938, when the *St. Louis Post-Dispatch* used its radio station to send a "Radio Edition" to printers at the homes of its staff. In the 1930s and 1940s more papers experimented with faxed newspapers; the *New York Times* still publishes TimesDigest (formerly TimesFax), a daily compilation of articles that is sent to hotels, cruise ships,

---

[6]Carla Kimbrough-Robinson, "News groups must innovate or die," *Quill*, April 2007, p. 37.

corporations and Navy ships and bases. However, the technology didn't catch on, partially due to the high expense of the equipment.[7]

Yet today's newspapers publish online as well as traditional print copies, and consumers have taken to this technology—which is not much different than daily faxes—in droves. Today's newspaper editors are just as likely to be worried about **RSS feeds**, page hits and blogs as they are about crafting the best headline for the top news story. The Internet has forced newspapers to rethink how they deliver their content. According to Nielsen//Net Ratings, the top-visited newspaper website, the *New York Times'* site, got 13,857,000 unique visitors in the six months from March to August 2007. Those readers looked at 27 pages per visit on average and spent an average of 20 minutes and 20 seconds on the site.[8] Moreover, research suggests that those who visit websites are "power users"— they are intensive Internet users who spent more time online than their peers, are likely to shop and make purchases online, and are younger, better-educated and more affluent.[9] It stands to reason that newspapers would want to cater to these users and their purchasing power.

> **RSS feeds**
> a family of *Web feed* formats used to publish frequently updated works in a standardized format

No More Paper Newspapers?[10]

Amid the cries of "Reinvent or die," "Go digital" and "Paper's a thing of the past," several Harvard researchers are finding that paper isn't likely to go the way of stone knives and bearskins—and that newspapers should not necessarily depend on the Internet for salvation.

Harvard media critic William Powers, in the provocatively titled research paper "Hamlet's BlackBerry: Why Paper is Eternal," suggests that paper has many charms that a website does not. Paper is tactile; you can write on it, underline and highlight things; it is less distracting than reading content on a website, where readers might be distracted by links and flashing colors. Moreover, it's easier on the eyes than reading a screen (as any researcher will tell you!). Therefore, readers may go to the Web for fast bits of information like sports scores and weather, but for longer reads, paper's where it's at.

In his paper, "Creative Destruction: An Exploratory Look at News on the Internet," Harvard researcher Thomas E. Patterson found that while traffic to national newspaper websites is continuing to grow, as is traffic to broadcast television and alternative

[7]George Mannes, "Delivering the FAX," *Invention & Technology Magazine*, Spr. 1999, Vol. 14, No. 4, http://www.americanheritage.com/articles/magazine/it/1999/4/1999_4_40.shtml.

[8]Newspaper Association of America Nielsen//NetRatings. Retrieved from http://www.naa.org/Trendsand Numbers/Newspaper-Websites.aspx#spotlight-Top-100-Newspaper-Websites.

[9]Brent Stahl, "Power Users 2006: An Engaged Audience for Advertising and News," June 2006, http://www.naa.org/TrendsandNumbers/~/media/PDFs/Power_users_2006%20pdf.ashx.

[10]Kelly Toughill, "The discreet charm of newsprint," *Toronto Star*, September 8, 2007, p. AA6.

news sites, visitors to daily newspapers in big cities and smaller towns are not coming in droves. He predicts that local newspapers will have trouble keeping their current readers, much less attracting new ones.

What does this pair of studies suggest? The need for more research to confirm or deny the findings. Why do we care? If newspapers go, there goes a lot of the investigative journalism that American democracy needs to survive. It isn't just about saving journalism—it's about keeping the public informed about the critical events of the day, helping them think critically, and enabling them to play a role as informed citizens in a democracy.

News Delivery

Marc Gunther wrote in 2007 that reporters at the *Washington Post* have become "platform-agnostic," which means that they realize that their content must be accessible in many different ways. Readers of the *Post*, noted Gunther, can experience news in many different ways and from many different perspectives: "They can join a lively global debate about religious faith, read hyper-local coverage of a fast-growing Virginia county, or watch daily video programs from the digital magazine *Slate*." The traditional business model of newspapers, driven by advertising revenue, is not as viable as it once was.[11] To survive, newspapers must reinvent themselves, and do so quickly.

Newspapers continue to experiment with different ways to deliver their content. Early newspaper websites were simply mirror images of what the print edition contained; they earned the dubious label of "shovelware" or "dumpware"

How can newspapers take advantage of the email addiction? © Zsolt Nyulaszi/Shutterstock

because the tendency was to put everything online instead of culling through the chaff for the wheat. Usability studies suggest that people browse Web pages differently than they browse printed products. Newspapers began to adjust to the notion that they had to edit material to go online as closely and carefully as the content that went into the printed product. They must also consider how to best design their home pages to maximize usability and access. Instead of looking like a traditional front page of a newspaper, with a few stories "above the fold," the home page of a newspaper's website will have more links and less actual content, to entice the user into clicking and reading.

According to AOL's third annual "Email Addiction" survey conducted in July 2007, the average email user checks email five times a day, and 59 percent of those with portable devices like BlackBerries check every time they get a new message.[12] How can newspapers take advantage

---

[11]Marc Gunther, "Hard News," *Fortune*, 8/6/2007, Vol. 156, Issue 3.

[12]http://press.aol.com/article_display.cfm?article_id=1271.

of that email addiction? Some deliver a morning email to their subscribers with headlines at a glance, followed by regular email notifications of news stories, customized to the user's preference. For example, subscribers can choose to receive the *Los Angeles Times'* daily summary, "Top of the Times," and may select additional email notifications or newsletters on topics like breaking news, food and drink, and travel. The *New York Times* offers both morning and afternoon summaries and other customizable alerts.

Want the news on your phone? Many newspapers have iPhone, cell phone and BlackBerry-friendly versions of their websites. Newspapers are also taking advantage of Web 2.0 features like blogs, podcasts, social networking syndication, and other interactive, user-created technologies that will be discussed in depth in Ch. 10.

Newspapers Go Niche[13]

Newspapers have traditionally tried to reach the largest audience possible. However, with readership declining, many papers are finding that it may be helpful to cater to a more narrowed audience. A niche newspaper may well turn out to be the best plan to counter the fall in print readers.

The tabloid *Quick* is aimed at a younger audience. Everything in the paper has a bit of attitude, even the weather. Instead of giving temperatures, the paper tells its readers what to wear. This approach is an attempt to make reading the paper more entertaining, in the hopes that younger readers will get into the habit of reading a daily newspaper.

The *Chicago Tribune* launched their niche paper, *RedEye*, in 2003. Their approach to gaining a new audience includes punchy headlines and attractive photography. "The idea was to try some approach to attract this hard-to-attract demographic group to the newspaper reading habit," said Don Wycliff, the *Tribune's* public editor.

Many have feared that these niche papers, especially the ones daily papers offer for free, would take away readership. The general feeling is that most young readers who pick up these tabloids would not be readers of the wider publication. And hopefully, by engaging young readers, these newspapers gain readers for the future.

Talking Back and Personalization

Traditionally, newspapers were a one-to-many medium. Readers could talk back in the letters to the editor feature or the op-ed pages, but this process took time. Also, editors could choose not to publish letters or articles on topics they did not like or that were critical of the news organization.

---

[13]Alison Miller. "Niche papers use 'attitude' to target new readers," The American Society of Newspaper Editors, April 19, 2004.

Many newspaper websites provide the option for readers to comment on stories, often in discussion board format. Readers can share their thoughts and ideas, usually subject to limitations on libel or profanity, related to the story. Many newspapers also permit users to post comments in the blog sections of their websites.

Newspapers also recognize that users want choices. As noted above, subscribers to the *Los Angeles Times'* email digest service can customize their topics and delivery options to their individual tastes. The idea of creating one's own newspaper dates to 1992 and an experiment by a class of freshmen at the Massachusetts Institute of Technology's Media Lab. The class assignment was to provide a news service for potentially homesick new freshmen at MIT by gathering news from their hometowns. The class developed fishWrap, a personalized news service that received data from the student, like hometown and special interests, and searched online wire services for stories matching that data. Users could refine their news each time they accessed fishWrap.

While most newspaper websites do not allow for that level of customization, and the newspaper staff usually prefers to retain control of how its home page is delivered, there can be no doubt that readers will continue to demand increased personalization options and turn to news outlets where that customization is possible. As discussed in Ch. 10, community journalism sites permit residents in a very local area to participate in discussions about issues affecting areas no larger than city blocks—perhaps the height of customized, personalized, hyper-local content.

CAREERS IN THE FIELD

The newspaper industry is a great field for individuals who excel at collecting information, writing, and editing. It is also good for people who enjoy having something new to focus on every day. Since the news is always changing, what you work on will always be new. Positions at a newspaper include reporters, writers, and editors. You might also find positions for layout design. Today you will likely even work on the newspaper's website doing design or maintenance. There are also many opportunities on the administrative side of the industry in departments such as public relations, marketing, or ad sales.

To start your career in the newspaper industry, you may only need to look to your school. Most universities and colleges have an on-campus publication that is developed by students. You may also try to find an internship at your local paper. Having experience will help you develop a portfolio, a collection of all the work you've done. This is especially important if you want to work as a reporter or a writer. Potential employers will want to see what you are capable of doing.

SUMMARY

- The first newspapers in America were one-sided printings called broadsheets that reported news from England.
- Colonial, minority, and abolitionist newspapers all included information that was involved in revolutions for their target audience.
- The introduction of the rotary press made possible the cheap mass production of newspapers.
- Yellow journalism became popular as an attempt to sell newspapers by depicting the seamier side of life.
- *USA TODAY's* short stories, informational graphics, and approach to news heralded the new age of newspapers—one that is built on adapting to fast-changing media preferences and savvy media consumers.
- Today, newspapers are continuing to take advantage of the Internet's content delivery opportunities to provide timely and complete coverage.

DISCUSSION QUESTIONS

1. Discuss the evolution of gossip and seedier stories in newspapers. What events help explain the introduction of gossip? What does the desire for these stories say about the change in readership?
2. Analyze newspapers as a means to insight revolution, including abolitionist papers and underground presses. How does the media lend itself to spreading individualized messages? What are the differences between revolutionary papers in the colonial period and those that exist nowadays? What explains the changes?
3. Identify the distinguishing factors between the various forms of journalism including public affairs reporting, yellow journalism, jazz journalism and investigative journalism. How do the differences explain the aims of the paper publishing the news pieces?
4. Discuss how Letters to the Editor changed the way people use newspapers. How do they bridge the gap between reader and reporting? How does this communication explain the natural progression towards online news?
5. Analyze the status of newspaper readership. Is online readership the solution or does it only give key headlines? Can newspapers find a way to start a resurgence in print readers?

SUPPLEMENTAL WEB SITES

MAGAZINES

CHAPTER OBJECTIVES

- Understand how the magazine differentiated itself from books and newspapers
- Explain how the magazine became a mass medium
- Understand the state of today's magazine industry and how magazines have moved from addressing a mass audience to addressing a specialized audience
- Discuss your thoughts on the future of the magazine industry and how digital media will affect the medium

KEY TERMS

cutlines	pass-along rate
ezines	photojournalism
muckraking	psychographics
newsweekly	sidebar
niche	webzines

INTRODUCTION

Next time you pass a newsstand on the street, your bookstore on campus, or a kiosk in the mall, take a look at the magazine racks. You'll be amazed at the variety of magazine titles you will see. The Audit Bureau of Circulations (ABC), an independent circulation-auditing organization, counts 802 consumer magazines, 213 business publications, and 23 farm publications among its members in 2008.[1] This number does not include many small and low-circulation magazines. Suffice it to say, magazines are numerous and highly specialized.

---

[1]Audit Bureau of Circulations—About ABC, May 13, 2008. Retrieved from http://www.accessabc.com/aboutabc/introduction.htm#members.

No matter what your interest is, there's probably a magazine for it.
© Tony Arruza/CORBIS

niche
a smaller subgroup with specific interests

A basic online search might unveil even more. Essentially there is a magazine for every taste, topic, hobby, lifestyle, and vocation you can think of and probably some you hadn't considered! If you enjoy fishing specifically for billfish, you can subscribe to *Marlin* to learn more about the sport. If you are intrigued by the field of civil engineering you can subscribe to *Pipeline and Gas Technology*. Perhaps you consider yourself to be a geek, you could subscribe to *Geek Monthly* to read about issues that affect your geeky lifestyle.

One of the themes that you have encountered and will continue to see in this textbook is the evolution of the notion of a "mass audience" and the rise of the specialized medium. The magazine industry has strongly adopted this position of specialized **niche** publications—perhaps more than other traditional media. While some general-interest magazines such as *Reader's Digest* and *People* continue to publish, most magazines in today's market are specialized to appeal to a very specific audience, segmented by profession, interest, age, or any number of other characteristics.

Magazine historian Frank Luther Mott believed that magazines perform three basic services to society:

- "They provide a democratic literature which is sometimes of high quality." Mott acknowledged that, in catering to popular tastes, magazines often provide frivolous fare, but that is balanced by the fact that most serious authors at one time or another have contributed to magazines because of their wide audience and undisputed impact.
- "The magazine has played an important part in the economics of literature." That role is somewhat diminished, but magazines still provoke interest in serious reading when editors print excerpts from forthcoming books.
- "Periodical files furnish an invaluable contemporaneous history of their times." By way of proof, the reference rooms of most libraries provide access to the *Readers' Guide to Periodical Literature* as well as many digital search engines for magazine articles, including Lexis-Nexis and InfoTrac, and it is there that many scholars begin their inquiry into research topics.[2]

While magazines still qualify as a "mass medium," the industry may well be on the cutting edge of determining what makes up a mass medium in the twenty-first century. In this chapter, we will follow the magazine industry's path from its beginnings as a general audience medium to its current segmentation.

THE DEVELOPMENT OF SPECIALIZED PUBLISHING

The word *magazine* comes from the Arabic word "makazin," or storehouse. The first publication to use the term *magazine* was, indeed, a storehouse of information. *The Gentleman's Magazine*, which appeared in England during 1731, was a

---

[2]Frank Luther Mott, *A History of American Magazines*, vol. 1 (Cambridge: Harvard University Press, 1968), pp. 1–3.

compendium of letters, planting tables, essays, reprints of business and political documents, gossip, and selections from current or forthcoming works of poetry and fiction. Still, the concept of the magazine existed before the term was widely used. Author and political activist Daniel Defoe created the first magazine in England and the first political magazine, *The Review*, in 1704. Defoe used the publication to express his comments on social politics and criticisms of local government. Other early European magazines such as *Tatler* and *The Spectator* were also used to express social and political commentary, which commonly came in the form of letters, essays, poetry, and prose. Colonial magazines in the new world followed suit.

Magazines in America

Magazine publishing started in the American colonies in 1741. Andrew Bradford's *American Magazine* was the first publication of its kind in the colonies. A mere three days later, Benjamin Franklin published, *General Magazine*. Both publications purported to discuss colonial, rather than British, interests. Unfortunately, they were short-lived endeavors: Bradford's magazine lasted three months and Franklin's, six. Over the next several years other publications emerged and addressed issues such as taxation, Indian relations, religious freedoms, education, and the end of colonialism. Prominent political figures such as George Washington, John Hancock, and Samuel Adams wrote for various magazines; Paul Revere contributed several illustrations. While many publications were short lived, important works such as Thomas Paine's *Pennsylvania Magazine* (1775–76), the *American Museum* (1787–92), and the *Massachusetts Magazine* (1789–96) made significant contributions to the social dialog of the new nation.[3]

The magazine industry in the colonies grew slowly at first, with only 23 magazines founded between 1741 and 1783, the end of the Revolutionary War. The medium started to pick up speed when the government established the Post Office as a permanent arm of the federal government in 1794. Through a federal post office, magazine publishers had a reliable way to distribute their publications to distant audiences. Two years earlier, in the 1792 Postal Act, the post office flat out refused to carry magazines. Six out of the 13 magazines operating at the time failed as a direct result. Due to induction of the post office and acceptance from postal officials, 844 magazines appeared between 1795 and 1825.[4]

By the beginning of the nineteenth century, most towns and villages had access to weekly magazines. The most popular magazines covered religion, but literary magazines such as the *North American Review* were in high demand as well. Mark Twain and Ralph Waldo Emerson were among many distinguished writers that contributed original pieces or book excerpts to literary magazines. Around this time, other, more specialized magazines

The April 1895 edition of *Harper's* magazine included the essay "Joan of Arc" by Mark Twain. © *Corbis*

---

[3]history of publishing. *Encyclopedia Britannica* at http://www.britannica.com/EBchecked/topic/482597/publishing. Accessed December 02, 2008.

[4]Heather A. Haveman, "Antebellum literary culture and the evolution of American magazines," *Poetics* 32 (2004) 5–28.

emerged and covered various vocations and lifestyles, creating new genres of magazines.

Not a Book, but Not a Newspaper

Early magazines borrowed heavily from books, newspapers, and other sources, as there were no copyright rules in colonial America (the first federal Copyright Act, which provided protection for intellectual property, was not passed until 1790). As the magazines developed, American magazines sought to differentiate themselves from other media. Not as transient as newspapers, but not as permanent as books, the magazine could discuss lingering issues that affect current events. They served audiences by providing information that was longer and more detailed than newspapers, but less time-consuming to read than books. Magazines often filled in the gap between newspapers and books by providing audiences with provocative and contemporary content.

Originally, magazines were book-sized, approximately six inches wide by nine inches tall, because the publishers printed them on book presses. Eventually, printers tried new styles, and the size of the magazine page grew from being twice as big as book pages to nearly as large as tabloid newspapers.

Magazines have always had a more "experimental" nature than newspapers or books. From colonial times until the present, editors and publishers have continually tried new concepts or gimmicks for fresh and exciting ways of attracting audiences. In the late 1800s, for example, *Peterson's Magazine* for women included fashion plates, large fold-out illustrations of the latest dresses and gowns. Each illustration was individually hand-tinted to add a splash of color to the black-and-white publication. The practice is outmoded, but the term *fashion plate* endures as an expression meaning one who wears the latest styles.

Most of the magazines founded in colonial times lasted only a few issues or a few months. It was the mid-1800s before readers could select from several magazines with proven records. Many of the most popular magazines in the mid-nineteenth century could be classified as literary periodicals: *Harper's Monthly*, *The Atlantic Monthly*, *Century*, and *Scribner's*. In fact, the more successful magazines were published by book companies that used the periodicals to build interest in their forthcoming books by printing excerpts and carrying advertisements for the new titles. Charles Dickens' books, for example, appeared in *Harper's Monthly*. Even today, new authors often begin their careers in magazines; Michael Chabon, author of *The Mysteries of Pittsburgh*, *Wonder Boys*, and *The Amazing Adventures of Kavalier & Clay*, published his early short stories in *The New Yorker*, *Vogue*, and *Mademoiselle*.

BEGINNINGS OF THE MASS AUDIENCE MAGAZINE

By the end of the 1800s, the magazine industry experienced a surge. The two contributing factors were the passing of the Postal Act of 1879, which gave magazines a lower postage rate, and improved printing technology, which dropped the price of a magazine to an amount that working class individuals could afford. By 1905, nearly 25 national magazines were available. The wide reach of national magazines enabled the medium to connect, inform, and influence a massive audience.

The Catalyst for Social Reform

The magazine format, with fewer articles than a newspaper and more pages for each topic, also lent itself to fuller treatment of exposés of government and business wrongdoing, complete with illustrations—at first cartoons and drawings and eventually photographs—that helped tell the stories in dramatic new ways. This type of investigative reporting, often called **muckraking**, was popularized by newspapers toward the end of the nineteenth century. The term *muckraker* was coined by President Theodore Roosevelt because these reporters would sort through the muck in society to uncover a story. Because magazines enjoyed national distribution, they had more impact than newspapers that served only one city. This put magazines on the front line in the fight for social reform. Muckraking magazines included *McClure's*, which published articles by early investigative journalists Ida Tarbell and Lincoln Steffens, and Frank Leslie's *Illustrated Newspaper*. One of Leslie's investigative pieces on New York's "swill milk" industry, revealed the abysmal conditions in which cows were raised and fed (often with distillery waste), which resulted in milk not fit for human consumption. The milk was often doctored with water, chalk, egg whites, and other additives to increase volume and conceal problems. Leslie's 1858 exposé resulted in a huge public outcry and eventual regulation of the milk-producing industry.[5]

muckraking
investigative reporting

The Saturday Evening Post: General-Audience Magazine

Although *The Saturday Evening Post* can trace its history back to Benjamin Franklin, the truly mass-appeal version of that magazine was developed in the late nineteenth century by its publisher, the Curtis Publishing Company, and flourished until the middle of the twentieth century. It finally closed its original publication in 1969. The formula developed by *Post* editors served as a model for *Colliers, McClure's,* and dozens of imitators: entertainment that included adventure fiction, travel pieces, biographical features about celebrated figures, humor, pictorial essays, and human interest stories, with the occasional political scandal investigation. Writing was simple and direct, always using vocabulary easily understood by the average citizen. By catering to the lowest common denominator, magazine publishers found they could sell a million or more copies. Consequently they could provide a truly national advertising medium. The resulting financial support enabled publishers to keep the price of their colorful and splashily illustrated magazines very low.

The Saturday Evening Post was a true family magazine. The writing level and line-drawing illustrations made the content accessible to anyone who was literate. More important, the mix of articles appealed to various tastes. They included fact

---

[5]Erna Melanie DuPuis, *Nature's Perfect Food*, (2002). New York University Press, New York.

The Saturday Evening Post provided good reading for a wide audience.
© *Bettmann/CORBIS*

cutlines
the line or paragraph of explanation below a photo

photojournalism
the use of photography to document life

and fiction, humorous articles to balance the serious pieces about government or science, and lots of profiles of movie stars, sports heroes, historical figures, and world leaders. Above all, the magazine had a down-to-earth feel. Its Norman Rockwell covers and the Ted Key cartoons, which featured saucy and wise "Hazel" (a maid to a middle-class family upon whom a 1960s sit-com of the same name was based), appealed to the everyday American. It was consistently wholesome, informative, and lively—something to curl up with on Saturday night before television was introduced.

While *The Saturday Evening Post* provided plenty of good reading in the pre-television era, it also was a "quick read." Readers could browse through it quickly because the cartoons and the simple layout kept the eye intrigued. This quick read formula was further refined when *Life* magazine appeared in 1936, then *Look* magazine in 1937. The line drawings of the earlier magazines were replaced by emotion-provoking pictures taken by the leading photographers of the day and accompanied by punchy captions and **cutlines**, the line or paragraph of explanation below a photo. *Life's* articles were short and easy to read, but it was the impact of the stunning photo layouts that attracted the audience.

Photojournalism

Magazines set themselves apart from all other mass media in the middle of the 20th century by creating an outlet for a special type of journalism called photojournalism. **Photojournalism** used photos rather than words to tell a story. Unlike photographs in newspapers, which would simply capture an image of an event, photographs in magazines would capture the emotions behind the event. Photojournalists during the 1920s and 1930s got up close with the events of the Great Depression. They took shots of not just bread lines, but the faces of the people standing in the bread lines. Photos from this era captured the desperation of the American worker in a way that words could not.

Life became the gold standard for photojournalism. Iconic photographs of famous figures such as Malcolm X and nameless faces such as the Migrant Mother graced the cover and pages of the magazine for over 30 years. The golden age of photojournalism ended when *Life* and other photo-based magazines ceased publication. Today, examples of photojournalism can still be found in a variety of magazines and newspapers.[6]

The Rise and Fall of General Interest Magazines

The general-interest magazines were the leading national advertising vehicle of their day. Soaps, toothpaste, kitchen appliances, cigarettes, automobiles, and eventually alcoholic beverages were the source of huge advertising revenues. Since each copy of *Life*, *Look*, and *The Saturday Evening Post* was typically read then

---

[6]Magazines and Photojournalism's Golden Age, *JPROF*. Retrieved from http://www.jprof.com/magazines/05goldagephotog.html.

passed along to several people, the advertised products had to appeal to almost everybody to make the magazine an efficient advertising vehicle. Ironically, when the first advertisements for home television sets appeared in the mass circulation magazines in the early 1950s it marked the beginning of the end of the era of general-interest periodicals.

One of the few general-interest magazines to continue today is the *Reader's Digest*. Established in 1922 by DeWitt and Lila Wallace, the publication originally contained condensed and reprinted articles from other magazines in a readable format void of interruptions by illustrations or other graphic elements. Today *Reader's Digest* mixes original articles with reprints, plus departments featuring inspirational ideas, slices of life, and down-home humor. Articles on health and marital relations frequently are bannered on the promotional stickers added to the covers to boost sales at the checkout counter.

Reader's Digest is one of the few general-interest magazines still printed.
© Justin Lane/epa/Corbis

Time Creates the Modern Newsweekly

When *Time* magazine appeared in 1923, it was not the first periodical to present the news of the week accompanied by illustrations and commentary; *Harper's Weekly* had done it half a century earlier, and the *Literary Digest* flourished as the leading news magazine of the early twentieth century. Nevertheless, the birth of *Time* can be looked on as an important turning point in magazine history. Its innovative techniques became the benchmark for the modern **newsweekly**, a magazine dedicated to summarizing the week's news in capsule form, categorizing content to fit in departments such as "The Nation" and "The World," and accompanying articles with **sidebars**, shorter pieces that provide background context or commentary. *Time* summarized the main points in a story with brevity, a service to busy readers that was further refined six decades later by Gannett's *USA TODAY* newspaper.

Henry Luce co-founded *Time* with Briton Hadden, and stamped his personal style on the magazine: breezy, pushy, irreverent, and even smart-alecky. His magazine was presumptuous enough to select a "Man of the Year" for the first issue every January and promote the choice as if the Nobel Prize had been awarded. The slogan of *Time* for many years was "Curt, Concise, Complete." *Time* made news itself when it chose "You" as the "Person of the Year" for 2006, trumpeting, "You control the Information Age." This declaration emphasizing the trend toward customization of content described throughout this textbook.

newsweekly
a magazine dedicated to summarizing the week's news in capsule form

sidebar
shorter pieces that provide background context or commentary to a main article

THE MAGAZINE INDUSTRY

The magazine industry has changed dramatically since the medium gained popularity in the early 1900s. Umbrella publications that cover various topics are no longer of interest to most readers—specialization is now the name of the game for magazine publishers. Additionally, the magazine industry no longer has to focus on differentiating itself from newspapers and books; its main concern is proving itself relevant in the digital world.

The Advent of a Specialized Industry

The shift from general-interest to special-interest magazines began with the television era. When *Life* ceased publication as a weekly in 1972, its parent company, Time, Inc., understood that the magazine business was changing profoundly. It had already introduced *Sports Illustrated,* which not only narrowed its area of coverage to sports, but did it in a manner that interested sophisticated readers.

That trend of specialization and niche marketing caused the demise of the mass audience for magazines, which continues today. In the 1980s, Time, Inc. spent tens of millions of dollars to test-market several specialized magazines. *Picture Week,* which could not find a niche that differentiated it from *People* magazine, was folded, as was *TV-Cable Week.* Other titles developed successfully by Time, Inc. show just how narrow the focus must be to convince advertisers they are getting a specific target audience. Those publications include: *Real Estate, Home Office, Cooking Light, Women's Sports & Fitness, Southern Living, Leisure,* and *Parenting.*

One of the biggest leaps toward segmented marketing of a magazine came with *Playboy's* introduction in 1952. Both advertising and editorial content were aimed at one gender and age segment—men 18 to 30 years old—and a higher-than-average level of education and potential income. The venture was hugely successful, generating a business empire as well as inspiring imitators. *Playboy* heralded the start of niche magazines that target consumers by gender, age, occupation, or class.

Circulation

As you know from flipping through your favorite magazines, advertisers use the audiences for niche magazines as ways to target potential customers for their products and services. But how many readers are those advertisers reaching? The Audit Bureau of Circulation (ABC) has been verifying and reporting circulation rates for both newspapers and magazines since 1914. Objective circulation rates are necessary to determine fair and accurate rates for advertising. Another organization, Business of Performing Audits Worldwide, provides similar auditing services in over 25 countries.[7]

The ABC audits publishers' records, matching circulation claims with audited results and reporting any discrepancies. An auditor's report includes an examination of several years of subscription and circulation rates and the recommendation of the auditor about the fairness of the publishers' circulation claims.[8] In the well-aimed specialized magazine, the reader may not even make a distinction between the advertisements and the editorial material—all are part of the same well-focused information package. For example, an environmental magazine that runs an article that outlines the benefits of organic hair products may also run an advertisement that features a particular brand of organic hair products.

---

[7] www.bpaww.com.

[8] ABC Home page, Sample report, retrieved at http://www.accessabc.com/resources/protos.htm.

Many magazines strive for a balance of newsstand sales and subscriptions. But subscriptions make up the lion's share of magazine distribution; in 2007, according to the Magazine Publishers of America, 87% of magazines were distributed by subscription, with only 13% as single-copy newsstand sales. In 2007, nearly 370 million magazine issues were distributed, with an average subscription price of $27.30 per year.[9]

Many magazines are shared or seen by multiple readers. The frequency at which a publication changes hands is called the **pass-along rate**. Two to three readers per copy is a standard pass-along rate for magazines like *Time*. Some very personal magazines, such as *Playboy* or *Coping* magazines, are seen mainly by the purchaser and have a low pass-along rate. Magazines commonly found in waiting rooms at hair salons and doctors' offices, typically *US Weekly*, *Newsweek*, or *Highlights*, may have an exposure rate far higher than the average. Some magazines have tried basing advertising rates on the actual size of the audience, which takes into account the pass-along rate. But advertisers appear more comfortable with rates based on circulation, assuming that at least one person reads each copy in some depth. Since 2006, the ABC has split out sponsored "public place" subscriptions, such as those in doctor's offices and hotels, into a new category for circulation counts.

Magazines found in waiting rooms have an exposure rate far higher than average.
© Monkey Business Images/Shutterstock

pass-along rate
the frequency at which a publication changes readers

Audiences for Magazines

The 2008 National Directory of Magazines reports that there were nearly 20,000 magazine titles published in 2007 (only a subset of these titles are recognized by the Audit Bureau of Circulation), and these titles are grouped into over 260 categories.[10] Magazines with a medical focus topped the list of largest magazine categories, containing 986 titles. The religious category came in second with 742 titles, and the regional interest, ethnic, and travel categories completed the top five. Magazine categories experiencing the most growth were interior design, lifestyle, and travel.

According to the Magazine Publishers of America, 84% of adults aged 18 years or older read magazines. The industry has enjoyed a 9% increase in adult readership over the last eight years. In 2007, 248 new magazines were introduced, and 27 of those new publications were craft, game, or hobby magazines.[11]

For nearly two decades *Reader's Digest* had the largest circulation of any magazine in the United States. During the 1980s, *Reader's Digest* and *TV Guide* were neck-and-neck in the circulation derby. Suddenly, in 1988, both were passed by a

---

[9]Magazine Publishers of America—The Definitive Resource. Retrieved at http://www.magazine.org/consumer_marketing/circ_trends/1318.aspx.

[10]The National Directory of Magazines at http://www.oxbridge.com/NDMCluster/theNDM.asp.

[11]Magazine Publisher of America—The Definitive Resource, New Magazine Titles by Interest Category 2007, retrieved from http://www.magazine.org/research/finance_and_operations/finance_operations_trends_and_magazine_handbook/26945.aspx.

magazine called *Modern Maturity*. Most college students have never heard of the magazine. This is not surprising, since it is a controlled-circulation publication not available on the newsstands. The only way to receive it is to be over 50 years old and a member of the American Association of Retired Persons (AARP). A membership costs only $12.50 a year, making it also the least expensive magazine available.

Modern Maturity changed names in April 2003 to *AARP The Magazine*. A May 2007 press release announced that *AARP The Magazine* audience had topped 30 million—equaling the viewerships of "American Idol" and making it the largest circulation magazine in the world.[12]

Marketing Magazines

Owners of all media are concerned with the demographics of their medium, meaning the characteristics of audience members such as age, education, sex, income, type of household, geographic location, and other factors that can be measured using census-type data. Magazine publishers go even further than other media, using research that attempts to measure the values and lifestyles of their readers, also referred to as **psychographics**. This approach to enhanced demographics takes all of the available data about buying habits and other characteristics of the mass audience into its computers and matches it with the content and circulation data about various magazines.

psychographics
the process of using research that attempts to measure the values and lifestyles of an audience

Various research organizations have developed different labels for categories of audience members. For example, Claritas' Prizm system includes "Young Digerati" (tech-savvy singles and couples living in fashionable neighborhoods on the urban fringe who are affluent, highly educated, and ethnically mixed), "Urban Achievers" (young singles and couples, typically college-educated and ethnically diverse, who live on the coasts), and "Simple Pleasures" (singles and couples over the age of 65 living in modestly priced homes who are very likely to have served in the military).[13]

According to psychographics research, certain groups are more likely to purchase luxury items such as PDAs, expensive jewelry, or overseas vacation while other groups are more likely to purchase practical items such as cleaning products, school supplies, or auto parts. For example, those classified as "Young Digerati" are most likely to purchase the latest BlackBerry, shop at Banana Republic, or wear Omega watches. "Simple Pleasures" are most likely to

Most magazines carry advertising that is carefully chosen to appeal to particular readers.
© *Lawrence Atienza/Shutterstock*

[12]AARP Press Center, Targeting America's Coveted 50+ Demographic, AARP The Magazine Announces 2007 Road Show Schedule, *AARP The Magazine*, May 02, 2007. Retrieved at http://www.aarp.org/aarp/presscenter/ pressrelease/articles/magazine_road_show.html.

[13]Clatias at http://www.claritas.com/MyBestSegments/Default.jsp.

purchase laundry detergent, shop at Target, and pick up new car tires. Since the need and desires of these groups are so different, their preference of magazine is likely to be different as well.

Most magazines carry advertising that is carefully chosen to appeal to their readerships. However, several notable magazines do not, relying on subscriptions and issue sales. The feminist-focused *Ms.* magazine started as a one-time insert in *New York* magazine in 1971. The magazine could not always reconcile its editorial concerns with commercial issues, and it began publishing without advertising in 1989. *Ms.* now has a circulation of over 200,000. *Consumer Reports*, starting in 1936 as an independent review of product safety, states clearly in its ethical guidelines: "We don't accept ads, free samples, or products or gifts of any kind. We pay our own way. We don't use CU's name or information for personal gain or to advance personal causes." *Consumer Reports* had a circulation of over 4.4 million in 2008.[14]

Magazines Online

Virtually every magazine has a Web site. Many magazines permit visitors to search archives, read additional information either on the site or off, post their own thoughts and perspectives, view related video files and find up-to-date information that does not appear in a print edition. The traffic on certain magazine sites can be amazing. For example, *Sports Illustrated's* Web site receives about 532,615,708 individual page views a month![15]

However, some magazines publish only online. Called **ezines** or **webzines**, these magazines function much like traditional print magazines, with regular updates and advertising sales. Some of the more well-known and established ezines include *Salon* (www.Salon.com), founded in 1995, and *Slate Magazine* (www.slate.com), founded in 1996 and owned by the Washington Post company. *Slate* is free, while *Salon* features a combination of free and paid subscriptions. *Slate* attracts over five million visitors per month; *Salon* brings in 4.4 million.

ezines
magazines that are only published online

webzines
magazines that are only published online

While *Salon* and *Slate* may lead the online magazine pack in circulation, there are countless smaller publications that cater to a variety of interests. Specialization is particularly simple on the Web, given the ease of Web site creation. It is impossible to know how many ezines or webzines there are on the Internet; however, several directories exist that categorize ezines. The Ezine Directory categorizes over 3,600 ezines, including over 350 entertainment ezines and over 100 family ezines.[16] Whatever your interest, just like in magazines, there is an ezine out there that will fit it.

---

[14]Consumer Reports 2008 Annual Report. Retrieved from http://www.consumerreports.org/cro/resources/streaming/PDFs/cu-annual-report-2008.pdf.

[15]Magazine Publishers of America, Top Ten New Media Boxscores. Retrieved from http://www.magazine.org/digital/22508.cfmcc.

[16]The Ezine Directory at www.ezine-dir.com.

THE FUTURE OF MAGAZINES

Will the online format drive traditional print magazines out of business? *The Magazine Handbook*, a publication of the Magazine Publishers of America, indicates that the number of magazines continues to grow, and magazine reading is evolving, with readers spending 44 minutes on average per issue. Many readers save and file their magazines and refer to them many times. For now, traditional magazines are portable and sharable in ways that a Web site is not, but as digital technology advances that may not be true for long.

The Supporters and Skeptics

The Magazine Publishers of America suggests that magazines capture advertisers. In a 2007 survey, magazines performed better than television or the Internet in driving purchasing intent. Magazines outdid both television and the Internet in enhancing brand familiarity and awareness.[17] So, of course, if there are advertisers ready to buy space, there will be a market for those dollars.

But some suggest that the magazine's days are numbered. David Renard, author of *The Last Magazine*, starts his book with the stark declaration, "Magazines, as we know them, are dying." Renard suggests that in 20 years, the pressure of digital media will have forced traditional magazines off the shelves. The "four horsemen" of the magazine's demise include readers becoming viewers; distribution and sales channels shrinking; environmentalists focusing on the waste of the industry; and advertisers moving into the online world. Renard suggests that mainstream magazines will eventually be digital-only publications (in accordance with their disposable natures), while smaller, independent magazines will continue to be created and distributed as part of the conservation of the printed art form.

Perhaps Renard's prediction is correct and the writing is on the wall for the traditional paper-and-ink magazine product. But what is clear is that magazine publishers, as well as other traditional print media such as books and newspapers, will have to adapt to a digital environment.

Texterity and Zinio

Texterity (www.texterity.com) and Zinio (www.zinio.com) are companies that hope to make digital magazine delivery fast and easy. Their Published Web Format (PWF) permits browsing a magazine online to be similar to paging through a print copy, but with more benefits. Texterity's technology is browser-based and requires no additional software or downloads. Zinio requires users to download the Zinio Reader.

A text search, a spread of the thumbnails for all the pages, and a quick way to e-mail content to a friend are all part of the Web format package. The entire print

---

[17]Heidi Dawley, "In Drives Sales Magazines Rank No. 1", *Media Life Research*, October 18, 2007. Retrieved from http://www.medialifemagazine.com/artman2/publish/Research_25/In_driving_sales_magazines_rank_No_1.asp.

magazine, including ads, can be easily browsed, shared, and even printed. For the publisher, key information is gathered and transmitted via the Web, including hits on advertiser Web pages. If a reader is interested in visiting a cosmetic Web site, for example, he/she merely clicks on the Web site address on the virtual advertisement page, and a browser window opens on that site. Click paths are recorded so publishers can see what paths the reader takes through the magazine. Publishers can also offer surveys that can provide fast reader feedback.

The main concern for readers is whether online magazines are comfortable to read. Texterity's 2007 survey of digital magazine readers suggests they do: 88% report they are satisfied or very satisfied with their subscriptions, and they like the format because it is easier to search, they can more efficiently save their copies, and the format is environmentally friendly. In 2006, the Magazine Publishers of America partnered with Zinio to offer free digital subscriptions of a number of titles to college students in an effort to entice them into reading more magazines. In 2007, Texterity announced an option to deliver magazine content to your iPhone, including *Every Day with Rachael Ray*, *Vibe*, and *Popular Science*.[18]

"Content"

Many people have heard the quote, "Content is king." As online information turns into "content," it is inevitable that companies specializing in content delivery would spring up to meet that need. Mochila is one company that offers writing for a price. Dubbing itself "The Media Marketplace," Mochila will syndicate the content that Web site operators desire—for a price.

A tour through Mochila's services reveals the ability of a prospective Web site owner to search for timely content in categories such as health, entertainment, sports, or business. Users can browse for articles written by Mochila editorial staff writers to feature on their Web sites. This content can be displayed as sidebars that can be formatted to individual tastes. Now, rather than just selling a product, an online business can provide that all-important content to its potential customers, pulling them in and keeping them longer.

What does this mean for budding magazine writers? As online writer Marcia Yudkin puts it, the content is the "reading material or information of value to [a web business'] target market."[19] Yudkin offers a list of possible ways to break into the content provider field, from reviews to Q&As to opinion columns to interactive material. The skills a content provider needs, according to Yudkin, are similar to those that freelance writers have always needed: self-editing, fast turn-around, a good business sense. The world a new magazine journalist enters today may be formatted and delivered as it never has before, but content is still king, just as it's always been.

---

[18]Julie Bosman, "Magazines Going to the Web to Get Students to Read," *New York Times*, September 7, 2006.

[19]Marcia Yudkin, "From Writer to Content Provider," Retrieved from http://www.yudkin.com/content.htm.

Magazines on Demand?

"I want my iMag!" exclaims Lisa Granatstein of *MediaWeek*, business magazine for media industries. And she's not alone. As Web 2.0 and the age of interactivity and customization take over, it stands to reason that media consumers will want more control over all their media products, including magazines.

It is clear to Granatstein that the magazine industry, while far from dead, should be more forward-thinking than it is. Far from its heyday, the magazine industry needs to think of more ways to adapt and flourish. Yes, there are companies like Texterity and Zinio, who are providing magazines in a digital format, but there is still the issue of choice, of customization. What if a user wants two articles from this month's *Cosmopolitan*, one from *Sports Illustrated*, one from *Wired*, and a couple from *Time*? Why shouldn't that be possible?

Why not, as Granatstein suggests, create a sort of iTunes for magazines, where, as she puts it, "for a fee I can cherry pick articles or individual issues and bundle them"? Since today's media is all about customization, selection, and choice, perhaps an iMag of sorts will be an option in the near future.[20]

George

Hey, Jon Stewart, get out your wallet—you owe a creative debt to the late John F. Kennedy, Jr. for his pioneering magazine *George*. The printed precursor to "The Daily Show" and its ilk, this political magazine debuted in 1995 and lasted six years, eighteen months after the death of its creator, but eventually folding in 2001. *George* focused on the kind of political discussions that most Americans ignored and that were addressed in more staid magazines like *The New Republic* or *National Review*. By blurring the lines between politics, entertainment, and popular culture, *George* broke new media ground, which is now occupied by Stewart and other popular comedic pundits such as Stephen Colbert. As *Boston Globe* journalist Richard Bradley put it, "Just as *George* did, 'The Daily Show' mixes substance with entertainment to reach an audience that shuns traditional political journalism."

Predicted to last under a year by political journalists and commentators, who feared that *George* would "dumb down" or otherwise trivialize serious political issues, the magazine contained ads from Gucci and Prada and featured supermodel Cindy Crawford in a George Washington wig on the inaugural cover. The magazine enjoyed an average 450,000 circulation during its six-year run. *George* broke the traditional format of political magazines by integrating a sizable dose of popular culture. Bradley

---

[20]Lisa Granatstein, "I Want My iMag," *Mediaweek*, May 22, 2006.

John F. Kennedy, Jr. unveils *George* magazine.
©*Reuters/CORBIS*

notes that *George* featured covered U2 lead singer Bono's humanitarian efforts long before the established newsweeklies and political magazines did so.

Whether or not one appreciates or enjoys the Stewart/Colbert approach to political commentary, it's important to recognize both its ubiquity and its creative foundation. As Bradley says, "Today I see signs of *George* everywhere I turn. Sometimes the fusion of pop culture and politics strikes me as populist and invigorating, other times as insufficient and immature. But *George* was right—that's democracy."[21]

How Many Online Readers?

How is online advertising priced and tracked? Is it about how many visitors to a site, how long they stay on a page, where they click, or some other factor? Here is an example. ZATZ, a self-described "independent digital media publisher," publishes newsletters, updates, and books on software and hardware and proudly proclaims, "Our publications are designed from the ground up, proud to be online, proud to be Pure Internet Publishing"[22] As an organization without a traditional print product, ZATZ must be careful in its determination of ad rates and circulation. It must explain to prospective advertisers the impact of advertising in its publications, but without traditional ABC statistics like single-copy sales and subscriptions.

In its Media Kit, ZATZ explains, "Our goal here at ZATZ is *not* to deliver you the most eyeballs, but to deliver you prospective customers who can understand, care about, recommend, and buy your products and services." ZATZ tracks click-throughs of online ads—when a visitor to a site actually clicks on a banner or other advertisement to get more information. ZATZ encourages text rather than graphic ads, and it

[21]Richard Bradley, "The *George* Effect," *The Boston Globe*, October 9, 2005, p. C5.

[22]Zatz at http://www.zatz.com.

cites research that viewers have *banner blindness*—a term coined in 2001 by the Center for Media Research that suggests that surfers tend to ignore banner ads, even if those ads have information they want. ZATZ then provides its "circulation" statistics: over a rolling, two-month period, there are 1,072,115 unique visitors to the ZATZ network; on any given day, 17,868 surfers visit; the typical reader reads eight pages per visit and spends 22 minutes on the ZATZ network per visit; and finally, over a rolling, two-month period, ZATZ feeds 16,928,749 pages (impressions) to readers. This data is a far cry from traditional ABC data, but it is clearly of importance to online advertisers.

How does ZATZ stack up against the big players? In 2007, CNN.com's ad rate page reports an average monthly usage of 1.6 billion total site page views, including 815 million visits to the home page alone, with average monthly unique users of 28.4 million.

CAREERS IN THE FIELD

The magazine industry is a great field for individuals who excel at collecting information, analyzing information, writing, and editing. It's also good for people who enjoy being creative and insightful. Individuals who work directly with magazine content tend to hold positions as reporters, writers, editors, or layout and design specialists. There are also many opportunities on the administrative side of the industry in departments such as public relations, marketing, or ad sales.

To start your career in the magazine industry, you may only need to look to your school. Most universities and colleges have an on-campus publication that is developed by students. You can also volunteer to create a publication for a club or nonprofit organization or create a magazine of your own. Software programs such as Photoshop, Quark, and Publisher can help your publication achieve a professional look. You can add examples of your writing or designs to a portfolio, which can help you acquire an internship or entry-level position at a publishing house.

As we have learned from this chapter, magazines have become very specialized, so as a professional in the magazine industry, you may have to be specialized as well. Consider taking additional courses in subjects such as photojournalism or creative writing to fine tune your skills. Perhaps one day you will introduce your own specialized publication to the world.

SUMMARY

- The magazine differentiated itself from books or newspapers, by discussing both current and dated topics that appeal to a wide variety of people.

- National magazines such as the *Saturday Evening Post* played an important role in establishing the magazine as a mass medium.
- Today, most magazines focus on specialized content that addresses the specific interests and needs of certain groups rather than the general interest of a large audience.
- In the future, the magazine will have to adapt to the digital age and possibly replace print publications with online versions.

DISCUSSION QUESTIONS

1. According to magazine historian Frank Luther Mott, what three services do magazines provide? Do you agree with his statement? Can you think of any other service magazines provide?
2. In its early development, what advantages did the magazine have over newspapers and books? Do magazines still have those advantages today?
3. What is photojournalism? How is it different from other forms of journalism?
4. Why are general interest magazines less successful today? What benefits do specialized magazines give readers? What benefits do they give advertisers?
5. Where do you see the magazine in ten years? Based on your own lifestyle, what role do you think magazines will play in your life?

SUPPLEMENTAL WEB SITES

SUPPLEMENTAL READING

"Hearst's Cathie Black: Teen Category Still Strong" by Lucia Moses. *MediaWeek*
Time Magazine: We the People, by Linda Schinke-Llano.

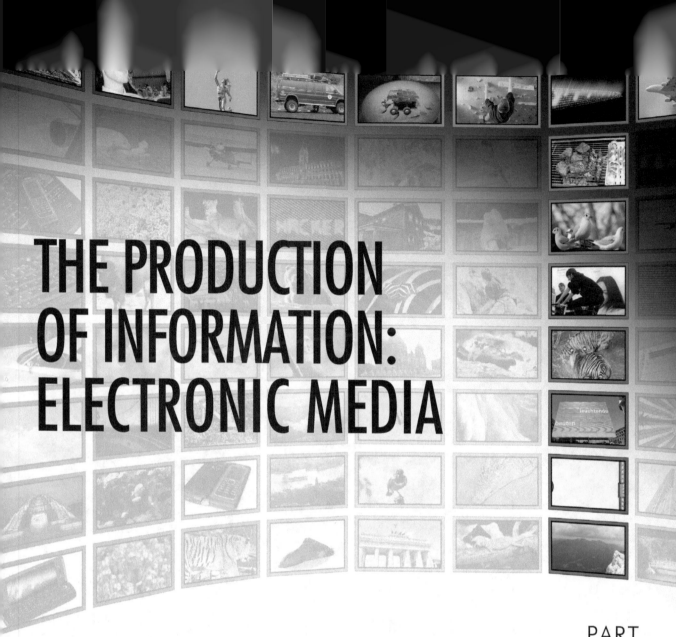

THE PRODUCTION OF INFORMATION: ELECTRONIC MEDIA

PART

3

MUSIC INDUSTRY AND A SHARED IMAGINATION

6

CHAPTER OBJECTIVES

- Understand the invention of sound recording
- Identify various recording formats
- Discuss the evolution of music since the early 20th century
- Discuss the role of rock and roll in American culture
- Identify controversies in the modern music industry

KEY TERMS

musical symbols
phonograph
nickelodeons
records
gramophone
Victrola
royalties
jukebox
stereo
digital recording
analog recording
Tin Pan Alley
jazz
ragtime
blues

R&B (rhythm and blues)
big band
rockabilly
folk music
punk
grunge
hip-hop
rap
gangsta rap
indie
artist & repertoire
    (A&R) representatives
rack jobbers
piracy
copyright

INTRODUCTION

Imagine you are in a crowded train, then a library, and then a gym. What do you see in each scene? Aside from people, you probably also see portable music devices, such as iPods and MP3 players.

Wherever you go, you see people tuned in to their own music.
© Radu Razvan/Shutterstock

musical symbols
handwritten accounts of musical notations

phonograph
earliest form of the record player

nickelodeons
parlors that allowed patrons to listen to recordings for a nickel

Music is an essential part of human life. We make music, we listen to music, and music surrounds us in most commercial settings. Music is a big business.

HISTORY OF THE MUSIC INDUSTRY

One basic method of music recording came through the use of symbols. **Musical symbols**, such as sheet music, were handwritten accounts of musical notations. The drawback to this form of recording was that it could only be performed by trained musicians who understood the notations. Other methods of production included the manipulation of wind or air and clockwork. The invention of the phonograph in 1877 by Thomas Edison made these previous reproduction methods obsolete.

The earliest form of the **phonograph**, or record player, was in the shape of a cylinder. Edison realized that sound could be recorded through the use of a horn, a stylus (needle), and a pliable material, such as tinfoil. The horn was connected to the stylus, and the stylus touched the tinfoil. When sound entered the horn, it caused the stylus to vibrate, which in turn created grooves in the tinfoil. To record the grooves, Edison spread the tinfoil around a wax cylinder. As sound entered the horn, the cylinder rotated to record the sound markings. To play back the sounds, a separate stylus moved through the path of the grooves and converted the vibrations into sounds. The first reproduction of a voice was not a great musical line; instead, it was Edison simply saying, "Mary had a little lamb." After Edison was satisfied with the phonograph, he sent word about the invention to prominent scientists throughout the United States and Europe. The cylindrical phonograph took off in Europe, and by the end of the 19th century, a phonograph factory in Paris had already cataloged 12,000 recordings.[1]

When Edison realized the potential for phonographs to provide entertainment, he opened phonograph parlors where patrons could listen to a recording for a nickel.[2] Soon phonographs became a popular attraction and were popping up in arcades. These amusement areas for recordings, and later on films, became known as **nickelodeons**.

The Gramophone

Soon after Edison's achievement, Emil Berliner, a German immigrant who lived in Washington D.C., expanded on the phonograph by taking away the cylinder and instead recording the vibrations onto a flat disc. In addition to changing the format, Berliner also realized that copies of the recording could be made by creating a negative mold of the original recording and using this mold to create copies. The

---

[1]music recording. *Encyclopedia Britannica* at http://search.eb.com/eb/article-9110130. Retrieved February 25, 2009.

[2]"The Thomas Edison Papers: Wax Cylinder Phonograph," Rutgers University, http://edison.rutgers.edu/cylinder.htm. Accessed February 25, 2009.

Nipper the dog became one of the most famous mascots in advertising history. © Richard Cummins/Corbis

The Victrola was a record player with a hand crank that was designed to look like a piece of furniture. © James Steidl/Shutterstock

copies became known as **records** and could be played on a specialized machine known as a **gramophone**.[3]

Once Berliner introduced the method of recording onto a disk, he helped found the Victor Talking Machine Company along with Eldridge Johnson. The company trademarked advertisements featuring a dog, Nipper, listening to a gramophone with the slogan, "His Master's Voice." This is one of the most famous mascots in advertising history.

The Victor Company prospered and went on to create the **Victrola**, a record player with a hand crank that was designed to look like a piece of furniture. The popularity of the Victrola cemented the disc as a superior format compared to the wax cylinder.

Radio

During this period before radio, major news stories were sometimes "re-enacted" and recorded on wax cylinders to give the audience a sense of far away events. David Sarnoff's idea of the radio as an entertainment device that would be found in every house in America was a visionary one that came true. Prior to this, radios were generally used for emergency and for voice communications, such as from ship to shore. Sarnoff wrote that:

> . . . a radio telephone transmitter having a range of, say, 25 to 50 miles can be installed at a fixed point where the instrumental or voice music or both are produced . . . The receiver can be designed in the form of a simple "Radio Music Box" and arranged for several different wavelengths, which should be changeable with the throwing of a single switch or pressing of a single button.[4]

records
copies of sound recordings that are in the shape of a flat disc

gramophone
early record player that played flat discs

Victrola
record player with a hand crank designed to look like a piece of furniture

[3]phonograph. *Encyclopedia Britannica* at http://search.eb.com/eb/article-9059766. Retrieved February 25, 2009.

[4]http://www.nbcuni.com/History/Radio_Music_Box.pdf.

Radio as an entertainment device took off during the 1920s and 30s. © Bettmann/CORBIS

The Radio Corporation of America (RCA) was founded in 1919, and radio as an entertainment device exploded during the 1920s and 30s. By 1938, 82% of American homes had a radio and by 1950 it was 91%. The mix of music and news was usually about 80% to 20%, although news programming increased during wartime.

During the 1930s and 40s, music on the radio was the major form of popular entertainment. Musicians—not singers—dominated broadcasts in the early days of recorded music because early microphones couldn't capture the nuances of singing and the human voice with enough fidelity for the radio. With demand for music on the rise from radio stations, inventors were tinkering with every aspect of the recording process. As the quality of recordings improved, pre-recorded music was used more and more as a major part of radio programming.

Radio Strikes

When radio stations began playing records on air instead of having live performers, this angered many people in the music industry who didn't receive compensation. The American Society of Composers, Authors, and Publishers (ASCAP) was organized in 1914 to help license and collect fees for musicians and composers, such as **royalties**, which are payments made to the author of a work for sales and live performances. By the 1940s, recordings had become the biggest segment of the money collected by ASCAP. Radio stations argued that they shouldn't have to pay for playing pre-recorded music because it was free advertising and would generate larger sales, and thus benefit musicians and composers.

James Petrillo, the head of the American Federation of Musicians (AFM), began to work with ASCAP to make sure the stations would have to pay for radio play. He led two musician strikes that kept the airwaves quiet for several years in the mid 1940s. The matter went to court. When the courts finally ruled that radio stations must pay a licensing fee for playing records on the air, a system of paying fees for playing recorded music on the radio was instituted.

Strikes and labor issues weren't the only reasons for the shift from live musicians to recorded music and the eventual rise of the vocalist as the dominant musical artist. Recording technology in the form of better microphones and better shellac for the surface of records was changing the way records sounded. As recordings sounded more "live," the need for live musicians on radio was reduced. Today, the occasional live musician heard on the radio is a notable special programming feature.

royalties
payments made to the author of a work for sales and live performances

Improvements in Technology

At the end of World War I, the popularity of the recording industry had declined. In an effort to attract buyers, the industry began using radio technology to produce electronic recordings. This helped the sound quality improve; unfortunately, by the Great Depression, money was too tight for many people to buy records.

The technology behind record making steadily improved as well. In 1915 the standard record was a 78-rpm. The 78 record spun at 78 revolutions-per-minute and could hold four-and-a-half minutes of a recording per side. Columbia Records introduced the long-playing (LP) record in 1948. The LP had fine grooves that could hold approximately 30 minutes of a recording per side and ran at 33.3-rpm. However, it didn't take long for additional improvements to be made. By the 1950s, RCA Corporation introduced the two-sided single to the market. These singles, or 45s (45-rpm) could hold up to 8 minutes of a recording per side. Stereophonic systems were also introduced which allowed one groove to hold two channels of information. By 1958, LPs, 78s, 45s, and stereos were all commercial items available for public consumption.[5] This technology was the primary mode of reproduction until the 1980s when cassette tapes and compact discs (CDs) took over.

> **jukebox**
> coin-operated electric record player that plays selected records

Just as the 78 replaced the wax cylinder, the 45 replaced 78s. In the 1960s and 70s, the LP began to replace 45s. These changes were obvious to consumers because each new song or album was another purchase. On the home front, these also required listeners to upgrade the "hardware" used to play the recordings. Victrolas gave way to turntables. At the height of the 45, turntables that could stack several records and play them sequentially were the mode. As the LP album gained popularity, record players featured dual speeds to play 45- or 33-rpm records.

After World War II, the recording industry grew. Developments that had not achieved commercial success during difficult financial times were given the opportunity to prosper. In 1927, the Automatic Music Instrument Company (AMI) created the first coin-operated electric record player that played selected records. This invention is also known as the coin-operated **jukebox**. During the war, jukeboxes were popular in underground bars and taverns, and after the war, popularity exploded. Jukeboxes spread to diners, drugstores, and bars across the country.

Jukeboxes gained popularity and eventually were found in diners, drugstores, and bars everywhere. © Genevieve Naylor/CORBIS

Stereo and Format Wars

More hardware changes resulted from the introduction of stereo sound in the early 1960s. Stereophonic sound, or **stereo**, is the reproduction of sound using multiple audio channels, such as speakers. The development of stereo led to a more natural sounding recording. With the introduction of concept albums and expensive

> **stereo**
> or stereophonic sound; reproduction of sound using multiple audio channels, such as speakers

---

[5]phonograph. *Encyclopedia Britannica* at http://search.eb.com/eb/article-9059766. Retrieved February 25, 2009.

turntables with stereo speakers, audiophiles shifted away from listening to music on AM radio due to poor sound quality.

In the golden years of analog recording, from the 60s to the 80s, the format of audio transformed quickly from records to audio tape. The high-end reel to reel decks audiophiles sought in the 50s and 60s were made obsolete by cassette tape. Cassette tape, with less audio quality but better marketing of its hardware (players) and tapes, won the battle for consumer dollars over the 8-track tape and its hardware. Yet by 1988, CD sales surpassed LP sales for the first time in history.

Technology disrupted the music recording establishment with digital recording, which freed "content" from "medium" more profoundly than had ever been done before. **Digital recording** involves breaking down a recording into numerical code using 0s and 1s, and recording this code onto magnetic tape or optical discs. Prior to this, **analog recordings** recorded sound waves directly onto records or cassettes. This change led to even more format changes. The Sony Walkman, introduced in 1979, rocked the world of music recording. In 1984, Sony's Portable CD player sent another technological tremor through an industry that wasn't sure where its future lay. With the introduction of the MP3 in 1997 and Napster's first incarnation in 1999, there had been a revolution in music and recording whether the music business knew it or not. With the first iPod shipment from Apple in 2001, it seemed that music producers and record companies were finally aware that business wouldn't be the same anymore.

Rapid and incessant change creates what Marshall McLuhan described as "disruptive technology."[6] Today the music industry is unsettled because its longtime economic models are being challenged on several fronts. There are more ways for people to listen to music than ever before. There are new ways for artists to connect with audiences that cut out traditional roles played by the big recording companies. Corporate consolidation means that recording companies might be owned by defense contractors. Artists and the creative work they produce are no longer evaluated on the basis of musical content, but are just another "widget" to corporate accountants and stockholders.

digital recording
recording method that breaks down a recording into numerical code using 0s and 1s and records this code onto magnetic tape or discs

analog recording
recording method that records sound waves directly onto records or cassettes

Muzak: It's Not Your Father's Elevator Music Anymore[7]

Technology makes it possible to tailor and deliver an unending stream of popular music to almost any environment. Technology is also putting the listener in control in ways that were not possible in an analog age. Movies aren't just for watching anymore, and music isn't just for listening to. The entertainment giants are looking for synergy between the content in various media in ways that would have been impossible to pursue in an age of analog sound.

---

[6]McLuhan, M. (1964). *Understanding Media: The Extensions of Man*, pp. 7–12, 41–47 (Original edition): pp. 19–24, 63–70 (Critical edition).
[7]David Owen, "The Soundtrack of Your Life," *The New Yorker*. April 10, 2006. http://www.newyorker.com/archive/2006/04/10/060410fa_fact. Accessed March 9, 2009.

The music environment in retail malls is designed to attract shoppers.
© Andresr/Shutterstock

Think for a moment how most commercial spaces—stores, shopping malls, elevators, doctors' and dentists' offices—provide occupants with a soundtrack. Today, the ubiquitous music environment formerly known as "elevator music" has been reimagined for today's consumer society as an "acoustic pheromone" designed to attract or repel shoppers according to their psychographic profile. In the article "The Soundtrack of Your Life," David Owen describes how Muzak, the nondescript elevator music of the 1950s, has moved into the "realm of retail theater."

Muzak sells about 80 pre-packaged programs and designs customized programs as part of its global business. The company has created a digital music inventory they call "the Well." In the Well are millions of commercially recorded songs classified by genre and even subgenre—jazz, shag, heavy metal, and more.

Today's Muzak is an expression of "brand." The company hires program designers who attempt to identify the psychological associations of songs and then connect the songs into an aural tapestry that appeals to the emotions of a shopper. The idea is to create an emotional soundtrack for a bar or retail store that affects a customer like an "aural pheromone." The sounds should attract some customers while repelling others to reinforce its emotional impact.

The program designers, called audio architects, alter the rhythms and song connections to get different moods going at different times of the day. The soundtrack gets louder and pushier around closing time. There is also different music for after hours when the customers are gone.

Because music makes emotional connections with us, the audio architectures Muzak creates are powerful and compelling whether we are conscious of it or not. Their biggest competitor, according to their marketing department, is silence.

Tin Pan Alley
area in New York, near Broadway, that was a popular source for sheet music before the popularity of radio and the record player

jazz
improvisational musical form developed from ragtime and blues

Louis Armstrong's jazz music is still popular today.
© CORBIS

ragtime
musical style that displaces regular accents by emphasizing weak beats

blues
style of African-American folk music that expresses emotions rather than telling a story

R&B (rhythm and blues)
musical form that is a combination of blues and big band and was influential in the formation of rock and roll

Popular Music

Prior to the phonograph, people still enjoyed music in their homes. Although they weren't able to listen to a song on a record player, people were able to play songs from sheet music. A small area in New York near Broadway, **Tin Pan Alley**, became a popular source for sheet music at the time. The name Tin Pan referred to the large number of musicians in the area who pounded on pianos in an attempt to sell their songs to producers.[8] At the time, sheet music was in such high demand that the terms "popular music" and "tin pan" became practically interchangeable. However, the name could also be considered derogatory in reference to the cheap pianos used by musicians. Unfortunately for the musicians and songwriters of Tin Pan Alley, once the record player and radio became staples in homes and businesses, the demand for sheet music sharply declined and the Tin Pan Alley era was over.

One of the most influential genres during the period of early radio was jazz. **Jazz** is an improvisational form developed from ragtime and blues. **Ragtime** is a musical style that displaces regular accents by emphasizing weak beats, and **blues** is a style of African-American folk music that expresses emotions rather than telling a story. Jazz was developed by African Americans and is constantly evolving, making a specific definition tricky. It is generally characterized as being improvised with deviations of pitch and syncopated rhythms, which emphasize beats that are normally not accented. However, this is not always the case.

During the 1930s and 1940s, jazz was extremely influential and dominated radio and record sales. Some of the most popular jazz musicians of the time include Louis Armstrong, Duke Ellington, and Benny Goodman. These musicians are still popular today.

Rock and Roll

By the end of the 1940s, six record labels controlled the majority of the music industry: Capital, Columbia, Decca, Mercury, MGM, and Victor. During this time period, labels pushed for a sen-timental style that popularized songs such as "How Much Is That Doggy in the Window?" By the 1950s, rock and roll exploded onto the music scene. Early rock and roll was a combination of country music and rhythm and blues that was fueled by black culture and white spending power.[9]

Rhythm and blues (R&B) played a central role in the formation of rock and roll. In fact, many legendary rock bands, such as the Rolling Stones and the Who advertised themselves as rhythm and blues bands. **R&B** itself is a combination of

[8]Tin Pan Alley. *Encyclopedia Britannica* at http://search.eb.com/eb/article-9072549. Retrieved February 26, 2009.

[9]rock and roll. *Encyclopedia Britannica* at http://search.eb.com/eb/article-9105870. Retrieved February 26, 2009.

blues and **big band**, which is a harder, but slower form of jazz. By the middle of the 1950s, R&B simply meant black popular music not focused on teenagers.[10]

Disc jockeys, such as Allan Freed, Dewey Phillips, and William Allen, helped create rock-and-roll radio, which spread this new musical style. White teenagers immediately gravitated to a sound that was sexy and exciting compared to performers of the 1940s and early 1950s. In fact, the term "rock and roll" was an expression used by African Americans to mean sex.

In 1954 the recording industry found a face that would further popularize the genre: Elvis Presley. Presley's appeal came from the fact that he was an attractive white man with the voice of a black man. It was this combination of cultures that acted as a catalyst for the rise of Elvis, but also of rock and roll. Elvis dominated the music charts from 1956–1958 and sent girls into a frenzy with his gyrations. Often when Elvis appeared on television shows, his entire body wasn't shown to the viewing audience. Instead, he was shown from the waist up.

Elvis was discovered by Sam Phillips, a disc jockey from Memphis who some have called "the man who invented rock'n'roll."[11] Phillips was willing to work with any performing artist, no matter their color. Because of this he was able to work with B.B. King and with Jackie Brenson and the Delta Cats. Phillips owned a recording service that allowed people to create their own records for a small price. He discovered Elvis Presley when Elvis came into the shop to make a present for his mother.[12] Phillips went on to open Sun Records and produced records for Johnny Cash, Jerry Lee Lewis, and Roy Orbison.

Phillips worked on combining the various musical styles of the South, such as blues, country, and gospel. This combination was one of the first versions of rock and roll, called rockabilly.[13] Elvis, Fats Domino, Little Richard, Buddy Holly, and Jerry Lee Lewis all performed rockabilly. **Rockabilly** is essentially a combination of rock and roll and hillbilly music. These performers appealed to teenagers across the country looking to rebel against the clean cut culture of early 20th century. In addition to music, teens embraced other rebellious figures such as James Dean and Marlon Brando. While the youth of America felt like they had found their own soundtrack, other cultural leaders condemned the style, going so far as to claim that rock and roll was "devil music."[14]

big band
musical form that is a harder, but slower, form of jazz

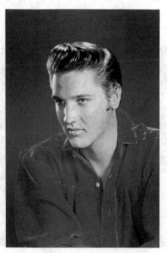

Elvis Presley dominated the music charts in the mid-50s.
© Michael Ochs Archives/ Corbis

rockabilly
musical form that is a combination of rock and roll and hillbilly music

---

[10]rhythm and blues. *Encyclopedia Britannica* at http://search.eb.com/eb/article-9063492. Retrieved February 26, 2009.

[11]"Sam Phillips: Rock'n'Roll Guru," BBC News, http://news.bbc.co.uk/2/hi/entertainment/827057.stm. Accessed February 26, 2009.

[12]Ibid.

[13]"Sam Phillips," The Rock and Roll Hall of Fame and Museum, Inc., http://www.rockhall.com/inductee/sam-phillips. Accessed February 26, 2009.

[14]rock and roll. *Encyclopedia Britannica* at http://search.eb.com/eb/article-9105870. Retrieved February 26, 2009.

The intensity that rock and roll started with didn't last long. By 1959, Elvis was drafted into the army, Little Richard left rock and roll for gospel, Buddy Holly died in a plane crash, and Jerry Lee Lewis was condemned for marrying his 13-year-old cousin. After the loss of so many stars so fast, rock was at a crossroads. Knowing the potential for record sales, labels frantically searched for the next crop of stars. However, the labels' interpretation of rock and roll was tame compared to the scene of the 1950s. In the early 1960s, the stars of rock and roll were Ricky Nelson, Frankie Avalon, Annette Funicello, and Connie Francis. These performers did not have the same impact as the performers of the 1950s.

The British Invasion

The Beatles brought innovation and style to the 60s rock and roll. © Gerhard Rauchwetter/dpa/Corbis

In 1964, the Beatles took the United States by storm. Compared to the toned down sound of rock and roll in the early 1960s, the Beatles brought innovation and style. Up until then, British bands were unsuccessful in replicating American rock and roll. However, by the beginning of the 1960s, many British teens were becoming well versed in the genre. The British invasion was in full swing by 1964. Along with the Beatles, England could also claim the Rolling Stones, the Who, the Animals, the Kinks, and Dusty Springfield. Whereas the Beatles were beloved by audiences and television, the Rolling Stones were a more polarizing group. The Rolling Stones were darker and more sexual than the clean-cut Beatles. These two roles eventually split rock and roll and changed the genre to simply rock. Both groups continued successfully performing and selling albums, but the Rolling Stones influenced hard-rock performers whereas the Beatles influenced a softer sound based on melody. The British Invasion helped change the face of American rock and roll. The Frankie Avalons were replaced with Steven Tylers, and the Annette Funicellos were replaced with Janis Joplins. The wholesome, clean-cut image of American rock stars evolved into an image of someone more intimidating.

Folk Music

folk music
musical style that uses traditional, often acoustic, instruments and has a political agenda

During the turbulent political times of the 1960s and 70s, with the Civil Rights and women's movements and the Vietnam War, music naturally became politically expressive. Although all genres were inspired by the state of the times, folk music spoke the loudest with regard to activism. Folk music originated from an oral tradition in rural areas. Songs were passed down through generations and learned through hearing. Modern **folk music** is characterized as having a political agenda and using traditional, often acoustic, instruments.

In the early 20th century, during the Great Depression, Woody Guthrie was the first major composer of protest music, including "This Land Is Your Land"

and "Union Maid." By the middle of the 20th century, folk music branched out to blend with other genres, such as rock and pop. Folk rock emerged through Bob Dylan, and folk pop gained popularity with the group Peter, Paul, and Mary.

Folk rock eventually split into two camps: folk rock from the United States and folk rock from Britain. Folk rock in the United States was characterized as youthful, rebellious protest music. Popular artists include the Mamas and the Papas and Simon and Garfunkel. On the other hand, British folk rock stuck more to tradition. Artists took established folk music, sometimes centuries old, and blended it with modern sounds. More recent folk rock and folk pop can be heard in the music of Bruce Springsteen, Tracy Chapman, and 10,000 Maniacs.

Alternative Rock

Similar to the situation in the early 1960s, by 1970, rock was once again at a crossroads. With the breakup of the Beatles and the deaths of Jimi Hendrix and Janis Joplin, rock would eventually split into smaller movements that would appeal to more specific audiences.

In the 1970s, the development of **punk**, an aggressive form of rock characterized by confrontational, socially aware lyrics and a sped-up style of music, tried to reawaken the energy that followed the early years of rock and roll. Punk acted as an urban celebration after years of hippie style and music. However, at the heart of punk rock was a rebellious attitude that went against the commercial nature of popular rock of the time. Even though punk never gained the widespread popularity of traditional rock, you can still see the impact and influence of early punk rockers on culture. Look around and you can probably spot one or two Ramones or Sex Pistols t-shirts. Another contribution made by punk rock was that it was able to usher in a sound that would help shape yet another movement in rock: grunge.

punk
aggressive form of rock music characterized by confrontational, socially aware lyrics and a sped-up style of music

grunge
musical form that is a combination of heavy metal/hard rock and punk rock

Grunge appeared in the early 1990s as a combination of heavy metal/hard rock and punk rock. The grunge movement emerged at an independent record label in Seattle, Sub Pop. Sub Pop helped launch the careers of Mudhoney, Screaming Trees, Soundgarden, and Nirvana. The popularity of grunge can be directly attributed to the release of the single "Smells Like Teen Spirit" from Nirvana's *Nevermind* album. After the suicide of Nirvana front man Kurt Cobain and Pearl Jam's rejection of commercial popularity, the popularity of grunge faded by the end of the 90s.

Alternative rock provided categorization for musical groups that went against the norm of the glamorous rock style of the 1970s, with David Bowie, and the hair metal of the 80s and 90s, with Poison and Motley Crue. It provided a landscape that would launch such long lasting groups as U2 and Green Day. Many alternative rockers appealed to a specific audience of white males, which left a void in musical options for many blacks. This void helped to spur a musical revolution in the 1980s: rap and hip-hop.

Pearl Jam's Eddie Vedder performs on stage during the height of the grunge movement. © Neil Preston/CORBIS

Hip-Hop, Rap, and Gangsta Rap

Hip-hop can be defined as many different things. It is the background music used for rap. It is a musical style all on its own that blends rhythmic beats and rhyming lyrics. Hip-hop also refers to a culture that includes deejaying, rapping, graffiti, and B-boying, which is a combination of dance, style, and attitude.

The hip-hop genre originated in the Bronx section of New York. DJ Kool Herc was one of the first major hip-hop deejays.[15] The Jamaican immigrant used two turntables to blend fragments of older songs with popular music, which created an almost endless flow of music at parties. Hip-hop deejays of the time were also famous for isolating a record's break beat, the part of a dance record where the drumbeats are the only sounds that remain. These break beats encouraged dancing and dance contents where break dancing was a popular style. Another famous hip-hop deejay, Grandmaster Flash, led innovations in turntable manipulations, such as needle dropping and scratching.

Rap, a vocal style characterized by rhythmical speaking, emerged when hip-hop deejays spoke over records. DJ Kool Herc is known as the father of modern rap.[17] However, there are many other influences that led to the modern sound of rap, such as talking blues songs, jailhouse toasts (poems reminiscing about misdeeds), dozens (an oral game exchanging insults), and toasting (a style of rhymed speech from Jamaica). The first nationally recognized rap song was Sugarhill Gang's "Rapper's Delight" (1979). Other pioneers of old school rap include Grandmaster Flash & the Furious Five and the Cold Crush Brothers.

In the 1980s, the introduction of MTV and a crop of new rappers spread the genre to many new listeners. Run-D.M.C. helped bring rap into the mainstream by combining rap with hard rock; the Beastie Boys, a trio of white rappers, helped broaden the audience even more for rap; the group Public Enemy rapped about socially conscious topics and black political ideology; and female rappers Salt-N-Pepa and Queen Latifah provided a balanced view of hip-hop culture by countering the misogynistic views of many male rappers.

Salt-N-Pepa provided rap from a female point of view.
© Marko Shark/CORBIS

By the end of the 1980s, Los Angeles responded to New York's rap and hip-hop sounds by further pushing the boundaries with a new style called gangsta rap and with the group N.W.A. (Niggaz With Attitude), who included Ice Cube, Eazy E, and Dr. Dre, among others. **Gangsta rap** is a form of hip-hop that provides a window into the lifestyle of poverty and drug use in many inner cities. Gangsta rap often contains

---

[15]hip-hop. *Encyclopedia Britannica* at http://search.eb.com/eb/article-9117537. Retrieved March 3, 2009.
[16]Ibid.

Tupac Shakur and Notorious B.I.G. were both murdered in the East Coast-West Coast gangsta rap showdown. © *Chi Modu/Diverse Images/Corbis (left)*; © *Shawn Mortensen/ Corbis (right)*

hyperrealism, thoughts of immortality, and a romanticized image of the outlaw. N.W.A.'s album *Straight Outta Compton* provided a graphic perspective of the life of violence that permeated many inner cities. Gangsta rappers, such as Tupac Shakur, were praised for telling the truth about life for many people, but criticized by others for glorifying a criminal lifestyle. Gangsta rap in the 1990s became a dangerous showdown for East Coast and West Coast rivals. After the murders of West Coast Tupac Shakur and his East Coast rival Notorious B.I.G., many thought the genre had gone too far.

During the late 90s and the early part of the 21st century, hip-hop, which is often synonymous with rap, emerged as the most popular musical genre in the United States. Rappers, such as Jay-Z and Sean Combs have transcended music to become moguls who design clothes, fragrances, and beverages. Rappers, such as OutKast, Kid Rock, and Rage Against the Machine, have also incorporated rock and pop into their music similar to Run-D.M.C. Although many genres of music have become diluted and commercialized for profits, many argue that rap has been able to withstand these temptations due to listeners' demand for authenticity.[17]

MODERN MUSIC INDUSTRY

The modern music industry is composed of people who develop and distribute music to the general public. With the rise of file sharing the in the early 1990s, the entire business plan for the music industry was turned inside out. Control over manufacturing, distributing, and promoting artists was lost to the Internet. Music was available for free (albeit illegally) on the Internet, and it was also unregulated. There was no worry of parental advisories or censorship.

---

[17]hip-hop. *Encyclopedia Britannica.* http://search.eb.com/eb/article-9117537. Retrieved March 3, 2009.

Record Labels

During the 1980s and 90s, record labels were shuffled around and consolidated leaving four major labels to produce 85% of all recordings in the United States: Universal Music Group (Geffen, Interscope, Motown), Sony BMG Music Entertainment (Arista, Columbia, Epic), EMI Group (Capital, Virgin), and Warner Music Group (Asylum, Atlantic, Reprise).[18] The remaining 15% of U.S. record production came from various independent labels.

Many artists start off with or develop their own independent label. An independent label, or **indie**, is a record label that is independently funded and not connected to a major label. They can range from a label with one artist that is run out of the artist's home to a large business that helps put a spotlight on up-and-coming acts. Because indie labels have limited funding, they do not have the same power and influence as one of the four major labels. However, one advantage of indie labels is their willingness to take a risk on an unknown artist. Major labels have reason to be skeptical of unknown artists because even seasoned performers can be unprofitable for the label. In 2001, Mariah Carey signed the largest contract of that time, an $80-million-dollar deal with Virgin Records. After Carey had a public meltdown, Virgin released her from her contract in 2002, along with $28 million dollars.[19]

indie
or independent record label; record label that is independently funded and not connected to a major label

Recording Artists

The most well recognized member of the recording industry is usually the recording artist. The recording artist is the person or group that struggles, often for years, trying to get discovered and gain a large audience. This is the name on the CD, download, and music video.

Successful recording artists need to be more than just good musicians. They also need to be negotiators aware of the business side of the music industry. Recording artists should be conscious of financial matters, such as contracts, copyright laws, and royalty payments. Infamous bankruptcy cases involving huge stars, such as M.C. Hammer, TLC, and Toni Braxton, are a reminder that dealing with record companies can be a very complicated process. Some artists, such as rocker Courtney Love, have been outspoken when it comes to record companies and payments. Love claims that record companies design contracts so that artists pay for the production of records. After the labels recoup these expenses, take their designated profits, and the artists pay their managers and lawyers, there is practically nothing left for the artist.[20] (See Profit Controversy.)

Artists must also be confident in their sound while straddling the line of being marketable. Kelly Clarkson gained fame by winning *American Idol* and releasing pop-infused songs such as "Since U Been Gone." On her third album *My*

---

[18]Bill Lamb, "Top 4 Major Pop Record Labels," About.com: Top 40/Pop, http://top40.about.com/od/popmusic101/tp/majorlabels.htm. Accessed March 3, 2009.

[19]Jason Ankeny, Artist Biography—Mariah Carey, *Billboard*, http://www.billboard.com/bbcom/bio/index.jsp?pid=48340. Accessed March 3, 2009.

[20]Courtney Love, "Courtney Love Does the Math," Salon, http://archive.salon.com/tech/feature/2000/06/14/love/index.html. Accessed March 3, 2009.

Profit Controversy

In 2000, rocker Courtney Love made a speech at the Digital Hollywood Online entertainment conference giving support to online downloading while bashing recording label practices. Love claimed that, "The system's set up so almost nobody gets paid."

Love presented a fictitious example of a band that ends up making a huge deal with a record label that includes a 20-percent royalty rate and a one-million-dollar advance on their contract. This may sound like the band in question has hit the jackpot; however, that million dollars doesn't line the musicians' pockets as one may think. Love breaks down the way this money is used to help jump start the band's album.

Love claims that $500,000 of that money is used to record an album. Then, out of the remaining $500,000, the band needs to pay their manager a 20-percent commission. That's another $100,000. Then, the band's lawyer and business manager are paid $25,000 each. This leaves $350,000 to be split among the band members. Let's assume there are four members. After $170,000 is taken out for taxes, that leaves $180,000 left for the group, or $45,000 each. This is the band's income for the following year until their album gets recorded and released.

It's not over yet. Now the band has to promote their album. Let's say the album is a huge success, sells a million copies, and the band releases two singles, both of which require videos. The combined total cost for the videos is one million dollars. The record label pays for this; however, 50 percent will be recouped by the label out of the royalties. Now the band needs to go on tour to further promote the album. This costs $200,000, which is again initially paid for the by label but is 100 percent recoupable. Love also claims that the record company will spend another $300,000 on independent radio promotion, which the band will eventually have to pay for. Plus, let's not

Courtney Love performs in concert with her band Hole.
© John Atashian/CORBIS

forget that the band has to pay back the original one-million-dollar advance. This leaves the band in debt to the record label for $2 million.

However, what about all those records that were sold? Love says that if all one million records were sold at full price and the band received 20 percent of the royalties, they should receive approximately $2 million. Because of the amount the band owes the label, they are left with nothing except the satisfaction of being popular and heard on the radio. In this situation, Love claims that the record label grosses $11 million. After subtracting expenses, the label stands to profit approximately $6.6 million.

December, released in the summer of 2007, Clarkson took artist control of the album and went in a darker direction. After a public feud with record label head Clive Davis (who questioned whether the record was a hit) less than expected record sales, and a cancelled tour, Clarkson quickly went back into the studio to work on a new album that was released in March 2009. Clarkson's fourth record, *All I Ever Wanted*, returned to the pop sound that helped make her a star.

While talent shows such as *American Idol* and *America's Got Talent* have been extremely popular with viewers, the vast majority of artists are discovered by A&R (artist & repertoire) representatives. **A&R representatives** are essentially talent scouts that are on the lookout for the next big artist. They listen to demo, or demonstration, tapes and go to live shows. A&R representatives may also work with artists in the recording studio, helping to develop the artist's sound or helping to produce or manage the artist.

artist & repertoire (A&R) representatives record company talent scouts

The Production Staff

A **record producer** has many jobs. The producer manages resources and budgets for equipment and background musicians and runs the recording sessions. Producers can also have some creative control over a record. The producer can make decisions to have an artist sing a track again or even delete a track from an album altogether.

Aside from the producer, there is also a staff of technical experts, such as audio engineers and sound mixers who work to make a record sound the best it can. These technical experts are managed by the record producer, so the work they do is based on requests by the producer.

Whereas the artists themselves are important to the sound of a track, the production is also highly important. Modern record production is more complicated than simply recording an artist singing or a band playing. Now different aspects of the track are recorded on separate audio tracks and then blended together. Once all of the tracks are recorded, the technical staff edits them. This can help explain why some of your favorite bands or singers don't sound as good performing live compared to the songs on their albums. Although there are other factors that contribute to this, it's difficult to produce a piece of live music that sounds like a track that had been labored over for hours.

While an artist is hard at work recording an album, a team of marketing experts is busy planning the marketing and promotion of that artist. This process includes organizing radio air play and advertising campaigns, such as television appearances, videos, and print advertisements. The marketing and promotion team is also responsible for coming up with catchy posters and displays.

Selling the Music

The two primary modes of distribution are retail sales and online sales. Direct music retailers, such as f.y.e., are focused solely on selling music and music accessories. Other retail shops, such as Best Buy and Target, sell music but are not focused solely on its sale. Stores like these use **rack jobbers**, or contractors hired by retail stores to stock and order music for the store. This frees up a store's staff to focus on other, potentially more important, merchandise.

rack jobbers
contractors hired by retail stores to stock and order music for the store

Online stores, such as Amazon and iTunes, have gained considerable popularity over the past 10 years. This has caused some direct retailers, such as Tower Records, to claim bankruptcy. Benefits of online stores include a large variety of options and the ability to preview a song or album prior to purchasing it. Shoppers also often have the option to purchase individual songs for less than $1. Online stores can charge a relatively inexpensive amount because there is no physical item to create. There is no expense for a CD, a case, liner notes, etc. There is also less potential to lose money due to excessive amounts of overstock.

Other less significant modes of sale are music clubs and specialty CDs, which can be sold through television, such as the compilation CD *Ultimate Power Ballads*.

CONTROVERSIES IN THE MUSIC INDUSTRY

Since 2000 and the rise of Napster, piracy has been a considerable problem for the music industry. **Piracy** is the illegal duplication of copyrighted works. A **copyright** is a law that gives the creator of the work ownership over that work. In the music industry, the artist is not necessarily the copyright holder of a song. Ownership can also be held by the record label or by an individual, such as a producer. For example, pop star Michael Jackson had partial copyrights to most of the Beatles' catalog of songs and received a percentage of the royalties that these songs generate.[21]

piracy
illegal duplication of copyrighted works

copyright
law that gives the creator of a work ownership over that work

During the rise of online pirating, from 1999–2002, music sales declined 31%.[22] Since then, the news for physical album sales in the United States has only gotten worse. The year 2000 was the pinnacle for physical album sales, selling 785.1 billion. In 2008, album sales were only 54 percent of that figure. However, downloads are not making up the difference.[23] According to the International Federation of the Phonographic Industry (IFPI), there were billions of illegal files swapped in 2007, and the ratio of unlicensed to licensed tracks downloaded is approximately 20:1.[24]

---

[21]"The Rights Stuff," Snopes.com, http://www.snopes.com/music/artists/jackson.asp. Accessed March 3, 2009.

[22]Peter Feuilherade, "Online Piracy Devastates Music," BBC News, http://news.bbc.co.uk/2/hi/technology/3532891.stm. Accessed March 4, 2009.

[23]Geoff Duncan, "Nielsen: U.S. Album Sales Down 14 Pct." Digital Trends, January 2, 2009, http://news.digitaltrends.com/news-article/18791/nielsen-u-s-album-sales-down-14-pct. Accessed March 6, 2009.

[24]International Federation of the Phonographic Industry, "IFPI Digital Music Report 2008," http://www.ifpi.org/content/library/DMR2008.pdf. Accessed March 6, 2009.

In an attempt to gain control of rampant piracy, the Recording Industry Association of America (RIAA) categorized peer-to-peer (P2P) file sharing as illegal and began suing people engaged in the activity. Many people assume that because something is able to be downloaded it is legal. This is not the case. Since the early 21st century, copyright holders have allowed particular websites legal access to music downloading. However, many illegal sites still exist. In 2009, several high-profile defendants lost their file-sharing cases in court, suffering fines of many thousands of dollars per song. The RIAA has since decided to change its approach and not sue individuals; instead, it plans to find other ways to combat music piracy.

Censorship

Censorship is nothing new. It has been around since the invention of the radio and the record. In 1939, Billie Holiday's song "Strange Fruit" was banned from the radio for protesting the lynching of blacks.[25] In 1966, the cover art for the Beatles' record *Yesterday and Today* album was changed by their record label. The original art depicted the band members sitting among butchered meat and decapitated baby dolls; it was replaced with a stock photo of the group.[26] In the 80s and 90s rap groups such as 2 Live Crew and N.W.A. dealt with censorship issues concerning explicit content. In 2006, country trio the Dixie Chicks remarked at a concert in London, "Just so you know, we're ashamed the president of the United States [George W. Bush] is from Texas."[27] This comment alienated many country music fans, and conservative radio stations went so far as to ban the group from having airplay. Now, after years of hindsight, many recognize these musicians as classic artists in their respective genres.

Musical censorship is a controversial issue that is still not resolved. How far can lyrics push the envelope before they become too explicit and potentially detrimental to the listener? How far can labels and stores go to censor albums before they are infringing on the artist's freedom of speech? There are no clear cut answers to these questions; however, here are a few of the arguments for and against musical censorship.

Those in favor of censorship often support traditional family values. They argue that children and teenagers should not be exposed to explicit, offensive, or violent lyrics. They point out artists such as Eminem and Marilyn Manson as influential artists who are causing impressionable children to turn to bad behavior. Parents claim that parental warnings such as "Explicit Content" are inadequate warnings regarding the content of the record. Advocates of censorship also suggest that record labels specifically target teens and tweens to boost sales and that explicit lyrics are included or added to records as a marketing strategy. Some groups, such as the American Family Association (AFA), claim to not

Those who are in favor of censorship often point out that artists such as Marilyn Manson are a bad influence on children.
© *Rune Hellestad/CORBIS*

[25]"1900–1949," USA/Canada, Free Muse, http://www.freemuse.org/sw20536.asp. Accessed March 4, 2009.

[26]"1960–1969," USE/Canada, Free Muse, http://www.freemuse.org/sw20694.asp. Accessed March 4, 2009.

[27]Peter S. Canellos, "Furor over country band echoes a nation's cultural discord," *The Boston Globe*, June 20, 2006, http://www.boston.com/news/nation/articles/2006/06/20/furor_over_country_band_echoes_a_nations_cultural_discord/. Accessed March 4, 2009.

specifically support censorship; however, they do encourage advertisers to only support "quality programming." This way entertainment that goes against traditional values does not have the financial support it needs to be successful.[28]

The other side of the argument is led by the RIAA. Often those who are against censorship use the First Amendment as proof that censorship is unconstitutional. Censoring music can also create a slippery slope that can lead to censorship of books, newspapers, and other artistic forms of media. Those who oppose censorship claim that music acts as a reflection of the current culture. Therefore, if music is filled with sex and violence, perhaps there are other, bigger problems that need to be addressed before censorship comes into play. Additionally, opponents argue that it is not the responsibility of an artist or the music industry to prevent a child from listening to an album. That is the responsibility of a child's parent or guardian. Obviously, some songs are not appropriate for everyone. This is why the RIAA has taken the opportunity to label certain records as having "Explicit content." The RIAA also suggests that music can act as the starting point for talking with children about themes in music and what these themes mean.[29]

Can Music Be Dangerous?

In October 1984, 19-year-old John McCollum committed suicide while listening to an Ozzy Osbourne record. In December of the following year, 18-year-olds Raymond Belknap and Jim Vance spent six hours drinking beer, smoking marijuana, and listening to Judas Priests' Stained Class album. Both men then attempted suicide; only Vance survived. Following these incidents, the victims' families filed lawsuits against the bands claiming negligence, liability, and intent.

In the case of Osbourne, his albums do contain songs about suicide and death. However, the Court of Appeals ruled that even though Osbourne's songs contained these themes, they did not stress immediate action. Music is still covered under the First Amendment—even music that propagates the idea of suicide—as long as it does not convey immediate action of the message.

Because of the ruling in the Osbourne case, prosecutors in the Judas Priest case claimed that Bleknap committed suicide because of a subliminal message on the album saying, "do it, do it," which suggests immediate action. Although the judge pointed out that there was a subliminal message that sounded like "do it, do it" on one song, he ruled that the message was the accidental noise of a guitar part.[30]

---

[28]"General Information," The American Family Association, http://www.afa.net/about.asp. Accessed March 4, 2009; "Analysis," http://www.geocities.com/musiccensorship/analysis.htm. Accessed March 3, 2009. Sarah McBride and Ethan Smith, "Music Industry to Abandon Mass Suits," *The Wall Street Journal*, Dec. 19, 2008, available at http://online.wsj.com/article/SB122966038836021137.html.

[29]"Tools for Parents and Educators," The Recording Industry Association of America," http://www.riaa.com/toolsforparents.php?content_selector=&searchterms=censorship&terminclude=&termexact=. Accessed March 4, 2009; "Analysis," http://www.geocities.com/musiccensorship/analysis.htm. Accessed March 3, 2009.

[30]Deflem, Mathieu. 1993. "Rap, Rock, and Censorship: Popular Culture and the Technologies of Justice." Paper presented at the annual meeting of the Law and Society Association, Chicago, May 27–30, 1993, http://www.cas.sc.edu/socy/faculty/deflem/zzcens97.htm. Accessed March 4, 2009.

Another famous case of critics questioning the safety of music is the 1992 controversy involving the song "Cop Killer" by the band Body Count and released by Time Warner. Body Count was a heavy metal band fronted by gangsta rapper Ice-T. The genres of heavy metal and rap have generally been followed by controversy; however, the timing of this release coincided with the beating of Rodney King by police officers and the Los Angeles riots that followed the ruling acquitting the police officers of criminal charges. The song "Cop Killer" is a first person account of a person angered by the King ruling and by police brutality. The song also became a hot issue during the 1992 presidential election, getting slammed by the candidates and police organizations. The attention and pressure, including death threats, became so overwhelming that Ice-T held a press conference to announce that any further reproductions of the album would not include the song "Cop Killer."[31]

Many people claim that violence in music contributes to violence in real life. However, others claim

Ice-T's song "Cop Killer" generated much unwanted attention for the rapper. © Scott McDermott/Corbis

that a person's response to themes like sex and violence are instilled in them by their family. However, it is difficult to make blanket statements about the effects of media on people because research on this topic is ever changing.

CAREERS IN THE FIELD

The music industry is a good fit for competitive people who have knowledge of various software programs and who are willing to work evenings, weekends, and holidays. The nature of the industry creates many specialized occupations, such as sound engineers that include audio technicians, sound mixers, and re-recording mixers.

Sound engineers set up and operate equipment that can record, synchronize, mix, and reproduce sound. They are also responsible for connecting the appropriate wires and cables and setting up mixing boards. Because recordings are now digital, understanding the equipment used in sound recording is vital. Specialized equipment has been replaced with computer software that can be found on your computer, and audio tapes have been replaced with computer hard drives.

---

[31]Deflem, Mathieu. 1993. "Rap, Rock, and Censorship: Popular Culture and the Technologies of Justice." Paper presented at the annual meeting of the Law and Society Association, Chicago, May 27–30, 1993, http://www .cas.sc.edu/socy/faculty/deflem/zzcens97.htm. Accessed March 4, 2009; Barry Shank, "Fears of the White Unconscious: Music, Race, and Identification in the censorship of 'Cop Killer,'" http://www.emayzine .com/lectures/rap.htm. Accessed March 4, 2009.

Often, audio skills are learned through on-the-job training, but having some formal education is beneficial. If possible, take a few classes in electronics or computer engineering, volunteer to work at your school's radio station, or start building electronic equipment as a hobby. When you start in the field, don't expect to work for a major label. Most large stations and labels only look for technicians with experience, so focus the beginning of your career on on-the-job training.

SUMMARY

- The first version of the phonograph was cylindrical, but it was eventually replaced with a flat disc, called a record.
- Radio was the first mass media after it became a major form of entertainment in the 1930s and 40s.
- The switch from analog to digital recording was revolutionary in freeing recorded content from the restrictions of various mediums.
- The music of rock and roll acted as a catalyst for teenage rebellion against the clean cut culture of the early 20th century.
- The combination of rock and roll and folk music led to the evolution of alternative rock, which included punk and grunge.
- The rise of alternative rock created a void for black listeners. This void led to the rise of hip-hop and gangsta rap.
- Controversies in the current music industry include piracy and censorship.

DISCUSSION QUESTIONS

1. Describe the mechanics of the original phonograph invented by Thomas Edison.
2. What led multiple musicians to strike in the 1940s?
3. What is digital recording? How is it different from analog recording?
4. Examine the origin of hip-hop. How was it formed? Who contributed to its popularity?
5. Describe the arguments for and against musical censorship. Where do you stand on the issue?

SUPPLEMENTAL WEB SITES

MOVIES, THEATER, SPORTS, AND EVOLVING FORMS OF ENTERTAINING

7

CHAPTER OBJECTIVES

- Understand how the entertainment industry performs many of the same roles as the news media
- Discuss how technological changes are challenging the paradigm of business conglomerates, who for years have been creating films based on the "blockbuster" mentality
- Discuss the rise of photography as a communication channel in the first half of the 20th century
- Define synergy and explain how modern entertainment corporations apply this concept to their business deals
- Explain how mass entertainment has evolved since the 1970s, with the increased popularity of theme parks, sports, and electronic games
- Discuss the idea of a current "attention economy" and what this means for the future of mass media

KEY TERMS

block booking
conglomerate
documentary
synergy
vertical integration

The iPod touch is just one of the many technological advances of the past few years. © Kay Nietfeld/epa/Corbis

INTRODUCTION

Consider the difference between the forms of entertainment you use every day and the sources of entertainment from a generation ago. Fifty years ago, people could only see movies in the theaters. But today, you have the option of going to the theater, watching movies on DVD or on-demand, or even downloading movies to your computer or iPod. Whereas your parents or grandparents would have gone to a stadium to watch a sporting event or listened to coverage of the event on the radio, you can turn to ESPN or watch videos on ESPN.com. And although your parents may have played early one- and two-player video games like "Pong," you now have the option of connecting with gamers worldwide via the Internet.

Entertainment is evolving. The motion picture industry, live theater, sports, newer mass media, such as video and online gaming, and popular theme parks mirror and comment on the larger society. The products created for these industries encapsulate slices of cultural history. They provide models for understanding the values and lifestyles in a culture. These media provide jobs and opportunities in art, communications, marketing, and advertising. It is important to understand the interactions between these media that can both define and reflect social trends. These are not news media, but they serve some of the same purposes as the news media.

ROLES OF THE ENTERTAINMENT INDUSTRY

The entertainment industries provide the public with information and entertainment, act as marketing tools, reflect changes in society, and satisfy our needs for communal activities. These roles are not entirely different from the roles of news media. And as we have discovered in our study of the "serious" mass media, the "fun" mass media—the entertainment industries—are being transformed by digital technologies at a very rapid rate. As these media are transformed, the interrelationship of the entertainment and news media grows.

Entertainment as Social Critique

The entertainment industries have become a prominent source of news, as new technologies, products, and business models provide vehicles to spread information. Entertainment productions bring up social issues such as gender, religion, bias, disease, crime, terrorism, and politics in myriad ways. In doing so, the entertainment industry helps inform, educate, and provoke discussion about these issues. Popular entertainment often pushes the envelope of what is socially acceptable.

Entertainment That Reflects Society

- *V for Vendetta* (graphic novel, motion picture)—addresses ideas of government repression and terrorism
- *The Sopranos* (cable TV, DVD)—long-running serial about an American family whose breadwinner just happens to be a mafia chief
- Grand Theft Auto (video game)—one version included pornographic images that could be unlocked after purchasing the game; these images were removed after the ESRB challenged the game company
- *The Warriors* (motion picture, video game)—a cult film hit from the 1970s, which was considered ultraviolent at the time; now a video game that contains "Blood, Intense Violence, Sexual Themes, Strong Language, Use of Drugs and Alcohol" according to the ESRB
- *Hairspray* (motion picture, live musical theater)—a wacky reminiscence about growing up in Baltimore where teens integrate a local television dance show, "The Corny Collins Show."
- The Holy Land Theme Park—"Visit Jerusalem in Orlando" featuring musical productions, live shows, rides, and shopping

Entertainment that produces discussion or controversy can energize people to take action in the real world. Interest groups or individuals frequently try to put pressure on legislators or regulators urging that media be censored or regulated due to its perceived negative effects on society.

The Southern Baptist Convention (SBC) ended an eight-year boycott of Disney parks in 2005. The SBC boycott was aimed at ending Disney's policy of extending benefits to homosexual employees and sponsorship of "Gay Days." The boycott had no discernable financial impact on corporate policy and ended when Disney studios and Miramax films split up.

Fines and threats have led to networks choosing censorship. Popular controversial radio host Howard Stern's move from public broadcast radio to subscription satellite radio was motivated in part by his reaction to FCC fines and his network's attempts to tone down his program.

The Entertainment Software Rating Board (ESRB) was started by electronic game companies to head off government regulation of violent or sexually explicit content in games. The game rating system is modeled on the Motion Picture Association of America (MPAA) movie ratings.

Information about each of the rating systems and how these ratings should help parents and others in guiding

Howard Stern moved to unregulated satellite radio after years of government fines for indecency. © Shannon Stapleton/Reuters/Corbis

Entertainment as Social Critique

Some entertainment goes beyond typical entertainment value and serves as a social critique.

- *JFK* (1991) by Oliver Stone—sets out to describe the situation surrounding President John F. Kennedy's assassination. The film won two Academy Awards and was nominated for eight, including Best Picture. JFK made Roger Ebert's top ten films of the decade list.
- *Three Kings* (1999) by David O. Russell—set at the end of the Persian Gulf War. Four soldiers steal gold that was stolen from Kuwait, but end up helping the victims of an oppressive regime and the Persian Gulf War.
- *Bowling for Columbine* (2002) by Michael Moore—documentary that explores the roots of America's predilection for guns.
- *The Passion of the Christ* (2004) by Mel Gibson—shows the last twelve hours of the life of Jesus Christ. This film was nominated for three Academy Awards. The film's dialogue is in Latin, Hebrew, and Aramaic, and was released with subtitles for international release.
- *Good Night, Good Luck* (2006) by George Clooney—a biographical treatment of Edward R. Murrow's confrontation with notorious bully Senator Joseph McCarthy.

entertainment choices for children and teens is carefully detailed by the American Academy of Pediatricians (AAP). According to the AAP:

> Ratings have become more common because research has shown how much children are influenced by what they see and hear, especially at very young ages. The effects don't seem to go away as the child gets older. One study of 8-year-old boys found that those who watched violent TV programs growing up were most likely to be involved in aggressive, violent behavior by age 18 and serious criminal behavior by age 30.[1]

MOTION PICTURE INDUSTRY: FROM PICTURES TO PIXELS

The film industry is subject to a wave of changes in how it creates, produces, markets, and distributes its creative content. Today, movies are made available to the public in theaters, on DVD, and online.

---

[1]American Academy of Pediatrics. "Entertainment Rating System—Why It Was Developed." 2001. Available from http://www.medem.com/medlib/article/ZZZRI81PASD. Accessed February 20, 2009.

Hollywood's "Golden Age"

In the early days of motion pictures, studios and movie theaters operated independently. As the industry matured, the studios moved to acquire control beyond the ownership of the talent, production facilities, and titles. They began to purchase movie theaters, from small town cinemas to grand movie palaces. This is called **vertical integration** because one company controls a product from its inception to its final form.

At one time, studios purchased movie theaters, thus controlling the product completely. © Suzanne Tucker/Shutterstock

Vertical integration enables a movie studio to set prices and policies from top to bottom. Actors, directors, writers, producers, and theater owners depend upon large consolidated studios for work. They also depend on these studios to distribute their work to audiences.

From its beginnings, Hollywood movie production moved toward consolidation. By the 1930s, Warner Bros., Paramount, 20th Century Fox, Loew's (MGM), and RKO (Radio-Keith-Orpheum) were the major players and had achieved vertical integration. Along with "The Little Three"—Universal, Columbia, and United Artists—these companies operated as a mature oligopoly. Eight companies essentially controlled the entire market.

vertical integration
a process in which one company controls a product from its inception to its final form

When their films came out, the studios took advantage of their vertical integration to force independent theaters to do **block booking**, where popular films were paired with B-list films that the theaters had to accept and screen, often sight unseen, as part of the deal.

block booking
the practice in which studios paired popular films with B-list films that the theaters had to accept and screen as part of the deal

In the 1940s, independent movie producers and exhibitors challenged the monopolistic behavior of the major studios. In the 1948 case *U.S. v. Paramount Pictures*, the studios were ordered to divest themselves of their theaters. The studios complied and this opened up the market. However with the post-war boom in television beginning in 1950, the economic model that had prevailed in the movie industry since the 1930s was further disrupted.

Hollywood's "Golden Age," when those eight companies had control of 95 percent of all film rentals and close to 70 percent of all box-office receipts, came to an end. There are parallels between those "Golden" days and today. Hollywood and the movies went through a difficult time when many predicted the demise of movies in the face of the "new media" of that time—broadcast television.

It is ironic that the "Big Three" television corporations, ABC, CBS, and NBC, established near-monopolistic control of television broadcasting only to face similar challenges with the rise of cable television and expansion of the number of channels available for programming.

Current Trends and the Impact of Technology

Current trends in entertainment include the rapid growth of video on demand and availability of television content on various kinds of digital playback devices, such as cell phones and iPods. Although unsettled and still in search of economically viable business models, these trends are further transforming the television industry. However, this move to unbundle content from any particular method of delivery is perceived as a threat by the movie industry. The motion picture industry lobbies Congress to "dumb down" playback devices and add "flags" and other copy-protection to some forms of content in an attempt to shore up analog business models in a digital world.

Meanwhile, technology continues to improve other parts of the movie industry. New digital formats designed for theater use can make the viewing experience more realistic, as HDTV is doing in living rooms everywhere. Re-fitting theaters with new projectors and sound systems is costly. The theater owners must find the appropriate price that an audience will be willing to pay for a better viewing experience in order to make the transition to digital projection systems work.

The Bureau of Labor Statistics notes that:

> Most motion pictures are still made on film. However, digital technology and computer-generated imaging are rapidly making inroads and are expected to transform the industry . . . Digital technology also makes it possible to distribute movies to theaters through the use of satellites or fiber-optic cable. Bulky metal film canisters can be replaced by easy-to-transport hard drives, although relatively few theaters are capable of receiving and screening movies in that manner now. In the future, however, more theaters will be capable of projecting films digitally and the costly process of producing and distributing films will be sharply reduced.[2]

This is causing major concern throughout the movie business. The move to digital production and projection means new methods of making pictures. Old jobs will be replaced by new ones to suit digital movie making. The entire industry needs to re-tool its equipment across production, distribution, and presentation in the transition to digital media.

Disney, Fox, MGM, Paramount, Sony Pictures Entertainment, Universal, and Warner Bros. Studios created Digital Cinema Initiatives in March 2002 to " . . . establish and document voluntary specifications for an open architecture for digital cinema that ensures a uniform and high level of technical performance, reliability, and quality control."[3]

Theater owners fear the expense of the changeover. Audiences would appreciate better images, but may resist higher box office prices. The Screen Actors Guild (SAG) has spoken out about actors receiving fair compensation for movies and television shows that are sold and downloaded onto iPods. In 2006, SAG president Alan Rosenberg accused ABC of selling *Lost* and *Desperate Housewives* for digital download to iPods without first bargaining with the Screen Actors Guild. ABC intends to pay residuals to performers based on the videocassette formula, which SAG doesn't believe is fair. SAG is going to take action to challenge ABC's decision.

[2]Bureau of Labor Statistics, U.S. Department of Labor, *Career Guide to Industries, 2008-09 Edition*, Motion Picture and Video Industries at http://www.bls.gov/oco/cg/cgs038.htm. Acessed February 20, 2009.

[3]Digital Cinema Initiatives, LLC, "About DCI." 2008. Available from http://www.dcimovies.com/. Accessed February 20, 2009.

Directors have to adapt their vision to the new medium. In the analog world, television and motion pictures were different media and each had its own aesthetic. From crew to cast to director and writers, working in the movies was similar but not identical to working in television. When "filming" a production or live event happens digitally, what is left to distinguish a motion picture from a television show or even from a news package? The resulting product is a set of moving images that have been recorded, edited, and packaged in a digital medium. Is it a film when it isn't captured on filmstock? Is it television if it's a movie that can be played back equally well in a theater, on a television set, or on a computer screen?

Compensation Changes

What kind of compensation will content producers receive when a work can be viewed on many platforms and the viewer has control over the medium for viewing? This question is debatable, but we can look at how the music recording and radio industries worked out similar issues involving analog recording.

In an era when pre-recorded music was becoming a staple of radio, musicians, composers, radio stations and networks faced fundamental changes in operations. This gave rise to disputes about fees and residuals. In 1914, Tin Pan Alley songwriters joined up with the American Society of Composers and Publishers (ASCAP), whose function was to set up and collect royalties each time a licensed song was played. Initially, most of the revenue ASCAP collected was generated by the sale of sheet music, variety shows, dance band programs, and the like that aired on radio. Later, prerecorded music became the biggest source of ASCAP's revenues.

PHOTOGRAPHY AS A COMMUNICATION CHANNEL

We live in an increasingly visual culture. In the early part of the 21st century, video seems to be the most dominant force in the entertainment industry.

The modern "picture press" began in 1842 with the *Illustrated London News*, taking a form we recognize as modern after World War I. Public interest in stories told with pictures, the brief rise of a free press in Germany after the war, and technology in the form of small, light, easy-to-use cameras gave rise to more printed photos.

World War II was the impetus that drove many European photographers and photo editors to emigrate to the United States. They gathered in New York City where Henry Luce ran the publishing empire that included *Life*, a showcase for photographers from advertising and journalism. The picture story captured the American imagination at the same time that it helped form America's idea of itself and present its face to the world.

Many modern photographers, such as Margaret Bourke-White and Edward Steichen, produced photographs we regard as art, as well as journalistic and advertising images. In the 1930s, these photographers, as well as filmmakers and writers, began to work in a style called **documentary**. These types of works looked with a critical eye at social issues such as poverty and injustice. Writer and critic

documentary
a style of photography, film, or writing that looks with a critical eye at social issues such as poverty and injustice

John Hersey (1914–1993) was an American writer and author noted for his documentary fiction about horrific events in the second World War. © Bettmann/CORBIS

Walter Benjamin made the distinction between an art photo without a news caption and "responsible image making." The art photo can transform poverty or pain into something beautiful to behold, but the photographer uses words to anchor the photo's meaning to the real world.

In the pre-television era before World War II, people read pictorial magazines eagerly and these magazines flourished in major cities around the world. The stories in these magazines became the narratives that helped create national consciousness in countries that had been wracked by war. The popularity and growth in the number of magazines that featured photo stories made it easy for photographers to become freelancers and leave their jobs at publishing houses. The independence of freelancers from strict editorial directives led to an era of creative, individualistic work.

During the 1950s and 60s, photographic images in narrative stories and advertising were one of the most influential mass media. However, the increasing availability of television, and especially the Vietnam War, began to draw viewers away from print to the television screen.

The large national magazines such as *Look* and *Life* couldn't compete with the six o'clock news and the visceral imagery of the ongoing casualties and process of the war. Color television became ubiquitous and was hungry for images that moved viewers.

The influential image-makers began to work in television and the movies. Theaters and TV sets became the primary media through which audiences were exposed to images.

LIVE PERFORMANCE: FROM THEATER TO TOURING

Theater is intertwined with American history. Like any mass medium, live theater entertains, educates, and mirrors society. Theater in the United States was star-driven when it began. Theater companies had their own playhouses in cities and towns across the country. They developed a set of plays to showcase their stars. As conditions shifted economically, and other mass media underwent some changes, live theater production changed as well.

Broadway

A collaborative system arose where a producer and director assembled a team including writers, actors, and stage designers to produce a play that would hopefully have a long, successful run on the theater circuit. These productions were typically large scale and often began on Broadway before moving out of New York to other cities and regional theaters.

By the 1960s, the heyday of Broadway was over. Playwrights from Chicago, Los Angeles, and other cities were writing plays that were produced outside New York. August Wilson, David Huang, Wendy Wasserstein, Des McAnuff, David Mamet, Tony Kushner, and Peter Sellars were a few of the playwrights of the time. For them, New York is an important place to show

Theater is alive and well today, though there are fewer performances than in days past. © Alan Schein Photography/CORBIS

off their work, but it isn't the ultimate destination. Theater is alive and well in the United States these days, though there are fewer theaters and performances going on today than there were in the 1900s. At that time, there were fewer other media to compete with live theater for an audience.

Today, Broadway features are often based on books or movies that were best-sellers or blockbusters. A success on Broadway frequently leads to a movie version for popular plays and musicals.

Synergy: Developing Conglomerates

Large media corporations look for what they call **synergy** in entertainment properties. In the 1980s, businesses began to grow by combining with other businesses into **conglomerates**. A single corporate entity would consist of many smaller businesses that did not all specialize in the same commercial enterprise.

For example, suppose a corporation purchases the rights to a good book. That book can then be adapted for screen and stage, be made into a show or ride at a theme park, or perhaps spawn an electronic game. As a result, these ventures would drive the market for retail merchandise such as dolls, toys, and costumes. That's synergy at work. The synergy builds additional opportunities for profit for large corporations from a single entertainment property.

Disney's "The Lion King," "Beauty and the Beast," and "Mulan" are examples of this type of corporate undertaking. The entertainment products include picture books, coloring books, videos, films, lavish traveling musicals, shows at ice arenas, and features at theme parks.

> **synergy**
> the working together of various entertainment ventures (such as a book, a movie, a theme park exhibit, and retail merchandise) that are all born from a single entertainment property

> **conglomerate**
> an organized group of many smaller businesses that do not all specialize in the same commercial enterprise

NEW MASS MEDIA ENTERTAINMENT: CAN WE HAVE YOUR ATTENTION, PLEASE?

Theme parks, sports, and electronic games represent new kinds of mass media that have been attracting growing audiences and experiencing revenue growth since the 1970s.

Theme Parks

The Disney theme parks are an important part of the corporate focus on synergy and creating demand for its entertainment products inside and outside the gates of the theme park. Disney remained the top chain, with 116.5 million visitors worldwide last year, followed by Merlin Entertainment with 32.1 million. Universal drew 26.4 million, followed by Six Flags with 24.9 million and Busch with 22.3 million. Cedar Fair came in sixth place, with 22.1 million visitors in 2007.[4]

Theme parks are expected to grow in popularity as Baby Boomers become grandparents. © Karin Hildebrand Lau/Shutterstock

---

[4]ThemeParkInsider March 14, 2008, "2007 theme park attendance report released" by Robert Niles. http://www.themeparkinsider.com/flume/200803/649/.

Sports

When the Entertainment and Sports Programming Network (ESPN) launched the first all-sports cable channel on September 7, 1979, its success was by no means a sure thing. Bill Rasmussen, formerly a semi-pro hockey team's PR man, fought to create the network, using Getty Oil money to get it off the ground. In its early years, ESPN wasn't profitable. With a limited budget and no connections to major sports programming, ESPN was forced to carry rarely watched sporting events. Unable to afford to carry football, baseball, or any of the other major sports, ESPN concentrated its efforts on its news programming. This proved to be a wise decision.

ESPN put its resources into its news show, Sportscenter, and network executives turned college basketball games and the National Football League draft into television events. They made masterful use of marketing and built audiences for sports television in new ways. By 1995, ESPN was the first cable network to make it into 70 percent of homes in the United States. By 2005, ESPN had surpassed 90 million households. Currently it is available in more than 98 million homes.[5]

ESPN's properties include ESPN, ESPN2, ESPN Classic Sports, ESPNews and ESPN The Magazine. ESPN Original Entertainment has developed the sports game show "ESPN's 2-Minute Drill" and the documentary "The Season" and continues to create new sports-based programming.

Old Media: Going Digital

Global spending on entertainment media dipped in 2000 after the dotcom boom but has steadied and was expected to reach $690 billion by 2009.[6] Demand for digital distribution of music, books, films, and video games is increasing.

The availability of high speed broadband is a major catalyst behind this trend according to industry analysts. Threats to growth in entertainment industries lurk in rising interest rates and skyrocketing energy costs. The demand for this kind of entertainment is increasing in developing countries, particularly China. This pressure will continue to increase overall spending on these media.

The recession will last longer than previous ones due to a steeper downturn and the impact on consumer spending will be much steeper than in the past, but spending on entertainment and media will continue to grow. Video games, online film rentals, digital distribution of music, music for mobile devices, e-books, video on demand, and satellite radio spending will grow by 2.7 per cent compounded annually for the entire forecast period to $1.6 trillion in 2013. The spending will likely see a 3.9 per cent drop in 2009 and a mere 0.4 per cent advance in 2010, with a period of much faster growth of about seven per cent in 2013. Video games, online film rentals, digital distribution of music, music for mobile devices, e-books, video on demand, and satellite (subscription) radio accounted for about $160 million in 2000. By 2004, this had risen to $11.4 billion.[7]

---

[5]http://www.espnmediazone.com/corp_info/corp_fact_sheet.html.

[6]http://paidcontent.org/article/419-global-internet-spending-expected-to-rise-107-percent-annually-through-/.

[7]http://www.pwc.com/gx/en/press-room/2009/global-entertain-and-media-outlook-2009.jhtml.

As demand for the electronic forms of media grows, sales of physical media continue to fall. Physical music (such as CDs), home video rentals, and PC games are examples of content that can be delivered as physical or electronic media. Increasingly, consumers favor electronic delivery.

Electronic Games

In the 1970s and 80s, arcade games like "Pac-Man" and "Pong" by Atari were popular in bars and restaurants. In 1972, Magnavox introduced the Odyssey game console that connected to a television set and played "Pong." The Odyssey system came with "Pong" but its program cards were removable like modern game systems such as Xbox and PlayStation.

The system was primitive by today's standards, but over 80,000 units were sold in 1972. Another 250,000-plus Odyssey machines were sold between 1973 and late 1975, bringing the total to over 350,000 units sold.[8] The system was removed from stores in late 1975 and replaced by a newer, simpler model: the Odyssey 100. As simple as it was, the Odyssey set the stage for increasingly sophisticated game boxes and online games such as the massive multi-player "World of Warcraft."

In 2005, video games brought in a record $10.5 billion in sales of hardware, software, and accessories.[8] Electronic games played on "game boxes" were initially connected to video outputs and limited to players who were together in time and space. "Mario Bros," "Pong," "Donkey Kong," and games of this generation had colorful animations and catchy background music loops. Players took turns competing against characters in the game.

Multiple player games were developed so that several players could compete against each other and against the game. Before the World Wide Web and broadband, there were a variety of games that allowed players to compete with one another online. The history of these games goes back to the time before the World Wide Web when text-based games such as "Zork" and "StarTrek" were played via CRTs (cathode ray tubes), using mainframe computers.

The number of these games has expanded since the 1990s. Many of them now have fan web sites that provide information about the games, fan art, and discussion forums. Some sites even include video and audio "mash-ups," in which fans use images from screengrabs and audio from the games to create their own videos and MP3s.

U.S. consumer spending on online games jumped about 20 percent from $73 million in 2003 to $88.8 million in 2004 and $54.4 million for the first half of 2005. It is projected that U.S. in-game advertising spending will increase from $295 million in 2007 to $650 million in 2012.[9] Spending for online games is expected to climb higher throughout the decade.

The attraction of these worlds is based on their interactivity and the way they evolve into social communities. With each improvement in computer graphics or broadband speed, the games become more entertaining and sophisticated.

Video games continue to grow in popularity and versatility. © *Erick Jones/Shutterstock*

[8]http://www.foxnews.com/story/0,2933,181816,00.html.

[9]http://www.emarketer.com/Reports/All/Emarketer_2000485.aspx

Although they are different than traditional entertainments that occur face-to-face in the real world, such as sporting events, concerts, or plays, the pleasure and problems of virtual entertainments appear to be no better or worse than traditional entertainments.

AND THE FUTURE WILL BRING . . .

Studies of people in their teens indicate that they are heavy users of all media, which is not surprising. However, the degree to which teens multi-task—for example, watch television while they type a paper on their computers and instant message with friends—represents something new in mass media. Media professionals who must connect with people to get their message across, whether it is news, entertainment or advertising, say we are in an "attention economy."

The message doesn't just need to get into the media; it has to break through a barrage of media to capture someone's attention. When individuals had fewer choices in mass media, media producers could better serve as the information gatekeepers who controlled what the viewers or listeners could tune in to, and when. Times have changed.

Analog technologies that made it difficult to combine content from different media are easier to work around and are being replaced in a world of digital information. The public audience is no longer a bunch of passive consumers. They are media makers, the editors and program directors in the "Me Media" environment today.

What lies ahead for mass media entertainment? More choices, more user control, more competition for attention and hopefully more fun as the existing businesses and industries adapt to our digital century or go out of style!

CAREERS IN THE FIELD

There are a wide variety of jobs in the entertainment industry. In sports, there are professional athletes, coaches, and referees. There are also business and administrative positions available within this field. For example, sports agents handle contract negotiations and other business-related matters. Tournament directors and sports program directors, however, handle administrative and management tasks.

In the theater arts, common occupations include actor, choreographer, producer, and director. Individuals who are involved in live theater may work in a range of different venues, from small community theaters to the larger theaters on Broadway.

Likewise, the jobs within the motion picture and video industries are quite varied. These jobs range from high-profile positions, such as actors, producers, and directors, to "behind the scenes" positions, such as film editors and sound engineers.

Over the next several years, the demand for arts and entertainment services is expected to increase. However, certain occupations within these industries will have better prospects than others. On one hand, there should be many opportunities for part-time, seasonal employees, such as amusement park workers.

On the other hand, professional athletes and performing artists will face stiff job competition.[10] Within the motion picture and video industries, there will be more job opportunities for those with technical skills, such as computer specialists, multimedia artists and animators, and digital film and video editors. Competition for the more high-profile jobs, such as actors and directors, is expected to be fairly high.[11]

SUMMARY

- The entertainment industry has taken over some of the roles of the news media, by informing, marketing, and creating public awareness of social issues.
- Filmmaking by business conglomerates was based on the "blockbuster" mentality but technological changes are challenging this paradigm. Electronic games—video games and especially massively multiplayer online role-playing games—are evolving forms of mass entertainment which allow players to interact in virtual worlds.
- After World War I, the American public developed an increased interest in stories told with pictures. The popularity of pictorial magazines such as *Life* and *Look* led to a documentary style of photography, in which photographers used their work to highlight social issues such as poverty and injustice. With this new style, photos were more than art. By adding captions, photographers were in the business of "responsible image making."
- In entertainment, synergy is the working together of various entertainment ventures (such as a book, a movie, a theme park exhibit, and retail merchandise) that are all built from a single entertainment property. Large media corporations look for synergy in the entertainment properties they purchase. For example, a corporation may purchase the rights to a popular children's book, adapt the book for a movie, create an electronic game based on the movie, and sell toys, costumes, and other merchandise related to the movie.
- Since the 1970s, new kinds of mass media have been attracting growing audiences and experiencing revenue growth. One example of new mass media are theme parks, which attract hundreds of millions of attendees each year. Another example is ESPN, which has greatly expanded its audience and its properties since its inception in 1979. A third example is video and online games. Video gaming systems and accessories account for billions of dollars in sales each year, and consumer spending for online games is expected to continue increasing throughout the decade.

---

[10]Bureau of Labor Statistics, U.S. Department of Labor, *Career Guide to Industries, 2008-09 Edition*, Arts, Entertainment, and Recreation at http://www.bls.gov/oco/cg/cgs031.htm. Accessed February 22, 2009.

[11]Bureau of Labor Statistics, U.S. Department of Labor, *Career Guide to Industries, 2008-09 Edition*, Motion Picture and Video Industries, on the Internet at http://www.bls.gov/oco/cg/cgs038.htm. Accessed February 22, 2009.

- Media professionals who must connect with people to get their message across, whether it is news, entertainment or advertising, say we are in an "attention economy." What this means is that the message doesn't just need to get into the media, it has to break through a barrage of media to capture someone's attention. The future of mass media lies in more choices for consumers, more user control, and increased competition for consumers' attention.

DISCUSSION QUESTIONS

1. Do you feel that it is appropriate for young children to receive the majority of their information about the world through television and video games?
2. Do you think that the government should develop its own standardized rating system for entertainment, or that private systems are effective as they are?
3. Are "business conglomerates," which make books, movies, video games, action figures, etc. from the same series, guilty of monopolizing a market?
4. Do you believe that role-playing computer games that connect players via the Internet are a valid form of socialization? In your opinion, are these games a healthy way for children to connect with one another? Why or why not?
5. Discuss the importance of human entertainment from an economic standpoint and from a psychological standpoint.

 ## SUPPLEMENTAL WEB SITES

RADIO

CHAPTER OBJECTIVES

- Discuss the early history of radio and how it was influenced by contributions from Heinrich Hertz, Guglielmo Marconi, Lee DeForest, Edwin Armstrong, and David Sarnoff
- Outline the transition of the radio from military equipment to home entertainment device in the 1920s
- Explain why individual radio stations began forming networks in the 1920s and 1930s
- List the first four major radio networks
- Discuss how the rise of talk radio affected AM radio
- Discuss Edward R. Murrow's contribution to radio news broadcasting
- Explain the impact of the Radio Act of 1927
- Discuss how the Telecommunications Act of 1996 has affected radio as we know it today
- Identify forms of global radio
- Explain how the emergence of satellite radio, CPB stations, Internet radio, and podcasts have altered the ways in which people listen to radio
- Identify two factors that currently limit job growth in radio broadcasting

8

KEY TERMS

Audion
cyberjock
daypart
economies of scale
electromagnetic waves
genre
narrowcasting

oligopoly
podcast
radio
ratings
satellite radio
shock-jock
voice-tracking software

How do the early days of radio compare with today? *(left)* © *Bettmann/CORBIS; (right)* © *Simon Marcus/Corbis*

INTRODUCTION

Radio is one of the oldest electronic mass medium in society. Over time, technology and public policy has caused radio's function and purpose to change. What was once just a few bleeps sent from one ship to another is now crystal-clear voices communicating around the world. Although radio waves float freely though the air, the contents of those waves are highly restricted. There are government regulations about who can own radio stations and who controls subject matter over the airwaves, in addition to economic models that dictate who pays and who makes money. These factors help determine how radio fits into a society.

In commercial radio, what news, information, and entertainment the audience wishes to hear and how they choose to receive that content have an influential role in how radio functions as well. The attention of an audience did—and can—create a "golden age" for the medium. However, just as quickly, a shift in attention can end one.

radio
telecommunication modulated by electromagnetic waves; may also refer to radio programming, modern music radio, the radio industry, or radio stations in general

To talk about radio, we need to know that **radio**, from a technological standpoint, means telecommunication modulated by electromagnetic waves. However, *radio* also may refer to radio programming, modern music radio, the radio industry, or radio stations in general. All these meanings of *radio* inform our understanding of radio as a mass medium.

Today there are more than 16,000 AM radio stations, 26,000 FM stations, and 1500 shortwave radio stations in the world. In addition, over 3 million people subscribe to satellite radio. As we'll explore in this chapter, modern radio only vaguely resembles the original concept of wireless electromagnetic transmissions. These days, people are as likely to be listening to what they call "radio" on an MP3 player, a computer, or via satellite transmission in their cars as they are to be listening to an AM/FM receiver.

A HISTORICAL OVERVIEW

It's hard to believe that what started as a few taps of Morse code in 1901 grew into the diverse multimedia outlet that is today's radio industry. Indeed, the history of radio is an ongoing story of vision, ingenuity, and rapid technological advancement.

Birth of a Medium—1888–1912

Although radio as we know it today has only been around for a little over a century, radio waves have been present as long as planets have orbited the sun. However, it took the innovative thinking of many scientists and inventors to make sense of these invisible waves. German physicist Heinrich Hertz was the first to prove the existence of radio waves in the late 1880s. His experiments proved that, like light, radio waves are a type of electromagnetic wave.[1] **Electromagnetic waves** are movements of energy that can travel at the speed of light in a free space detached from wires. Soon after Hertz made these discoveries, scientists were eager to find a way to use radio waves to carry sounds, including voices.

The early tapping of Morse code evolved into radio as we know it today. © Anyka/Shutterstock

electromagnetic waves
movements of energy that can travel at the speed of light in a free space detached from wires

As a young man, Guglielmo Marconi read about Hertz's work and began conducting his own experiments in a quest to develop wireless telegraphy. By 1901, Marconi had transmitted the first radio message across the Atlantic Ocean—Morse code for the letter "S." Over the next several years, radio came to be used as a form of ship-to-shore communication. In 1912, wireless operators were onboard both the *Titanic* and the ship that rescued its survivors, the *Carpathia*. Marconi's technology allowed radio operators to transmit information about the disaster and ask for assistance before the *Carpathia* reached its port in New York City.[2]

Meanwhile, Lee de Forest was developing his own innovations for radio, including the **Audion**, a device that he patented in 1907. De Forest's device was used to convert radio frequency into audio frequency, so sounds could be transmitted and amplified. The Audion made live broadcasting possible and later became a key component of all telephone, television, and radar systems before the invention of the transistor.[3] Although some admirers refer to de Forest as the "father of radio," some critics of his time claimed that he merely patented many ideas that others had generated.[4]

Audion
a device used to convert radio frequency into audio frequency, so sounds could be transmitted and amplified

Ironically, de Forest brought similar claims against another pioneer of early radio, Edwin Armstrong. In 1912, Armstrong took de Forest's invention of the Audion one step further by devising a way to improve the amplification by a thousandfold, so the sound generated could be heard across a room. The most impressive part of Armstrong's take on the Audion—later named the regenerative circuit—was that it could serve as an oscillator as well as a receiver. This allowed

[1]"Heinrich Rudolf Hearst," Physicists' biographies at http://phisicist.info/hertz.html. Accessed July 17, 2008.

[2]Helen Briggs, "Profile: Marconi, the wireless pioneer," *BBC News Online*, December 11, 2001, at http://news.bbc.co.uk/2/hi/science/nature/1702037.stm.

[3]"de Forest, Lee," *Encyclopedia Britannica*, at http://search.eb.com/eb/article-9029588. Accessed July 21, 2008.

[4]"The Complete Lee de Forest," *Perham Collection*, History San Jose, 2003, at http://www.leedeforest.org. Accessed July 17, 2008.

the device to both generate and obtain radio waves. Shortly after receiving a patent for his idea, he crossed paths with de Forest, who claimed ownership of the idea. Although de Forest eventually won a lengthy legal battle on the basis of a language technicality, Armstrong is still credited with the invention.[5]

As illustrated by de Forest and Armstrong, the development of radio in its earliest forms depended on the ingenuity and, at times, fierce competitiveness of pioneering scientists.

From Work to Play, Tool to Toy

Radio communications were a vital link in the military chain of command during World War I. This caused the U.S. government to place heavy restrictions on radio broadcasting. At the end of World War I in 1918, many of those restrictions were lifted and radio broadcasting was ready to take on a new purpose. David Sarnoff, a Russian immigrant who had worked for the Marconi Company during the war, had a vision of radio as a home entertainment device. Sarnoff believed that radio could bring music into the home in a way no one else had imagined. He also envisioned a radio receiver in every home. Sarnoff's tenacious efforts helped him rise to fame as one of the first on-air radio personalities and a leader at Radio Corporation of America (RCA).[6]

A radio in every home was a visionary idea for a time when there was no mass communication beyond print brought directly to the individual. KDKA, the first commercial radio station, which began broadcasting in 1920, changed all that. It featured music and entertainment, but it also carried the election returns for the 1920 presidential election.

The main downfall of radio was the high operating costs. Running a broadcasting station required strong financial backing but realized little or no profit. However, as radio stations began to rise in popularity and value, businesses started to view radio as a good platform for advertising. Eventually, advertising became the primary means of support for radio broadcasting in the United States.

As its popularity grew, large corporations wanted to get into the business of radio. In 1926, Sarnoff brought together the resources of RCA, General Electric, and Westinghouse to purchase WEAF in New York. WEAF eventually became the anchor station for the National Broadcasting System (NBC). NBC soon swelled to 25 stations nationwide and became the first broadcasting network. In 1927, NBC was able to broadcast the Rose Bowl from California to New York through the use of long-distance wire telephone lines. Fans from coast to coast could hear the football game for the first time.

Still, music was the "killer app" that Sarnoff believed would make radio a household necessity. From the beginning, the success of radio and the success of music recording industries have been intertwined. Americans bought radios so live

---

[5]Armstrong, Edwin H. *Encyclopedia Britannica* at http://search.eb.com/eb/article-410. Accessed July 22, 2008.

[6]broadcasting. *Encyclopedia Britannica* at http://www.britannica.com/EBchecked/topic/80543/broadcasting. Accessed July 21, 2008.

music could be delivered directly into their homes. In turn, radio spurred the sales of records, as listeners sought out their favorite songs or bands after hearing them on the radio. Sarnoff's hunch that broadcasting and music recording would influence one another over time turned out to be accurate.[7]

Reporting and News Radio

Although much of radio programming in the 1920s and 30s revolved around music and entertainment, there was an interest in radio news as well. In addition to the 1920 KDKA broadcast of the election, news events such as presidential inaugurations, baseball's World Series, and aviator Charles Lindbergh's safe landing in Paris after his solo flight across the Atlantic were broadcast on the radio. However, regular newscasts didn't catch on until the mid-1930s. These first newscasts consisted of summaries of the headlines from the morning newspapers read over the air.

Newspaper publishers feared that radio would lure their audiences away, and many refused to print radio schedules in the early years. The newspaper publishers blocked the press associations (AP, UP, and INS) from selling news for radio broadcasts until the 1940s.

The radio networks understood the potential of broadcast news and began to create syndicates and the capability for reporting national and global events. With the start of World War II, radio became the most important link between the public, Washington, D.C., and the rest of the world. With their loved ones thousands of miles away, listeners tuned in to the familiar voices of correspondents who reported from abroad to "bring home" news of the war to the United States.

Edward R. Murrow of the Columbia Broadcasting System (CBS) was in Europe when the war began. He quickly assembled a team of reporters to report nightly to London on the progress of the war. Honest, urgent, and live at the scene, these broadcasts came to define broadcast news for decades.

In the new medium of radio, there were no models for reporters to follow. Murrow didn't have formal training as a journalist. He thought that made it easier to report for radio because he didn't have to unlearn anything before jumping into radio reporting.

One of his innovative broadcasts features the sound of British civilians entering an air-raid shelter. Murrow set the microphone on the ground to record the quiet, orderly footsteps that reinforced his words about the courage of the average citizen during the London Blitz.

Edward R. Murrow and his team of reporters became the model for all the networks of his time. © CORBIS

Murrow and his team of reporters, called his boys, set an example at CBS that became the model for all the networks. Investigative reporters and political correspondents adopted the blunt style of the reporter, microphone in hand, who steps up to politicians, generals, corporate leaders, or John Q. Public and asks the tough questions, demanding to know the truth. This style came to define hard-hitting journalism and also migrated to television with Murrow and his protégés.

---

[7]"About RCA: Linking the Nation," *RCA*, at http://home.rca.com/en-US/ PressReleaseDetail.html?Cat=RCA History&MN=7. Accessed July 16, 2008.

From Novelty to Network

Due to the influence of World War I (1914–1918) and the Great Depression (1929–1939), the structure of radio broadcasting developed under different economic and social conditions than those that exist today. The radio industry was based on a different set of assumptions about programs, producers, technology, and consumers.

Newspapers were the dominant medium at the time of radio's introduction into the world of mass communications. Radio stations had to find **economies of scale** through the wire services that allowed companies to pool their resources in order to extend their coverage. Creating these networks also allowed stations to share the expense of producing and transmitting content. Juggernauts of the industry quickly emerged.

After NBC was created, the company formed two semi-independent radio networks, the Blue Network (WJZ) and the Red Network (WEAF). The Red Network flourished and, by 1938, carried 75 percent of NBC's commercial programs. The askew performance of the two networks prompted NBC to sell the Blue Network, which eventually became the American Broadcasting Company (ABC), in 1943.[8]

economies of scale
the decreased per-unit cost as output increases; this is because some resources are less expensive in bulk

Shortly after NBC's conception, a cigar-business owner named William S. Paley combined the United Independent Broadcasters and the Columbia Phonograph Company to create the Columbia Broadcasting System (CBS). A businessman at heart, Paley strove to turn a struggling radio network into a success. The key to this accomplishment was advertising. He offered free programming to affiliated stations if those stations would designate slots of airtime to network shows that were sponsored by advertisers. Paley's gimmick helped CBS expand from 22 stations in 1928 to 144 stations over the course of a decade. Although CBS produced many successful radio shows that featured stars such as Fred Allen, Bing Crosby, and Kate Smith, the network's repertoire grew considerably after Paley's raid of NBC's talent pool. Paley was able to coerce stars such as Jack Benny, George Burns, and comedy duo Amos 'n' Andy to join the CBS network. This attack hurt NBC even more when the age of television approached, as these personalities proved to be as popular on the screen as they were on the air.[9]

CBS produced many successful radio shows that featured stars such as Bing Crosby.
© Bettmann/CORBIS

Not all radio networks were created to compete on a national level. In 1934, the Mutual Broadcasting System (MBS) was developed as a cooperative network shared by WOR in New York, WGN in Chicago, WLW in Cincinnati, and WXYZ in Detroit. Unlike the larger networks, MBS had no production studio or centralized corporate owners. The network catered mostly to small, rural markets and carried popular programs such as the *The Lone Ranger* and *The Green Hornet*.[10]

The rise of radio networks gave way to a new generation of radio listeners. No longer a system of amateurs broadcasting to a puny local audience, radio became a medium to which people from all over the nation could connect and enjoy the

---

[8]National Broadcasting Co., Inc. *Encyclopedia Britannica* at http://www.britannica.com/EBchecked/topic/404533/National-Broadcasting-Co-Inc. Accessed July 22, 2008.

[9]CBS Corporation. *Encyclopedia Britannica* at http://www.britannica.com/EBchecked/topic/100876/CBS-Corporation. Accessed July 22, 2008.

[10]"History of Radio," http://history.sandiego.edu/GEN/recording/radio.html. Accessed July 22, 2008.

same entertainment, share information, and exchange opinions. In 1935, two out of three homes had a radio set, and broadcasting could be heard 24 hours a day. By 1950, there were radio sets in 40 million homes, and 63 percent of Americans claimed radio as their primary source for news. This era of initial excitement and respect for the medium is often referred to as the "golden age" of radio. However, the golden age came to gradual extinction as radio became a victim of its own growth. More stations meant more competition, and a swollen market meant less revenue to go around.[11]

The Rise of FM

Although Lee de Forest criticized Edwin Armstrong for being an unoriginal thinker, Armstrong proved himself as an inventor with the creation of frequency modulation (**FM**) broadcasting. Unlike standard amplitude modulation (**AM**) broadcasting, which varies the amplitude, or power, of radio waves to create sound, FM varies the frequency of radio waves across a wide band of frequency, creating a clearer sound.[12] Still, AM radio dominated the broadcast band until the 1960s. Although the technology for the static-free sound of FM broadcasting had been around for nearly 30 years, concern for sound quality did not equal the concern for bandwidth exertion. Finally, in 1961, new Federal Communications Commission (FCC) regulations opened up more bandwidth on the FM dial. The combination of newly introduced stereo sound, the transistor radio, and high-fidelity records helped FM radio become the home for music.

As a larger audience began to tune in, FM stations became more specialized. Tailored formats such as easy listening or rock and roll started to emerge. Baby boomers, who were becoming teenagers during FM's emergence, could listen to music specifically targeted to their generation. FM radios were showing up in people's homes, cars, and even in their hands. In the early 1960s, Japanese electronics company Sony perfected the transistor radio with the TR-63. The small, stylish, and battery-powered FM radio could be carried in a front shirt pocket. The transistor radio allowed people to stay connected to music, news, and entertainment while on the go, similar to the way MP3 players do today.

As contemporary music continued to change throughout the 1960s, station formats became more experimental. DJs started to do more than just play records; they indulged in political debates over controversial issues such as the Vietnam War, civil rights, and the draft.[13] The "free-form" format of FM stations helped shape the music and

The transistor radio allowed people to stay connected wherever they went.
© Wire_man/Shutterstock

---

[11]Steven Schoenherr, "Golden Age of Radio 1935–50," *Recording Technology History* Accessed July 6, 2005, at http://history.sandiego.edu/gen/recording/notes.html.

[12]modulation. *Encyclopedia Britannica* at http://www.britannica.com/EBchecked/topic/387402/modulation. Accessed July 22, 2008.

[13]*Historical Dictionary of American Radio*, edited by Donald G. Godfrey and Frederic A. Leigh (Greenwood Publishing Group, 1998).

politics of the 1960s and 70s. This mini renaissance for radio faded as baby boomers aged and as FCC rule changes in the 1990s made it easier for large corporations to purchase multiple independent stations.

Talk Radio

AM radio was shedding audience in the 1970s, as the best music migrated to FM. In the 1980s, however, the talk format caught on and flourished, revitalizing AM radio. The AM frequencies that couldn't handle high-fidelity audio well were fine

for transmitting the sound of the human voice. The 1987 repeal of The Fairness Doctrine (see Figure 8.1) further hastened the rise of talk radio. Previously, the Fairness Doctrine had required broadcasters to balance shows in terms of their political points of view. The idea was that the need for the public to have access to a variety of viewpoints outweighed commercial needs of broadcasters. With the law's repeal, however, political commentators such as Rush Limbaugh could bring a blend of news, entertainment, and partisan analysis to AM. Although the politically charged broadcasts of commentators such as Limbaugh often spark controversy, they also attract listeners. Talk radio is the top choice for about 15 percent of the radio audience, and it dominates AM radio today. Listeners are mostly male, but otherwise fairly diverse.[14]

Rush Limbaugh's radio show sparks controversy and attracts listeners. © Mark Peterson/CORBIS

INSIGHT

Section 315 Affects Candidates for Office

Perhaps the best-known part of the Communications Act of 1934 is Section 315, which stipulates that if a broadcast licensee permits one legally qualified candidate for public office to use a broadcasting station, equal opportunity shall be afforded to all other candidates. The licensee has no power of censorship of material broadcast under provisions of Section 315, nor does that licensee have any obligation to allow the use of the station by any candidates.

Subsequently the act was amended so that appearance by a legally qualified candidate on a bona fide newscast, news interview, documentary, or spot coverage of news events is not covered by the provisions of Section 315.

Every four years, Congress usually passes special legislation exempting presidential contests from the provisions of Section 315 so that national debates can be held without affording "equal opportunity" to fringe candidates who have no realistic chance of garnering enough votes to be serious contenders.

Section 315 applies only to appearances by the candidates themselves, not their supporters or discussions of their views or platforms. When a candidate is a movie or television star, broadcast stations refuse to run the candidate's entertainment material for the duration of the contest. For that reason, none of Ronald Reagan's old movies were shown on television during his campaigns.

FIGURE 8.1

RULES AND REGULATIONS

From the beginning, the radio industry has been subject to a variety of government rules and regulations. As times and technology have changed, so too have many of the rules governing the medium.

The Early Years

Signal interference arising from broadcasts airing on the same frequencies is a technical issue requiring a large-scale solution. Unless a station was granted a "clear channel" to broadcast on the same frequency across the entire country, radio stations from different locations broadcast on the same frequencies. Trouble arose when stations strayed into each other's frequencies or when their signals were too powerful. The result was static, dissonance, and disgruntled audiences.

In the United States, radio was a commercial affair almost from the beginning. Herbert Hoover served as Secretary of Commerce under presidents Harding and Coolidge before being elected president in 1928. He favored the allocation of radio frequencies to large corporations as a solution to the problems of interference, ownership, and funding.

In 1923, three kinds of stations were created by allocating bands of frequencies. These included high-power "clear" channels, medium-power channels, and low-power channels. The Radio Act of 1927 set up the Federal Radio Commission (FRC) with responsibility for regulating radio frequency usage. In 1928, the FRC's General Order 40 shifted most radio stations' frequencies so that 23 of the first 25 clear channels were assigned to affiliates of NBC. Formed in 1926, NBC had 48 affiliate stations, sold "sustaining" programs to affiliates, and broadcast "sponsored" programs produced by advertisers such as the American Tobacco Company.

The FRC's favoritism toward commercial interests gave rise to a radio reform movement beginning in 1930. An examination of the impact of radio and newspaper publishing on democracy in 1934 by the Hutchins Commission helped lead to the establishment of the FCC to replace the FRC. Many of the problems identified by the Hutchins Commission—such as the distortion and neglect of news coverage by large corporations and the control of news by advertising and commercial interests—remain relevant today.

The ownership caps and other rules and regulations put in place by the FCC in 1934 grew out of the Hutchins Commission recommendations. This 1934 legislation, updated by amendments, still influences policy today.[15]

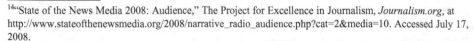

[14]"State of the News Media 2008: Audience," The Project for Excellence in Journalism, *Journalism.org*, at http://www.stateofthenewsmedia.org/2008/narrative_radio_audience.php?cat=2&media=10. Accessed July 17, 2008.

[15]Christopher H. Sterling, "U.S. Policy: The Communications Act of 1934" *U.S. Museum of Broadcast Communications Archives*, at http://www.museum.tv/archives/etv/U/htmlU/uspolicyc/uspolicyc.htm. Accessed July, 17, 2008.

The 1980s and Beyond

As a result of further technological developments in the telecommunications industry, such as the introduction of cable television, the FCC continued to update its rules and regulations over the years. In the 1980s however, President Reagan began actively moving to deregulate industries. His efforts had their greatest impact on radio with the Telecommunications Act of 1996, which President Clinton signed into law. This act includes many sections and deals with television, cable, telephony, radio, and more. Its impact on broadcast radio in the United States has been far-reaching.[16]

Before 1996, corporations were not allowed to own more than 40 radio stations. Deregulation in the 1980s and 1990s, however, relaxed these limits. Business strategists sought to make money by consolidating smaller independent companies into large corporations. By exploiting economies of scale, giant corporations produced economic gains for their stockholders.

After the deregulation in 1996, media consolidation snowballed in AM and FM radio in the United States. Today, six companies own the majority of the nation's radio broadcasting frequencies and therefore dominate broadcast radio. These **oligopolies** exert economic dominance over radio and related media enterprises such as advertising, performance venues, and recording contracts for music artists and merchandizing. Clear Channel, one of just a handful of companies that control most of broadcast radio frequencies, aggressively acquired stations when the ownership limit was relaxed, and today they control over 1,200 radio stations nationwide.[17] They dominate broadcast radio in 100 of the 112 major media markets.[18]

oligopoly
control of the market by only a few, rather than many, companies

Increased media consolidation led to a decline in FM radio's individuality and local character. Most owners were increasing the number of ads per hour and decreasing the number of songs in their playlists. Restricted playlists with as few as 100 songs became commonplace. In 2005, on Clear Channel stations, commercials took one minute in five of typical broadcasts. Audiences began to turn away from programming that trailed in importance to advertising.

Public Interest Rouses FCC

Although the Telecommunications Act of 1983 did remove many of the regulatory controls on commercial radio, the broadcast airwaves continue to belong to the public, and the FCC still retains responsibility for regulating them.

In 2003, the FCC moved to relax the rules on media ownership further. This may have been a tipping point, because public outcry calling for limits on media

---

[16]Fritz J. Messere, "U.S. Policy: Telecommunications Act of 1996," *U.S. Museum of Broadcast Communications Archives*, at http://www.museum.tv/archives/etv/U/htmlU/uspolicyt/uspolicyt.htm. Accessed July 17, 2008.

[17]Clear Channel Communications Homepage. *Clear Channel Communications, Inc.*, at http://www.clearchannel.com/. Accessed July 17, 2008.

[18]Jeff Perlstein, "Clear Channel: The Media Mammoth that Stole the Airwaves," *CorpWatch.com*, November 14, 2002, at http://www.corpwatch.org/article.php?id=4808. Accessed July 28, 2008.

concentration was fierce. Nearly 3 million people contacted the FCC calling for media reform in 2003. The issue brought together groups from both the left and the right, including the National Rifle Association, Common Cause, MoveOn.org, the Traditional Values Coalition, and Mediareform.org.

The matter went to court. There was no further relaxation of ownership limits, and the FCC decided not to appeal the matter. As a result, the FCC had to rewrite its policy pertaining to serving local interests and promoting access to the airwaves by diverse groups.[19]

DEVELOPMENTS AND ISSUES IN CONTEMPORARY RADIO

The radio industry has experienced dramatic changes in the recent years. For us in the 21st century, the consumer is king of mass media. With digital media and broadband networks, consumers can get content wherever, whenever, and however they want. Broadcasting is giving way to **narrowcasting** in radio, as well as other mass media. The question isn't AM or FM, nor is it what station to tune in. Today's listener wants "me media" that provides whatever content he or she wants at the time and place demanded by the listener. Today, radio transmissions are often "narrowcast" to listeners on demand.

narrowcasting
creating a media channel that is aimed at a niche audience

Satellite Radio

The rise of **satellite radio** in recent years marks an important development in the radio industry. Subscribers to satellite networks pay a monthly fee and get access to commercial-free programming, some of it directly from broadcast radio, and other stations that are only heard via satellite.

satellite radio
radio created from digital signals sent through satellites in space; allows for commercial-free broadcasting over a broad geographical area

Satellite radio operators have made deals with car manufacturers so that all new vehicles have built-in satellite radio receivers, and most come with a complimentary subscription to the first several months of satellite radio.

Portable satellite radios are also available. These devices can download and play individual songs like MP3 players can, as well as play programming streams from satellite radio.

Other listeners time shift their favorite radio programs by subscribing to RSS (real simple syndication) feeds that automatically download the most recent episodes of a program to their computer and transfer the segments to their MP3 players.

How has satellite radio changed the industry?
© Brant Ward/San Francisco Chronicle/Corbis

[19]Paul Davidson, "Looser media rules tossed," USA TODAY, June 24, 2004, at http://www.usatoday.com/money/media/2004-06-24-fcc-overturned_x.htm. Accessed July 28, 2008.

shock-jock
a slang term for a disk jockey or talk show host who pushes the boundaries of what is offensive

In 2006, **shock-jock** Howard Stern moved to satellite radio. The move was closely watched throughout the radio business. He commanded an audience of 10 million with his morning show on FM radio. Following crackdowns on profanity over the airwaves from regulators and the threat of fines or censorship from his employer, Stern decided to make a decisive move off the public airwaves and onto subscription radio broadcast via satellite. With his move from FM broadcast radio to satellite radio, his new employer SIRIUS saw its subscription base rise above the 3-million mark.

In the past several years, satellite radio subscriptions have continued to increase. After the 2008 merger of SIRIUS and XM, the combined company had over 18 million subscribers.[20] That same year, a study conducted by the digital technology research firm Parks Associates predicted that by 2012, satellite radio subscribers would increase to 39 million.[21]

Public Broadcasting

More than 26 million people listen to Corporation for Public Broadcasting (CPB) stations and support news shows like "All Things Considered," long-form radio entertainments like "This American Life," and a variety of musical offerings on public radio stations through pledges. The audience for CPB had remained steady, but has declined slightly between 2004 and 2005. Competition for listener attention is fierce, and the hours per day that individuals can engage with mass media can't expand indefinitely. It may be inevitable that as more varied devices are available, the number of listeners in the audience for any one device may decrease.

Now it's easier than ever to listen to exactly the music you want, anytime and anywhere. © Ronen/Shutterstock

Internet Radio and Podcasting

Innovative radio broadcasting stations of all kinds are presenting supplemental content via downloads for listeners who have special interests. News radio 780, one of the only all-news AM radio stations still broadcasting, has put press conferences and uncut interviews on its Web site where listeners can listen, download, or subscribe to news of their choice. The Internet has allowed the station, and others like it, to reach audiences far beyond their over-the-airwaves reach.[22]

Nowadays, even individuals with computers and inexpensive software can provide competition for

[20]"SIRIUS XM Radio Provides Merger Update," September 9, 2008, SIRIUS Satellite Radio News Releases, http://investor.sirius.com/ReleaseDetail.cfm?ReleaseID=333252&cat=&newsroom. Accessed September 12, 2008.

[21]"Almost 70 Million Consumers Will Have Either an HD or a Satellite Radio by 2012," *Reuters*, January 8, 2008, at http://www.reuters.com/article/pressRelease/idUS204500+08-Jan-2008+PRN20080108. Accessed September 12, 2008.

[22]WBBM 780 homepage, at http://www.wbbm780.com/. Accessed July 18, 2008.

listeners. It is simple to create online music or talk programming. Digital audio, such as **podcasts** (digital recordings of radio broadcasts or similar programs made available on the Internet),[23] can be uploaded to the Internet and downloaded for listening on computers or MP3 players. This is yet another form of competition for the attention of listeners.

podcast
a digital recording of a radio broadcast or similar program, made available on the Internet for downloading to a personal audio player

Revenues and Ratings

Radio revenues are dependent on advertising. But how do radio stations know how large the audience is for various programs, and how do advertisers verify that the claims made by station owners are correct? They turn to Arbitron Inc., an "international media and marketing research firm serving radio broadcasters, radio networks, cable companies, advertisers, advertising agencies, outdoor advertising companies, and the online radio industry in the United States, Mexico, and Europe."[24] In a joint venture with VNU, Inc., Arbitron provides media and marketing research services including market **ratings** to broadcasters and advertisers.

ratings
statistical measures of listeners or viewers of broadcast programming

Radio shows are programmed around a set of genres. A **genre** is a style. Like any other fashion or any other style, music genres go in and out of popularity with audiences. Arbitron also provides data on audience demographics for different genres and for various **dayparts**.

genre
a style

The amount of money that broadcasters can use for advertising time is tied to ratings. Arbitron and similar companies provide ratings information for major markets. These resources provide an interesting way to learn about radio and are essential for those who intend to pursue a career in radio.

daypart
a subsection of the day used in radio or television programming

Responding to Competition

With satellite radio, Internet radio, and podcasting bursting onto the media scene, there are suddenly many more alternatives for the listening audience.[25] To stay in business, the radio industry looked to new formats as a way to be competitive in a world in which competition comes from the Internet, MP3 devices, cell phones, or anyone who has a computer with a microphone and Internet connection.

cyberjock
sometimes pejorative term for a disk jockey who hosts a radio show from a single locale that is broadcast widely and uses computer software to localize weather, traffic, and advertisements

In 2002, an alternative format called "Jack" was trademarked in Canada. With the slogan "Playing what we want," "Jack" stations typically have a playlist of 1,000 songs. They are classified as variety or adult hit by radio research companies.[26]

By 2004, "Jack," "Bob," and even "Dave" radio, based loosely on the "random shuffle" concept, were taking over American airwaves. Several of these alternatives to the Clear Channel **cyberjock** model began to advertise fewer commercials per hour. Although they denied they were responding to the competition, Clear Channel moved to reduce the number of commercials on its stations in 2005.

---

[23]podcast. *New Oxford American Dictionary* at http://www.bbn.com/utility/glossary/p. Accessed July 18, 2008.

[24]About Arbitron. *Arbitron, Inc.*, at http://www.arbitron.com/about/home.htm. Accessed July 18, 2008.

[25]Podcasting News homepage at http://www.podcastingnews.com/. Accessed July 17, 2008.

[26]Lou Pickney, "Variety Hits-History of the Format," at http://www.varietyhits.com/variety/history.shtml. Accessed July 17, 2008.

voice-tracking software
computer software used in radio programming that allows a DJ to hear the end of one song and the beginning of another so he or she can record the voice tracks so they sound live, though it is played back at a later time. After recording the "break", the song is encoded and can be transmitted anywhere on radio or Internet.

In addition, companies such as Clear Channel responded to mounting competition by seeking to cut expenses by achieving economies of scale. Clear Channel is a leader in using **voice-tracking software** to customize their programs to make it sound as if the DJs are actually local residents. With digital equipment, local traffic and weather information can be interlaced into a broadcast from a single point, like Clear Channel's San Antonio studios. When the broadcast goes out across the airwaves, listeners think the DJ is local because of the customized traffic and weather segments. The use of cyberjocks cuts the cost of producing radio shows, but at the same time it can rob the airwaves of diverse voices and local perspectives.[27] Other changes evolve from the consolidation of radio ownership.

BEYOND NATIONAL BOUNDARIES: GLOBAL RADIO

Although radio is an old medium, it is still one of the most vital forms of communication outside the United States. There are about 44,000 radio stations in the world according to the CIA World Factbook, and only one in three of these is in the United States.

The BBC

In the United States, the airwaves were largely put into commercial use. In the United Kingdom, the British Broadcasting Corporation BBC, or the "Beeb" as it is called by millions of listeners, was established with public support and a royal charter in the 1927.[28] The effort to keep the BBC independent of commercial and government influence was led by John Reith, the BBC's first general manager, who believed in "an independent British broadcaster able to educate, inform, and entertain the whole nation, free from political interference and commercial pressure."[29]

In 1937, the BBC established a network designed for its empire and the rest of the world, which is called the World Service today. The BBC was broadcasting television by 1936, but had to suspend television broadcasts during World War II.

The coronation of Queen Elizabeth in 1952 drew the largest audience in BBC history and set the stage for television to become the premiere broadcast format. BBC programming was solid, but competition from Independent Television (ITV) captured many viewers during the 1950s and 1960s. In the 1970s, the BBC linked with the Open University to create the University of the Airwaves. In the 1980s,

---

[27]Anna Wilde Matthews, "Clear Channel Uses High-Tech Gear To Perfect the Art of Sounding Local," February 25, 2002, at http://stayfreemagazine.org/public/clearchannel.html.

[28]BBC Radio homepage, at http://www.bbc.co.uk/radio/i/. Accessed July 17, 2008.

[29]"The BBC Story: History of the BBC, the 1920s" at http://www.bbc.co.uk/heritage/story/index.shtml. Accessed July 17, 2008.

Margaret Thatcher's government cut back funding, but the BBC streamlined and in the 1990s launched the highly respected BBC Online. By January 2005, BBC Internet radio listenership had jumped 70 percent from the previous year, with a total of over 7 million listeners.[30] Today, the BBC Web site and Internet radio broadcasts continue to gain an audience.

Shortwave Broadcasts

Many radio stations that are widely accessible are shortwave broadcasts. Shortwave signals can be aimed at the earth's ionosphere. When they strike the ionosphere, they bounce back to Earth and can skip from one part of the globe. This is called the skywave effect, and it helps the waves continue or propagate over long distances.

Solar emissions can affect the reflectivity of the earth's atmosphere, but if conditions are right, a shortwave radio in the United States can pick up stations from Africa, Asia, Australia, and East Asia.

Avid shortwave listeners are known as Dxers from the old telegraph term meaning "Distance." They search out broadcasts that fall into three main categories: broadcast, clandestine, and amateur or utility. Broadcasts consist of music, cultural, religious, and political programming. "Pirate" and other unlicensed radio stations, including some anti-government broadcast material, fall into the clandestine category. Utility broadcasts include weather information, world clocks, Morse code, and radio teletype.

CAREERS IN THE FIELD

According to the 2008–09 edition of the Bureau of Labor Statistics (BLS) Occupational Outlook Handbook, there were about 67,000 jobs for news analysts, reporters, and correspondents working in radio in 2006.[31] During that same year, there were about 71,000 announcer jobs in radio. About 30 percent of these positions were held by freelance announcers and close to half (42 percent) of radio announcer jobs were part time.[32] In addition, there were about 105,000 jobs for broadcast and sound engineering technicians and radio operators in 2006.[33]

---

[30]"BBC internet radio users up 70% on 2004," *BBC Press Office*, February 28, 2005, at http://www.bbc.co.uk/pressoffice/pressreleases/stories/2005/02_february/28/radio.shtml.

[31]"News Analysts, Reporters, and Correspondents," Occupational Outlook Handbook, 2008–09 Edition, *U.S. Department of Labor, Bureau of Labor Statistics*, December 18, 2007, at http://www.bls.gov/oco/ocos088.htm.

[32]"Announcers," Occupational Outlook Handbook 2008–09 Edition, U.S. Department of Labor, Bureau of Labor Statistics, December 18, 2007, at http://www.bls.gov/oco/ocos087.htm.

[33]"Broadcast and Sound Engineering Technicians and Radio Operators," Occupational Outlook Handbook 2008–09 Edition, U.S. Department of Labor, Bureau of Labor Statistics, December 18, 2007, at http://www.bls.gov/oco/ocos109.htm.

Announcer jobs are one of the many positions available in the radio industry. © Tsian/Shutterstock

According to the BLS, "job growth in radio and television broadcasting will be limited by consolidation of ownership of radio and television stations and by labor-saving technical advances, such as computer-controlled programming and remotely controlled transmitters."[34] In addition, the BLS reports that ownership consolidation reduces employment "because one or a few technicians can provide support to multiple stations."[35]

SUMMARY

- Much of the early history of radio, during the second half of the 19th century, is the story of inventors and scientists making sense of invisible waves and how they could be harnessed to carry sounds and voice.
- In the early 1900s, David Sarnoff, an employee of the Marconi Company, had a vision of radio as a home entertainment device. The first commercial radio station began broadcasting in 1920, leading to the first golden age of radio in the 1930s and 1940s.
- In the 1920s, individual radio stations began pooling their resources to create "economies of scale." The first major networks that emerged were the Red Network and the Blue Network, which evolved into the National Broadcasting Company (NBC) and the American Broadcasting Company (ABC). The Columbia Broadcasting System (CBS) and a fourth network, Mutual Broadcasting System (MBS), followed in the 1930s.
- Radio became an important news medium during World War II when broadcasts from Europe by Edward R. Murrow set a new standard for broadcast reporting. That style of news broadcast on the radio later influenced television news.

[34]Ibid.

[35]Ibid.

- With the introduction of high-fidelity audio, more listeners began tuning in to FM stations for music. Talk radio revived AM. After the Fairness Doctrine was repealed, early talk radio hosts such as Rush Limbaugh provided a model for aspiring shock-jocks.
- Radio licensing by the government requires broadcasters to serve the public interest. The Federal Communications Commission (FCC) regulates broadcasting to protect that interest, but deregulation under President Reagan in the 1980s culminating in the Telecommunications Bill of 1996 may have weakened the protections.
- Digital radio, satellite radio, and podcasting promise to alter radio listening because of the quality of sound and type of programs available. However, the advances will mean purchasing new equipment.
- As technology, regulation, and economic factors change, the radio business is changing and so are the employment opportunities in radio. Advances in technology and media consolidation are two contributing factors to the limited job growth in radio and television broadcasting.
- Shortwave radio signals allow radio stations to broadcast globally. Internet radio, such as the BBC's Internet broadcast, has become popular as another form of global radio.

DISCUSSION QUESTIONS

1. Why is radio regulated?
2. Are podcasts, Internet radio, and streaming music "radio"? Why or why not?
3. What effect will satellite radio and high-definition radio have on standard radio?
4. How did the Fairness Doctrine work to ensure AM radio stations would stay on air?
5. What are your thoughts on media consolidation? Has this practice had a positive or negative impact on radio?

SUPPLEMENTAL WEB SITES

TELEVISION, CABLE, AND THE FUTURE

9

CHAPTER OBJECTIVES

- Understand how the television set and television broadcasting was developed
- List the different types of television programming
- Describe how television networks develop programming
- Understand how cable television was developed
- Give examples of future trends in the television industry

KEY TERMS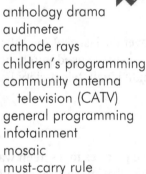

anthology drama
audimeter
cathode rays
children's programming
community antenna
  television (CATV)
general programming
infotainment
mosaic
must-carry rule

narrowcasting
photoelectricity
reality TV
scanning
share
situation comedy
sketch comedy shows
soap operas
superstations
variety show

INTRODUCTION

Since television entered people's homes in the 1940s, it has been a primary source of entertainment for many American families. Whether you watch one hour or 20 hours of television a week, the medium most likely plays some sort of role in your life. You may have learned your ABCs from a children's program, watched your favorite sports team win a championship, or witnessed the Twin

Television brings sight and sound together to make you feel like you're there in person.
© Monkey Business Images/Shutterstock

Towers go down on September 11th through the power of the television screen. Imagine if you were unable to connect to the world in this way. How would you stay informed or entertained? While newspapers and radio can provide adequate information, they do not have the multi-sensory effect of television. You can listen to a space shuttle launch on the radio and hear the command tower count down to blast off. In a newspaper, you can see an amazing picture of thick smoke building up beneath the shuttle as it lifts into the sky. However, television has the power to bring sight and sound together to create an experience that makes viewers feel like they are witnessing an event in person.

Television often gets a bad rap. It has been given names like the "boob tube" or "idiot box", and those who are avid television watchers are often categorized as "couch potatoes". But television is much more than meaningless images with synchronized sound. It is a portal to a world that one would not see if not for the connective power of television. It is also an amazing piece of technology that required the efforts of many innovative individuals.

To understand how television has become such an important part of our culture, let's review the birth of the medium, examine how programming is developed, and discuss how new technologies have transformed the nature of television.

THE ADVENT OF TELEVISION

Television has taken many different shapes over the last century. Like many forms of media, it started as merely a concept and was developed into an industry. This industry was almost overlooked, as many individuals felt society had no use for television.

The Early Stages

While developing the technology to bring live pictures to a screen was a long and meticulous process, one of the first inventions that made television broadcasting possible came about accidentally. In 1872, English telegraph worker Joseph May made an unusual discovery about the element selenium. While examining materials for use in the transatlantic cable, the first telegraph cable to cross the Atlantic Ocean, May randomly placed a strand of selenium wire on a table near a window. As beams of sunlight passed through the window onto the wire, May noticed that the sunlight caused the electric conductivity of the selenium wire to change. Upon further investigation, he realized that the amount of electricity produced by the wire was in direct relation to the amount of light that fell on it. While this discovery was only of minor importance at the time, it provided the foundation for **photoelectricity**, or turning light into an electric signal.

photoelectricity
the act of turning light into an electric signal

Over the next few years, various inventors such as George R. Carey attempted to use this discovery to create electric images. They used selenium cells to break up a picture and sent the pieces over a wire to small electric lamps. Once the selenium cells reached the electric lamps the image would be recreated in a mosaic. A **mosaic** is a television tube that consists of many tiny photoelectric particles that convert light to an electric charge.[1] To recreate the image, the electric lamps would be turned on, turned off, intensified or dimmed. The more lamps used in the mosaic, the more detailed the picture. However, this process required an outrageous amount of wiring and an impractical setup of electrical lamps. To reach the level of detail in a modern day 23 inch television, it would take 350,000 lamps, each no more than one-fortieth of an inch in diameter.[2]

mosaic
a television tube that consists of many tiny photoelectric particles that convert light to an electric charge

In 1884, German inventor Paul Nipkow avoided the problems of a mosaic device by applying the principle of scanning. **Scanning** involves viewing all the elements of a picture successively, rather than all at once, and sending them in a specific order over a single circuit. In this principle, a photoelectric cell would scan, or look over, only one portion of a picture at a time—going right to left then down a row, just as a person would read a book. Nipkow developed a rotating disk, called a scanner disk or Nipkow disk, which allowed information-filled cells to be sent from a transmitter to a reception point where the original image is recreated line by line. At the time, this technology was viewed as impractical. However, the concept of using a single wire to transmit an entire image became, and still remains to be, the basis of all television.[3]

scanning
the act of viewing all the elements of a picture successively, rather than all at once, and sending them in a specific order over a single circuit

More than forty years later, the concept of scanning was used to create the first successful televisions. While the machines may not be considered televisions by today's standards, they could transmit pictures. In 1922, Charles Francis Jenkins of the United States created a machine that sent still pictures through radio waves, but perhaps the more true form of television was created by John Baird in 1925. Baird's machine created a transmission of a live human face. The inventions of Jenkins and Baird were not immediately hailed as revolutionary technology. Critics felt the cost of building such systems would never be repaid and that the world did not have much use for television. Still, Jenkins and Baird, as well as companies like American Telephone and Telegraph Company (AT&T) and General Electric Company (GE) worked to further develop television technology. In 1928, Jenkins began to sell television kits that allowed consumers to build their own televisions. He also established his own television station and produced animated programs. In 1929, the British Broadcasting Corporation (BBC) allowed Baird to produce and broadcast a half-hour television show. These programs were made for extremely small audiences, as very few people owned television sets. However, in the following years, audiences would grow from tens to thousands as

---

[1]mosaic. In *Merriam-Webster Online Dictionary* at http://www.merriam-webster.com/dictionary/mosaic. Accessed November 13, 2008.

[2]Christopher H. Sterling, John M. Kittross, *Stay Tuned: A history of American broadcasting.* Lawrence Erlbaum Associates: 2002.

[3]television. *Encyclopedia Britannica* at http://www.britannica.com/ EBchecked/topic/1262241/television. Accessed November 13, 2008.

Television

The word *television* was coined by a Frenchman named Constantin Perskyi at the 1900 Paris Exposition. On August 25, 1900, he read a paper to the International Electricity Congress and used the word to describe a device that could send images through electricity. Strangely enough, at the same exposition, a set of trading cards, titled "In the Year 2000" displayed images of inventions that were expected to emerge by the year 2000, one of which resembled a television. Little did they know that the *television* would reach their homes in only a few decades.[4]

One of the "In the Year 2000" trading cards showed communication as they envisioned it in the 19th Century.
© *Stefano Bianchetti/CORBIS*

viewers were purchasing or constructing their own television sets just to catch a glimpse of a few flickering images on a dim receiver screen.[5]

Steady Progress

Determining who invented the television is a difficult task, as the efforts of many inventors played a role in the development of technologies used in a television system. However, two individuals played a major role in developing television into a mechanically sound and economically viable system. Vladimir Zworykin was a Russian immigrant who worked at Westinghouse Electric Company, a subsidiary of Radio Corporation of America (RCA) in Pittsburgh, Pennsylvania. In 1923, while working for the company, Zworykin filed a patient application for an all-electronic television system. Despite the fact that Zworykin was unable to build and demon-

[4]Television History: The First 75 Years. (2006). *TV History.* Retrieved from http://www.tvhistory.tv/1890s%20Victorian%20Trade%20Card.htm.

[5]television. *Encyclopedia Britannica* at Encyclopædia Britannica Online: http://www.britannica.com/EBchecked/topic/1262241/television. Accessed November 13, 2008.

strate the system due to lack of funding, he managed to convince David Sarnoff, vice president of RCA, to provide $100,000 in funding on the promise that in two years he would produce a usable electronic television system. As Zworykin worked on building his system, another inventor by the name of Philo Taylor Farnsworth was demonstrating his basic version of an electronic television system called an Image Dissector. Farnsworth was an ambitious young man from Utah with only a high-school education. He learned about electronics though technology magazines and his own experimentation. Farnsworth secured funding for his project by gathering investors who hoped to gain a profit from marketing an affordable television system that was consumer friendly. While Farnsworth was able to develop his system for only $5,000, a fraction of Zworykin's cost, it would take many years and nearly $50 million dollars before anyone could create a television that was profitable.[6]

Utah inventor Philo T. Farnsworth displays his image dissector. © Bettmann/CORBIS

With the initial funds provided by RCA, Zworykin developed the Kinescope, a cathode-ray receiver that could project images onto a glass tube. **Cathode rays** are beams of electrons used to project images on to florescent screen inside a vacuum tube. Meanwhile, Farnsworth worked on perfecting his Image Dissector. A functional television could have been created more quickly and for less money if the two men were able to collaborate, but competition between RCA and Philco, Farnsworth's partnering company, kept the two innovators apart. In 1930, RCA attempted to purchase the patent to Farnsworth's Image Dissector for $100,000, but was turned down. RCA and Zworykin were able to learn enough from the Farnsworth's Image Dissector to develop the Iconoscope camera tube, which became their first working electronic television system.

cathode rays
beams of electrons used to project images onto a florescent screen inside a vacuum tube

This development created conflict between RCA and Farnsworth. In 1932, both parties met in court to determine who invented the electronic television. After a long process, the court eventually ruled in favor of Farnsworth, and in 1939 RCA agreed to pay royalties to Farnsworth Television and Radio, Inc, the firm Farnsworth created after leaving Philco. Still, RCA was able to gain a fair share of the credit for the television through its various publicity events. Later that year, RCA demonstrated its system at the 1939 World's Fair in New York City. At the official opening ceremonies, Franklin Delano Roosevelt became the first U.S. president to be televised. Some media outlets hailed television as a technology that would change the American home, but others, including *The New York Times*, described it as a gimmick without useful applications.

Television Reaches the Public

In 1941, the Federal Communications Commission (FCC) decided that the technology was well developed enough to be introduced to the public. In that year, fewer than 10,000 regular viewers were able to receive television transmissions

---

[6]Ibid.

from a handful of stations. Television sets were a very significant investment for a middle class family. A black-and-white receiver with a five-inch screen cost about $1,000, at a time when a Chevrolet cost $2,000. Still, the public was growing curious about television. Unfortunately, the attack on Pearl Harbor and World War II greatly delayed the widespread adoption of television by the public, partly because most electronic companies diverted their resources for the war effort. Many American television stations reduced their schedules or simply went off air. American electronic companies such as Bell labs, General Electric, and Westinghouse focused their efforts on using television to guide missiles, long-range reconnaissance, and other military endeavors. RCA's David Sarnoff proclaimed to President Franklin Roosevelt that, "all our facilities and personnel are ready and at your instant service."[7]

In the mid-50s, thanks to mass production and competition in the industry, many American homes had a television. © *Bettmann/CORBIS*

The war ended in 1945, and television expanded rapidly. By 1948, nearly 70 television stations were on air. The expansion was quickly halted by a second delay. Due to concerns regarding the limited space available in the VHF (very high frequency) band, the FCC administered a 4-year freeze on all new station licenses. In 1952, the organization opened the UHF (ultra high frequency) band to allow more space for television transmission and resumed issuing new licenses. By 1955, the cost of a television began to drop thanks to mass production and competition in the industry. That year, nearly 67 percent of Americans were equipped to receive programs in black-and-white. That figure grew to 87 percent by 1960.[8]

Television in Color

Just like black-and-white television, color television gained popularity slowly. In the 1940s, Peter Carl Goldmark of the Columbia Broadcasting System (CBS) introduced the first color television system. Subsequently, RCA developed a technique for color broadcasting that, unlike CBS's version, would be compatible with black-and-white broadcasting. This type of compatible broadcasting was approved by the FCC in 1953. Within the next year, RCA started to manufacture color television sets known as the CT-100 color receiver. The high price and questionable quality of color television sets caused the majority of consumers to stick to black-and-white sets. But over the next ten years, the price of color TV sets dropped and the quality improved dramatically. By 1967, color television sets outsold black-white-televisions for the first time, and in 1973 more than half of American households had a color set. Today, 98 percent of Americans have a color TV in their home.[9]

---

[7]RCA Press Room, About RCA - Television, Retrieved at http://home.rca.com/en-US/PressReleaseDetail .html?Cat=RCAHistory&MN=9.

[8]http://www.history.com/encyclopedia.do?articleId=203824.

[9]Associated Press. "Color TV Hits 50th Anniversary in U.S." *USA Today*, March 24, 2004. Retrieved from http://www.usatoday.com/life/television/news/2004-03-24-color-tv_x.htm.

Television Goes Digital

In December 2005, the U.S. Congress approved new legislation requiring broadcasters to end all analog transmission of television signals. As of February 2009, any viewer using an antenna to receive television signals would need to acquire a converter box in order to receive programming. Digital TV transmission, already a reality for many cable and satellite service providers and consumers, promises better image and sound quality. The approved legislation also allocated up to U.S. $1.5 billion for consumer purchase of converter boxes that will allow all analog TV sets to receive the new digital signal.[10]

Digital television transmission, coupled with technological innovations on the receiving end, such as high definition television (HDTV), liquid crystal display (LCD) and plasma screens, and high quality audio systems, are poised to revolutionize the way most people watch TV. These new technologies have prompted a growing number of consumers to set up sophisticated home-theaters—entertainment centers comparable to the best theater-going movie experience.

The development of the technology behind television sets and television broadcasting took many years and numerous people to bring the technology to its present state of development. Similarly, the development of programming for television was, and still is, a painstaking process.

A growing number of people have set up sophisticated home theaters with the latest technology.
© pics721/ Shutterstock

THE FORMATION OF TELEVISION PROGRAMMING

While creating the technology that made television possible was a tremendous feat, deciding what should be broadcast on television was an equally challenging task. After the initial excitement of seeing live people appear on a screen wore off, it was apparent that quality programs would have to be developed if the medium was going to continue to grow and surpass radio. Different television genres and formats have been popular over the decades. While some of those faded into oblivion, some continue popular to this day, while others have disappeared just to re-emerge later completely reformatted.

From Radio to Television

Early radio programs—variety shows, dramatic productions, comedies, and quiz shows—were performed live for simultaneous transmission throughout the country. So important was the supposed dynamic of a "real" event that announcers at one radio network were required to wear tuxedos; the management was convinced

---

[10]Digital TV 2009.

that this made them speak with distinction and moreover it both impressed the studio audience and sparked their earnest participation.

When many of the popular radio programs and formats moved to television, the tradition of presenting them live continued, if for no other reason than because it was quicker and cheaper than filming and editing them. Newscasters had to learn to look at the camera from time to time, but basically they were the same radio news readers with a microphone and a sheaf of papers in front of them, with little in the way of graphics or film footage to illustrate what they were reporting.

Television as Entertainment

Variety shows were a natural for television. Whereas radio had been limited to presenting musical acts that could be appreciated by the ear alone, television could use baton twirlers, jugglers, tap-dancers, wire-walkers, puppeteers, and animal acts. **Variety shows** were presented live, sometimes from a hastily refurbished Broadway theater with an announcer standing in front of the curtain and ballyhooing the next act much as a vaudeville host might have done. Ed Sullivan's *Toast of the Town* long reigned as television's quintessential variety show. *Arthur Godfrey and His Friends* was an extended family of young performers chaperoned by a father-figure host, while Milton Berle's popularity stemmed from the comedian's willingness to go to any extreme to pull off a ridiculous skit. These types of programs paved the way for modern sketch comedy programs. **Sketch comedy shows** often contain a series of short comedy scenes, referred to as sketches. Sketches are about five to ten minutes long and typically performed by ensemble casts. NBC's *Saturday Night Live* is an iconic sketch comedy show that has aired for over 30 years. Variety shows have made a bit of a comeback in recent years with shows such as *American Idol* and *America's Got Talent*, but modern shows have added a competitive twist to the formula.

Dramatic television also made a smooth transition from radio to television. Radio drama had been fairly simple to produce live, because actors only needed to sound like the characters they played, and sound effects took care of setting the scene. Nonetheless, drama made the move to television with considerable success. A new generation of playwrights, directors, designers, and actors presented **anthology dramas**, high-quality original hour-long and 90-minute plays weekly on such shows as *General Electric Theater*, *Playhouse 90*, and *Studio One*. Eventually these live dramas were replaced with prerecorded dramatic programs.

Some lament the passing of live dramatic television. But a look at those old shows reveals that their production values were quite basic, and the look was flat in texture. Today we expect more polish and excitement from prerecorded programs.

Still, some entertainment programs such as talk shows maintain a live or partially live format. NBC pioneered the talk show format, wherein personalities provided a blend of entertainment, information, and service material. *Today* was the prototype for the early morning news-weather-feature-chatter wake-up format, and *The Tonight Show* paved the way for countless desk-and-couch late-night programs in which a genial host does an opening monologue, interviews a handful of

variety show
a live show that features numerous acts such as dancers, musicians, and comedians

sketch comedy shows
a program with a series of short comedy scenes

anthology drama
high-quality original hour-long and 90-minute plays that aired weekly, often aired live

celebrities, banters with the band and the audience, and bumbles through a topical comedy sketch.

Early television broadcasting was carried for only a few hours each day, mainly in the evening when whole families could watch. As programming was expanded into the daylight hours, children's programming was added. **Children's programming** consists of television shows that are appropriate and often educational for children under the age of 12. Sitting on bleachers or benches in tiny, cramped studios, an audience of a few dozen kids would be entertained by puppets, perpetually cheerful adults, a clown, and a few zany characters. Buffalo Bob was the host-sidekick to the freckle-faced *Howdy Doody*, in one of the earliest children's programs. It became the forerunners of popular children's programs such as *Sesame Street*, *Barney*, and *The Wiggles*.

children's programming
television shows that are appropriate and sometimes educational for children under the age of 12

The situation comedy is a staple of television programming. A **situation comedy**, or **sitcom**, is a program that typically consists of a group of characters placed in a familiar setting or situation that ultimately generates humorous activity. Traditional sitcoms are filmed in front of a live studio audience and allow viewers to hear the emotional reactions of audience members. *I Love Lucy*, a popular situation comedy of the 1950s, was the first television program to be filmed and then broadcast at a later time. The show pioneered the three-camera set-up, with one camera in the center used for the establishing shot of the Ricardos and their neighbors in the living room, and the other two focusing on the faces of Lucy and the person with whom she was speaking. On this program the bedroom—if pictured in any episode—showed two separate beds so as not to violate the moral sensitivities of 1950s viewers.

situation comedy
a program that typically consists of a group of characters placed in a familiar setting or situation that ultimately generates humorous activity

Today, notice how often the "situation" in a situation comedy revolves around a family or group of characters gathered around a familiar setting—the living room or a bar or an office or a coffee house—and the three-camera set-up moves the action along swiftly in a manner that is easy to follow on the small screen. This classic form of situation comedy is used in shows such as *Two and a Half Men* and *Everybody Loves Raymond*. Other shows such as *The Office* and *Scrubs* have scrapped the studio audience and added more cameras to create a program that is more like a movie than a television show.

The classic form of situation comedy where the same characters are gathered in a familiar setting is still used in shows today. © *Photofest*

Other popular programs that have evolved over the years have been detective shows and westerns. The shows are typically filmed on location and edited into a one-hour format, with commercial breaks nicely worked in at planned pauses in the action. Crime dramas joined sitcoms as the main programming for prime-time television. Networks and their advertisers wanted to train audiences to watch the same programs regularly, so they encouraged producers to develop familiar and likable characters who could be shown in standardized yet slightly different situations week after week.

Game shows were popular programs on radio, but they became even more popular on television as the agony or glee of the contestants could be seen in all its human glory. Easy and cheap to produce, the games became not only words, bells, and buzzers, but giant boards with flashing lights, handsome hosts, and maybe even beauty queens modeling or presenting the prizes.

For a short while game shows disappeared from television when it was discovered that some contestants on the most lucrative prime-time shows, including *The $64,000 Question*, had been coached in ways that prepared them to answer difficult or obscure questions. The quiz show scandals of the 1950s shook the public's confidence in the integrity of television programming. While it may have taken longer to win back the public's trust, games shows returned to television after four years. Today nationally syndicated shows such as *Jeopardy* and *Wheel of Fortune* are still extremely popular, attracting large audiences on a nightly basis. In the late 1990s, U.S. networks successfully imported and adapted European game shows such as *Who Wants to Be a Millionaire*, which gained daily slots on ABC's prime-time schedule, and even topped the most-watched charts for a short time.

Another format that made the transition from radio to television was the soap opera. **Soap operas** are serial stories told through a series of characters, usually in installments. Named "soaps" because their earliest sponsors were often personal hygiene and house cleaning products and companies, these radio dramas thrilled generations of listeners before making their move to television. Initially, because of their storylines and daytime broadcast schedule, the characters and plots were of interest mainly to young and middle-aged women. But as storylines diversified and diverse characters were brought in, many men became big fans of television soaps as well.

soap operas
serial stories told through a series of characters, usually in installments

Quiz Show Scandal of 1959

The most notorious case of game show rigging occurred in 1959 on the show *Twenty-One*. The program required contestants to go head-to-head in a trivia contest and answer enough questions to reach 21 points in order to receive a cash prize. Charles Van Doren, an English professor at Columbia University, was a celebrated winner on the popular game show, winning more than $130,000 and many admiring fans, but he soon found himself in the center of controversy. Around the time of Van Doren's win, rumors began to spread that game show executives fed certain players answers to questions in an effort to heighten drama and allow a more likeable contestant to win. During a congressional investigation, which was coordinated to examine the rumors, Van Doren admitted to cheating during his 15-week run on the show. The scandal followed Van Doren for many years, forcing him to retire from his position at Columbia and publish books under a pseudonym.[11]

---

[11]The American Experience, Quiz Show Scandal, People & Events, *Public Broadcasting System*. Retrieved from http://www.pbs.org/wgbh/amex/quizshow/peopleevents/pande02.html.

Telenovelas

Soap operas are popular not only in America but around the world. Latin American countries have been very successful developing their own brand of soaps, called *tele-novelas*. These serial dramas, developed in countries such as Brazil, Mexico, and Venezuela, are exported all over the world, and shown on prime-time in countries as diverse as China, Turkey, or Italy.

The addition of visual components to the soap opera meant that several story lines could be followed at once. Along with the usual middle-aged characters developed in the radio format, television added plots involving more glamorous young people. Soap operas became so popular for a while that, in the 1980s, producers and networks moved to nighttime with dramas such as *Dallas* and *Dynasty*, which explored more mature themes. Many of the weekly one-hour prime-time dramas that were created in the 1990s such as *Melrose Place* and *Dawson's Creek* and up to today, such as *Desperate Housewives* and *Gossip Girl*, were heavily influenced by the original soap opera format and language.

Televised sporting events are one of the main features that set television apart from all other media. Sports events are complicated in terms of camera placements, following the action, and cutting from close-ups to the entire field of action. But they were quickly embraced by television programmers because they attracted large audiences; they were fairly inexpensive to produce; and advertisers liked the tie-in with popular hometown teams. In addition to baseball, which radio had covered for decades, television elevated professional sports to new stature. It also brought wide popularity to boxing, professional wrestling, bowling, and even marginal sports-entertainment attractions such as the roller-derby competition.

Televised sporting events set television apart from all the other media. © *David Lee/Shutterstock*

Reality programming is one of the newer forms of television programming and has become a very successful genre. The term **reality TV** is generally applied to describe programs that focus on non-actors that produce unscripted dialog. The format has been so victorious on TV that it has gained its own Emmy category. Although many question the label itself, since it has revealed several circumstances in which reality was tweaked to produce more desirable results, reality shows have made a strong mark on the network's schedules, and at least at this point don't seem to be losing steam.

reality TV
programs that focus on non-actors that produce unscripted dialog

Ranging from the prosaic—talent shows such as *American Idol*—to the bizarre—survival shows such as *Survivor* and *The Amazing Race* that test contestants' mental and physical strength. These reality shows are relatively cheap to produce and generate enough buzz to gain their own free publicity. Many analysts have also credited their success to the fact that they give audiences the sense of being able to watch themselves through the eyes and experiences of "real people."

Television as an Informer

In the early stages of development, many supporters viewed television as a revolutionary way to inform and educate the masses. Today we take for granted the ability of network and local news departments to provide complete (and many times live) coverage of presidential elections, natural disasters such as the 2004 tsunami, space shuttle launches, terrorist attacks, sport events, wars, inaugurations, and just about any other newsworthy event. Yet, these news functions were developed and perfected in little more than one generation.

Early television was not capable of providing much more than the 15-minute reading of the news that radio offered. Gradually, film footage and then live transmissions were added. Because of the addition of visual images, news broadcasts were allotted more time. By the end of the 1960s, first with the civil rights movement and then with the Vietnam War, television news had guaranteed a significant, permanent, premium (and much longer) space in the networks' schedules.

Coverage of the political nominating conventions marked the 1950s and made the careers of seasoned journalists such as Edward R. Murrow, David Brinkley, Mike Wallace, and Walter Cronkite, who had all migrated to TV from traditional media such as radio and newspapers. The presence of TV cameras in those conventions made them not only more relevant for the audience, but also made the medium much more attractive as a workplace for those seasoned reporters. Television made the nominating conventions a prime-time show, just like the World Series of baseball or the Miss America Pageant.

Because of their prominence at historic events, the network anchors were elevated to positions of power and respect unusual for anyone in American society. That's why Walter Cronkite, who consistently had the highest believability ratings before his retirement from the anchor seat in 1981, came to be known as "Uncle Walter" for the American public. The viewers felt he not only brought them the news, he in fact embodied the news.

In one decade or so, the era of the news reader was over. The all-powerful anchor and the participant journalist were now the norm on TV. The same way cameras, and later transmission dishes, made images and live transmissions an essential part of television journalism, it quickly became apparent that the anchors and other on-air personalities didn't have to remain tied to the New York or Washington studio. Instead they could be expected to travel with the President to a summit, attend the Olympic Games, and even visit the war front as Cronkite and others memorably did during the Vietnam War.

infotainment
a form of programming
that combines current
news and feature stories

Some news programs began to take an unlikely turn in the 1980s, as infotainment became a hot new format. **Infotainment** is a form of programming that combines current news and feature stories. Programs such as *Entertainment Tonight*, and *Extra*, presented soft celebrity or crime news. The fast-moving, easily digestible format blended the structure of a news program with the easygoing style

Walter Cronkite and Tim Russert

Nothing attests as much to the power of the television newsman or newswoman than our ability to recall important historical events based on how well-known journalists delivered those events into our living rooms. Two recently deceased television journalists, Walter Cronkite and Tim Russert, have come to symbolize (or even become synonymous with) television news for several generations of viewers.

When Cronkite died on July 17, 2009, the *New York Times* noted in its obituary how "from 1962 to 1981, Mr. Cronkite was a nightly presence in American homes and always a reassuring one, guiding viewers through national triumphs and tragedies alike, from moonwalks to war, in an era when network news was central to many people's lives." For many of our parents and grandparents, Cronkite's self-assured and reassuring demeanor became indelibly associated with some of the important events of their generations. His passing at age 92 reminded many of the golden age of television news, when nightly newscasts neatly summarized the news of the day, and no one could have anticipated an era of 24-hour news cycles and countless news blogs.

Tim Russert's death a year earlier at the age of 58 marked a different kind of passing. For many television observers, if Cronkite had a successor, his name was Russert. With his sharp and inquisitive mind hidden behind an affable Midwestern persona, Russert was able to deliver (and discuss) political news with the same kind of gravitas Cronkite employed to interview presidents and announce life-changing events. In its obituary of Russert, the *New York Times* called attention to the fact that he had come to play "an increasingly outsize role in the news media's coverage of politics." It may well be the case that Russert's death will come to symbolize the end of "personalized" political coverage. As blogs and Web sites multiply endlessly, it becomes harder to imagine any one political journalist coming to embody the "everyman quality" Russert brought into television news.

of a talk show. The anchorpeople are encouraged to be personalities themselves, and to feature the same stars that the audience read about in *People* and other similar news-gossip magazines.

It was just a matter of time before the success of such infotainment shows rubbed off into the traditional news shows. Currently, even the networks' serious news shows, such as *60 Minutes* or *Primetime Live*, have either generated their own spin-offs or incorporated many of the blended features popularized by infotainment. As recently as ten years ago, no one could imagine that the traditional news magazines would be racing to scoop each other on topics such as celebrity infidelity, Britney Spears, or New York socialites. Many in the news business defend themselves by pointing toward the audience, and saying that they are only giving the public what it wants.

Similarly, many news talk shows and news segments have become glorified soap boxes for celebrities to promote their latest films, books, or CDs. Shows such as the highly successful *Today* and *Good Morning America*, which are currently competing for the top morning ratings spot, have also incorporated infotainment into their format, transitioning easily from serious news segments to celebrity talk to cooking and fitness tips.

Since the events of September 2001, as the general public turned once again to the networks for reliable information, broadcast TV's news audience seems to have stabilized, after a brief increase in numbers. The competition from 24-hour news channels such as CNN and Fox News spurred the networks to reinvest in their coverage, a fact that became clear during the first stages of the Iraq War, when every single major news outlet had their own ground crews—and sometimes their anchors and star reporters—in the battlefield.

TELEVISION NETWORKS AND PUBLIC BROADCASTING

Each of the major radio networks entered the television business in the late 1940s, with NBC and CBS signing up affiliates in most of the 100 major markets, while ABC and Dumont—the long-forgotten fourth network—lagged far behind. Dumont dropped out of competition in the mid-1950s, and ABC became the dark horse in the network field, a role that it would hold until its ascendancy in the 1970s as the premier sports network.

Early Network Programming

In the early stages of the medium, there was insufficient programming for round-the-clock broadcasting. Typically, the station of the late 1940s and early 1950s came on the air with a "test pattern" around 5 p.m., carried one or two local programs, including the reading of the news in the early evening, and then joined the affiliated network for three hours of programming—the beginning of the concept of prime time. That paralleled radio network programming, and the format remained the heart of the network-affiliate concept even after the networks began to provide soap operas and game shows during the daytime hours.

Because the art of television production would take time to develop, each network carried movies that filled almost the entire three-hour prime-time slot at least one or two evenings a week. Each network began to work with advertisers and film producers to develop continuing half-hour and one-hour programs. Soon certain nights took on a distinctive flavor. Saturday emerged as comedy/variety night, with CBS's popular *The Jackie Gleason Show* and NBC's *Your Show of Shows*. CBS established several situation comedies on Tuesday night and the other networks accepted its domination in that segment of programming, much the way in which the other networks conceded in the 1990s and early-2000s that Thursday nights were NBC's "Must-See TV" nights, where the network reigned unchallenged with its popular sitcoms.

The networks gradually developed the capability of filling every night of the week with original programming, and they had to do it 52 weeks of the year because they had no ability to store and reuse television programs. Filmed "kinescopes" of television programs were useful for archival purposes, but they were not of broadcast quality. The introduction of the videotape—an electronic means of recording and storing television programs—meant that the networks could make just 26 episodes of a weekly program and show "reruns" during summer months.

By the 1960s, the networks had developed the practice of introducing most of their new shows one or two weeks in the middle of September. Shows that did not find an audience fairly rapidly were canceled and replaced with other programs whose pilot episodes shown the summer before did not win them a slot in the opening fall line-up. This practice is still used by the networks, with the possible difference that now unsuccessful shows typically get canceled much faster than they did before.

Late night talk shows have been a successful and enduring staple of network television. The most famous and longest running of them, the *Tonight Show* on NBC, started in 1954, when the network decided to broadcast nationally a local New York City talk show with host Steve Allen (*Television Talk: A History of the TV Talk Show*, by Bernard M. Timberg and Robert J. Erler, University of Texas, 2002). The genre was a direct successor to similarly formatted radio shows. Entertaining and cheap to produce, late night talk shows proved to be a great success with audiences, mixing sketch comedy, stand up bits, live music and celebrity interviews conducted by an affable, easy-to-relate-to host who normally stayed away from controversial issues and hardball questions.

Hosted successively by Steve Allen, Jack Paar, Johnny Carson, Jay Leno, Conan O'Brien, and Jay Leno again, the *Tonight Show* generated other successful imitators in competing networks, *Late Night with David Letterman* being the most famous of them. Written off by many as a dying format, the late night talk show genre has, time and again, showed its enduring appeal and relevance—throughout the 1990s with the rivalry between Jay Leno and David Letterman, and more recently with the addition of O'Brien into the mix. The format has also sparked a sub-genre in the political satire talk show category, with Comedy Central's *Daily News with Jon Stewart*, and the *Colbert Report* with Stephen Colbert, and HBO's *Real Time with Bill Maher* creating a whole new generation of viewers and admirers.

FCC Examines the Role of Networks

Ever-mindful of its mandate to prevent monopoly control of the information carried on the public airwaves, the Federal Communications Commission began the first of several inquiries into program production and distribution in the late 1950s. In 1970 the FCC passed the "Financial Interest and Syndication Rules," a document that forced the networks out of the business of syndication. A network could no longer control the profits from reruns of its shows. Shortly thereafter, the federal government filed antitrust suits aimed at curtailing network control of programming. By the end of the 1970s, all three networks had signed consent decrees that limited the number of programs they could own. Syndication and program control were profitable for the networks, so the FCC limitations, while they prevented a monopoly in the production and distribution business, also precipitated the decline of network revenues.

Network Affiliates

Companies such as NBC, owned by RCA, transferred an adapted version of the radio network system studied in the previous chapter to the newly-developed medium of television. The very profitable and accommodating corporate parent-affiliate relationship proved to be an even greater success on TV. In the largest and most profitable markets, such as New York and Los Angeles, the corporate parent also owned the station, but ownership limitations imposed by the FCC left the ownership of most stations to local, and at the time family-owned, companies.

The affiliation system has survived for so long because it is based on a close-knit relationship beneficial for both parent network and affiliates. Through this system, local stations receive network programming from the parent station (which they rebroadcast for a fee); produce local programs such as regional newscasts; and also purchase nationally syndicated programs, which help to fill the stations' daily schedule. In return, besides paying fees for the shows they receive, affiliates also pay to the parent network a percentage of the income generated by local advertising, and receive a percentage of the nationally broadcast commercials. In many cases, particularly in special programs and sporting events such as the NFL and NBA seasons and the Olympic Games, network and affiliates strike deals on how to finance the costs and divide the profits. These deals are not always easy to arrange, but the survival of the affiliation system speaks for its mutually beneficial aspects.

Indeed, by the beginning of the 1990s, as the share of audience and the revenues from the networks plummeted, the FCC began to relax its restrictions on the networks. The Fox Broadcasting Company, bidding to become the fourth network, was granted a waiver by the FCC to program 18 1/2 hours a week without being subject to the syndication rule.

In 1991, the FCC made some concessions to the networks, allowing them to keep resale rights to as much as 40 percent of the programming they produced, and to earn royalties on reruns of other programming. From 1991 on, the FCC has reviewed many of its ownership rules in a way that greatly benefited the networks and the parent companies that own them.

Networks Loss Profits

The networks began the 1980s with a combined share of 91 percent of the television viewing audience. By the early 1990s they had about 60 percent. By the turn of the century, the networks had lost 44 percent of the 1980 nightly TV audience to other media such as basic and premium cable as well as satellite, dropping their combined share to approximately 50 percent of the audience.[12] This decline

---

[12]"What's Really Going On In The Media World" by E.W. Brody. *Public Relations Quarterly*, Vol. 49, Issue 1, pg. 9, 2004.

translates into lost advertising revenues, because shrinking audiences put the advertisers in a much stronger bargaining position when they haggle with networks over "upfront" sponsorship of shows—committing themselves in advance to pay for advertising that will put a show on the air. This also signaled another significant phase in the demassification of a unified mass audience for TV.

The networks have struggled hard not only to stop this audience decline but to regain some of the lost market share. They have also tried to find different ways of increasing their profitability. Inventing or "reinventing" genres and formats such as reality TV and game shows has been one of these tactics. By creating or betting on these formats that are cheaper to produce and seem to attract new viewers, networks hope to stop some of their losses.

Networks are struggling to stop audience decline and regain lost market share.
© Evok20/Shutterstock

Another area that has seen a lot of investment—and a great deal of return for television channels—is DVDs and digital media files. These pieces of technology are a cash cow for networks and cable channels, as well as the programs' producers. They are very cheap to produce and release—recent and even "classic" sitcoms, dramas, miniseries, and TV movies have already been produced and only have to be repackaged. In some cases, programs are loaded with extras and bonuses, such as cast commentaries and deleted scenes. The costs involved usually relate additional copyrights and bonuses for the cast, creators and producers, as well as marketing and publicity.

Public Broadcasting

Not all forms of television broadcasting seek to make a profit. **Public broadcasting**, unlike commercial broadcasting, is meant to be used as resource for the public, not a means to turn a profit for a corporation. The advent of television was hailed as an opportunity for new and unparalleled efforts to educate the masses with the new technology. Unfortunately, commercial interests were so strongly opposed to reserving part of the broadcast spectrum for educational television that educational forces had to pressure the FCC in a systematic and sustained way. Once the network licensing freeze was over in 1952, the FCC agreed to reserve one channel out of every eight for noncommercial use.

While noncommercial programming does not generate revenue, it still costs money to produce. Therefore, funding is an essential part of its survival. Universities sponsored the first educational television stations, but financial support was difficult to find. The Ford Foundation, which helped educators put pressure on the FCC, continued its support by underwriting National Educational Television (NET), a consortium of nonprofit stations that formed their own sort of network. Rather than feeding programs electronically from a central location, as the commercial networks did, they merely mailed or delivered recorded programs to one another to rebroadcast.

By the late 1960s, there were nearly 200 educational television stations, and it was apparent that they needed to be put on sounder footing. The Public Broadcasting Act, passed by Congress in 1967, created the Corporation for Public

Broadcasting (CPB) to foster the growth of nonprofit radio and television stations and facilitate their linkage for the purpose of sharing production costs. Two years later, the Public Broadcasting Service (PBS) was created specifically to facilitate nonprofit television programming. The CPB is a primary supporter of PBS.

The Public Telecommunications Financing Act of 1978 requires the CPB to submit to the president and Congress a "comprehensive and detailed inventory of funds distributed by federal agencies to public telecommunications agencies." Up until the 1980s, the federal agencies contributed the most to CPB's budget. Then, federal support for public television was seriously cut back. More and more, public television turned to funds from viewers and the business community. Pressured by a lagging income, in 1988 PBS changed its rules to permit the mention of one specific product or service each time a corporation received credit for funding a program.

Today, only about 14 percent of the funds that support public broadcasting come from the federal government. The rest is spread among state governments, the business community, and the general public, through personal donations.

Pressure on the Networks

The chief programmer at each of the major broadcast networks spends a lot of time studying the scheduling board on the office wall that shows the three hours of prime-time programming—8 to 11 p.m. in the East and West, 7 to 10 p.m. elsewhere—for seven nights a week—22 hours (Sunday nights carry an additional hour of prime time) for each network to fill, 88 hours of programs for the four major networks combined. Because about half will be 30-minute episodes of situation comedies and dramas, and each network offers at least one 2-hour movie each week, the total number of prime-time programs each network offers at any one time is around 30.

Trying to decide what will constitute an effective lineup of shows each night in terms of holding an audience from one show to the next is complicated enough. The problem is compounded by the necessity of competing with other major networks, independent stations, public broadcasting, cable, DVDs, Internet, video games, and other distractions. But *scheduling* is only part of the complex business of network programming. There are other pressures on the chief programmer, all of them pushing the network toward decisions that result in "lowest common denominator" programming that makes it difficult for anything but mediocre programs to survive the process.

Among the groups that affect the networks' decisions are:

* Advertisers
* The viewers
* Government regulators
* Advocacy groups and television "watchdogs"
* The competition—all television, not just other networks
* Packagers—studios and independent producers of programs
* Artists and creative people, many of whom control their own shows
* Affiliated stations

Any of these groups, when and if they become actively involved, have a veto power over the network. When you are dealing with such a large audience and such high production costs, you cannot afford to ignore or offend any segment of society. That's a dilemma that confronts network television more than any other medium.

Advertisers want popular programs that attract everybody and offend nobody. The stations that affiliate with the network have much the same outlook. In addition, the affiliates often have concerns that are regional: Stations in the conservative, religious regions of the country are more likely to drop a network show with too much emphasis on sex and violence or controversial topics, while outlets in the major urban centers might complain about programs that do not provide enough thought-provoking material.

NETWORK RATINGS

Every mass medium has a method for measuring the size and composition of its audiences. Audited circulation figures enable advertisers to know how many people read a newspaper or magazine, and surveys provide specific information about which people make up the audience. Box office figures measure theater attendance, and theater producers can observe the house to know which segments of the audience are responding to the program.

But broadcast media, as we saw previously, pose a special problem because the consumers can change the station they are watching from minute to minute, and there is no way for the broadcaster to observe or calculate which family members are in the audience for particular programs. A special form of research, then, is needed to measure who is watching what. In order for the information to be useful, it has to be quantified quickly for programmers and the advertisers they must satisfy.

What Is a Rating?

The firms that measure the reach and penetration of television programming know how many homes in the country have television. It is against this total number of potential viewing units that the ratings are calculated. The ratings for a given half-hour never add up to 100 percent, since 100 percent of homes with television aren't viewing at any one time. The top program in prime time may have a 30 rating, and all of its competitors in that time slot may have a combined 40 rating, for a total of 70—meaning that 30 percent of the sets in the area measured were not turned to any program.

Ratings are most significant in evening prime time, when most people are likely to be at home and free to watch television. This is the period when the major manufacturers of consumer goods and services want to reach the largest possible audience. Ratings are far less significant in the middle of a weekday morning, when as few as 5 percent of households use television.

share
a measurement that is used to express a network's percentage of the viewing audience

At times of the day other than prime time, the measurement known as the **share** is more significant. It is possible for a local show to have a rating of only 7, which means that 93 percent of the area homes with television were not tuned in. But the show could have a 40 share, meaning that 4 out of every 10 sets that *were* turned on at that time were tuned to the program.

National advertisers of cars, soaps, and soft drinks that want to reach every consumer probably will not be impressed with a 40 share when they discover that it is coupled with a 7 rating. But a station that has the most popular program in the cheaper time slot will attract plenty of local and specialized advertisers.

Ratings systems have relied on everything from telephone interviews, personal interviews, and written surveys. © Doug Stevens/Shutterstock

audimeter
a device that can record when a radio set or television set is turned on and to which station

Development of the Ratings Systems

The first ratings systems, developed for radio use in the 1930s, involved telephone interviews ("What program are you listening to at this time?"), face-to-face interviews at the door ("What stations have you listened to in the past 24 hours?"), and even postcard reply surveys ("Please check off which stations were listened to this past week, and by which family members"). All of the systems relied on the cooperation of those who responded, and on their recall ability. Clearly a system that monitored broadcast consumption as it occurred would be preferable.

The AC Nielsen Company acquired the rights to a device, invented by two professors at MIT, called the **audimeter**, which could record when a radio set was turned on and to which station. When a family agreed to be one of the 1,000 Nielsen families across the country, they were visited monthly by a technician who removed the punched tape carrying the listening information. The data might be nearly two months old by the time Nielsen could assemble them for use by broadcasters and advertisers.

By the time television was introduced for home use, however, the audimeter had been improved so that the consumer could remove the tape and mail it in. Nielsen shifted from radio measurement to rating the television programs, and by the 1960s the technology had improved to the point where data was automatically fed to the company over phone lines, making the data available to the producers within a few days. Today, both Nielsen and its main competitor, Arbitron, supplement electronic data with the phone surveys in major markets when instant information is demanded by the industry.

Critics of the Nielsen technique point out that a television set may be put in use merely to provide background sound, to keep a pet or baby company, or to convince burglars that someone is home—with nobody really *watching* television; and thus no consumer paying attention to the advertising messages. The rival Arbitron system for a while required family members to make notations in a diary concerning the times when the set is on; to which channel, and, most importantly, which members of the family were watching. Critics questioned whether the diaries were kept carefully and accurately.

Neither method measured "why" or "how intently" the program was watched, or what value the audience put on the message after they had watched it. That is why the ratings firms augment their usual measurements with telephone surveys that go into greater detail.

CABLE TELEVISION

The concept of *broad*casting is exciting because information is beamed out for anyone to receive—a true and democratic *mass* communication system. Still, there are problems with broadcasting. The signal goes only so far, depending on the power of the transmitter. Signals can be lost if mountains or tall buildings intervene. Perhaps more importantly, the number of signals that can be carried on local airwaves is limited. Within 30 years of the advent of broadcasting, it was clear that technical improvements were needed in order to ensure that clear and adequate signals could be supplied to every consumer, and that many more choices could be added to the average consumer's television "menu."

Transmissions take barely a fifth of a second, and thus **superstations**— broadcast stations that decided to serve the entire country instead of just their local broadcast area by offering themselves to cable operators—in Atlanta, Chicago, and New York can be viewed in places thousands of miles away. Entertainment and news services also are fed to foreign countries, so the same movie, sports event, or 24-hour news can be viewed simultaneously in Detroit, Madrid, Cancun, or Hong Kong.

superstations
broadcast stations that decided to serve the entire country instead of just their local broadcast area by offering themselves to cable operators

How Cable Works

At its simplest, an old-fashioned cable system consisted of:

- An *uplink*—the earth station that sends signals carrying programming up to a satellite. The satellite may then beam the information to yet another satellite serving another sector of the globe.
- A *headend*—the electronic center where signals are captured by an antenna. When satellite transmissions are involved, the headend is a *downlink*. Signals at the headend may be scrambled to prevent unauthorized use by anyone who is not a subscriber.
- *Trunk lines* that carry the signals into districts—a neighborhood, community, or small town—where feeder cables go down each street either on poles or underground, generally following telephone lines.
- A *drop line* to the individual customer. Inside the subscriber's house, a converter attached to the television set transforms the electronic signal into an unscrambled picture.

Cable Begins as CATV

community antenna television (CATV)
a method of broadcasting that uses tall antenna towers to reach remote areas that are cut off from broadcasting centers

By 1950, **community antenna television (CATV)** was bringing signals to remote areas and those previously cut off from broadcast centers by intervening terrain, such as the mountains of Colorado. CATV entrepreneurs erected tall antennas to capture distant or blocked signals, and then ran coaxial cable to the homes of subscribers who were happy to pay for the service. Eventually CATV operators began to "import" programs from beyond the area served by their antenna, and the concept of cable television began to develop.

The first technical problem occurred when the fledgling cable companies went to string their wires. Some planned to run the cables from house to house, but that was feasible only in areas of dense settlement. The obvious solution was to use the poles owned by the telephone company, as other utilities have done. But telephone companies set rates in many areas that added greatly to the cost of cable. Managers of the AT&T system forecast correctly that cable—far from being just a means of improving the television signal—was an alternative means of bringing many kinds of information into homes electronically. That put the cable companies in potentially competitive conflict with the phone companies.

Cable Growth

The flurry of interest in cable distribution of programming in the 1950s led some to predict that the entire nation would soon be wired. However, 50 percent penetration of American homes was not realized until 1988. One hundred percent cable availability was not a reality until the 1990s, when alternative systems such as satellite TV began to cover areas that were previously bypassed by traditional cable. Just as it did with broadcast television, the FCC has had to work its way through several difficult issues to ensure that all customers are served adequately and fairly, and to guard against domination of the field by any one economic group or interest.

In 1959 a U.S. Senate subcommittee considered legislation to require licensing of CATV operators, who were not regulated by any agency. Lacking information about the scope of cable and unsure of the many ramifications of the new technology, the legislators argued the bill furiously. At that point, states and municipalities jumped into the regulation of cable, forcing owners to obtain local franchises in order to string wires through or under the streets and requiring them to return a percentage of the income to the municipality in return for that franchise. The borough of Manhattan was among the first areas to be served by cable because its tall buildings make broadcast reception difficult. Many areas of New York City took longer to adopt cable because of the high costs. This situation was symbolic of the chaos and uncertainty of cable distribution.

Regulating Cable

The FCC did not get involved in regulating cable until 1965, when it ruled that programs imported from more than 60 miles away could not duplicate any local broadcast in the preceding or following 15 days. That restriction prohibited a cable operator, for example, from using a satellite to pick up a concert that was broadcast live in another market but that was scheduled to be shown on tape locally at a later date. This "syndicated exclusivity" regulation pleased the broadcasters but angered the cable operators, who joined forces to lobby against it. They succeeded in convincing the FCC to shorten the exclusivity period to just one day. It was the first event in an ongoing struggle that saw the cable operators gaining strength and forcing the FCC not to automatically favor the entrenched broadcasters.

In 1968, the U.S. Supreme Court rejected the argument by cable operators that cable was not interstate and therefore not subject to regulation by the federal government. Moreover, it said FCC regulation of cable was necessary in order to carry out the mandate of congress to develop the dissemination of electronic information in the best interests of the public. That decision laid the foundation for the FCC's heavy involvement in regulating cable.

In the 1970s, cable companies began to offer original programming, and they broadened the information they could offer by receiving signals from satellites. Now homes wired to cable could receive programs from anywhere. When cable differentiated itself as the "multi-channel medium" with the most variety to offer, it became attractive even to those in populated areas who did not need CATV in order to receive a signal.

The 1972 Regulations

The FCC issued a set of regulations in 1972 that put cable's house in order, superseding earlier decisions as well as a jumble of state and municipal regulations. Among the most important provisions were the following:

- *Certificate of Compliance.* While municipalities could still franchise cable owners, each system operator was required to obtain a "certificate of compliance" from the FCC. The granting of the certificate was virtually automatic, but the process alerted the FCC to verify that the operator was capable of providing service and that the municipality stayed within guidelines in setting reasonable franchise fees.
- *"Must Carry" Rule.* To ensure that cable operators would not carry just the most popular and profitable programs, all local signals had to be carried on cable if it is requested by a local station. The **must-carry rule** was popular with stations but unpopular with cable operators who preferred to pick and choose among local stations to maximize their profitability.
- *Importation of Signals.* Cable operators were permitted to import signals in order to carry all three major networks and adequate independent stations. There were several rules governing how many stations could be imported, and operators could not bring in a network affiliate hundreds of miles away that was available closer to the home region.
- *Anti-siphoning.* Cable systems were allowed to offer pay channels carrying movies, sports, and concerts. However, siphoning of events and programs that previously appeared free on broadcast television was prohibited. The FCC administered a rule in 1968 to prevent popular broadcast programs such as the

must-carry rule
a FCC regulation stating that all local signals had to be carried on cable if it is requested by a local station.

Super Bowl, the World Series, and the Olympic Games from being expropriated by pay television.

- *Multiple Ownership.* Owners of television stations could not operate a cable franchise in the same community, and the television networks were prohibited from owning cable channels.
- *Local Origination.* Cable operators were required to provide local origination programming. In the 100 largest markets, these included "access" channels available to individuals or groups who wanted to get their information on the air.

The 1972 regulations required cable operators to provided original material "to a significant extent," but start-up costs made it difficult to build and equip studios. In the large markets where local access was required, franchisers provided little more than a rented storefront equipped with one or two cameras and tape recorders supervised by a single technician. Long-winded speeches by minor politicians, artistic presentations by those with marginal talent, and low-budget news programs have been carried by the public access channels in some large cities. On the positive side, schools and colleges have been encouraged to create and broadcast programs using their own television production facilities and crews.

Deregulation Gives Cable Greater Freedom

The 1984 Cable Communications Act eased regulation on the industry. It came after lobbyists for cable owners successfully convinced congress to shield them from controls by municipalities and states. The owners argued that the prime responsibility of the operator should be to the subscribers of cable television, not to government bodies, and that the market would determine the prices people wanted to pay for various services.

In 1985, the must-carry rule was struck down by a federal court and the FCC did not fight the move. The chair of the FCC said the decision "takes the first step toward a true marketplace for the distribution by cable systems" and "represents a positive step toward full First Amendment protection for all forms of electronic media." The demise of the must-carry rule occurred after Supreme Court Chief Justice Warren Burger refused to heed the call of broadcasters, especially owners of the smaller UHF stations, who wanted to ensure that cable had to carry their programming. The president of the National Association of Broadcasters called the action, "a blow to the localized system of broadcasting in this nation." Even some FCC staff members feared that greedy cable operators would ignore local needs and offer only the most profitable programming. New York City cable operators immediately dropped the New Jersey public broadcasting channel, although many New Yorkers work or travel in New Jersey and could be interested in news and programs from their neighboring state.

Cable operators proclaimed they would continue to fight regulation by the FCC and other authorities on the grounds that they should have all the freedoms accorded to the print media. They argued that they must have the flexibility to find programming that is different from broadcast fare. They also wanted to explore the concept of **narrowcasting**—offering channels for specialized audiences such as children, rock music fans, sports enthusiasts, and hobbyists.

narrowcasting
the act of offering channels for specialized audiences such as children, rock music fans, sports enthusiasts, and hobbyists

In 1988, the Reagan Administration released a report by the Commerce Department's National Telecommunications and Information Administration that called for even further deregulation of cable in order to foster more competition. The report was aimed at ensuring that a few large companies would not dominate the industry. While it did not suggest that telephone companies should be allowed to enter the cable industry, it did suggest that telephone lines could be used as common carriers to help more cable companies gain access to information.

Re-regulation or Continued Deregulation?

In 1990, the head of New Jersey's Board of Public Utilities claimed that cable television in the state of New Jersey was a monopoly and suggested that permitting more than one cable company to operate in a town would benefit subscribers by giving them a choice of providers and lower rates. Cable companies argued that federal deregulation precluded states and communities from interfering with their franchises. While cable rates and programming policies cannot be dictated by states or communities, local authorities can set service requirements for utilities. New Jersey has strengthened rules that require quicker response to service outages and billing credit when service outages occur.

Bills working their way slowly through Congress at the beginning of the 1990s would allow cities to regulate rates in areas without two or more cable operators, limit the number of subscribers nationally that any one cable operator could serve, regulate the prices of premium channels, and reinstate the must-carry rule. Cable operators, who argued that they spent extraordinary amounts of money to develop almost a million miles of system in just one decade, nevertheless prepared themselves for some form of re-regulation. In the summer of 1991 the FCC reinstated local rate regulations for many cable operations. Working in favor of the cable companies was the fear on the part of many in congress that allowing states and municipalities to control rates and decide on the number of franchises would lead back to the corruption and chaos that marked the early days of cable regulation.

In the fall of 1992, the pendulum continued its swing back toward regulation of cable when both houses of Congress passed a bill to regulate rates for basic cable services and spur competition. Consumer groups and broadcasters were among the biggest supporters of the measure, which passed with sufficient majorities in both houses to override the expected veto from President Bush. Nevertheless, in January 1992, the Senate handed cable operators a setback by passing legislation that would strengthen both local and federal regulation to limit the increases in cable rates. Siding with broadcasters, the legislators brought back the must-carry rule in the Cable Act of 1992. The rule was upheld as both content neutral and necessary by the Supreme Court in two related cases in 1994 and 1997. Stations could either choose the must-carry option or a retransmission consent option. If they chose the must-carry option, cable systems had to carry those stations but did not need to pay for them. If the stations chose retransmission, they could be carried for some kind of compensation. Most large stations chose the retransmission option. The must-carry rule is being challenged in court again in 2010 by Cablevision, an east-coast cable company.

Cable Matures as a Business

Through the 1980s, the popularity of cable grew at a tremendous rate. More than 4,000 new systems were launched in that decade—a new system virtually every day. Initially many were owned by local entrepreneurs. Some had media experience, others were businesspeople eager to make a profit, and still others were engineers who had expertise in the technology. Eventually many of those that didn't have an understanding both of the technology and the business sold out to companies that did. Many of the new owners were parts of chains, and some of the largest chains were owned by large communication companies.

Westinghouse, the electric manufacturing company, for example, entered the cable business in 1981 by purchasing Teleprompter, the firm that wired the northern half of Manhattan in New York City. Just five years later Westinghouse put Teleprompter's parent company, Group W Cable Inc., up for sale and turned a profit. Westinghouse management had decided to concentrate on broadcasting, where the investment offers a quicker return to stockholders. Warner Communications (now part of Time Warner) formed Warner Amex, but a few years later bought out American Express's share in order to form a new cable venture with Viacom. Ownership patterns were in a state of flux throughout the 1980s as communication companies tried to figure out whether cable belonged in their mix.

Eventually chain ownership became the norm. The government's encouragement of further deregulation at the end of the 1980s was based partly on a concern that a few companies were cornering a large segment of the market. The largest, Telecommunications Inc., had 20 percent of the nation's 42 million cable customers. Deregulation was seen as encouraging more players to enter the market.

Cable Becomes Profitable

Among the largest cable services, only one was profitable in 1983: TBS, the Atlanta-based Turner superstation. Five years later, however, most of the top advertiser-supported services made money, led by TBS, Turner's Cable News Network (CNN), and ESPN. In fact, each of those top three cable services made more profit than CBS and ABC combined. Under deregulation, the networks were free to enter into ventures with cable services, and so the combination of players was constantly shifting throughout the 1990s and into the new century.

Cable's profitability can be exemplified by the increased costs of cable subscriptions. At one time the average consumer paid less than $10 a month for cable. Now, many subscribers pay a basic rate over twice or three times that much and add premium services that may bring the monthly bill to over $100, when taxes, fees and Internet services are added.

Eventually—assuming that the FCC decides to require competition in the market—cable will approach 100 percent penetration of the American market and consumers will draw the line on how much they are willing to pay and how many services they need. When that happens, the cable industry will "shake out," meaning that many companies will exit because they cannot make a profit, and the remaining companies will solidify their holds over the segment of the market they control. Rather than being producer-driven the industry will be equally consumer-driven. There will be a balance that involves information being created, priced, and delivered by the producers according to the needs and interests of the consumers.

Users Shape the Medium

Most mass media have to poll their audiences to find out what they like and don't like. Cable gets constant indications of the popularity of its services. Subscribers call to add the Disney Channel or drop HBO. They write letters to say that they would like to see their service add C-Span, which covers Congress, or perhaps an additional Spanish language station. They realize they have more control over the information they receive than they do with most other mass media.

Some cable operators questioned the concept of offering a basic service for a fixed rate. The basic service system provides consumers with 20 to 30 channels for one standard price. Each additional premium channels cost more. Instead, cable companies started to sell channel packages, which meant that subscribers had to choose between groups of channels and options, without the option to ungroup them.

Recent research, however, indicates that consumers are not staying in their niches. In fact, many viewers are watching the broadcast network-type programming on such services as USA Network and TNT more heavily than the narrowly focused programming designed for well-defined audiences. Convinced that consumers really do like network-type shows, TBS and other cable channels have experimented with running sitcoms in blocks when the broadcast networks are showing news or public affairs programs, so that viewers who want light-hearted entertainment can find it on cable when it isn't on the networks.

THE FUTURE OF TELEVISION

We have discussed throughout this book an important trend toward demassification of mass media, and the situation could not be different with television. If network television reigned supreme from the 1950s to the 1970s as the main provider of entertainment and information to the masses, that situation started to change dramatically in the 1980s and 1990s, with the addition of cable channels, videocassettes and DVDs, video games and the Internet as providers of thousands of additional information and entertainment alternatives to an ever-growing and more demanding media audience. As we discussed in this chapter, network television went from being the main purveyor of news and entertainment—and coming close to being the only medium capable of fostering a shared political agenda for a mass audience—to being just one more voice in the wilderness competing for the attention of a shattered and fragmented audience.

This fragmentation also carried a financial price for television. As broadcast and cable networks lose revenue to other forms of media, it has become clear that television must reinvent itself in order to survive in the future. This reinvention may require altering traditional methods of programming and adapting to new technology.

Market Segmentation

Market segmentation seems to be one of the strategies devised by the networks to survive and prosper in the television business. In the 1950s, 1960s, and 1970s the networks remained unchallenged in the market, and had to design their schedules in a way that reached the widest and largest audience possible. This attitude helped to solidify the idea that the networks should always provide **general programming**—shows that included a mix of dramas, comedies, sports, news, game shows, variety, talk shows, and other genres aimed at the widest general audience possible.

general programming
shows that included
a mix of dramas,
comedies, sports, news,
game shows, variety,
talk shows, and other
genres aimed at the
widest general
audience possible

With the advent of cable and satellite technologies, and the market fragmentation we have witnessed since the late 1970s, the networks began to question if their old market strategy was still sustainable. During the 1980s, the three networks resisted and delayed the necessary changes as much as they could. However, Fox emerged in the early 1990s as a viable network exactly because it dared to do things differently. Originally aiming its programming at ethnic minorities and younger audiences, it claimed niche markets obviously underserved by the traditional networks.

Fox emerged as a viable network by aiming its
programming at niche markets.
© Monkey Business Images/Shutterstock

Despite the fact that, as Fox grew and solidified in the 1990s it also veered toward a more traditional general programming format, beefing up its sports and news divisions, for example, its initial success shook up the market, and made it clear for the three major networks that adaptation to the new reality was crucial for their survival. The market segmentation and experimentation by the networks seen in the 1990s and 2000s might be considered a direct effect of both Fox's emergence and the necessity to respond to the market segmentation introduced by cable television.

As a result, the networks have toyed with new ideas and formats since the mid-1990s. Instead of targeting the widest, broadest general audiences possible, these formats have been clearly designed to attend particular segments or niche markets, an unthinkable idea 15 years ago. Thus, CBS and ABC have alternated between trying to reach younger and older, urban and rural audiences, with short-lived programs that are dropped the next season. At least CBS's and ABC's market segmentation have paid off, as the networks enter the 2006–2007 season with high ratings. Tellingly, NBC, the network that has most resisted market segmentation and experimentation, has been struggling with dipping ratings for the past two seasons.

Television On Demand

In order to stay up-to-date with the desires of the public, broadcast networks and cable networks need to adapt the content of their programming to the match the likes and dislikes of the public and adjust program scheduling to adapt to the viewing habits of the public. With the arrival of the Internet, we have turned into an on-demand society. Many people don't wait for the morning paper or the nightly news to learn about a breaking news story, they go to the Internet to pull up the information when they demand it. Similarly, many viewers do not sit down and watch a television show during its scheduled time. Through the use of Digital Video Recorders (DVRs), viewers can record a program, shut off the set or watch a different program, and then watch the recorded program whenever they choose.

Other forms of on-demand viewing are available on the Internet. Most major networks have full episodes available for free on the networks' Web sites or for sale on Web sites such as Amazon and iTunes. While using the Internet to keep up with on-demand culture will be an important part of network television's survival, it also opens the industry up to more competition. YouTube and other video sharing Web sites offer thousands of hours of original programming that can pull viewers away from network programs that are available on television and on the Internet. To keep viewer's eyes on network television programs, networks such as CBS and BBC have partnered with YouTube to provided collaborative programming to viewers.[13]

On-camera positions are more high profile, but television has many other jobs behind the scenes.
© claudia veja/Shutterstock

In the future, television programs may permanently move from the television screen to the computer screen, couch potatoes may turn into mouse potatoes, and audiences may become their own programmers. But just as it has for the last 100 years, television will continue to grow and evolve with technology.

CAREERS IN THE FIELD

When a television show ends and the credits begin to scroll, many viewers change the channel and move on to a new program. However, those who stay tuned will notice the numerous roles involved in producing a television show. Positions like director, camera operator, and costume designer may be self-explanatory, but other positions such as key grip, gaffer, or vision mixer may be a mystery to those outside of the television business. Television offers a wide range of career opportunities to people with various talents and interests. On screen talent may experience the more glamorous side of television, but the true magic occurs behind the scenes. Behind the scenes positions occur in four different areas: pre-production—producers, casting directors, and writers; production—floor managers, boom operators, and technical directors; control room—television director, video tape operator, and graphics operator; post-production—sound editor, composer, and special effects operator. The size of a television crew depends on the complexity of the production.

The news side of television and cable also provide a similarly wide variety of opportunities. Being an on-camera news anchor or reporter carries its own brand of glamour and celebrity, but it takes a large group of reporters,

---

[13]Thom Patterson, "Is the Future of Television on the Web?" *CNN.com*. Retrieved from http://www.cnn.com/2008/SHOWBIZ/TV/05/01/tv.future/index.html.

researchers, producers, writers and editors to put together even a 30-minute local newscast. In addition to those, sport shows also generate many jobs in the field.

If you are interested in a career in television it is important to decide on an area in which you would like work so you can tailor your education and build the proper experience. A great way to discover which area you are most interested in is to find an internship or entry-level position at a television station or production company. Positions such as runners and production assistants (PAs) are sometimes available to individuals with little or no experience. If you are outside of a major city, look to your local cable station or university station for opportunities.[14] If you are technically savvy, you can build experience by producing your own show though a podcast over the Internet.

Getting your foot in the door in the television industry may be a difficult process, but positions are available to those who are willing to work their way up the ladder. Whether you aspire to be a technical director or an executive producer, knowing as much as you can about the medium will only help you in your journey. Who knows, in only a few years, maybe television viewers will see your name scroll across the screen at the end of a program.

SUMMARY

- The development of television technology started in the late 1800s and involved with the invention of the cathode-ray tube, scanning disk, and Image Dissector.
- Many of the first television programs were based on radio programs. Over time such as situation comedies, prerecorded dramas, and reality television emerged.
- Cable television created more competition for broadcast networks and more options for television viewers.
- Television programs are slowly moving to the Internet to attract more viewers.

DISCUSSION QUESTIONS

1. Name two individuals that played an important role in the development of the television. What contributions did these individuals make?
2. What is infotainment? How has it affected news programs?
3. How is public broadcasting different from other forms of broadcasting?

---

[14]Dave Owen, "How to Get a Job in Television" *Media College*. Retrieved from http://www.mediacollege.com/employment/television/find-job.html.

4. What was the purpose of the must-carry rule? How did it affect cable operators?

5. How has the Internet affected television?

SUPPLEMENTAL WEB SITES

SUPPLEMENTAL READINGS

Tube: The Invention of Television by David E. Fisher, Marshall Fisher
Defining Vision: The Battle for the Future of Television, by Joel Brinkley

THE INTERNET

CHAPTER OBJECTIVES

- Discuss the early history of computer systems and the purpose they served in the 1960s and 1970s
- Explain how the concept of connecting computer networks became the Internet
- Discuss the roles Vinton Cerf and Tim Berners-Lee had in creating the modern Internet
- Identify the challenges and opportunities the Internet introduced to traditional media outlets
- Explain the difference between one-to-many and many-to-many media
- Discuss how citizen journalism affects the way we receive and interpret news and information
- List four major concerns regarding the Internet
- Explain the role of social networking Web sites in society

10

KEY TERMS

ARPANet
citizen journalism
e-commerce
hypertext transfer
   protocol (HTTP)
many-to-many model
modem
network
one-to-many model

open architecture networking
packet switching
social networking
streaming
transmission-control
   protocol (TCP)
uniform resource
   locator (URL)
viral videos

179

How has the Internet changed the way you get information? © Monkey Business Images/Shutterstock

INTRODUCTION

When was the last time you picked up a newspaper to check the weather forecast, purchased a CD in a music store, or sent a handwritten letter to an out-of-state friend? Chances are you have not participated in one of these activities in quite sometime. For members of generations X and Y, and even some tech savvy baby boomers, most of these tasks are performed using the Internet. With Web sites that allow users to track weather patterns and get up-to-the-minute predictions, Internet-based e-mail that lets individuals send messages to acquaintances across the country instantly, and online retailers that permit consumers to purchase and acquire products on demand, it's no wonder why more than 70% of the U.S. population is connected to the Internet. That means more than 212 million people, in urban and rural areas alike, are able to search for and acquire information 24 hours a day, seven days a week. Internet usage is not exclusive to populous and highly developed countries. Internet rates are even higher in smaller countries such as Iceland (86%), New Zealand (75%), and Portugal (74%).[1]

As an international juggernaut, the Internet has changed the way the world sends and receives information. It has created a subculture of interconnected individuals with fervor for around-the-clock access to news, sports, and entertainment. But does more information mean we are better informed? Does faster access to information mean more accuracy? Does more communication create a united world? While there are no definitive answers to these questions, they certainly evoke an interesting discussion. In this chapter we will touch on these subjects as well as the emergence of the Internet, how it affects other forms of mass media, and how we will adapt to a digitally dominated society in the future.

WEAVING "THE NET"

As the Internet has become a popular medium for social networking, digital media, and shopping, it is sometimes forgotten that the Internet was created and developed mainly for strategic military purposes. In fact, the British Colossus system, one of the first computers invented, was created to crack German military codes during World War II. Similar proto-computers such as the famous Enigma machine were also used in WWII to decrypt secret messages and track the movement of troops, warships, bombers, and missiles. During the 1960s and 1970s, the United States military started to realize the full potential of computer systems by connecting each unit together through a system called a network. A **network** is a

network
a number of interconnected computers that are able to share data electronically

---

[1]Nielsen/NetRatings, December 2007 Global Index Chart at http://www.netratings.com/resources.jsp?section=pr_netv&nav=1. Accessed September 10, 2008.

number of interconnected computers that are able to share data electronically. The AUTODIN I, a defense command-and-control system, was one of the first computer networks created. Like most networks of its time, the AUTODIN I was a special-purpose system that was created with very clear strategic goals in mind.

The Primary Purpose

The Internet as we know it today was preceded by one of the first general purpose networks called the ARPANet, which was created in 1969 by the Advanced Research Projects Agency (ARPA) of the U.S. Department of Defense. The **ARPANET** was a network that connected computers at government-supported research sites, such as universities and government laboratories and allowed information and computational resources to be shared. A group of ARPA scientists invented the basic packet switching technology that is still one of the main pillars of the Internet. **Packet switching** takes large chunks of computer data and breaks them up into smaller, more manageable pieces, or packets, that can move through any open circuit to a specific destination. Once the packets reach the destination, the pieces are reassembled into readable data. Because packet switching does not require a single dedicated circuit between each pair of computers for communication, through the use of a **modem**, computers can "talk" and exchange data by using existing telephone networks.

During the 1970s the ARPA, later renamed the Defense Advanced Research Project Agency (DARPA), investigated other methods of connecting computer systems such as satellite-based and ground-based packet networks.[2] The

The Enigma machine helped decrypt secret messages and track troops during World War II. © markrhiggins/ Shutterstock

ARPANet
a network that connected computers at government-supported research sites, such as universities and government laboratories and allowed information and computational resources to be shared

packet switching
a form of technology that takes large chunks of computer data and breaks them up into smaller, more manageable pieces, or packets, that can move through any open circuit to a specific destination

modem
a device that allows computers to "talk" and exchange data by using existing telephone networks

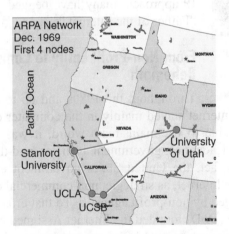

FIGURE 10.1 The first four nodes of the ARPA Network connected Stanford University, University of California Los Angeles, University of California Santa Barbara, and University of Utah.

---

[2]Internet. *Encyclopedia Britannica* at http://www.britannica.com/EBchecked/topic/291494/Internet. Accessed September 10, 2008.

open architecture networking
a process in which networks with fixed standard interfaces would be interconnected by open "gateways"

transmission-control protocol (TCP)
an official procedure, which allowed computers to communicate efficiently and consequently be joined in a coherent network of servers

satellite-based packet networks allowed the United States to connect with several European countries and other remote regions, while the ground-based packet radio network allowed computers to connect to mobile terminals. Soon it was clear that in order to connect to the greatest amount of systems in the most efficient ways, the networks would need to be connected to one another. Thus, the concept of the Internet was born.

The idea of the Internet was embraced by the DARPA. They established a program called Internetting, which was based on the concept of open architecture networking. In **open architecture networking**, networks with fixed standard interfaces would be interconnected by open "gateways." However, the concept was easier on paper than in practice. In order for the system to work, new protocol and system architecture had to be designed and developed. In 1974, a Los Angeles-raised mathematician Vinton Cerf from Stanford University in California collaborated with the DARPA on a report that established the proper protocol and system architecture for this type of networking—namely the **transmission-control protocol (TCP)**—which allowed computers to communicate efficiently and consequently be joined in a coherent network of servers. The TCP also included the Internet protocol (IP), which was a global addressing device that permitted routers to transmit data packets to their end user. By the early 1980s this system of open architecture networking was adopted by the U.S. Department of Defense, and later the TCP/IP system was accepted and endorsed by governments, researchers, and businessman from around the world. For his accomplishments in constructing the TCP/IP approach, many have pegged Vinton Cerf as the "Father of the Internet."[3]

Vinton Cerf is considered by many to be the Father of the Internet. © Shamshahrin Shamsudin/epa/Corbis

From Non-Profit Entity to Commercial Behemoth

Throughout the 1980s and up to the mid-1990s the buzz surrounding the Internet stayed mainly in the computer community. While the system was accessible to the mainstream world, it was primarily used by scientists, researchers, academics, government agencies, and the military to store and exchange data. In fact, the United States government essentially saw the ARPANet, and then the Internet, as strategic, non-commercial entities that should be regulated and managed by non-profit agencies. To that effect, in 1988 the U.S. Department of Defense (DoD) founded the Internet Assigned Numbers Authority (IANA), a non-profit agency created by a contract between the ARPA and the University of Southern California to administer and manage the daily operations of this incipient network. It was up to the IANA, for example, to keep a registry of addresses, servers, and top-level domains.

---

[3]"Tim Berners-Lee," *Internet Pioneers* at http://www.ibiblio.org/pioneers/lee.html. Accessed September 10, 2008.

While still under some government control, the Internet inevitably experienced rapid commercialization. The introduction of the personal computer in the mid-1980s made mainstream citizens more comfortable with computer technology and by the end of the decade opened the door for the Internet phenomenon. One of the first commercial movements was through the connection of commercial e-mail services to the Internet. In 1988 the Corporation for National Research Initiatives connected MCI mail to the Internet. It was the first connection with a provider outside of the research community. By 1993, federal legislations opened up space in government-sponsored networks for commercial users. The transition from a researched-based Internet to a commercial-based Internet was eased by the introduction of a computer program known as a browser. Tim Berner-Lee, an Oxford-educated Englishmen who worked for the European Organization of Nuclear Research (CERN), created one of the first Internet browsers known as the World Wide Web (WWW). The WWW was a virtual "space" in which scientists could store information that could be retrieved by colleagues throughout the world. In addition, Berners-Lee also invented **Hypertext Transfer Protocol (HTTP)**, the "language" computers would use to send and receive documents over the Internet. What's more, Berners-Lee also created the **Uniform Resource Locator (URL)** address system to store and locate information. Berners-Lee's achievements gave the world their first glimpse of the modern Internet and ignited a commercial explosion.

hypertext transfer protocol (HTTP) the "language" computers use to send and receive documents over the Internet

Piggybacking on the access protocols and standards developed by Berners-Lee, researchers at the University of Illinois created a user-friendly browser called Mosaic. The browser allowed users to point-and-click through the interface, an action previously unavailable to Internet users. In 1994, the Netscape Communications Corporation streamlined the Mosaic program and made it available for commercial use. Soon after, software titan Microsoft developed a Web browser called Internet Explorer, which was also based off of the Mosaic program. By the late 1990s there were approximately 10,000 Internet service providers in the world, with the majority located in the United States.[4] To create more efficient and profitable services many small- and moderately-sized providers merged and created industry leaders such as America Online, Inc. (AOL) and Yahoo. With a virtually endless arena in which to sell advertising space, Internet providers saw sky rocketing advertising revenues into the year 2000. Businesses with Internet connections saw sales and consumer traffic increase at an exponential rate. By the turn of the century more than ten million businesses and government agencies had Web sites. Today that number has increased to more than 70 million active Web sites and 175 million hostnames.[5]

uniform resource locator (URL) an address system to store and locate information

The Internet phenomenon hit its peak with the introduction of search technology. Search engines such as Google took the vast amount of information on the Web and organized it based on keywords and Web hits. So something that

---

[4]Internet service provider. *Encyclopedia Britannica* at http://www.britannica.com/EBchecked/topic/746032/Internet-service-provider. Accessed September 10, 2008.

[5]"August 2008 Web Service Survey," *Netcraft* at http://news.netcraft.com/archives/web_server_survey.html. Accessed September 10, 2008.

The Internet is where people go now to get information.
© Feverpitch/Shutterstock

once served as a carrying case for the world's information was now a virtual answer machine. The Internet is often the place people look for answers. What's the best driving route to take to work? What year was *War and Peace* first published? What is the president's position on immigration? With a few clicks of a mouse this information can be displayed in front of us almost instantly, a process unmatched by any other form of media. So how does the Internet affect other types of media like books, radio, newspapers, and television? And how does using the Internet as a primary source of information affect society? We will discuss these topics in the following sections.

CONSEQUENCES TO OTHER MASS MEDIA

What are the implications of this Internet revolution, and in what way does it affect traditional mass media operations? In previous sections of this book, we have examined how digital production and distribution are changing the media. In fact, digital production and distribution of mass media content have become the cornerstones of the whole industry. Nowadays, most, if not all, media outlets participate in some type of digital distribution. While digital media enables traditional media sources to reach a larger audience and expand business, the transition can stir up uncharted issues.

For example, from November 2007 to February 2008 members of the Writer's Guild of America (WGA), a union that represents writers working for the entertainment industry, battled with TV and movie producers for more control of media content produced and distributed electronically. After a 14-week standoff an agreement was reached that gave writers an increase in the residual rate for all movies and TV shows sold online and assured the union's authority over content created specifically for the Internet.[6] However, the writers' strike was about much more than being paid for media content streamed online—it was about how to adapt to this new electronic reality, and how writers and other content producers can keep control of (and be compensated for) the products they create for a media market that is in a huge state of flux. The strike also highlighted the fact that electronic distribution of entertainment will come to play a major role in the way we receive our favorite music, movies, news, and TV shows.

Let's now see in more detail some of the challenges and opportunities posed by the Internet to traditional media.

---

[6]Rebecca Winters Keegan, "Writers Guild Strike Nears End" *Time*, February 10, 2008. Accessed September 8, 2008 at http://www.time.com/time/arts/article/0,8599,1711750,00.html?iid=sphere-inline-sidebar.

Books

Book publishing has been big business for over five hundred years. From the Gutenberg Bible to the Harry Potter series, readers have long enjoyed the feel of soft paper on their fingertips as they flip through pages and the sense of accomplishment they acquire when the back cover is finally closed. It's these tangible aspects of a printed book that have kept book publishers from surrendering to the digital era completely. With their cumbersome size and expensive production cost, you would think that books would be the first form of traditional media to go completely digital, however printed books still account for the majority of revenue acquired by book publishers. Since the early 90s, companies have tried

Readers still enjoy the feel of a real book in today's digital world. © Zsolt Nyulaszi/Shutterstock

to market digital readers to consumers. Companies such as Adobe, Microsoft, Palm, and Franklin Electronic Publishers have tried to sell digital readers that mock the look of an actual book and give consumers the ability to purchase thousands of titles online, but the public didn't bite. In 2002, less than 500,000 electronic books were sold in the United States, far less than the 1.5 billion printed books sold in that same year.[7] However, new products and initiatives have helped push books in the digital direction.

While recreational readers are still more likely to purchase the latest title from Tom Clancy in hard cover than as an e-book, digital books are becoming extremely useful for researchers and students. Initiatives like The Internet Public Library and Project Gutenberg have brought all the information that was once only available in a bound book to the computer screen. Project Gutenberg is the first and single largest collection of free electronic books. Hundreds of volunteers work to convert printed works from the public domain into digital form and make them available online.[8] This process eliminates the need to go to a library and search through the stacks for classic works such as Shakespeare's *The Comedy of Errors.* However, most online libraries only have a fraction of published works available, requiring people to log off the Internet and flip through some pages.

Bringing works from the past into the future may be a slow-moving process, but the book publishing industry is not shying away from the electronic revolution. Kindle, an electronic reading device created by Amazon, is the latest gadget to attempt to convert print book readers to e-book readers. With sales toping 240,000 units in 2008, the moderate success of the product is a sign that hard covers and paperbacks may make a slow retreat in the future.

---

[7]"E-Books, Once Upon a Future Time," *Wired* September 14, 2003 at http://www.wired.com/techbiz/media/news/2003/09/60435. Accessed September 10, 2008.

[8]"Gutenberg: About," *Project Gutenberg* at http://www.gutenberg.org/wiki/Gutenberg:About. Accessed September 10, 2008.

Books Gone Cellular

In 2007, five out of the ten best-selling books in Japan were "cell phone novels"—books written by authors on their mobile phones as text messages and uploaded, one message at a time, to Web sites and blogs. The way they were produced and delivered is not the only different thing about these "text-messaging books." Most of them were written by young, female, first time authors, as they rode the subway to school or work, or killed time between other activities. The serialized character of these novels, partial chapters, or short sentences is uploaded as they become available. The completed book is then published in hard or soft cover. The characters and plot development of these novels are more like soap operas and Harlequin novels than complex, rich literary achievements, but popular just the same.[9]

Radio

Since the emergence of companies like XM Satellite and Sirius Satellite Radio, it has been well publicized that standard AM/FM radio stations have been losing listeners to popular satellite radio stations, but traditional radio has also been losing listeners to Internet music and broadcasting sites. While 90% of people in the United States still listen to traditional radio, even avid listeners spend 14% less time listening to their radios than they have in previous decades.[10] The cause of radio's diminishing audiences is a combination of listeners choosing to replace traditional broadcasting programs with those found on the Internet and seeking new music from digital-music Web sites.

Since the late 90s, **podcasting** has become a popular form of Internet broadcasting. The phrase podcasting comes from a combination of *iPod* and *broadcasting*, as many podcast files are downloaded onto portable digital music players such as iPods. Although the essence of podcasts existed before Apple released the iPod in 2001, the medium was not as popular before that time.[11] Podcast programs can range in format from that of a traditional radio program featuring a well-known figure to a simple rant expelled by an ordinary person. Through this medium virtually any person with a computer and webcam or microphone has the ability to create and share their thoughts, opinions, or music tastes with the entire Internet community.

Since the Internet has the ability reach farther than radio waves, many radio stations have opted to stream their programs through a station-sponsored Web site

[9]Norimitsu Onishi, "Thumbs Race as Japan's Best Seller Go Cellular," *New York Times*, January 20, 2008 at http://www.nytimes.com/2008/01/20/world/asia/20japan.html. Accessed September 10, 2008.

[10]Richard Siklos, "Is Radio Still Radio if There's Video?" *New York Times* February 14, 2007 at http://www.nytimes.com/2007/02/14/business/media/14radio.html. Accessed September 10, 2008.

[11]Media convergence. *Encyclopedia Britannica* at http://www.britannica.com/EBchecked/topic/1425043/media-convergence. Accessed September 10, 2008.

in addition to the airwaves. **Streaming** is a method of relaying video or audio material over the Internet. Streaming corporate radio programs online has become a popular choice for many listeners. A 2007 study by Credit Suisse evaluated the performance of the twelve leading Web-radio sites and found that the amount of Internet radio listeners increased by 33.5% since the previous year.[12] These streamed programs not only allow radio station to cultivate an audience outside of their local listeners, it keeps them competitive in a changing market. The inclusion of the Internet is vital to radio's survival as the amount of money spent by corporations on online advertising is expected to surpass the amount spent on radio advertising in the next year.[13]

In order to stay relevant in the digital world it seems that the radio industry needs to change some of its signature characteristics—like being heard but not seen. Taking a cue from popular radio hosts like Howard Stern, Don Imus, and Danny Bonaduce, many radio programs set up webcams in the studio and broadcast video on the Internet. This new format combines the Internet's innovative form of communications with radio's traditional strength of using on-air personalities and local flavor to interest listener.[14] Whether or not this new format can still be considered "radio" is up for debate, nevertheless the medium has accepted that traditional radio needs to change and adapt in order to survive in the twenty-first century.

streaming
a method of relaying video or audio material over the Internet

Newspapers

The Internet and the digital revolution have profoundly affected the way newspapers work. On the editorial side, online media affects the way writers and editors gather information and designers layout and produce their pages. On the business side, executives must change the way advertising space is sold, subscriptions are marketed, and circulation numbers are measured to adapt to the Internet era. While these changes may deviate from the traditional methods used in newspaper work, they often serve as an opportunity to increase readership. Still, the Internet poses some enormous challenges to other aspects of the newspaper industry, forcing many newspapers to maintain a shaky balance between print and digital mediums.

During a six-month period in 2007, the *Denver Post* and the *Rocky Mountain News*, popular regional daily papers based in Colorado, saw their paid circulation numbers drop an astounding 12%. The dramatic drop puzzled newspaper executives, as the periodical's level of quality and trustworthiness had not changed. What did change, however, was the character of the newspaper business.[15] The two

---

[12]Media and Publishing. *Encyclopedia Britannica* at from http://search.eb .com/eb/article-257962. Accessed September 10, 2008.

[13]Catherine Holahan, "Advertising Goes Off the Radio" *Business Week* December 7, 2006 at http://www .businessweek.com/technology/content/dec2006/tc20061207_485162.htm. Accessed September 10, 2008.

[14]Richard Siklos, "Is Radio Still Radio if There's Video?" *New York Times* February 14, 2007 at http://www.nytimes.com/2007/02/14/business/media/14radio.html. Accessed September 10, 2008.

[15]David Milstead, "Denver papers' Circulation Falls" *Rocky Mountain News* April 28, 2008 at http://www .rockymountainnews.com/news/2008/apr/28/denver-papers-circulation-slide-continues/. Accessed September 10, 2008.

respected Colorado papers are not alone. As more and more readers migrate to the online versions of their favorite newspapers, dailies from coast to coast are struggling to maintain their paid circulation numbers. Lost circulation numbers means fewer paid advertisers, and that is a lethal combination that translates to lost revenue. While each of the top fifty most read newspapers in the United States offer an online version, the print versions of newspapers are still viewed as the mainstay of the industry.[16] Realizing the obvious impact of the Internet, the Audit Bureau of Circulations (ABC), an industry non-profit that computes newspapers' circulation, measured the reach of newspapers by combining both paid circulation and Web site readership for the first time in 2007. This new rating system legitimized online versions of newspapers and gave industry executives and advertisers a more accurate look at a changing market.

Not only do online versions offer newspaper companies the ability to update information twenty-four hours a day, fill a virtually unlimited amount of ad space, and save money on print production and delivery costs, it also allows the publication to reach a wider audience. A man from Topeka, Kansas can read the Miami Herald and a woman in New York City can read the Birmingham News. But with this increased reach, comes an increase in competition. Because the Internet has created an open market for online news outlets, newspapers have significantly expanded their local coverage and gone out of their way to convince readers (online or otherwise) that they remain an essential local news delivery outlet that is tailored to the local reader's needs. One of the newspaper industries' main tasks, right now, is to nurture a new generation of faithful readers who will trust, rely on, and stay loyal to their local dailies even as their digital options expand.

"Innovate or become extinct" has become the mantra for newspapers large and small. The addition of online versions has kept newspapers alive for now, but one must wonder what the future holds. The young, highly sought after audience that online versions attract, are luring advertisers away from print versions.[17] This natural progress may cause newspaper companies to abandon what was once their bread and butter and go completely digital.

Will printed newspapers soon become a thing of the past? © Stephen Coburn/Shutterstock

Television

Digital video production and editing, high definition television, digital cable, satellite delivery, and digital video recording devices such as TiVo are not the only technological advancements that are affecting the television industry. As we discussed earlier, the Hollywood writers' strike shed some light on how

[16]Richard Perez-Pena, "More Readers Trading Newspapers for Web Sites" *New York Times* November 6, 2007 at http://www.nytimes.com/2007/11/06/business/media/06adco.html?n=Top/Reference/Times%20Topics/ Organizations/A/Audit%20Bureau%20of%20Circulations. Accessed September 10, 2008.

[17]Ibid.

important digital delivery (and control of the delivery) has become to television and cable.

A new generation of mass media consumers, who have grown up with the Internet, seems to have no problems conforming to this new reality, watching shows on their laptops, desktops, phones, PDAs, and iPods; legally or illegally downloading movies, shows, and clips on the Internet; or streaming podcasts, radio shows, or even live TV as soon as they become available. However, as broadcast and cable channels watch their audiences shrink, they worry that Internet delivery might be threatening their very survival. A study in England found that young adults, ages 16–25, spend on average 40% more time online than they do watching TV (19.3 hours per week online, compared to 13.5 hours watching TV). Online use also topped other forms of media such as radio (8 hours) and newspapers (5.1 hours).[18]

To keep up with the lifestyle of the cyber generation, most major networks allow viewers to stream full episodes of select programs for free. This offering has the potential to attract views that may not otherwise tune in to a particular program, but it also has the potential to pull viewers away from their TV sets and push them towards the convenience of online viewing. Networks are forced to closely monitor the ever-changing balance between TV and online viewership, as online broadcasts are less profitable than the traditional method. While some networks have trouble maintaining that balance (see below), other networks are tipping the scale and proactively developing new methods of reaching a larger Internet audience. In 2007, ABC, CBS, NBC, and Fox all announced initiatives to make more programs and materials available online. ABC partnered with America Online (AOL) to offer full episodes via AOL; CBS launched the CBS Audience Network, which delivers content worldwide through multiple partners such as Yahoo, MSN, Comcast, and YouTube; and NBC and Fox worked together to create hulu.com, a Web site that allows viewers access to videos from more than 90 content providers.[19] These types of partnerships have allowed networks to maintain their brand and have more control over copyrighted content.

Viewers Must Flip on the TV to Get the "Gossip"

In 2008, the CW, a television network owned by CBS corp. and Warner Bros., found out just how hard it is to maintain a profitable balance between online and on-air audiences with their hit program "Gossip Girl." Originally the network offered viewers the ability to watch full episodes of the show for free via the CW's Web site. However, after the show saw its TV ratings drop 20%, network executives decided to pull the

---

[18]"Media Literacy in Regions Revealed," *Association of Online Publishers* at http://www.ukaop.org.uk/cgi-bin/go.pl/research/article.html?uid=952. Accessed September 10, 2008.

[19]"In the Growing Market for Online Video, TV Networks Want a Piece of the Action" *Knowledge at Wharton* October 3, 2007 at http://knowledge.wharton.upenn.edu/article.cfm?articleid=1814. Accessed on September 10, 2008.

online viewing options, forcing audiences to watch the program the old fashioned way: on a television set. The decision came with a dose of irony, as the Internet is integral to the plot of the show (episodes are narrated by an anonymous blogger), and the target audience is 18–34 year olds, which is a demographic that is most comfortable watching online entertainment.[20] Executives admitted to making a risky and myopic decision, but hoped it would not alienate its key audience. To keep the Internet audience's interest, the network offered free behind-the-scenes footage and two-minute recaps on its Web site and the ability to purchase full episodes on Apple's iTunes. The removal of free online streaming may have annoyed faithful viewers, but it did not deter them, as the second session of "Gossip Girl" brought in 3.4 million viewers, giving the CW its best Monday night ratings in two years.[21]

Will the Internet surpass television as a source of entertainment programming?
© junjie/Shutterstock

viral videos
videos that are passed on from user to user

For now, network television seems to be adapting well to the Internet age and succeeding in staying relevant in the industry, but there is no certainty that traditional television broadcasting can maintain that relevancy in the future. Soon, watching live television may be considered passé. Since the market is in a state of disequilibrium, it is hard to determine if and when the Internet will surpass the television as a source of entertainment programming, but television networks seem determined to evolve and adjust their business models rather than become obsolete.[22]

Changing the Game for Advertisers

Big changes in mass media mean big changes in the world of advertising. The introduction of the Internet has created a new medium on which advertisers can reach potential customers. While advertisers can still follow familiar advertising methods by purchasing banner ads or commercial space online, they are also presented with new options such as search related advertising and product focused viral videos. Search related advertising gives companies the option of putting their Web site at the top of a search engine list and increases the chance that Internet users will visit the company's Web site. It is not surprising that search engine giant Google controls about 75% of all search-related Internet advertising.[23] **Viral videos**, digital videos that are passed on

---

[20]Meg James, "CW to Stop Free Streaming of 'Gossip Girl'" *Los Angeles Times* April 18, 2008 at http://www.latimes.com/business/la-fi-gossip18apr18,1,1364751.story.

[21]Benjamin Toff, "Gossip Girl Rating 3.4 Million Season Premiere Lifts CW to Best Monday Ever," *The Huffington Post* September 2, 2008 at http://www.huffingtonpost.com/2008/09/02/gossip-girl-ratings-34-mi_n_123337.html. Accessed September 10, 2008.

[22]"In the Growing Market for Online Video, TV Networks Want a Piece of the Action" *Knowledge at Wharton* October 3, 2007 at http://knowledge.wharton.upenn.edu/article.cfm?articleid=1814. Accessed on September 10, 2008.

[23]"Microsoft Seen Losing Ground In Next-Gen Ad Technologies" 7 February 2008. Dow Jones News Service.

from user to user, have also emerged as a unique way for advertisers to reach potential customers. They even created a new marketing method called viral marketing. In 2004, Burger King created a viral video called the Subservient Chicken, which features a person dressed in a chicken suit taking commands from an off camera man. The ad was to promote the idea that you can get "Chicken the way you like it" at Burger King. More than 385 million people have viewed the ad. While this new form of advertising may be bizarre to some, they can generate $100 million to $150 million dollars a year for advertisers.[24]

ONE-TO-MANY, MANY-TO-MANY

As we have discussed, in some ways the Internet and other forms of mass media work hand-and-hand: you can stream radio through a Web site, read a book online, or watch a network news program via an online media player. But when Web pages break away from traditional media sources the connection is lost and concerns over content arise. As we saw in previous chapters, a communications model in which a centralized cluster of producers tightly controls the content that is created and distributed to consumers characterizes traditional mass media. This communication system has been called a **one-to-many model**. However, the Internet has created a **many-to-many model** in which information flows in a much more decentralized way. Content, in the form of Web sites, search engines, blogs, discussion groups, multiplayer universes, and even e-mail is easily created by millions of users and dispersed to millions of other users, without any need for centralization or control. Technology has allowed for the extreme democratization

one-to-many model
a model in which a centralized cluster of producers tightly controls the content that is created and distributed to consumers

many-to-many model
a model in which information flows in a decentralized way

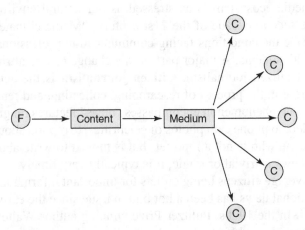

FIGURE 10.2 Traditional Mass Media Model (One-to-Many)

[24]Catherine Holahan, "The Web's Most Viral Ads," *Business Week* at http://images.businessweek.com/ss/06/07/viral_marketing/index_01.htm. Accessed September 10, 2008.

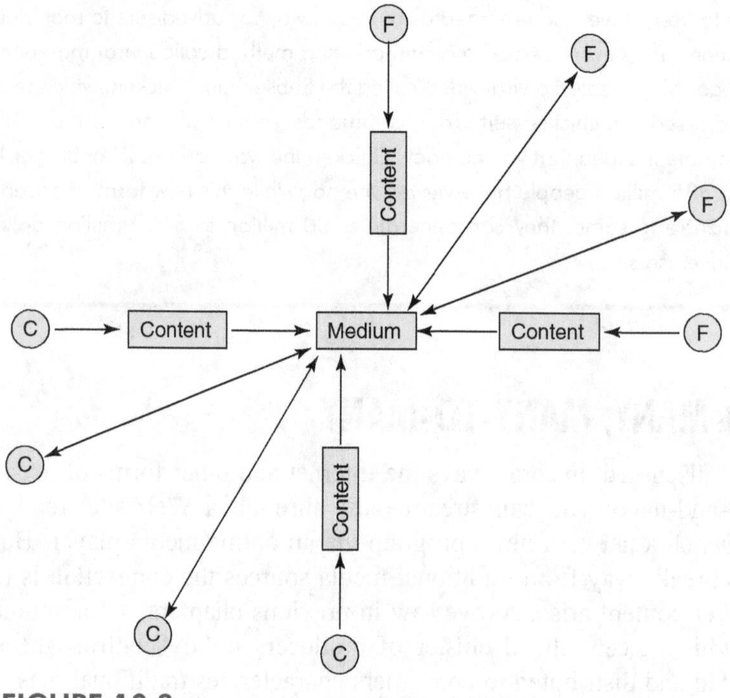

FIGURE 10.3 Internet Mass Media Model (Many-to-Many)

of information and turned everyone with access to a computer and basic content-production skills into a potential mass media mogul and raises concerns about citizen journalism.[25]

Citizen Journalism

Currently, the media ecosystem is as stressed as our natural environment as it heads toward the second decade of the 21st century. "Media climate change" is one way to describe the conditions facing communication professionals, journalists, educators, and students. A major part of this change can be attributed to the materialization of citizen journalism. **Citizen journalism** is the act of citizens taking an active role in the process of researching, collecting, and reporting news and information. The phenomenon encompasses "news" features ranging from the Rodney King video, to phone cam photos of celebrities, to reports about local government by someone who is not a reporter, but is moved to write about an issue. Whether citizen news is trivial or tragic, it is typically very timely.

The idea of average citizens being outlets for important information regarding local and international news has been a hot button issue since the early part of the twentieth century. In the 1920s, Pulitzer Prize winning author Walter Lippmann argued that the modern world is too complex for the average citizen to understand without help. He called for a "journalistic elite" to analyze complex issues facing the nation and boil down complexity for the common person. He felt that the news

citizen journalism
the act of citizens taking an active role in the process of researching, collecting, and reporting news and information

---

[25]"Commercial Scenarios for the Web: Opportunities and Challenges" by Hoffman, Novak and Chatterjee *Journal of Computer-Mediated Communication*, Vol. 1, Issue 3, 1995.

is so important to our democracy that only a special trusted source, the elite journalist, could frame it and present it to the public—a passive mass audience of listeners and viewers. Philosopher and psychologist John Dewey countered Lippmann's philosophy by arguing that what people know, news included, is hammered out through public participation, discussions, and communication about ideas and events. He felt that news is a civic conversation generated by all kinds of people. Therefore, being a part of this civic conversation is what it means to be a good citizen. For Dewey, a responsible journalist revealed and reported on issues in order to strengthen and inform the civic conversation. He saw this as the way to keep a democracy healthy.[26]

During the 1950s and 1960s, radio and television as a news medium offered limited access and minimal or nonexistent audience interaction. The natural result is that the words of a journalist whose news is heard or seen regularly by a passive, mass audience are viewed as more important than the views of common people. Into the 1970s, the model of a good journalist was a sober, well-dressed, well-educated, usually male and white anchor whose presence exuded authority and whose pronouncements were taken as undisputed truth. When Walter Cronkite, ranked in surveys in the 1970s and 80s as the "most trusted man in America," ended his news broadcasts with the sign-off line, "And that's the way it is," most people believed it.

Let's click ahead to the early 21st century. The Internet, and the penetration of high-speed broadband, provides an arena for many-to-many communication media. Today, being connected in the developed world allows inexpensive public conversation between everyone. With very few barriers, more people have a chance to be heard and get their ideas into the global conversation, including the news. Though Walter Lippmann successfully promoted his model of the journalist as an elite news provider, the model contained the seeds of its own demise. Becoming part of an elite brings with it pressure to serve those in power. The journalist gets distanced from the public he or she is supposed to serve.

In 2000, Christopher Locke, Rick Levine, Doc Searls, and David Weinberger put the Cluetrain Manifesto online. It was signed by thousands of people and became the best-selling business book of 2001. Ironically, the entire text was available for free, online. They opened the Cluetrain Manifesto, with these words, "A powerful global conversation has begun. Through the Internet, people are discovering and inventing new ways to share relevant knowledge with blinding speed."[27] Similarly, knowledge-sharing Web sites such as Wikipedia, established in 2001, allow any person to share their expertise in various subjects and basically create an online database for the world's knowledge.

As the 21st century opens, there are tools to talk to one another live, forums for debate, and video-casting tools, podcasts, and audio, video, and text blogs that

---

[26]Dewey (New Republic May 3, 1922) and in The Public and Its Problems. Also: The Public and Its Problems (New York: Holt, 1927; London: Allen & Unwin, 1927); republished as The Public and Its Problems: An Essay in Political Inquiry (Chicago: Gateway, 1940).

[27]Levine, Locke, Searls & Weinberger *The Cluetrain Manifesto: The End of Business as Usual* (2001) at http://www.cluetrain.com/book/index.html. Accessed September 10, 2008.

maintain an open global dialog. These are some of the many-to-many communication tools available to everyone—school children, soccer moms, and senior citizens—not just corporate news outlets. But eliminating the corporations from the news delivery process also eliminates accountability. What stops a teenage blogger from spreading a nasty rumor about a celebrity or a World War II enthusiast from unintentionally providing false information on a knowledge-sharing Web site? These types of issues fuel many of the concerns and controversies surrounding the Internet.

CONTROVERSY AND CONCERNS

The Internet's ability to reach a wide audience and that audience's ability to create, change, and access its contents can create many concerns. While the severity of these concerns is gauged by personal opinion, they are still issues that affect all Internet users. Let's take a closer look at some of these concerns.

Credibility

With the wealth of information available on the Internet it is hard to distinguish facts from fiction. Putting information on Web pages is relatively cheap, easy, and unmonitored, and there is no authorized authorities to remove false information. This forces Internet users to determine legitimacy on their own. Is a blog a good place to find information about the government's role in a foreign conflict? Is a knowledge-sharing Web site a good source for a research paper? Since reliability is a subjective term, determining what is a reliable source and what is not can create gray areas. Typically a domain type of .edu or .gov indicates that there is some content supervision by a respected institution, however there is no guarantee. Many educational institutions, as well as business, have created their own criteria for evaluating online sources. This is an attempt to take advantage of the easily accessible knowledge on the Internet without sacrificing the quality of information.

TABLE 1	Domain Types and Their Meanings
Domain Type	**What It Means**
.com	a company, commercial business, or organization
.edu	an academic institution, such as a college or university
.int	an international organization
.gov	a non-military government entity, such as state park
.mil	a military organization
.net	other organizations: nonprofit, nonacademic
.uk, .au, ca, jp, etc.	country codes indicating servers found in other countries

Copyright Infringement

Napster, the pioneer of digital music, was also the pioneer of copyright infringement laws involving the Internet. As a Web site that allowed users to exchange
digital music files for free, Napster and its founder Shawn Fanning came under
fire after record companies and recording artists claimed the Web site was illegally
distributing copyrighted materials. Do to a lawsuit filed by the Recording Industry
Association of America against Napster, the Web site eventually had to convert to
a paid subscription format.[28]

More recently YouTube, a video sharing Web site, has been at the forefront of
the copyright controversy. YouTube regularly removes a large amount of material
that infringes copyright, but because Internet users mostly control the site, many
copyrighted videos still manage to sneak through. Hollywood has a love-hate relationship with YouTube: marketers love it, legal staffs hate it. A media organization
may have a relationship with YouTube in which it is promoting its own content
while at the same time going after infringers posting material without its consent.[29]

Some critics argue that media companies are having such a hard time with the
digital age because the decentralized, tough-to-control character of the Internet
has threatened the well established, commercially driven media model. Others
say that an intense emphasis on short-term profits has blinded media companies
to the long-term (positive) effects the Internet might bring. Media companies, on
the other hand, counter argue that the commercial, private model that we have
come to know and cherish is what allows for creativity and innovation to thrive.
If movie, TV, and music studios are not collecting the profits, how can they keep
financing expensive movies, shows, and other media products? If artists, writers,
directors, and stars are not being paid for what they do, what incentive will they
have to create?

It can be said that when it comes to the Internet, media companies want
to "have it both ways"—while they are not shy to use the free-for-all, chaotic
character of the Internet to generate buzz and hype and to freely promote their
movies, shows, records, and stars, conglomerates become eager to draw a line
when they sense that this "free publicity" might be eating into their profits.

Cybercrime

The Internet offers a new gateway for criminal activity. **Cybercrimes,** crimes
committed through the use of digital technology, can range from selling illegal
prescription drugs to identity theft. Now, criminals no longer have to stand in dark
alleyways to solicit customers, they can do it anonymously from a computer. As
of 2005, the U.S. Drug Enforcement Administration (DEA) has investigated 236
cases of illegal drug trafficking on the Internet and seized more than $14 million

---

[28]Computers and Information Systems. *Encyclopedia Britannica* at http://search.eb.com/eb/article-215140.
Accessed September 10, 2008.

[29]Ben Fritz and Michael Learmonth, "Showbiz's site fright: Web seen as both a threat and a gold mine,"
Variety, March 10, 2007 at http://www.variety.com/article/VR1117960880.html?categoryid=13&cs=1.
Accessed September 10, 2008.

in cash.[30] Identity theft is also a crime that has been accelerated by the Internet. In 2003, the U.S. Federal Trade Commission released the first national survey on identity theft. The report estimated that 3.3 million Americans had their identities fraudulently used to open financial accounts such as bank accounts and credit cards. The crimes caused a loss of $32.9 billion to businesses and $3.8 billion to individuals.[31] These types of crimes generate concern over what information is safe to offer on the Internet. It also forces Internet users to decide between the convenience of storing personal information online and the security of keeping your identity safe.

Internet Addiction

It may seem bizarre, but it is certainly not farfetched to claim that many people struggle to step away from their computer screens. In South Korea, two-thirds of the population is on the Internet, and most of them have fast broadband connections, making South Korea one of the most wired countries in the world. Consequently, it is also a country with the highest rates of Internet addiction.[32]

Are you constantly connected to your PDA?
© iofoto/Shutterstock

In November 2007, a story in the *New York Times* reported on the popularity of Internet "rehab centers" in South Korea. These rehab centers receive mostly teenage boys whose parents worry that the long hours spent by their children online have begun to have serious negative effects on their daily activities and school work, not to mention their social lives and even their health.[33]

Internet addiction does not only affect teenagers. Since the introduction of personal digital assistants (PDA) and portable browsers such as the BlackBerry and iPhone, young professionals have problems stepping away from the Internet and resisting the need to continuously check e-mail. The MIT Sloan School of Management conducted a study that showed 90% of participants felt some degree of compulsion in their BlackBerry usage.[34] This type of compulsion can lead to increased stress and anxiety at work and at home. While one of the many advantages to the Internet is that it helps us stay connected to friends, work, and various other entities, we have to wonder, is that always a good thing?

Overall many critics of the Internet are concerned about a potential "dumbing down" effect, in which new generations of users might abandon

---

[30]"DEA Congressional Testimony" *U.S. Drug Enforcement Administration* at http://www.usdoj.gov/dea/pubs/cngrtest/ct121305.html. Accessed September 10, 2008.

[31]Cybercrime. *Encyclopedia Britannica* at http://search.eb.com/eb/article-235700. Accessed September 10, 2008.

[32]Caroline Gluck, "South Korea's Gaming Addicts" *BBC News* November 22, 2002 at http://news.bbc.co.uk/2/hi/asia-pacific/2499957.stm. Accessed September 10, 2008.

[33]Martin Fackler, "In Korea, a Boot Camp Cure for Web Obsession" *New York Times* Nov. 18, 2007 at http://www.nytimes.com/2007/11/18/technology/18rehab.html?_r=3&scp=1&sq=korea+internet+addiction&st=nyt&oref=slogin&oref=slogin&oref=slogin. Accessed September 10, 2008.

[34]Margaret Locher, "BlackBerry Addiction Starts at the Top," *PC World* March 6, 2007 at http://www.pcworld.com/article/129616/blackberry_addiction_starts_at_the_top.html. Accessed September 10, 2008.

more rigorous entertainment or research procedures in favor of fast, superficial, pre-digested content. Defenders of the Internet are quick to point out that some of those same criticisms were raised when new media such as television or comic books came about. They note that, historically, whenever a new mass medium surfaces, there is always a period of confusion and adjustment, as society and traditional media struggle to understand it and adapt to the new reality. Furthermore, some critics contend that in essence, the Internet is only a neutral new delivery system, and that it will be up to society and all of us to determine how this new technology is used.

SOCIAL ASPECT OF THE INTERNET

While issues and concerns may circulate about the positive and negative effects the Internet has on mass media and society, there is no denying that the Internet has brought the world closer together and created its own unique culture. Social Web sites are a key part of this developing culture. If you have a personal page on a Web site like MySpace or a Facebook page you are one of millions to do so. You are also participating in a phenomenon called **social networking**, a trend in which users connect with one another based on shared interests, geography, history, or other factors. Early social network sites such as Classmates.com, created in 1995, focused on reconnecting with high school classmates. Other social networking Web sites catering to young adults soon followed.

social networking
a trend in which users connect with one another based on shared interests, geography, history, or other factors

TABLE 2	Worldwide Growth of Selected Social Networking Sites June 2007 vs. June 2006		
Total Worldwide Home/Work Locations Among Internet Users Age 15+			
	Total Unique Visitors		
Social Networking Site	**June 2006**	**June 2007**	**% Change**
MySpace	66,401,000	114,147,000	72
Facebook	14,083,000	52,167,000	270
Hi5	18,098,000	28,174,000	56
Friendster	14,917,000	24,675,000	65
Orkut	13,588,000	24,120,000	78
Bebo	6,694,000	18,200,000	172
Tagged	1,506,000	13,167,000	774

Source: comScore World Metrix, http://www.comscore.com/press/release.asp?press=1555

Social Networking

MySpace and Facebook are the sixth and seventh most-visited Web sites respectively, according to Alexa, an online traffic-monitoring site. Users can customize personal Web pages to their own tastes, post pictures or blogs, and chat or leave messages for friends. According to Facebook, two million people establish accounts every two weeks. In May 2007, Facebook created a utility that permits individuals to program third-party extra applications for the site. These utilities include trivia contests, video games, puzzles, and more—over 10,000 such applications existed as of December 2007. Users can also create customized groups to gather together online in support of a person, purpose, or event.

YouTube is also another form of a social networking site. Owned by Google (purchased in 2006 for $1.7 billion), YouTube permits users to upload and view videos on its site and currently hosts about 6.1 million videos. While YouTube is often used to post humorous videos and entertaining TV and movie clips, it is also used for more serious purposes. Political parties have been using YouTube to advertise their candidates. Users can see statements from the candidates and respond to them by uploading their own videos. In the fall of 2007, YouTube partnered with CNN to televise debates by the Democratic and Republican presidential hopefuls featuring questions submitted by YouTube users.[35]

Personal Privacy

The enormous popularity of social networking sites makes issues of privacy and identity protection even bigger. According to several 2007 reports from the Pew Internet and American Life Project, 64% of online teens ages 12–17 have participated in content-creating activities, like social networking sites, picture or video posting, or standalone Web sites. Although 66% of those teens do restrict access to their personal information, 32% report that strangers online in some way have contacted them. A majority use their first names on their sites (82%), their city or town (61%), and photos of themselves (69%). Twenty-nine percent include an e-mail address, and 2% post a cell phone number.[36]

For most users, social networking and other participatory sites are ways to keep in touch with old friends, make new ones, market goods and services, and be entertained. They allow individuals to be creative, connect with people from different cultures, and become involved with social issues. Whether the content on social networking sites is trite or imaginative, exclusive or inclusive, lackluster or inspirational it all contributes to the global conversation and brings us closer together as a world.

Throughout this chapter we have discovered how the Internet was born and developed. Overtime the simple idea of sharing information has morphed into something that has changed the world. The Internet is a piece of technology that

---

[35]"CNN, YouTube To Unveil Presidential Debate Details Thursday" by Caroline McCarthy. CNET News, June 13, 2007.

[36]"Internet News Audience Highly Critical of News Organizations Views of Press Values and Performance: 1985-2007," The Pew Research Center for the People and the Press. Released August 9, 2007.

A Social Networking Page Could Cost You a Job

Public information is not just a problem for teenagers; many employers report that they surf social networking pages to find details about potential employees that may not be discussed in an interview. As one career developer points out, employers are looking at more than just the resumes of their prospective employees; they are concerned about all publicly available information: "The term they've used over and over is red flags. Is there something about [a prospective employee's] lifestyle that we might find questionable or that we might find goes against the core values of our corporation?"[37]

transcends social, economical, and demographic lines and, for better or worse, changes the way people live their lives. If you don't think that the Internet greatly affects your existence, just imagine your life without it. In a few years, many people will not have to. To future generations the Internet will no longer be a revolutionary form of media; it will be as common as the radio and TV, and perhaps we will have a new form of media to which to adapt.

e-commerce
the act of buying or selling of goods or services over an electric system such as the Internet

CAREERS IN THE FIELD

As we have learned, the Internet has changed the way corporations do business and the way people work, it has also created new career choices. Electric commerce, or **e-commerce** is the buying or selling of goods or services over an electric system such as the Internet. E-commerce professionals can work in various facets of the industry. Web site design and development, content development, Web programming and application development, and database administration are just a few options. Naturally, as the Internet becomes a more popular way for consumers to purchase goods and services, the more in-demand the field becomes. E-commerce is offered as a major at many colleges, universities, and through some MBA programs.

SUMMARY

- The Internet was originally developed for strategic military purposes, before the technology was made available for commercial use.
- Vinton Cerf created the transmission-control protocol (TCP), which allowed networks to connect. Tim Berners-Lee created the World Wide Web, which allowed users to browse the contents of the Internet.

---

[37]Alan Finder, "For Some, Online Persona Undermines a Résumé," New York Times, June 11, 2006. Accessed September 10, 2008.

- Books, radio, newspapers, and TV are all positively and negatively affected by the Internet. Each media outlet has changed its traditional business model to adapt to new technology.
- Traditional media sources are represented by the one-to-many model, which is a centralized cluster of producers that tightly control the content that is created and distributed to consumers. The Internet is represented by the many-to-many model, which involves information that flows in a much more decentralized way.
- Citizen journalism has taken the responsibility of reporting news and information away from the "journalistic elite" and placed it in the hands of the common citizen.
- Concerns regarding the Internet include content quality, copyright infringement, cybercrime, and Internet addiction.
- Social networking sites allow groups of individuals to communicate with one another and contribute to the global conversation.

DISCUSSION QUESTIONS

1. During the 1960s and 1970s who were the primary users of computer networks? What purpose did they serve?
2. Does the Internet offer more opportunities than challenges for radio? Newspapers? TV?
3. How do you personally participate in the many-to-many media model?
4. Does citizen journalism help or hinder the global conversation?
5. What other concerns does the Internet generate? What issues concern or affect you the most?

 ## SUPPLEMENTAL WEB SITES

SUPPLEMENTAL READINGS AND VIDEO

"Citizen Journalism" at Online Newshour, http://www.pbs.org/newshour/bb/media/july-dec05/citizen_11-16.html#

Thomas L. Friedman, *The World Is Flat 3.0: A Brief History of the Twenty-first Century* (2007) New York: Picador

Henry Jenkins Convergence Culture: Where Old and New Media Collide http://books.google.com/books?id=RlRVNikT06YC&ie=ISO-8859-1

Mark Whipple, The Dewey-Lippmann Debate Today: Communication Distortion, Reflective Agency, and Participatory Democracy. Sociological Theory. 23:2, June, 2005

MESSAGE MAKING

PART

4

PUBLIC RELATIONS

CHAPTER OBJECTIVES

- Trace the development of the public relations industry, from inception to present day
- Discuss the contributions of pioneering figures in the field of public relations, including P.T. Barnum, Ivy Lee, and Edward Bernays
- Identify the four PR models, and outline their major elements
- Discuss the components involved in implementing a PR plan
- Identify and discuss the varied roles and functions of public relations in the contemporary global marketplace
- Understand the skills necessary for professionals to succeed in the public relations industry

11

KEY TERMS

corporate social responsibility (CSR)
damage control
focus group interview
greenwashing
issues management
MBO
media facilitators
press agent/publicity model
propaganda

public information model
public opinion poll
public relations (PR)
RACE formula
rebranding
spin
subpublics
two-way asymmetric model
two-way symmetric model

INTRODUCTION

In 2000, Turkcell, one of the three main mobile phone providers in Turkey, learned from a customer survey that its subscribers wanted to see the company more involved in the community, particularly when it came to supporting educational projects. As a result, the company joined nonprofit organizations in launching a campaign, "Contemporary Girls of Contemporary Turkey," that aimed to increase educational opportunities for Turkish girls, especially in impoverished rural areas.

As part of this ongoing public relations campaign, scholarships were offered in the first year to 5,000 girls in 28 rural areas. Because of the campaign's dramatic success, those numbers were increased in successive years, reaching 35 areas and benefiting thousands of girls who would have not been otherwise able to attend primary and secondary schools.

public relations (PR)
the business of bringing about public awareness, understanding, and goodwill toward a person or organization

For Turkcell, the campaign changed people's general views of the company, earned them three major social responsibility awards in the program's first three years, and generated not only positive publicity, but also popular support and goodwill toward the organization.[1] In 2007, the program won the prestigious Golden World Award from the Institute of Public Relations.[2] This campaign provides an excellent example of how companies are using public relations—that is, the business of bringing about public understanding and goodwill toward a person or organization—to improve their image and build a more positive relationship with consumers.

Aristotle's *Rhetoric* is considered by some to be one of the earliest volumes on public relations. © Panos Karapanagiotis/Shutterstock

EARLY PUBLIC RELATIONS: A HISTORICAL OVERVIEW
The Origins of Public Relations

While the term **public relations** probably is barely over a century old, one finds ample instances of such activity among the ancients. Aristotle's *Rhetoric*, for example, is considered by some to be one of the earliest volumes on public relations. In this work, the ancient Greek defined rhetoric as the "art of oratory, especially persuasive use of language to influence the thoughts and actions of listeners"—a primary concern in any public relations campaign, past or present. Moreover, the authors of the first major public relations textbook indicate that "Caesar carefully prepared the Romans for his crossing of the Rubicon in 49 B.C. by sending reports to Rome on his epic achievements as governor of Gaul.[3] Others suggest

---

[1]Aydemir Okay and Aylar Okay, "Contemporary Girls of Contemporary Turkey: Case Study of a Public Relations Campaign." In *The evolution of public relations: Case studies from countries in transition*, Judy VanSlyke Turk and Linda H. Scanlan, eds. pp. 23–33. Gainesville, Florida: The Institute for Public Relations Research and Education, 2004. Available at http://www.instituteforpr.org/files/uploads/Int_CaseStudies.pdf.

[2]Turkcell, Communication Activities. "IPRA Golden World Awards, 2007 Competition." Available at http://www.turkcell.com.tr/c/docs/ic/TURKCELL_SNOWDROPS.pdf.

[3]Scott M. Cutlip and Allen H. Center. *Effective public relations*. Englewood Cliffs, New Jersey: 1952.

that the gospels (*gospel* means "good news") were written "more to propagate the faith than to provide a historical account of Jesus' life."[4]

The groundwork for much of modern public relations thought can likewise be traced to the American colonial era. Founding fathers, including Benjamin Franklin, Thomas Jefferson, and John Adams, used propaganda techniques familiar to today's public relations practitioners. Samuel Adams spelled them out:

- Formation of an activist organization
- Using many media
- Creating events and slogans
- Orchestrating conflict
- Sustaining an information campaign over time until the minds of the public were won over to the cause.[5]

Although conceived of during the eighteenth century, these public relations tenets remain relevant today, particularly within the political arena.

From Press Agentry to Public Policy

Politics remained an integral venue for the development of public relations throughout the 1800s. Andrew Jackson, the first "common man" to assume the presidency (from 1829–1837), felt more responsible to the masses than had previous presidents. Distrustful of those who traditionally held power, he surrounded himself with a "kitchen cabinet" of advisors more in tune with his populist views. Among his confidants was Amos Kendall, a former newspaper editor who took on many of the duties now associated with the White House press secretary.

Kendall's approach was that of a press agent—catering to the needs of the press. He wrote speeches for Jackson to deliver, conducted straw polls on public opinion, and built Jackson's image as an honest and resourceful president. By shaping the way Jackson was represented in the press through words, action, and the strategic release of information, Kendall became a model for public relations practitioners to follow for years to come.[6]

P.T. Barnum can be credited with translating the emerging public relations industry, and its reliance on press agentry, into the world of entertainment. Barnum not only catered to the press, but in fact courted them with bold, sensational stunts and spectacles meant to capture the world's attention. And he became, indeed, a master of publicity: exhibitions at his American Museum sold

P.T. Barnum became a master of publicity with his "Greatest Show on Earth." © *CORBIS*

[4]James E. Grunig and Todd Hunt, *Managing Public Relations* (New York: Holt, Rinehart & Winston, 1984), p. 15.

[5]Scott Cutlip, "Public Relations and the American Revolution," *Public Relations Review*, Fall 1976, pp. 11–24.

[6]Fred F. Endres, "Public Relations in the Jackson White House," *Public Relations Review*, Fall 1976, pp. 5–12.

millions of tickets.[7] And he is perhaps best known for proclaiming his eponymous circus to be "the greatest show on earth."

By the beginning of the twentieth century, the term public relations had come into use. It generally was interpreted to mean the way business explained itself to the people and attempted to convince them that it was working for their general welfare. American Telephone & Telegraph Company (AT&T) president Theodore Vail gave the term legitimacy when he directed that the company's 1908 annual report be titled "Public Relations." The publication focused on the firm's responsibility to make a fair profit, to treat its employees well, and to answer any questions that could reduce conflicts between itself and its publics.[8]

Ivy Lee: Informing the Public

As the twentieth century began, American business was under attack as a force that dominated society and trammeled individuals. Magazine muckrakers took industry to task for dehumanizing the workplace and putting worker comfort and safety second to profits. As a result, unions organized and legislators began to enact laws to limit business practices. A former New York newspaper business reporter, Ivy Ledbetter Lee, saw the need for industry to do a better job explaining itself to society. Lee's message to business was: "Let the public be informed!"

Business had always tended toward secrecy, but Lee advised business leaders that openness could help win the support of distrustful publics, including legislators. Lee opened one of the first publicity agencies specializing in providing information about business to the media. Lee centered his agency's services around his Declaration of Principles, which spelled out how his firm intended to give editors accurate, complete information and to answer inquiries from the press as swiftly as possible.[9]

One of Lee's greatest PR successes occurred within the coal industry. Lee provided news on behalf of the coal operators to counter information supplied by local labor unions. He convinced John D. Rockefeller to visit the family's mines in Colorado to offset criticism in a labor dispute. Eventually he was able to change the senior Rockefeller's image of detached aloofness to one of a charitable and concerned leader of business.

Edward Bernays: Shaper of the Profession

While Ivy Lee is considered a pioneer in the PR field, the name Edward L. Bernays is synonymous with the shaping of public relations as we know it today. More than any other work, his *Crystallizing Public Opinion*, published in 1923, ushered in the era of scientific persuasion within the public relations realm. Scientific persuasion effectively replaced Ivy Lee's construct of public relations as

[7]Irving Wallace, "P.T. Barnum." *Encyclopedia Britannica* at http://search .eb.com/eb/article-9013431.

[8]Edward L. Bernays, *Public Relations* (Norman: University of Oklahoma Press, 1952), p. 70.

[9]Ray E. Hiebert, *Courtiers to the Crowd* (Ames: Iowa State University Press, 1966), p. 48.

the simple dissemination of information, which had previously supplanted press agentry—the hype and hoopla associated with P. T. Barnum.

Born in Vienna and a nephew of Freud, Bernays once was a press agent—the person who contacts the media to promote theatrical events—for the great tenor Enrico Caruso. A journalist by training, he was called to serve on the American government's Creel Committee for Public Information during World War I, which gave him a better understanding of the workings of **propaganda**—information deliberately spread to help or harm the reputation of an individual, organization, or country.

His second book, *Propaganda*, published in 1928, was based on the concept that "the conscious and intelligent manipulation of the organized habits and opinions of the masses is an important element in democratic society. Those who manipulate this unseen mechanism of society constitute an invisible government which is the true ruling power of our country."[10]

Bernays coined the phrase "engineering public consent" as a synonym for proactive public relations. He argued that facts and events could be arranged and presented to convince an audience that one course of action was preferable to another. His textbook *Public Relations* was published in 1952, and he continued as a spokesperson and advocate for public relations past his hundredth birthday in 1991.

Bernays, who died in 1995, also coined the phrase "public relations counsel" and suggested that it was a profession, not merely a craft or trade.[11] Unlike press agents and publicists, who care only about getting publicity for their clients, Bernays suggested that the public relations counsel should use the techniques of the social sciences to understand how public opinion is created and thus how public opinions can be swayed through scientific, ethical, and socially responsible techniques.

MODERN PUBLIC RELATIONS: MODELS, CONCEPTS, AND PROGRAM BASICS

PR Models

As with many subfields of mass communication, it can be helpful to conceptualize public relations in terms of theoretical models. Two leading public relations scholars and theorists, James E. Grunig and Todd Hunt, characterize Edward Bernays as responsible for developing two new models of public relations, which joined two earlier models.[12] P. T. Barnum personified the **press agent/publicity model**, with his shameless promotions based more on fancy than fact. Ivy Lee, in contrast, represented the **public information model**, with his emphasis on

propaganda
information deliberately spread to help or hurt the reputation of an individual, organization, or country

press agent/publicity model
a PR model, favored by P.T. Barnum, that emphasizes promotion and publicity with little regard for facts

public information model
a PR model, favored by Ivy Lee, that emphasizes one-way (source-receiver, or producer-consumer) dissemination of truthful information

---

[10]Edward L. Bernays. *Propaganda.* New York: Horace Liveright, 1928.

[11]Edward L. Bernays, *Crystallizing Public Opinion* (New York: Liveright, 1923).

[12]James E. Grunig and Todd Hunt. *Managing Public Relations.* New York: Holt, Rinehart, Winston, 1984.

one-way (source-receiver, or producer-consumer) dissemination of truthful information.

The writing and practice of Bernays led to the development of what Grunig calls the **two-way asymmetric model**. This model uses formative research—research conducted before beginning an information campaign—to ascertain the attitudes of the target publics. While the flow of information is imbalanced in favor of the producer, feedback from the consumer can and does influence the producer. The two-way model represents a necessary way of conceiving public relations when the actions and behaviors of consumer publics affect the actions and behaviors of producers in the competitive business system.

As Bernays worked with educators and professional leaders, he came to realize that in businesses subject to heavy government regulation, or where the activist consumer has as much influence as the producer, balanced communication is necessary to adapt the organization to the realities of society. Grunig calls this fourth situation the **two-way symmetric model**. Examples might include an energy utility wishing to open a nuclear power plant, or a pharmaceutical company hoping to introduce an experimental drug. Consumer feedback and, ultimately, approval, is critical in such situations in order to ensure success for the business.

With the popularization of the Internet and other media technologies that facilitate the speedy dissemination of information, it is possible to say that consumers and clients have attained a new level of power over all realms—business, politics, and entertainment. Nowadays, it is virtually impossible for most industry sectors to succeed without fully taking into account the opinions, needs, and desires of their target publics. In this sense, the two-way symmetric model has become the most important and widely used public relations model.

Table 11.1 summarizes the characteristics of the four models of public relations. Note that the development of the models follows public relations history over the last century.

Although the two-way symmetric model tends to dominate the field in today's age of information, all four models still coexist. The astute public relations practitioner is the one who knows how to choose the correct one to fit the situation at

two-way asymmetric model

A PR model in which formative research is used to ascertain the attitudes of the target publics before a PR plan is implemented; it recognizes that the actions and behaviors of consumer publics affect the actions and behaviors of producers in the competitive business system

two-way symmetric model

A PR model most often applied to businesses subject to heavy government regulation, or where the activist consumer has as much influence as the producer; it recognizes that balanced communication is necessary to adapt the organization to the realities of society.

TABLE 11.1	Four Models of Public Relations
Model	**Characteristics**
Press agent/publicity	Emphasis on promotion, sensationalism, persuasion and/or manipulation of public, sometimes at the expense of facts
Public Information	Emphasis on one-way dissemination of truthful information
One-way asymmetrical model	Emphasis on formative research to determine wants, needs, and attitudes of target consumers
Two-way symmetrical model	Emphasis on balanced communication between producer and consumer

hand. Your own college or university, for example, might use publicity to promote the institution and its offerings to prospective students, public information to tell about a research project, two-way asymmetric public relations when dealing with student protesters, and the two-way symmetric model when trying to convince a foundation to fund a major grant.

Facilitating the Flow of Information

Preceding chapters have examined the functions of specific news and entertainment media. However, the subject of this chapter, public relations, as well as the topic of Chapter 12, advertising, are not media in themselves. Instead, they may be conceptualized as **facilitators** and they also utilize media to disseminate their messages. That is, public relations and advertising make the creation and distribution of mass media possible because, directly or indirectly, they underwrite the cost of disseminating information cheaply to large audiences.

media facilitators industries, such as public relations and advertising, that make the creation and distribution of mass media possible because, directly or indirectly, they underwrite the cost of disseminating information cheaply to large audiences

Advertisers, as we shall see in the next chapter, provide the cornerstone of financial support by purchasing time or space in the mass media. Public relations, on the other hand, bestows what some have called a "subsidy" because it involves the supply of information, which the media otherwise would have to pay to gather, for free. In fact, without the financial support of public relations and advertising, the forms of media that we consume on a daily basis would be astoundingly expensive—a newspaper might cost a couple of dollars, instead of 25 or 50 cents, and magazines might run $15 each.

In addition to providing financial support, PR has, over the past few decades, transformed from a "behind the scenes" entity to a powerful, highly visible, and influential industry at the forefront of media, culture, and business. In his 1986 book *Goodbye to the Low Profile,* Herb Schmertz, former vice president of public affairs at Mobil Oil, highlighted and described this rapidly changing role of public relations.[13]

Without the financial support of public relations and advertising, everyday media would be very expensive.
© arteretum/Shutterstock

Schmertz had once been considered controversial among public relations practitioners because of his willingness to inject his own forceful personality into the debate on oil companies and their policies. For years, it had been assumed that PR people worked quietly behind the scenes, avoiding conflict and perpetuating the fantasy that events happened naturally without the assistance of public relations. As the title of his book suggests, Schmertz believed it was time to reinvent the popular concept of public relations, acknowledging the role of PR in fostering open and full debate on public issues.

While not all PR professionals agree with his assertive techniques, most appreciate that public relations, once considered an apologist and publicist for big business, has become a force for building alliances, influencing

---

[13]Herb Schmertz, *Goodbye to the Low Profile: The Art of Creative Confrontation.* New York: Little Brown, 1986.

In order to implement a PR program, you need to tailor the message for a specific audience.
© Monkey Business Images/Shutterstock

discussion of public issues, and facilitating the flow of information between producers and consumers of products, services, and ideas. Public relations clients in today's global marketplace thus need, and demand, sophisticated, multi-faceted PR programs that require and depend on astute research and novel, persuasive devices.

Program Implementation

The implementation of a modern PR program is a complex operation that varies greatly, depending on the account and client. However, a few components tend to remain consistent across all situations.

Identifying Subpublics

These days, PR professionals realize that modern consumers have effects on the producers that are as important as the effects producers hope to have on consumers. The mass public rarely acts in a unified way. As a result, one key component in implementing a PR program for any organization or purpose is to determine the characteristics and behaviors of the target consumer, or **subpublics.** This is not a totally new concept: magazines and radio, responding to the competition from television, learned to tailor their messages for specialized audiences with specialized information needs and interests.

Some of the subpublics a large organization such as a corporation must identify and plan communication programs for might include:

subpublics
specialized audiences with specialized information needs and interests that PR professionals must identify before implementing and specifically targeting a program

- Employees
- Consumers of products or services
- Other individuals or organizations providing raw materials or services to the organization
- The surrounding business community and local chambers of commerce
- Stockholders in a company or members of an association
- Municipal governments and state and federal regulatory and legislative bodies that can pass laws affecting the organization
- Political and activist groups
- Professional groups that determine norms and standards for a field
- Minorities
- Voters
- The news media
- Trade publications serving a particular industry

Each of these categories of subpublics can be further divided. Employees, for example, would include part-time workers, blue-collar personnel, clerical staff, managers, and supervisors. Catering to the information needs of every group complicates the job of public relations agents in an organization.

At your college or university, for example, the PR staff working for the administration or development office likely divide the alumni subpublic into smaller categories. Alumni subpublics might include:

- Wealthy graduates of 50 years ago who might just come forth with a few million dollars if buildings were named for them
- Football fanatics whose loyalty depends largely on the win-loss record of this year's team
- Parents who are thinking of sending their children to the school from which they graduated
- English majors who now head corporations and think the school should offer a degree in business
- Engineers who work for industry but return to campus occasionally for refresher courses
- Scholars who earned Ph.D. degrees and are now college professors

Each subgroup is potentially helpful and influential, and thus the PR staff likely works hard to carefully target their messages and requests to each one. For example, a university may develop a dozen different publications catering to these subpublics, rather than relying on a single alumni magazine to satisfy everyone's needs and interests.

Setting Objectives

When implementing a program, PR professionals must also set clear goals and objectives. Press agent/publicity and public information specialists may be concerned with getting information to consumers, creating enthusiasm for an idea, motivating actions, or instilling confidence in a person or project. Thus their objectives are relatively simple and obvious: "Fill the stadium on Saturday" or "Let people know about the many uses of our products." In the two-way models, however, objectives are more complex: "Gain compliance with the new recycling laws" or "Help our employees find educational resources that will promote their career advancement."

Whatever the model, public relations people have to set specific objectives—the number of people reached or the number of consumers behaving in a certain manner—and specific time frames and deadlines so that the effects of the public relations program can be measured and demonstrated to management in numerical terms.

Planning the Program

To ensure that they have followed all the steps in implementing a successful public relations program, many professionals follow a plan modeled after John E. Marston's **RACE formula**.[14] The letters stand for research, action, communication, and evaluation. Since evaluation at the end of a program is a kind of research that may lead to modifications or changes in the public relations program, the

RACE formula
John E. Marston's construct for the implementation of a successful public relations program involving four steps: research, action, communication, and evaluation

---

[14]John E. Marston. *Modern public relations*. New York: McGraw-Hill, 1979.

formula can be seen as a spiral that continually renews the process of analysis, program design, and communication.

Research includes measuring public opinion, analyzing all information currently available to publics, considering options, pretesting messages, assessing the impact of information channels, and making qualitative assessments of ideas that may prove effective. *Action* means laying out the program that will get the message across—planning events and organizing information that will persuade the consumer to accept the views (or product or candidate) put forth by the organization. *Communication* involves creating and conveying messages to audiences, and the *evaluation* of feedback as to whether and how the messages have been received and interpreted.

THE ROLES AND FUNCTIONS OF PUBLIC RELATIONS IN TODAY'S GLOBAL MARKETPLACE

In today's global marketplace, where communication is lightning fast, new technology is constantly developing, and many organizations aim to reach consumers all over the world, public relations continues to grow in prominence and importance. Moreover, the roles and functions of public relations continue to expand and evolve in response to these changes and challenges. Indeed, public relations today fulfills a variety of functions within a diverse set of contexts. While the following discussion is not exhaustive, it is a useful sampling of some of PR's most important roles.

Crisis Management

damage control
the first phase of crisis communication in which PR practitioners identify how the crisis has negatively affected the public's perception of the organization and demonstrate that the organization is taking responsibility and has a plan for solving the crisis

In the last few decades, one of the most important roles PR departments have played in many large organizations has been within the context of crisis management. Developing a crisis communication plan comprises one of the most important responsibilities of many PR bodies. Crisis communication consists of two important phases. The first is called **damage control**. It involves finding out what has happened and how it has negatively affected the public's perception of the organization. The immediate task is to demonstrate that the organization is taking responsibility and has the means of solving the crisis.

issues management
the second phase of crisis communication in which PR practitioners aim to demonstrate to the public that the organization is working to solve or alleviate the problem through cooperation or negotiation with other organizations

The second phase involves moving the organization from the crisis footing to one of **issues management**. While it may not be possible to undo the effects of the crisis or make it go away, it is possible to demonstrate to the public that the organization is working to solve or alleviate the problem through cooperation or negotiation with other organizations.

An example is the exposure of a nonprofit charity organization whose executive director has been discovered misappropriating contributions and putting them to personal use. The damage control phase consists of showing that the wrongdoing has been stopped and the wrongdoer has been relieved of duty. The issues management phase consists of a program to reassure contributors that their money is

Historical Case Study: The Tylenol Tragedy

In September of 1982, several deaths in the Chicago area were traced to arsenic-laced Tylenol capsules. When it was revealed that the medicine was made by a subsidiary of Johnson & Johnson, the company's stock fell sharply in value.

The swift response of the J&J public relations department was to counsel management to remove the product from the shelves immediately. A team rushed to Chicago to work with the police in getting information to the public, and a national hotline was set up to answer questions from consumers. The chief executive officer of the company served as spokesperson throughout the crisis, and he assured the media and consumers that the company would put consumer safety before profits.

Rather than abandon the successful Tylenol brand, the company reintroduced it in tamper-resistant packaging after research showed that consumers trusted the company as a result of its handling of the Tylenol tragedy. Johnson & Johnson's management of the crisis became a model for industry to follow.

being applied to the charitable programs for which it was intended, and that those programs continue to be worthy of public support.

High profile examples of poor crisis communication—the 1979 Three-Mile Island nuclear power plant accident, for instance, in which the federal government and plant operators took three days to effectively address the public—have set examples for today's corporations on how such crises *should not* be handled. As a result of these historical failures, many corporations nowadays specifically mandate how quickly media requests for information must be met in the event of a crisis, as well as which officer will serve as spokesperson for the company when a catastrophe occurs.

In 2007, after many of their toys were discovered to contain dangerous levels of lead paint, Mattel Inc. found itself mired in a serious crisis. In response, CEO Robert A. Eckert issued a direct apology on the company's Web site. The company then enacted a recall, followed by a revised safety plan that required more rigorous inspections for its products.[15] As Mattel demonstrated, effective public relations planning can mitigate a crisis, winning support for an organization by showing its willingness to talk openly about its mistakes. In following, a poor PR response to crisis can result in total loss of public trust and, potentially, loss of business for a company.

Robert Eckert testifies before the Senate about toys manufactured in China that needed to be recalled for safety issues. © *Stefan Zaklin/epa/Corbis*

---

[15]Nicholas Casey and Nicholas Zemiska, "Mattel Does Damage Control After New Recall" August 15, 2007, *Wall Street Journal* [Online Edition]. Available at http://online.wsj.com/article/SB118709567221897168.html?mod=googlenews_wsj.

Corporate Rebranding

rebranding
the process through which a product, service, or organization is marketed and associated with new, different, and improved identity

corporate social responsibility (CSR)
the actions or programs adopted by organizations that reflect an interest in and concern for social and environmental issues

Another important role of public relations within a corporate context involves **rebranding**—that is, implementing initiatives that cause consumers to associate an organization with a new and improved identity. In some instances, rebranding may overlap with or follow crisis management, serving as a means to rehabilitate and change the image of a company marred by scandal or tragedy. In other cases, rebranding may represent an organization's attempt to increase their appeal to consumers, and in turn, their potential profits.

The demonstration of **corporate social responsibility**, or CSR, is at the heart of many PR rebranding efforts. The Turkcell case study that opened this chapter is just one among many examples of how companies today use PR to revamp their images, benefit society, and augment their bottom lines.

Case Study: A "Green" Oil Company?

British Petroleum (BP), a major oil and chemicals company that operates across six continents to the tune of $277 billion in revenues in 2007, has tried, at least since the mid-1990s, to clean up its image and brand itself as the "environmentally responsible" oil company.[16] Its advertising and public relations campaign, which in the U.S. had adopted slogans such as "bp: beyond petroleum" and "bp: better petroleum," has been largely successful in changing the company's image.

BP's rebranding effort can be traced to the mid-1990s, years before the company's purchase of Amoco, a competing oil giant, and several years before its incorporation of ARCO, another major player. In 1996, BP resigned from and distanced itself from the Global Climate Coalition, a lobbying group that ridiculed the science behind global warming and tried to undermine the Kyoto treaty discussions. The move coincided with the promotion of John Browne as BP's CEO.

In 2000, BP hired Ogilvy & Mather Worldwide, one of the largest global advertising and PR firms, to design and launch the $200 million public relations and advertising campaign responsible for the "bp: beyond petroleum" slogan and the company's new yellow and green sun logo.[17] BP's public relations effort also includes publicizing the company's research into alternative energy sources, as well as its attempts to cut greenhouse gas emission levels in its refineries.

Despite some recent setbacks—in July 2006, BP had to shut off its gigantic Prudhoe Bay oilfield in Alaska, after a corroded and poorly maintained pipeline caused an oil spill in the area; in 2005, an explosion at a Texas BP refinery killed 15 workers—the BP rebranding effort has been mostly successful. In a field where consumers are hard pressed to find "good guys" among many perceived villains, BP has been able to elicit positive reactions from the general public.

[16]Fortune Global 500 2007. *fortune* [Online edition at cnn.money.com] Available at http://money.cnn.com/magazines/fortune/global500/2007/snapshots/6327.html.

[17]Sourcewatch, "BP". Available at http://www.sourcewatch.org/index.php?title=BP.

In recent years, the burgeoning Green Movement—an increased concern on sustainability and environmentally-friendly practices—has incited many organizations to emphasize their products or practices as environmentally altruistic. Critics refer to this PR tactic as **greenwashing**, and accuse organizations of exaggerating their environmental contributions or misrepresenting their practices for PR and monetary gain. In some instances—the development of a hybrid locomotive by GE as part of their Ecomagination initiative, for example—companies do seem to be making valid, and valuable, efforts to improve the environment.[18] Other cases, such as the BP example outlined above, remain more ambiguous. Regardless, greenwashing will surely remain a key issue in public relations for years to come.

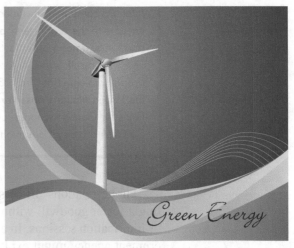

Green Energy

In recent years, more companies have emphasized their environmentally-friendly products in PR campaigns. © Yaraz/Shutterstock

Governments and Goodwill

The work of public relations is not limited to the business sector; public relations practitioners are key players in government agencies at the local, state, and federal level alike. Building strong ties with the community through programs and initiatives, keeping citizens informed about government issues, decisions, and services, and encouraging the public to participate in government-sponsored activities are a few of the varied functions of public relations within this realm.

greenwashing
the practice of companies expressing environmental concerns and/or making their products appear to be environmentally sound

Case Study: Reducing Violence in Central America

Since the late-1990s, public weapons buyback and exchange programs have been successfully implemented in Central and South America in an attempt to reduce societal violence. In countries such as Panama and El Salvador, which pioneered these programs, the campaigns' success can be largely credited to well-executed public relations campaigns set up by local and federal governments, in collaboration with social institutions and private companies.

In the mid-1990s, the United Nations warned that small weapons posed a very significant threat in developing (and developed) countries that had a history of civil unrest. Working with nonprofit organizations such as Rotary International and the Ford Foundation, the U.N. called for a "microdisarmament" that would reduce this threat.

Countries such as Panama and El Salvador were quick to respond to this call and set up comprehensive public relations and education campaigns that called on the general public to give up their guns in return for toys, food, or even cash. The public

---

[18]"GE Ecomagination: Hybrid Locomotive" GE Corporate Web Site. Available at http://ge.ecomagination.com/site/#hybr.

relations campaigns included public announcements in the mass media; press conferences with the organizers; paid advertisements in newspapers, radio and television; and flyers, among other tactics.

As a result, some areas that implemented the program in Panama registered a drop in violent crime from 5,124 cases to 1,588 cases in one year. In El Salvador, the United Nations observer mission collected more than 10,000 weapons, and the Guns for Goods exchange program collected 9,527 weapons, 3,157 magazines and 120,696 rounds of ammunition over four years.[19]

Public relations officers at local and state health departments, for example, might foster goodwill within the community by promoting free health screenings or information sessions. In addition, public information specialists at a given government agency might explain the reasons for controversial policies or decisions to affected citizens. On a national level, PR programs have been implemented by governments in response to a variety of societal issues, from deterring alcohol and drug use, to preventing forest fires, to reducing violence through weapons buy-back programs as mentioned in the case study from Central America.

Politics and Entertainment

During the Presidential campaign, Barack Obama represented "change."
© U.S. Air Force photo by Staff Sgt. Paul Gonzales

One need look no further than the 2008 U.S. Presidential election campaigns for evidence that public relations and politics go hand in hand. Interestingly, many of the principles applied to business apply to politics as well, albeit in slightly different ways. Politicians are often "branded" and "rebranded" in the hopes of capturing the public's attention and allegiance— John McCain and Sarah Palin, for example, were "mavericks, "while Barack Obama and Joe Biden represented "change." Developing a strong image for politicians is a key concern for PR people within this realm.

Moreover, crisis management also comes into play frequently in politics. When a scandal emerges surrounding a key political figure, PR people spring into action with plans to contain the damage and move forward as quickly as possible.

PR fulfills a similar role within the entertainment sector. When a major celebrity is involved in a scandal or breaks the law, a publicist usually scrambles to release a statement explaining or apologizing for the behavior. Many celebrities employ a team of public relations professionals who help shape the image of their

[19]Mark Hucklebridge and William Godnick, "Public Relations Campaigns Reduce Violence in Panama and El Salvador." In *The evolution of public relations: Case studies from countries in transition*, Judy VanSlyke Turk and Linda H. Scanlan, eds. pp. 135–147. Gainesville, Florida: The Institute for Public Relations Research and Education, 2004. Available at http://www.instituteforpr.org/files/uploads/Int_CaseStudies.pdf.

Historical Case Study: Selling Kitchens . . . and Nixon

The American public's opinion of Vice-President Richard Nixon in the 1950s soared when he visited an American exhibition in Moscow. He was shown forcefully lecturing Soviet Premier Nikita Khrushchev about the benefits of the American way of life in front of a model American kitchen. One might suspect that Nixon's staff arranged the event. But it was the public relations man for the kitchenware firm who created the moment spontaneously. "Right this way, right this way!" he shouted at the two leaders as they moved through the exhibit. They moved toward the kitchen, and Nixon made an assertive gesture toward the American hardware. An Associated Press photographer tossed his camera to the public relations man inside the exhibit, who took the famous "Kitchen Debate" photos.[20] The public relations man, William Safire, became President Nixon's speechwriter a decade later, and now is a respected syndicated columnist.

clients by coordinating interviews and television appearances, orchestrating photo ops, and ensuring that their client's projects receive ample press attention and coverage.

In both politics and entertainment, **spin**—a PR tactic in which a specific point of view of interpretation of an event is presented with the intention of influencing public opinion—often comes into play. Successfully convincing the public to see ideas or actions that they may not understand or agree with in a positive light comprises a key preoccupation of many PR practitioners.

> **spin**
> PR tactic in which a specific point of view of interpretation of an event is presented with the intention of influencing public opinion

SKILLS AND TACTICS OF THE PR PROFESSIONAL

Because of the diversity of the field, today's PR professionals must possess a multitude of skills, employ a variety of tactics, and stay informed about key issues in the field.

Relations with the News Media

The most critical skills for public relations practitioners are those necessary for placing stories in the news media. Editors must be convinced that a story is interesting, factual, and relevant. While the advertising agency pays to insert its message in commercial space or time, the public relations counsel ethically cannot pay to control what goes in the news columns. The apparent newsworthiness of the item is what wins it credibility.

---

[20]Art Stevens, *The Persuasion Explosion* (Washington: Acropolis Books, 1985), pp. 70-71.

Not surprisingly, many of today's successful public relations professionals are former journalists who understand the workings of the newsroom. Fundamental skills for dealing with the press include:

* Writing an interesting news release following the journalistic format and style used by the news media.
* Explaining to a busy editor on the phone in just a few minutes why a story is interesting and important.
* Providing the contacts or resources the journalist needs to write a story; helping the journalist get through to the spokespeople for your organization.
* Arranging a press conference that is well-timed for the media and produces useful information.
* Understanding the special needs of the print and broadcast media, which often have different priorities.

Two-Way Benefits

When we discussed the creation of news in Chapter 11, we acknowledged the special relationship between the press and public relations professionals. Former Mobil vice-president for public affairs Herb Schmertz, to whom we referred early in this chapter, counsels public relations professionals to maintain good relations with reporters and editors because "information is currency. If you build a good relationship with a reporter, you may find you'll learn as much from him as he'll learn from you. . . when you talk with someone who's well-informed, not all of the information flows in the same direction."[21]

That special relationship between journalists and public relations people suggests they can be placed simultaneously as producers and consumers of information. For example, a public relations person may have information for a journalist about a company's efforts to comply with new pollution standards set by the state government. The reporter's questions in response to the briefing may reveal what the reporter has heard about another company's efforts to forestall enforcement of the new regulations. That information, in turn, may help the public relations person to advise management about the climate of opinion surrounding the issue.

Press conferences ideally provide useful information for the media. © Monkey Business Images/Shutterstock

Management by Objectives

MBO

management by objectives, a technique used by professional managers and borrowed by public relations professionals; it involves laying out specific, quantifiable goals for PR campaigns

In recent years, public relations has borrowed a business management technique known as **MBO**—management by objectives—in order to clearly demonstrate the worth and impact of their programs. In the past, when public relations departments made such promises as to "improve our organization's image" or "celebrate the organization's contribution to the community," they found it difficult to show their contribution to the bottom line of the organization. That is to say, they could not

---

[21]Herb Schmertz, *Good-bye to the Low Profile* (Boston: Little, Brown, 1986), p. 126.

show that they enhanced the making of a profit or, in the case of nonprofit organizations, that they served the main goal of the organization.

However, by adopting MBO, public relations people developed the ability to demonstrate the worth of their programs in terms business people can understand. Today, PR professionals can use MBO to state the impact of PR program through quantitative measurement. Here is an example: "The information project reached 40,000 residents, and over half of them requested our information packet—three times as many as last year, when there was no information program."

Research Applications

The typical public relations professional of a generation ago was a former news reporter or editor hired to deal with former colleagues in the press. Today's public relations practitioner needs an important new skill: the ability to use research to understand how a public thinks and behaves in regard to issues that affect a client organization.

Just as the advertising industry became more sophisticated when it learned to measure the consumer's preferences and needs, so too has the public relations industry evolved as it has realized the importance of consumer research. Understanding the attitudes of consumers is critical to effectively reaching target publics with a message and persuading them to change their behaviors.

As with advertising, the survey or **public opinion poll** is a major research tool for public relations people. Another is the **focus group interview**, in which small groups of selected consumers are interviewed in a formal but open-ended way that allows them to make known to the researchers their interests, preferences, and concerns. Studying behaviors and quantifying them is another valid technique: How many people of what type attended an event, and how many of them subsequently requested information using the phone number provided?

The rise of research by public relations practitioners relates directly to the increase in MBO techniques. Research is needed to demonstrate exactly how and why an objective was set, and whether or not it was achieved.

public opinion poll
a research tool in which a large group of randomly selected consumers are surveyed on their opinions on a given topic

focus group interview
a research tool in which small groups of selected consumers are interviewed in a formal but open-ended way that allows them to make known to the researchers their interests, preferences, and concerns

Writing: The Essential Skill

Critics of public relations practitioners assume that the chief talent of the "PR person" is the ability to talk a good line, coupled with a propensity to "like other people." This limited view assumes that persuasion is accomplished by overwhelming another person with one's personality and depth of conviction.

In truth, persuasion is best accomplished by presenting factual data in a comprehensible, interesting, compelling, and believable manner. Consumers of the information should have the opportunity to think about the arguments, weigh the evidence, and persuade themselves that the idea or cause presented is the best one.

This is why writing is the basic skill of public relations. And this is also why, historically, so many public relations people have come from the ranks of reporters

A focus group interview gives researchers information on consumers' interests, preferences, and concerns.
© Monkey Business Images/Shutterstock

and editors. A premium is put on the individual who can gather information accurately, organize it coherently, and present it in a straightforward manner.

Journalistic writing, both feature articles and hard news reporting, provides the models that public relations people imitate when attempting to place a client's stories in the news media. The closer they come to the ideal, the greater the chances of placement. Because public relations also involves supporting the marketing of products and services, promotional writing modeled after advertising copy is a specialized writing skill that may prove helpful. Similarly, writing for the ear and following tight time formats are desirable specialized skills for public relations people who target the broadcast media.

Capitalizing on Emerging Technology

PR professionals need not only be skilled in media relations and writing, but also in the strategic use of the newest, cutting-edge technologies. Blogs and personal media such as Facebook provide forums for both research for and implementation of PR programs. Many corporate executives maintain blogs on their corporation's Web sites in order to appear accessible to consumers, for example, just as many actors, actresses, and music artists maintain personal pages or fan sites to promote their projects. In addition, podcasts, e-mails, and text messages can be keys to success in PR programs, keeping consumers informed and helping them to feel connected to a given cause or organization. In future years, the importance of emerging technology will likely only grow within the field of public relations.

CAREERS IN THE FIELD

A compelling reason for studying public relations is that the field, far from being static in terms of growth as many other mass media fields are, provides increasing numbers of entry-level jobs for college graduates. Opportunities abound in a variety of areas, including government, education, nonprofit and social programs, business, politics, and entertainment.

Some organizations handle all public relations in-house, meaning they put together their own publications, do their own lobbying with legislative bodies, and prepare campaigns aimed at diverse external publics, from stockholders to customers to community groups. Most corporations, and many government bodies and trade associations, give several important segments of their public relations work to specialized agencies. These organizations often turn to agencies for campaigns aimed at promoting specific products, lobbying, community relations, and media relations.

Some agencies specialize by topic: politics and public affairs, health care, insurance, environmental concerns, or new product introductions. Other agencies specialize in types of service: video news releases, special events, publications, or crisis communication. Small agencies may consist of a principal and one or two assistants, while freelancers may handle only two or three accounts; the largest agencies, with dozens of account teams, serve dozens of clients in a variety of ways.

In public relations, the quest for credibility has raised questions about the need to accredit or even license practitioners, much as lawyers are admitted to the bar, doctors are licensed to practice, and accountants must pass exams in order to pursue their trade. The Public Relations Society of America (PRSA) and the International Association of Business Communicators (IABC) both offer accreditation exams. However, because accreditation is not necessary to practice public relations and because the majority of practitioners do not join either organization, professional accreditation is not yet as meaningful as it is in the fields of law, medicine, and accounting. Accredited or not, today's public relations practitioners find that the field is maturing, gaining acceptance, and taking an increasingly important role in the management of complex organizations that depend on the support of consumers in order to survive.

SUMMARY

- The concepts central to modern public relations can be traced to ancient texts, including Aristotle's *Rhetoric* and the Bible, as well as to the ideas of the founders of the United States.
- Amos Kendall and P.T. Barnum may be considered two of the earliest press agents; Barnum, in particular, was known for enacting elaborate publicity stunts. Ivy Lee pioneered the concept of public relations as a tool for businesses to gain support from consumers. Edward Bernays, with his emphasis on proactive public relations and astute analysis of target publics, shaped public relations as we know it today.
- The press agent/publicity model, public information model, two-way asymmetric model, and two-way symmetric model comprise the four theoretical constructs for approaching public relations. Although the two-way symmetric model tends to dominate in the contemporary landscape, all four models continue to coexist and may be used to achieve specific PR goals.
- The modern public relations industry is a media facilitator. Identifying subpublics, setting objectives, and implementing Marston's RACE formula are key components of effective PR programs.
- Public relations plays key roles in crisis management, corporate rebranding, government, politics, and entertainment.
- Cultivation of media relationships, management by objectives, research, writing, and the use of emerging technologies are integral skills for success in the public relations field.

DISCUSSION QUESTIONS

1. Discuss the ethical implications of the press agent/publicity model favored by P.T. Barnum. Is the predominance of hype over truth ethical? Why or why not? What contemporary examples illustrate this potential conflict?

2. Analyze the factors that have contributed to the predominance of the two-way symmetrical model in PR communications in recent years. What advantages does this model offer over other techniques? What potential problems can occur as a result of its use?

3. How would you characterize the "special relationship" that exists between public relations professionals and the media? How can it be helpful, and/or detrimental, to both parties? What about the public? Explain your response.

4. Consider how you would design a PR program to rehabilitate the image of an organization in crisis. If possible, choose a current example from the news to illustrate your ideas. What steps would you take? What objectives would you delineate? How, and why, would your program be effective?

5. What impact have technological, political, economic, and/or cultural developments of the past decade had on the PR industry as a whole, and, more specifically, on the skills necessary to succeed in the industry?

SUPPLEMENTAL WEB SITES

ADVERTISING

CHAPTER OBJECTIVES

- Explain how the advertising industry has evolved over the last three hundred years
- Describe how advertisements are used in mass media
- Explain how advertisements benefit the consumer and media outlets
- Understand how the government regulates advertisers and how advertisers regulate themselves
- List four future trends in the advertising industry

KEY TERMS

advertising	guerrilla marketing
bait and switch	outdoor advertising
consumerism	paid search
direct mail	pay-per-click
fairness doctrine	point-of-sale advertising

INTRODUCTION

From the moment you wake up in the morning until the time you go to sleep at night, how many commercial messages do you think you are exposed to? If you watch TV or read the newspaper regularly, you many think you are exposed to a hundred or so messages. If you rarely give attention to major forms of mass media, you may think the number is even lower. The reality is that the average American is exposed to 3,000 commercial messages a day, that's over one million a year.[1] That number may seem inflated, however,

[1]Brenda O'Neill, "Can you feel sorry for an ad man?" *BBC News* November 21, 2005 at http://news.bbc.co.uk/ 2/hi/uk_news/magazine/4456176.stm.

if you really think about the words and images that are communicated to you over the course of a day you can see the truth behind this staggering number. As you get ready to leave the house in the morning you may flip on the radio or morning news and hear numerous broadcast commercials. When you pour your cereal, you may notice a promotion for an unrelated product printed on the back of the box. On your way to work or school you are exposed to hundreds of messages: the billboard for a vacation package alongside the road, a sign for a brand of shampoo on the side of a bus, or a bumper sticker on the car in front of you. You may be exposed to some commercial messages without even noticing: the Nike logo on your friend's shirt, the Starbucks coffee cup on your neighbor's desk, or the Jansport label on your backpack.

Commercial messages are all around us, and corporations are making it increasingly difficult to avoid them. Nearly $450 billion is spent annually to lure customers to certain products or services. Promoting commercial messages is called advertising. **Advertising** is essentially the act of calling the public's attention to a product, service, or need. Advertising is commonly found in different types of mass media in the form of radio or television commercials, newspaper spreads, or billboard announcements. However, as we discovered earlier, advertisements can be found almost anywhere.

Advertising the act of calling the public's attention to a product, service, or need

New York's Time Square shows just about every kind of advertising you can imagine.
© Alexey Malashkevich/Shutterstock

ADVERTISING BEFORE THE 21ST CENTURY

Advertising has existed in the United States for over three hundred years. The first known advertisement was placed in a newspaper, the *Boston News-Letter*, in 1703. The advertisement, or ad, publicized the sale of an estate in Oyster Bay Long Island. Years later Benjamin Franklin began running advertisements in the *Pennsylvania Gazette*. The first true pioneer of advertising did not emerge until 1833. Printer Benjamin Day found a way to bring advertising to the masses by creating the first successful penny newspaper, the *Sun*, in New York. Within four years of its first edition, the publication's circulation reached 30,000, making it the most widely read newspaper in the world. As the 19th century progressed, advertising became an important part of business development for major companies. Advertising agencies formed, companies hired full time advertising copywriters, and major corporations invested unprecedented amounts of money in ad placements. In 1882, Procter & Gamble Co. started an advertisement campaign for Ivory soap with an $11,000 budget, an amount that was unheard of at the time.

Modern advertising began to emerge in the 1900s with products such as Kellogg's cornflakes. In 1906 WK Kellogg created a widespread campaign by placing its advertisements in six Midwestern magazines. By 1915 Kellogg was spending more than one million dollars a year on national advertising, creating a benchmark for the future of advertising. By 1921, RJ Reynolds was designating $8 million to advertising, most of which was spent on promoting Camel cigarettes.

The investment proved to be successful as by 1923 Camel controlled 45% of the U.S. cigarette market.

As advertising became more popular, the government became involved in the process. The Section 5 of the Federal Trade Commission Act, passed in 1914, declared that the Federal Trade Commission (FTC) can issue cease-and-desist orders against any company that engages in dishonest or misleading advertising. Companies were now liable for any claims made in advertisements. Cigarette companies found themselves in hot water because of this act.[2] We will learn more about tobacco advertising and government regulations later on in this chapter.

A Changing Market

As public preference changed, so did the approach of advertisers. During the early part of the 20th century radio emerged as a popular form of media. Soon companies opted to spend their advertising dollars on the airwaves rather than print pages. By 1938, radio exceeded magazines in advertising revenue. But again, the market changed. Advertisers turn to television as a new way to reach consumers. On July 1, 1941, NBC's WNBT aired its first telecast. A close-up view of a Bulova watch opened and closed the telecast, marking one of the first instances of product placement on television.

Other changes in advertising occurred around this time. The US government started to use advertising to help build support for World War II. The War Advertising Council gained free advertising for public service messages. Popular campaigns such as "Buy War Bonds" and "Loose Lips Sink Ships" were placed in magazines and radio broadcasts across the United States. After the war, the War Advertising Council was renamed the Advertising Council and proceeded to

Advertisers and Athletes: The Start of a Love Affair

In 1905, three-time National League batting champion Honus Wagner became the first person to sign an endorsement contract. Wagner's deal with bat company Hillerich & Bradsby, Co. allowed the company to engrave his signature on Louisville Slugger bats and sell them to eager fans. Since 1905, more than 7,000 endorsements deals have been created between Louisville Slugger and professional baseball players. Wagner's deal sparked an ongoing trend in endorsement relationships between corporations and professional athletes that is highly prevalent in the advertising world today.[3]

---

[2]"Advertising Age: The Advertising Century" *Ad Age* at http://adage.com/century/timeline/index.html.

[3]Scot Mondore "One Hundred Years of Player Endorsements: Honus Wagner and Louisville Slugger" The National Baseball Hall of Fame and Museum February 19, 2007 at http://www.baseballhalloffame.org/news/article.jsp?ymd=20070219&content_id=859&vkey=hof_news.

advertise public service campaigns such as Smokey the Bear, McGruff the crime dog, and "Just Say No" to drugs.[4]

Advertisers' approach to choosing the perfect medium for their products changed with the emergence of AC Nielsen's machine-based rating system for television. The system made it possible to track how many households view certain television programs. Nielsen's machine allowed companies to find out on which programs their advertising dollars would be most wisely spent.

As the 20th century progressed, advertising companies became more methodical about where, when, and how they placed certain ads. Advertisements were no longer just used to persuade consumers to buy a product; they were used to encourage the public to embrace a brand. "The Pepsi Generation" was an advertising campaign initiated in 1963. It projected the image that all those who are young, or young at heart, should drink Pepsi brand cola.[5]

Soon after the MTV era introduced new, flashier forms of advertising during the 1980s, the Internet introduced new, high-tech forms of advertising in the 1990s. By 1993, the Internet enlisted five million users and emerged as a profitable medium for advertisers. Before the end of the century, well over $2 billion was spent on Internet advertising. Today over $24 billion dollars is spent on Internet advertising adding to total of $450 billion spent on advertising worldwide.[6] To understand why so much money is spent on advertising, let's examine why we need it.

A CULTURE OF CONSUMERISM

Consumerism the theory that an increase in the consumption of goods and services will benefit the economy

With billions of dollars being spent every year to convince consumers to buy certain products, one must question the necessity of advertising. Why can't the consumer just decide what products and services to purchase on their own? That question cannot be properly answered without understanding consumerism. **Consumerism** is the theory that an increase in the consumption of goods and services will benefit the economy.[7] In short, the more we buy the more we thrive. Americans adopted a culture of consumerism at the start of the 20th century. People began to work fewer hours, acquire higher paying jobs, invest in the stock market, and buy luxury items like cars, washing machines, and expensive clothing.

The culture of consumerism is clear in today's society. Americans purchase more than $6 trillion dollars in goods and services each year, and they rely on advertisements to inform them about new products. Gone are "mercantile days" when each shopkeeper waited on every customer by taking and filling their order

---

[4]The Advertising Council, "Ad Council: The Story of the Ad Council" at http://www.adcouncil.org/ timeline. html. Retrieved October 10, 2008.

[5]http://wehner.tamu.edu/mgmt.www/v-buenger/466/Coke_and_Pepsi.pdf.

[6]"Mobile Advertising" *The Economist* October 4, 2007 at http://www.economist.com/business/displaystory .cfm?story_id=9912455.

[7]Merriam-Webster at http://www.merriam-webster.com/dictionary/consumerism.

personally, acting as clerk, cashier and then often as salesman, describing new products and discussing the merits of various goods. How does the consumer today learn about the amazing plethora of goods and services available in today's expanding marketplaces? For better and worse, this is where advertising comes in.

Advertising and the Consumer

Advertising may not seem like a benefit because of the negative connotations connected to the practice. Consumers sometimes feel that advertisers are always trying to sell them something they don't need. However, in many cases advertisers are promoting goods and services that support our basic needs. Food, clothing, shelter, and other goods that aid us in our daily lives are products that are advertised. Sure, we may not need brand name clothing, but a Gore-tex jacket may help you keep warm in the winter. Without advertising, consumers may never learn about new product that can improve their health and well being.

How does advertising financially benefit the consumer?
© Jim Barber/Shutterstock

Advertising also has financial benefits for the consumer. Advertising promotes competition within the market, which drives down prices and increases product availability. It also helps consumers decide where to get the best price and what products have the best value.

Advertising and the Media

Advertising is the foundation of the economic health of our nation's media. Broadcast television and radio are solely supported by the revenue brought in by advertising. Newspapers, magazines, cable television, and Internet outlets rely on subscription fees as well as advertising revenue to support their businesses. Without revenue from advertising many media outlets would not exist and those that could survive would come at a substantially higher cost to the consumer.

Because advertisers allow media outlets to function with little to no cost to the consumer, more outlets are able to flourish, giving consumers more choices in news and entertainment. For example, in the 1950s television viewers were only offered three broadcast networks. Today, they have their choice of six broadcast networks and hundreds of cable channels. Advertising had the same effect on print media. In 1960 there were 312 morning newspapers, and today there are over 700. The number of consumer magazines has increased as well. In 1988 there were almost 13,000 publications, and today that number is more than 18,000.[8]

Advertising is also an integral part of the Internet. Paid advertisements make many of the most popular sites such as Google, Mapquest, and YouTube free to Internet users. Without revenue from advertisers there would be little incentive for Web site administrators to develop new Web sites. But when it comes to advertising and the Internet, the benefits run both ways. As we will discuss later on in the chapter, the Internet has become a large part of the future of advertising.

---

[8]"The Role of Advertising in America" Association of National Advertisers at http://www.ana.net/advocacy2/content/advamerica.

Now that we know why advertising is important to the consumer and the media, let's see how it is used.

THE MANY FACES OF ADVERTISING

Traditionally, advertisements appear in media in the form of print or broadcast. Print advertisements usually contain pictures or photos, catchy headlines, and occasionally coupons and can appear in newspapers, magazines, or flyers. Broadcast advertisements consist of brief 15-20 second audio and/or video pieces designed for television or radio. In addition to traditional advertising, methods such as direct mail, outdoor signage, and point-of-sale advertising can also make a big impact on consumers.

Direct Mail

Direct mail a type of advertisement sent through the postal service

Direct mail, sometimes referred to by consumers as junk mail, consists of advertisements sent through the postal service. Direct mail advertisements typically promote special sales or offers to select consumers. It can be a very useful form of advertising because companies can create mailing lists that only target consumers that are most likely to purchase their goods or services. Grocery store circulars and "pre-approved" credit card offers are common direct mail pieces. While direct mail pieces often receive a bulk rate for postage costs, it can still be rather expensive. The advertisements can also be viewed as a nuisance and be thrown away unopened.

Direct mail advertisements can be sent to mailing lists that target specific consumers.
© GWImages/Shutterstock

Point-of-Sale

Point-of-sale advertising is the placement of products, promotions, or other offers on or near a checkout counter. The candy in a grocery store checkout line and the flyer asking you to try a new style of burger on the counter of a fast food restaurant are both forms of point-of-sale advertising. Point-of-sale advertising has become high tech in the last few years. At coffee retailer Aroma Espresso Bar, customers who approach the counter may be greeted by a cashier and video screen that displays images of the various breakfast items available for purchase. Through this type of advertising, customers who entered the shop with the intention of only purchasing a cup of coffee may be encouraged to also pick up a croissant or muffin.

Point-of-sale advertising the placement of products, promotions, or other offers on or near a checkout counter

Point-of-sale advertising can be very beneficial to advertisers because most purchasing decisions are made in the store and advertisers have a chance to appeal to consumers' impulses.[9] However, point-of-sale-advertisements, especially the kind that involves technology, can be expensive and sometimes overlooked.

[9]Jennifer L. Schenker, "Point-of-Sale Advertising Goes High Tech" *BusinessWeek* September 22, 2008 at http://www.businessweek.com/globalbiz/content/sep2008/gb20080922_109810.htm.

Outdoor Advertising

Outdoor advertising is another way to reach consumers outside of their homes. Traditionally thought of as billboard signs, outdoor advertising has changed a lot in the last ten years. Outdoor media now includes park benches, public transit vehicles, or bus shelters that are wrapped with images and text promoting various products.

Some outdoor advertising methods can range from silly to bizarre. In Times Square in New York City a glass elevator was designed and built to simulate an Oreo cookie being dunked into a glass of milk. In London, a group of individuals were paid to walk on to a subway train wearing jackets with video screens in the arm pits. When a person would raise their arm, a video ad for Right Guard deodorant would play for the whole crowd in the train to see. While this method of advertising may sometimes be viewed as precarious, advertisers are willing to spend big, $7.3 billion in 2007 according to the Outdoor Advertising Association of America, in order to get their message out to the public.[10]

Outdoor advertising the placement of ads outside in the view of the general public, typically on billboards, signs, or other outdoor objects

Advertisers are willing to do just about anything to get their message out to consumers.
© emin kuliyev/ Shutterstock

The Internet

While advertisers are getting more creative with the way they execute advertising in traditional mediums, nothing has shaken up the advertising world more than the Internet. As we discussed in Chapter 10, the Internet is becoming a dominate force in media. In many ways the Internet works like a television or a newspaper. Advertisers can place an electronic banner ad, similar to a print ad in a newspaper, on a home page or a select page of a Web site. They can also place a pop-up or side bar video, similar to a television commercial, on a partnering Web site. These types of advertisements are increasing as more people are looking to the Internet to read up on the latest news or watch their favorite TV program.

Paid search a form of advertising used on a search engine Web site, which allows companies to have a brief advertisement placed on top or next to search results when certain keywords are used

The Internet also offers advertisers other ways to reach consumers that are unmatched by newspapers or television. Paid search and pay-per click advertising has come forward as one of the fastest growing methods of advertising. **Paid search** is a form of advertising used on a search engine Web site, which allows companies to have a brief advertisement placed on top or next to search results when certain keywords are used. For example, when a user types in the keywords "hair salon Miami" a small add for Gabriella's Unisex Salon in Miami may appear at the top of the search results page under a paid advertisements section. In **pay-per-click** advertising, Web page administrators allow outside companies to place advertisements on their Web pages in exchange for a small fee, which is paid to the Web site administrator, when a user clicks on the ad. For example, Sarah

Pay-per-click a form of advertising in which Web page administrators allow outside companies to place advertisements on their Web pages in exchange for a small fee, which is paid to the Web site administrator, when a user clicks on the ad

[10]Stephanie Clifford, "Summer Silliness Brings a Pizza Field and a Giant Oreo" *The New York Times* August 1, 2008 at http://www.nytimes.com/2008/08/01/business/media/01adco.html?pagewanted=1&_r=1.

Hawkins has a Web site for her event planning business. To make some extra cash for her business, Sarah allows Larson's Limousine Services to place a small ad on her Web page. Sarah may receive about 10 cents from the limo service every time a user clicks on the ad.

Paid search and pay-per-click were first implemented and mastered by Google founders Sergey Brin and Larry Page. Called AdWord (paid search) and AdSense (pay-per-click), these forms of advertisements are a key part of what has made Google the multi-billion dollar company it is today.[11] In 2007, Google made over $16 billion in advertising revenue and that number is projected to grow even larger in the next few years.[12]

Companies are drawn to this type of advertising because it allows advertisers to more accurately measure how many potential customers they are reaching, and it also guarantees that consumers are actively viewing the advertisement. Unlike a television commercial that can be missed when a viewer leaves the room or a print ad that can easily be passed by, paid search and pay-per-click advertising is actually initiated by the consumer, increasing the chances that the ad will be thoroughly viewed.

In a 2010 Supreme Court decision called "Citizens United," the justices removed limits on corporations' independent spending during campaigns for the Presidency and Congress. The decision will have an important impact on political advertising in future elections.[13]

Political Advertising: The Living Room Candidate

During election season in the United States, television viewers may notice more ads for political candidates than ads for fast food restaurants. Since the 1950s, television has changed the game for political candidates. Through television, candidates can enter voters' homes and influence their decision making through images, slogans, and rhetoric. The use of television ads for political advertisings was not in vogue until the 1952 election between Dwight D. Eisenhower and Adlai Stevenson. Previous candidates such as Governor Thomas Dewey viewed political television ads as "undignified" and refused to use them in his 1948 campaign.

Diverging from this view, Eisenhower embraced television ads, creating several 30 seconds spots titled "Ike for President" that featured animated characters, songs, and the now famous slogan, "I like Ike." Eisenhower's campaign merchandised the candidate just as a corporation would merchandise a new product. So it is not surprising that the same ad agency that created M&M's slogan "melts in your mouth not in your hand," developed the "Eisenhower Answers America" ad series. In these television

[11]Google Web site at http://www.google.com/ads/.

[12]Google Web site Investors' information at http://investor.google.com/fin_data.html.

[13]http://www.scotuswiki.com/index.php?title=Citizens_United_v._Federal_Election_Commission.

ads Eisenhower responded to questions from ordinary citizens. Forty spots, recorded in one day and then broadcast throughout the campaign season, aired before popular shows such as I Love Lucy. The spots helped Eisenhower enter his constituents' living rooms on a nightly basis and be viewed as a man of the people.

Stevenson never warmed up to the idea of using television to market a candidate. He publicized his disapproval of the process with the statement: "I think the American people will be shocked by such contempt for their intelligence. This isn't Ivory Soap versus Palmolive." Stevenson created television spots promoting his campaign; however they were often long and dull and aired during late hours. Viewed as nothing more than on-camera radio spots, Stevenson's television ads did little for his campaign.[14]

Dwight D. Eisenhower won the 1952 election by a large margin. His campaign changed the way Americans view their candidates, but also the way candidates make their appeal to the American people. In the 2008 presidential campaign, candidates spent nearly $3 billion on political television ads.[15] Whether they are used to promote a candidate's views and proposed policies or to portray competitors in negative light, political television ads have become an important part of the election processes.

Advertising Agencies

The forerunner of the advertising agency as we know it today was founded in 1841 by Volney Palmer, whose Philadelphia brokerage service specialized in buying advertising space from newspapers at a volume discount, then selling parts of that space to individual advertisers at a markup. To this day advertising agencies gain part or all of their compensation through the discount they receive from publishers bringing in ads. It is a service to the publishers to have large blocks of ads coming in without having to work with individual merchants or manufacturers.

It was not until the 1870s that advertising agencies emerged to serve manufacturers who needed advice on how to package their products and promote them to consumers. The N. W. Ayer and Son Agency, also of Philadelphia, was among the first to provide the service of studying a product and developing a "campaign" or strategy, for making that product familiar and desirable. The Ayer agency is responsible for many of the advertising slogans that have become part of our cultural lexicon, like "Diamonds are forever," and "When it rains it pours."[16]

---

[14]"The Living Room Candidate: 1952 Eisenhower vs. Stevenson" Museum of the Moving Image at http://www .livingroomcandidate.org/commercials/1952.

[15]Mark Preston, "Political television advertising to reach $3 billion" CNN October 15, 2008 at http://www.cnn .com/2007/POLITICS/10/15/ad.spending/.

[16]N.W. Ayer & Son. *Encyclopedia Britannica* at http://www.britannica.com/EBchecked/topic/1349123/ NW-Ayer-Son. Retrieved October 17, 2008.

MONITORING ADVERTISING INFORMATION

As we discovered earlier in this chapter, advertisers will go to great lengths to draw consumers to their products. However extreme, silly, or idiotic the ploy, advertisers still have to adhere to certain standards set by the advertising community and the federal government. Unscrupulous advertising is a major concern for media outlets and consumers alike. Publishers, networks, and other communication companies must be sure not to align themselves with companies that make false claims or promote dangerous products. False advertising cannot only damage the reputation of a media outlet, it can also harm the consumer. In the following section we will look at how Americans have monitored advertising using a mixture of government surveillance, consumer advocacy, media self-regulation, and industry self-regulation.

Government Regulations

The first casualty of government regulations in advertising was the pharmaceutical industry. Fed up with false claims and dangerous ingredients, the medical community joined with consumers and publishers to press Congress for the passage of the Pure Food and Drug Act in 1906. The law prohibited claims of undocumented cures, forbade manufacturers to misrepresent the efficacy of their products, and required all ingredients to be identified on the product label. This act particularly exposed the use of alcohol and drugs such as morphine in many pharmaceuticals. While these products apparently produced miraculous effects, more serious problems of addiction or complications were likely to follow the initial relief.

Soon after the Pure Food and Drug Act, the Federal Trade Commission (FTC) was established in 1914. The agency was authorized to regulate advertising and prevent deceptive practices. The FTC monitors and corrects claims of products that "cure" the common cold, guarantee "permanent weight loss," or "reverse baldness." As the FTC grew stronger, it became more proactive in its supervision of advertising practices; rather than merely handling complaints, the agency studied abuses and issued reports that attacked deception and the dissemination of misleading information.

Bait and switch a method of fraudulent advertising in which a company advertises a product at an unprofitable price then reveals to a potential customer that the product is unavailable

In the 1950s, the FTC began to crack down on "bait and switch" ads that lure consumers with a "low-ball" price. **Bait and switch** is a method of fraudulent advertising in which a company advertises a product at an unprofitable price then reveals to a potential customer that the product is unavailable. The FTC charged that many merchants used pressure sales tactics to convince the consumer to "move up" to higher-priced products after claiming that the advertised items were out of stock or not really of satisfactory quality. The FTC also investigated the misuse of the word free in advertisements for products that weren't really free but required the purchase of other goods.

Beginning in the 1970s, the FTC took a hard look at "Brand X" ads, which compared a sponsor's product with an unnamed competitor. The government agency pushed advertisers to (1) name the competitor so the consumer would know which two products were being compared; and (2) cite impartial research data as proof that one product is better or more effective than another.

In order to protect the rights of companies and consumers, the FTC can issue a cease-and-desist order or can levy a fine against advertisers whose messages it feels have injured another firm or a consumer. In the 1970s, the agency began to require "corrective advertising" to offset the effects of long-running campaigns that had misled the public. Profile bread was required to explain to consumers that its claim of having fewer calories per slice was true only because its slices were thinner than those of the competitor, and that using the product would not cause weight loss. The FTC forced Profile to spend one fourth of the company's advertising budget to correct this misleading claim. Some companies have used sneaky maneuvers to sidestep FTC rulings. Ocean Spray, the maker of various juices, was ordered to spend a portion of its advertising budget one year to correct a false claim. The company simply decided not to advertise that year. They rested on the claim that one quarter of zero dollars is zero dollars.[17]

More than 20 U.S. government agencies are empowered to regulate one or more forms of advertising. The U.S. Postal Service screens catalogs and other direct mail advertising for information that would constitute "using the U.S. mail to defraud." The Securities and Exchange Commission keeps an eye on any claims that would tend to create undue expectations for the rise in the value of a stock. The Food and Drug Administration oversees the dissemination of any information concerning foodstuffs, health care products, cosmetics, and drugs. A current area of concern for the FDA is the proliferation of health claims that seek to take advantage of the public's concern about fitness and dieting. In 1991, the agency announced new rules that would curb claims like that of Quaker Oat Bran, which allege to "reduces cholesterol," unless such claims could be substantiated by independent authorities such as the Surgeon General or the National Academy of Sciences.

Manufacturers and the advertising industry constantly pressure government agencies to ease up on regulations for fear that regulations will become as stringent as they are in some other countries. In Malaysia, television ads that show a car driving fast and even flying through the air—a common way of demonstrating the handling of an automobile in American ads—are prohibited because uneducated viewers might attempt to emulate the behavior. Malaysia's strict code controlling TV ads also stipulates that speakers in commercials must use the correct pronunciation of the official Maylay language, not dialects of Chinese or Indian.

Most Americans value their right to receive information without interference. They would not welcome or tolerate government control of entertainment or educational information for reasons of cultural purity or governmental preference. On the other hand, they place great value on receiving accurate information, especially about health and personal products. That is why there has been little or no protest from citizens as legislative and regulatory bodies have become more stringent with advertisers.

---

[17]*Age of Propaganda: The Everyday Use and Abuse of Persuasion* by Anthony Pratkanis and Elliot Aronson. New York: W. H. Freeman (2001).

Subliminal Messages

Surely one of the most pervasive hoaxes of the twentieth century was the notion that "subliminal" advertising was used to make people desire an alcoholic drink, buy a certain make of car, or dash off to a restaurant lusting for a plate of clams. Gullible people with little understanding of psychology—including some state legislators who have introduced bills that would ban "subliminal" ads—fall prey to books and articles suggesting that words hidden in ice cubes, shapes concealed in the folds of a garment, or symbols worked into pictures of food have the power to make the consumer jump up and rush to the store, controlled by some unknown force.

In fact, in certain New Jersey theaters in the 1950s, movie audiences were exposed to images superimposed over the last scenes of films, exhorting them to "Drink Coca-Cola" and "eat popcorn." That caused newspaper editorialists to raise a hue and cry against the "alarming and outrageous" mind-fooling technique they supposed would put consumers in a trance. But it doesn't take much to stimulate a movie audience to get up and move to the refreshment stand during intermission. The "subliminal" trickery was hardly necessary.

Psychological research indicates that intense stimuli have a much greater effect than subtle stimuli. Messages hidden within other images certainly are far too subtle to equal the effects of obvious and overt advertising techniques. Despite these findings, legislators in the U.S. government proposed a ban on subliminal advertising in all forms of media.[18]

The Attack on Cigarette and Liquor Advertising

Because of the wealth of information regarding the health problems caused by cigarette smoking and second hand smoke, cigarettes have been under attack in the United States for nearly half a century. In 1965, a series of findings by the Surgeon General led to required warnings on all cigarette packages and advertisements.

In 1971, after a long congressional debate, cigarette advertising was prohibited from the broadcast media by the federal government, which has more direct control over broadcast media than over print media. The tobacco industry and the broadcast industry maintained—and continued to argue—that the ban was unconstitutional. The temporary setback in advertising revenues for the broadcasters was a gold mine for the print media, which had lost billions of dollars to television over the preceding decade.

Pushed by the American Medical Association in the mid-1980s, Congress debated whether cigarette ads should be banned from the print media as well. The growing number of regulations imposed by the industry on smoking in the workplace

---

[18]Chris Sharp, "Subliminal Messaging: A life changing phenomenon" Helium at http://www.helium.com/items/383493-subliminal-messaging-a-life-changing-phenomenom.

and the decision by the military to restrict smoking helped fuel the spread of anti-smoking information. The industry responded with its own arguments that smokers should be allowed to choose whether to use the product and whether to receive information about it.

Lawyers for the RJ Reynolds Tobacco Company, for example, successfully fought the Federal Trade Commission's decision that one of the firm's advertisements misrepresented the results of a government study of smoking. The ad said that the results of the study were inconclusive. RJ Reynolds contended that the company's interpretation of the study was corporate opinion, and was thus protected by the First Amendment. The FTC simply saw the ad as one of many false claims about a scientific study by the tobacco industry.

What demographic do cigarette ads appeal to the most? © Netrun78/Shutterstock

Research shows that today more college women than college men smoke cigarettes, which researchers attribute to the fact that the tobacco industry is successfully linking smoking by women with images of glamour, success, and equality, as well as a means of staying thin and attractive. All of these charges are denied by the tobacco industry, which maintains that cigarette advertising is now directed only at people who already smoke.

The drive to prohibit all advertising of harmful substances such as tobacco and alcoholic beverages is being spearheaded by the medical community. Ironically, it came shortly after the medical professional societies finally altered their own ethical standards to permit "tasteful and restrained" advertising for doctors and medical institutions—a practice long prohibited by the profession.

Joe Camel

During the 1990s, Joe Camel, the cartoon spokesman for Camel brand cigarettes, was one of the most recognizable characters in American culture. With his dark sunglasses, slick clothes, and entourage of gorgeous friends, Joe Camel stood for all things cool. The Camel cigarette dangling from the corner of his mouth connected the cigarette brand to a favorable image. The fact that Joe Camel was an animated character concerned many consumers. Opponents of the character felt RJ Reynolds Tobacco Company, maker of Camel cigarettes, was using Joe Camel to appeal to children and young teens. A study conducted in 1991 by The Journal of the American Medical Association showed that 6-year-old children were just as familiar with Joe Camel as with Mickey Mouse.[19] The study also showed a connection between the Joe

---

[19]Jane E. Brody, "Study Ties Women's Brands To Smoking Increase for Girls" *The New York Times* February 23, 1994 at http://query.nytimes.com/gst/fullpage.html?res=9405E5DB113BF930A15751C0A962958260&sec=health&spon=&pagewanted=all.

Camel campaign and an increase in teenage smoking. RJ Reynolds denied that it tailored its advertisements to children and conducted its own studies that contradicted those of the American Medical Association.

Still, in 1997 the FFC declared that the Joe Camel campaign violated federal law because of its harmful effects on minors. RJ Reynolds decided not to fight the ruling and chose to replace Joe Camel with a realistic non-animated outline of a camel.[20] Today the stylish image of Joe Camel can only be seen in back issues of magazines or faded billboards; however, the character's impact is still visible in the demographics of today's smokers.

The national debate over the effects of advertising on people who abuse substances has become heated and emotional. A former "Winston man" quit smoking and testified before Congress stating: "My job was to encourage, entice, and lure. I became a high-priced accessory to murder." The National Association to Prevent Impaired Driving, a coalition of a hundred traffic safety, health, and public policy groups, issued a study titled "Beer and Fast Cars" that criticized the brewing companies for sponsoring auto races and putting their emblems on cars. The practice, said the report, targets young blue-collar men, the group with the highest incidence of auto accidents and arrests for driving under the influence of alcohol.

A study conducted for *The Wall Street Journal* showed that U.S. citizens overwhelmingly opposed the illegalization of alcoholic beverages and tobacco products, but their attitudes toward dissemination of information about the substances are quite different. By a substantial majority, the respondents favored banning beer and wine ads from television (hard liquor was already banned) and banning all alcohol and tobacco advertising from print media as well.

Consumers with a Voice

In 1989 advertisers including Ralston Purina, General Mills, and Domino's Pizza canceled their advertising on NBC's controversial sketch comedy show "Saturday Night Live" at the urging of a religious group that viewed the show as objectionable. "It's a difficult time for advertisers," said an NBC spokesperson. "There are a lot of pressure groups out there."

Pepsi discovered that statement to be true when it presented a commercial featuring recording artist Madonna shortly after the controversial music video for her song "Like a Prayer" hit the airwaves. Some religious groups opposed Madonna's use of Christian symbols and deemed the video and the artist distasteful and offensive. Pepsi canceled the Madonna ad feeling its association with the artist would create negative publicity. Pepsi found itself in the same situation again in 2002. However, it only took a complaint by one person to cause the company to change its advertising campaign.

[20]"Joe Camel Advertising Campaign Violates Federal Law, FTC Says" Federal Trade Commission Press Release May 28, 1997 at http://www.ftc.gov/opa/1997/05/joecamel.shtm.

On his news show *The O'Reilly Factor* political commentator Bill O'Reilly questioned Pepsi's use of rapper Ludacris as a company spokesperson, claiming the rapper espouses violence, degrades women, and promotes substance abuse.[21] Pepsi later dropped Ludacris as its spokesperson, but still received negative responses from consumers, and the rapper, who were disappointed that the company gave into pressure from one conservative figure.

It is not the opinions of well know figures that truly concern advertisers, it is the opinion of the American people. Irate individual consumers have always fired off letters and e-mails complaining about ads, but it is when special interest groups get involved that advertisers begin to worry. Groups such as the American Family Association's OneMillionMoms.com often participate in large-scale letter writing campaigns that aim to encourage advertisers to pull spots from television or radio shows that are considered immoral, violent, vulgar, or profane. The group takes credit for convincing large retail chains such as Lowe's to pull advertising from popular, but morally questionable, shows such as ABC's *Desperate Housewives*.[22] Organizations such as the American Family Association petition the advertisers of "distasteful" entertainment in attempt to pull funding from shows the organization finds offensive. A reduction in the number of paid advertisers may cause the entertainment industry to remove certain content from their products.

Today more than ever, advertisers have to walk a fine line in order to avoid offending one or another side of almost any issue. Advertisers must sometimes choose to alienate one segment of the population in order to appeal to their target audience. Still advertisers keep their ear to the ground when it comes to the opinion of the American consumer. A tarnished brand image can result in a major loss in revenue for advertisers.

ACT Against Predator Advertising

Action for Children's Television (ACT), a grass-roots organization formed by Peggy Charren in 1968, was created out of concern regarding the lack of suitable television programs for children. The group also had concerns about the type of advertising shown within children's programming. In 1989, ACT served as a consultant to the Consumers Union's holiday special, a program aimed to educate parents and children on the seduction of toy advertisements around the holiday season. "Buy Me That!", broadcasted on HBO, dissected several misleading techniques, including the implication that toys can walk and talk, the suggestion that a toy house or gas station comes with all the people and cars shown in the ad, and the failure to make clear that "some assembly required" may mean that an adult has to build a toy from parts before a

---

[21]Bill O'Reilly "Challenging Pepsi" *The O'Reilly Factor* August 28, 2002 at http://www.foxnews.com/story/0,2933,61546,00.html.

[22]Frank Rich "The Great Indecency Hoax" *The New York Times* November 28, 2004 at http://www.nytimes.com/2004/11/28/arts/28rich.html?pagewanted=print&position.

child can play with it. The program also revealed how ads that show children happily bouncing around on Pogo Balls and tossing Flip Balls with the ease of Olympic athletes are the results of editing, and it is unlikely that most kids will be able to perform with the same happy satisfaction as those depicted on the screen.[23]

ACTs most successful campaign occurred when the organization helped pass the Children's Television Act of 1990, which increased the quality of educational and informational television. Shortly after the act was passed, Charren closed ACT and suggested that it was now up to parents to police the airwaves and decide for themselves what type of programs are best for their children.[24]

Media Self-Regulation

Mass media producers usually exercise their rights to refuse advertising that is in bad taste or that makes questionable claims and they are also in the position to reject spots that touch on controversial political issues. On the night of the 1984 presidential election, the WR Grace Company began running an "issues" spot on network television that depicted a baby crying when it was handed a bill for $50,000—the child's share of the national deficit. Two of the networks accepted the ad, but one rejected it. In 1986, the company submitted a new version of the ad to the networks depicting an elderly man on trial in the year 2017 for failing to do anything to halt the growing national debt. This time all three networks would not accept the ad, stating that it was too controversial and exposed the networks to possible complaints under the **Fairness Doctrine**, a policy created by the FCC that required the coverage of all controversial issues to be fair and balanced.

Fairness Doctrine a policy created by the FCC that required the coverage of all controversial issues to be fair and balanced

J. Peter Grace, chairman and chief executive officer of the firm, responded: "They sell commercial time to advertise detergents, lingerie, hamburgers, appliances, and beer. Can it really be argued that selling time for conveying facts or ideas on important public issues will be detrimental to the interests of the country or the three networks?" Grace scoffed at the networks' contention that their news departments could do a better job of covering political issues than could business interests using advertising as a tool of information.

Most of the American advertising industry agreed with Grace and saw the network move as an attempt to pressure the Congress to do away with the Fairness Doctrine. In other words, the issues ads were being used as bargaining chips by the networks in their quest for less regulation. In 1987, the FCC finally did abolish most provisions of the Fairness Doctrine, but the regulatory body announced that it would continue to enforce the provision stating that issues currently the subject of voter referenda come under the Fairness Doctrine. Thus, opponents have to be given free air time to respond to statements made by another side on the issue.

---

[23]Walter Goodman, "TV VIEW; A Cautionary Guide for Little Customers" *The New York Times* December 3, 1989 at http://query.nytimes.com/gst/fullpage.html?res=950DE1D61030F930A35751C1A96F948260&sec=&spon=&pagewanted=all.

[24]William Richter, "Action for Children's Television" The Museum of Broadcast Communication at http://www.museum.tv/archives/etv/A/htmlA/actionforch/actionforch.htm.

For a long time the National Association of Broadcasters code was another media mechanism that affected what advertisers could do. First drafted in 1929, the code did not have the force of law; it was accepted by individual stations as a condition of membership in the NAB. When a suit resulted in the 1982 court decision that such a code unduly restricted the freedom to communicate information through advertising, the NAB withdrew it. Nevertheless, many of its provisions had been adopted as part of the standards and practices followed by individual stations, and thus they survive today.

The NAB code prohibited or limited the presentation of some products, which is why you never see hard liquor in commercials, and nobody actually *drinks* the beer or wine being advertised. Actors in commercials are permitted to be shown only lifting the glass or bottle toward or away from their lips. The film editor cuts away from the action during the moment when the liquid ostensibly is being guzzled.

Without the authority of the NAB code, broadcast stations are finding it more and more difficult to explain what messages are acceptable for commercials or public service announcements, and why. For example, a station had a long-standing policy of refusing messages advocating birth control, explaining that "controversial issues" were not suitable for ads and were more properly covered by public affairs discussion programs. The station decided to accept condom ads, however, if they were presented as part of a campaign to slow the spread of HIV/AIDS or other sexually transmitted diseases.

Did you ever wonder why you never see anyone actually DRINK the wine they're advertising?
© iofoto/Shutterstock

Most media will not accept an anonymous advertisement that discusses a public issue or in any way takes a political stand. The name of at least one sponsoring person must be placed in the ad. The media will refuse the ad if they cannot verify that the sponsoring name is a valid one. The media also rejects advertisements they feel may open them to libel suits; in the eyes of the law it is the media who publish the defamation and thus share the responsibility for it, even if the damaging words were written by the sponsor.

Industry Self-Regulation

In order to forestall regulation, the business community and the advertising industry try to prevent abuses that might lead to public outrage and government interference. Most advertisers support their local Better Business Bureaus in the campaign to warn consumers about fraudulent claims and deceptive practices. The local telephone company's yellow pages will not accept advertising it deems to be misleading, and merchants must prove claims they are the "best" or the "only" before the telephone book will carry those words.

The National Advertising Review Council (NARC) was formed by the national Better Business Bureau, the American Advertising Federation, the American Association of Advertising Agencies, and the Association of National

Advertisers—in short, the major forces in the advertising industry—for the purpose of self-regulating advertising. The investigative body of the NARC is the National Advertising Division (NAD), which is empowered to initiate inquiries into deceptive or misleading advertising and to hear complaints from both consumers and advertisers.

In a typical complaint to the NAD, Orville Redenbacher popcorn charged that General Mills' Pop Secret cheese flavored microwave popcorn claimed consumers preferred its product to Orville Redenbacher's cheese flavored popcorn, but the test was taken before Redenbacher had reformulated its product and the ad was run after the new product was on the market. In a later test, Redenbacher claimed, its popcorn scored higher. General Mills said its ad had completed its run, and new ads would not be run until after further testing. Case closed.

A more exotic complaint was lodged by the Children's Advertising Review Unit of the NAD against a copying machine company whose ads showed frustrated business people throwing their copiers out of windows. The complaint said that the dangerous act of throwing things out windows might lead impressionable children to imitate the practice, and the scenes of copying machines crashing on the sidewalk might cause anxiety in young children. The sponsoring firm agreed to consider those concerns when planning new ads.

The NAD does not have the power to censor ads, impose fines, or bring any other sanctions. But both the act of review and the publication of the results in the leading trade publications are instructive to the advertising community and help prevent future abuses or excesses. In practice, the NARC and NAD have been effective forces in serving the information needs of the consumer.

THE FUTURE OF ADVERTISING: KEEPING CURRENT

With the introduction and expansion of new media, the advertising industry will have to continue to evolve. While traditional media such as television, newspapers, and radio will still be important outlets, advertisers must look at the cultural trends to determine the best way to reach consumers.

New Technology

Since a growing number of people are looking to the Internet to stay up-to-date on news and entertainment, advertisers are going to look to the Internet to spend large portions of their budgets. Paid search and pay-per-click advertising is just the beginning. Viral videos and blogs will emerge as an effective way to reach consumers.

Mobile phones have also changed the game for advertising. As a device that people rarely leave home without, mobile advertising is riding on the heels of the Internet as the newest way to deliver commercial messages to consumers 24 hours a day. Today's mobile phones are far more advanced than the two-pound clunkers introduced in the 1980s. With the ability to browse Web pages and send e-mails, mobile phones are like handheld

Advertisers may start sending full length commercials to consumers' PDAs. © Monkey Business Images/Shutterstock

computers. Now that many cell phone makers are creating phones with flash technology, it can be possible to send full length commercials to thousands of consumers via their mobile phones.

Product Placement

When you watch episodes of your favorite TV show or movie you may notice the main character is drinking a Vitamin Water and wearing a Ralph Lauren Polo shirt. Those items were not randomly placed in the scene; they were put there by advertisers. Advertisers hope that consumers see a character wearing or using a certain product then want to emulate that character's choices.

The practice of inserting advertising into film and television entertainment came under scrutiny when consumers started to take notice. The executive director of the Center for Science in the Public Interest used the op-ed page of *The New York Times* as a forum for alerting the public to the amount of advertising that is finding its way into the movies we pay to see. In one movie, "Bull Durham," he counted the presence of Miller beer products or signs 21 times, along with obvious plugs for a soft drink, a brand of bourbon, and even Oscar Mayer wieners—a total of 50 brand names on screen for an average of one every two minutes.

Today, some television shows can have up to 7,500 instances of product placement in a single season. TV executives may worry that too much product placement may harm the integrity of a show, but as more and more advertisers are choosing the Internet over TV, they welcome the revenue. For advertisers looking to continue marketing products on television, product placement will be an increasing force.

Guerrilla Marketing

Traditional advertisements like the 30 second commercial and the newspaper insert will soon take a back seat to more exciting and cost-effective forms of advertising formulated by guerrilla marketing. **Guerrilla marketing** is an unconventional form of advertising that attempts to get the maximum result from minimal resources. Examples of this type of advertising could involve a person running the New York City Marathon in a chicken suit and signs advertising a new fast food restaurant chain. The gimmick may cost a few hundred dollars, but the message could reach over one million spectators and possibly get news coverage.

Guerrilla marketing
an unconventional form of advertising that attempts to get the maximum result from minimal resources

Guerrilla marketing is not always used for a cheap laugh; it can sometimes call attention to serious issues. At Taiba Hospital in Kuwait, administrators painted pink strips on a speed bump at the entrance of the hospital. A sign next to the speed bump said, "Feel the bump? Have your breasts checked." The ad was a high impact way to remind women to get a yearly breast examination.[25]

In the next decade we will see a lot of changes in the way advertisers deliver their commercial messages and the number of commercial messages we are exposed to will continue to grow. Whether these changes and increases will

---

[25]"Taiba Hospital: Feel the bump? Have your breasts checked" www.Jazzarh.net March 18, 2008 at http://www.jazarah.net/blog/taiba-hospital-felt-the-bump-have-your-breasts-checked/.

benefit us as consumers or saturate our lives with unneeded products is unclear. However, good or bad advertising will still remain an integral part of our economy and culture.

Social networking and social media are upending some ideas about how advertising works because people often hear about products from friends via Twitter or Facebook, and bypass advertising agencies and media organizations altogether. This is a new phenomenon and its full impact on advertising and messaging is as yet unknown.

Predictions about Advertising

- The 30-Second Spot will finally die. The funeral will be attended by the 60-Second Spot, the Radio Ad, the Infomercial, and the Bumper Sticker.
- Blogs will change everything. For marketers, the blogosphere will prompt them to think very seriously about their business models.
- The consumer will be boss.
- The FDA will crack down on illegal drug marketing via the Internet.
- Advertising "one-stop shops" will thrive. As marketers are pressed to find ways to reach consumers, advertising holding companies like WPP and Interpublic will continue to evolve into "one-stop shops" for everything from advertising to guerrilla marketing to package design.
- The Hispanic consumer will arrive. After years of treating the Hispanic segment as an afterthought, marketers will shift more money to addressing the demographic with a much greater amount of TV, print, and online ads featuring Latinos.
- Marketers will continue to fear Google.

Todd Wasserman

CAREERS IN THE FIELD

After seeing a commercial have you ever thought to yourself, I could come up with a better way to deliver that message? If so, perhaps you should consider a career in advertising. The field of advertising can be very exciting for creative and managerial types alike. However, advertising involves more than just coming up with catchy jingles or clever slogans. It involves a high level of research, analysis, and at the heart of it all, salesmanship. There are different facets of advertising that job seekers might find interesting. On the administrative side, positions include account management, media planning, and market research. When hiring for these positions, agencies look for candidates with a strong business mind, effective communication skills, and leadership experience. On the creative side, openings are in copywriting and art direction. Agencies typically look for copywriters and art directors with the ability to think outside of the box and come up with innovative ideas that will benefit the client and the consumer. Jobs in advertising are a bit scarce and competition for positions, especially on the creative side, can be tough. However, if you have the right combination of business sense and creativity, you might just stand out in the crowd.[26]

SUMMARY

- Americans are exposed to thousands of commercial messages a day from various types of media outlets.
- Advertising has evolved over the years to adapt to the changes in mass media.
- Advertisers go beyond standard television and radio commercials to advertise products. They use methods such as direct mail, point-of-sale advertising, outdoor signage, and the Internet to promote their message.
- Government agency, community groups, and the media regulate advertisements to ensure they are not dishonest, misleading, or distasteful.
- Advertising is a continuous force in our economy, and advertisers are finding new and inventive ways to reach consumers.

DISCUSSION QUESTIONS

1. How aware are you of the advertising in your environment? Do you think you have ever been swayed to purchase a product without being aware of the commercial message that prompted your purchase?
2. Do you think you benefit from advertising? Do you use it to help make decisions about what products to buy?
3. Do you think that banning tobacco advertising is against the first amendment? Should tobacco companies have the same rights as other companies?
4. Do you think advertising has become too intrusive? Would you be willing to pay more money to media outlets if they removed advertising?
5. What examples of guerrilla marketing have you noticed in the last few years?

SUPPLEMENTAL WEB SITES

[26]"Guide to Careers in Advertising" Advertising Educational Foundation at http://www.aef.com/industry/careers/1422#3.

LAW AND ETHICS

CHAPTER OBJECTIVES

- Define and distinguish among law, policy, and ethics
- Understand the history, theories, and interpretations of free speech and free press in the United States
- Identify legal, ownership, and regulatory issues faced by the mass media
- Understand the ways in which ethics is relevant to individuals in the media, as well as to media organizations

13

KEY TERMS

actual malice
censorship
clear and present danger
    doctrine
commercial speech doctrine
common law
copyright law
ethics
fair use doctrine
false light
imminent lawless action
    doctrine
indecency
intrusion upon seclusion
laws
libel

marketplace of ideas
misappropriation
negligence
obscenity
patent law
plagiarism
policy
prior restraint
prior review
profanity
reckless disregard
sedition
social responsibility model
tort
trademark law

Most of us don't feel bad about speeding until we get caught! © Lisa F. Young/Shutterstock

INTRODUCTION

In theory, the laws of society are based on the ethical morals and values of the people living in it. For the most part, this theory is true, and many laws uphold what most of us know to be fundamentally wrong, such as murder and theft. Other laws, however, are commonly broken. When was the last time you drove a car above the legal speed limit? Traffic laws are among those that many of us break—and usually feel little remorse for doing so. The gray areas between these extremes reflect the fact that we all have our individual beliefs about right and wrong, and we often disagree about legal matters. Controversial moral issues such as immigration, abortion, and the death penalty have been issues of contention in the United States for decades. While legislative decisions determine the legality of these issues, members of society continue to argue about the ethics of them.

On a smaller scale, individuals work out their disputes about who is right and who is wrong in small claims and divorce courts. Our litigious society is so rife with these squabbles that we can even watch as other people's petty tiffs are mediated on television by the likes of Judge Judy. According to the National Center for State Courts, state trial courts averaged about one incoming civil, domestic relations, criminal, juvenile, or traffic case for every three American citizens in 2003. That's over 100 million cases in state systems alone![1]

Lawsuits aren't only born of the disputes between individuals; media and other organizations also contribute to this case crunch. The Recording Industry Association of America reported that it brought suit against 8,650 file sharers in 2005, many of them students using university high-speed connections. This organization alone brought to court an average of over 700 lawsuits a month. While the debate over the legality of file-sharing may have some ethical concerns, this controversy highlights how disputes about morality may be veils for disputes about money and the competing interests not of consciences, but of cash.

In this chapter we will look at the landscape of media law and ethics, how they interact, and how they affect media organizations and professionals.

policy
an overarching plan or goal of a country or an organization

laws
statutes passed by legislative bodies at federal, state, or local levels; administrative mandates from agencies like the Federal Communications Commission; or rulings handed down by judges to implement policy plans or goals

LAW, POLICY, AND ETHICS

While legislation often overlaps with our morals, it is important to recognize the different definitions for terms involved in a discussion of these issues. **Policy** is an overarching plan or goal of a country or an organization, and **laws** are put into place to implement a policy plan or goal. Laws can take the form of statutes passed by legislative bodies at federal, state, or local levels; administrative mandates from

---

[1]National Center for State Courts, "*National Center for State Courts Overview,*" retrieved November 12, 2008 from http://www.ncsconline.org/D_Research/csp/2004_Files/EWOverview_final_2.pdf February 2005.

agencies like the Federal Communications Commission (FCC); or rulings handed down by judges—**common law**. **Ethics**, on the other hand, often informs law but, more specifically, involves balancing competing interests to determine the "right" or "correct" course of action.

As an example, the United States has a policy that government should be generally open to its constituents. In other words, most governing should not take place in secrecy: the House and Senate are presumed to have open sessions unless there is a need to close them, and all states have open meetings and records laws. Ethics informs the open government idea by suggesting that having "government in a fishbowl" is morally correct in a democracy, where

The Supreme Court is the highest judicial body in the U.S. © Liz Van Steenburgh/Shutterstock

the rulers rule with the consent of the governed. In the case of executive agencies, like the FCC, the Food and Drug Administration, and the Federal Aviation Administration, the policy of openness of records is codified into law by the federal Freedom of Information Act (FOIA). The FOIA requires agencies to make requested records available to the public unless the records fall under nine exemptions to openness, such as harming national security interests.

In the United States, the highest judicial body is the Supreme Court. Made up of nine men and women and based in Washington, D.C., the Supreme Court is responsible for deciding some of the most controversial and morally charged cases. Unless Congress passes a law or a Constitutional amendment is passed to contradict the Court's ruling, these decisions are final and make up the body of common law, also referred to as case law.

common law
rulings handed down by judges

ethics
a set of principles and beliefs intended to guide people to act in a "right" or "correct" way

The Supreme Court

The Supreme Court is at the top of the American judicial system, the court of last resort. Made up of nine men and women (only two African-Americans and three women have ever served), the Court's members are appointed by the President, confirmed by the Senate, and serve until they retire, die, or are impeached. Only 111 individuals have served on this prestigious Court, and 17 of those have been chief justices.

The current chief justice is John Roberts, appointed by President George W. Bush in September 2005. He replaced William H. Rehnquist, who died that same month. Chief Justice Roberts presides over eight associate justices who range in age from late-50s to late-80s. Justice John Paul Stevens was appointed by President Gerald Ford in 1975 and is the oldest member of the Court at age 90. Justice Stevens announced his retirement in 2010, giving President Obama his second opportunity to appoint a Supreme Court justice. His first appointment was Justice Sonia Sotomayor, the third woman and first Hispanic to serve on the Court.

How does a case get to the Supreme Court? Some would say it takes a lot of luck: most of the Court's caseload is discretionary. The justices pick and choose the cases they will hear; from the more than 7,000 petitions they receive, they will vote to hear about 100 per term and issue written opinions in 80 to 90 of those cases. Four of the nine justices must vote to allow a case to have oral arguments before the full Court.

The Court has occupied its current building in Washington, D.C. since 1935. Prior to that, other branches of the federal government lent the Court space to meet in their buildings. The current Supreme Court building is classic Corinthian style and features many sculptures that memorialize important figures and concepts in the law. It is open to the public for tours, and interested individuals may even watch oral arguments take place in the Court's main courtroom.

The Constitution contains a Bill of Rights which gives important protections to individuals.
© Onur ERSIN/Shutterstock

HISTORY OF FREE SPEECH AND PRESS IN AMERICA

The Constitution of the United States contains a Bill of Rights, which gives important protections to individuals in America. It reads, "Congress shall make no law respecting an establishment of religion, or prohibiting the free exercise thereof; or abridging the freedom of speech, or of the press; or the right of the people peaceably to assemble, and to petition the government for a redress of grievances." Within that amendment are five discrete rights: free speech, free press, freedom of religion, freedom of assembly, and freedom to petition the government. We will focus primarily on the free press aspect, although a free press is of course closely related to freedom of speech.

As we will see, even though the First Amendment explicitly says that "Congress shall make no law . . . abridging the freedom . . . of the press," Congress makes laws affecting the media all the time. Most of the body of First Amendment law is made up of limitations on governmental power to regulate speech and press.

The Zenger Trial: The Importance of Truth

A significant landmark for free speech and press occurred in 1735, when John Peter Zenger's newspaper, the *New York Weekly Journal,* criticized William Cosby, governor of New York. The governor put Zenger in jail for violating the law of **sedition**, which was quite clear at the time: Criticism of the government or its officials, even if true, that aroused the sentiments of the people against the government or the officials would be considered seditious libel, and there was no defense.

Zenger hired renowned Philadelphia attorney Andrew Hamilton, who took a unique approach to the problem. He knew that Zenger had, under the law, libeled Governor Cosby. Instead of trying to argue that Zenger had not libeled the

sedition
criticism of the government or its officials

governor, Hamilton instead attacked the law itself. He asked the jury to consider whether truth should not be considered to be a defense to libel: "I hope it is not our bare printing and publishing a paper that will make it a libel. You will have something more to do before you make my client a libeler. For the words themselves must be libelous that is, false, scandalous, and seditious or else we are not guilty." To drive home the point, Hamilton added, "Truth ought to govern the whole affair of libels."[2]

The jury went into deliberation and returned a verdict of not guilty, and Zenger was freed. The Zenger case remains important for several reasons. It is one of the earliest and most famous jury nullifications, in which the jury gives a "not guilty" verdict despite the fact that they believe the defendant was responsible for the action because they believe the law itself is wrong; and second, it is a strong statement of the importance of truth in American media law.

Early Theories of Free Speech and Press

There have always been individuals hostile to attempts by the government to regulate their speech, either through **prior review**—forcing material to be shared with the regulating body prior to its publication or broadcast—and **prior restraint**—banning the publication or broadcast of the material after reviewing it—or **censorship**—prohibiting the publication or broadcast of certain material. In England in 1644, John Milton wrote *Areopagitica: For the Liberty of Unlicensed Printing* in response to a licensing order from Parliament. The order required authors and creators to submit their works to licensors for permission to publish. In the pamphlet, Milton denounced the licensing arrangement and called for government to hold publishers and authors accountable for what they wrote after it had been published, instead of engaging in prior review. Milton too supported truth as the ultimate goal of publication: "And though all the winds of doctrine were let loose to play upon the earth, so Truth be in the field, we do injuriously by licensing and prohibiting to misdoubt her strength. Let her and Falsehood grapple; who ever knew Truth put to the worse in a free and open encounter?"

In 1859, John Stuart Mill, an English philosopher and theorist, added his book *On Liberty* to the lexicon of defenses of free speech. He proposed a "harm principle," in which he suggests that the only legitimate way in which society can interfere with the free action of another is to prevent harm: "The sole end for which mankind are warranted, individually or collectively, in interfering with the liberty of action of any of their number, is self-protection. That the only purpose for which power can be rightfully exercised over any member of a civilized community, against his will, is to prevent harm to others."[3] Mill argued that free speech is necessary for a self-governing nation. Without free discourse, truth may never emerge and individuals will never be able to examine their beliefs with an open dialogue to be sure that those beliefs are correct.

prior review
the process of regulating speech by reviewing it in advance of publication

prior restraint
banning the publication or broadcast of material after prior review

censorship
the process of regulating speech by prohibiting its publication or broadcast

---

[2]Lief, Michael S. and Harry M. Caldwell. And the Walls Came Tumbling Down: Closing Arguments that Changed the Way We Live, from *Protecting Free Speech to Winning Women's Suffrage to Defending the Right to Die*. New York: Simon and Schuster, 2004.

[3]Mill, John Stuart. *On Liberty*. Edited by David Bromwich and George Kateb. Binghampton: Vail-Ballou, 2003.

marketplace of ideas
a theory of free speech and press asserting that all ideas should be permitted to be published and disseminated so that consumers may pick and choose from among them

Mill's writings form the foundation for the **marketplace of ideas** theory of free speech and press. Under this theory, all ideas should be permitted to be published and disseminated so that consumers may pick and choose, culling through the falsities and bad ideas to find the good ones. Thus, the government should not engage in censorship because it is important to a free flow of information and ideas that all ideas, no matter how farfetched, dangerous, or seditious, must be allowed to be distributed.

EARLY INTERPRETATIONS OF THE FIRST AMENDMENT

Although the Bill of Rights was ratified in 1791, it was not until the early 1900s that the First Amendment would first be interpreted—and in the context of free speech, not press. In several cases during World War I that involved individuals opposed to the draft (*Schenck v. United States* and *Abrams v. United States*, both in 1919) the **clear and present danger doctrine** was suggested. Under this doctrine, the government may only punish a speech act if it invokes a clear and present danger of harm. For example, if an individual falsely shouts fire in a crowded theater and causes a panic when patrons trample each other to the exits, the government may punish the shouter for causing a clear and present danger. This doctrine is still in use today, although it was modified in 1969 in *Brandenburg v. Ohio* to become the **imminent lawless action doctrine**, whereby the government may only punish speech that directly provokes imminent lawless action. In *Gitlow v. New York* (1925), the Supreme Court made the First Amendment applicable to the states via the Fourteenth Amendment.

clear and present danger doctrine
a doctrine asserting that the government may only punish a speech act if it invokes a clear and present danger of harm

imminent lawless action doctrine
a revision to the clear and present danger doctrine asserting that the government may only punish speech that directly provokes imminent lawless action

More important for the press, however, was a 1931 case that made the press nearly immune from most censorship. Jay Near published a rabblerousing newspaper called *The Saturday Press* in Minneapolis. The paper was anti-Semitic, anti-black, anti-labor, and anti-Catholic, and Minneapolis officials ordered the paper shut down under a nuisance law. Near appealed, and his case went to the Supreme Court.

In *Near v. Minnesota* (1931), the Supreme Court said that in most cases, prior restraint would be illegal in all but three instances: the publication of troop movements during wartime could be subject to prior restraint, as could obscene speech and incitements to violent overthrow of the government. This case had the ultimate effect of barring most censorial actions by the government on the media, and its ruling was relied upon in the famous "Pentagon Papers" case of the 1970s (*New York Times Co. v. United States*, 1971), which permitted the *New York Times* to publish classified information about the war in Southeast Asia that the government had not proven would cause "grave and irreparable" damage to national security concerns.

LEGAL ISSUES FACING THE MASS MEDIA

With great freedom, as the American press has, comes great responsibility. As noted above, the courts and Congress regularly make laws that affect the media. These laws exist to protect consumers and give them recourse if they have been harmed by the media in some way. Many of the laws are a check on the media's power to harm—either through falsities, shabby reporting, invasion of individual privacy, or infringement of intellectual property rights.

American broadcasters operate under a more restrictive regime of laws than newspapers, magazines, and other print media. Under this dual system of regulation, the broadcast media—over-the-air "free" television and radio—are subject to additional regulations on what they may or may not do. These restrictions were originally put into place because the broadcast media are trustees of what was believed to be a scarce, public resource (the airwaves). Now, as cable, satellite, and high-definition TV and radio are becoming more and more popular, these regulations have outlasted the original justifications for them.

Issues of ownership and access have been important areas of concern for both media professionals and the public. Who gets to participate in the marketplace of ideas, and whose ideas will not see the light of day? How is media concentrated, and who owns what? All of these questions are important to understanding the role of mass media in a modern age. Despite the rise of Web 2.0 and the participatory Internet community, many individuals still get their news and information through traditional media like television and newspapers, and the owners of these media have a large, and arguably disproportionate, ability to affect what we believe to be important (see the discussion of agenda-setting in Ch. 11).

Why are the broadcast media subjected to more restrictive regulation than print media?
© Florian ISPAS/Shutterstock

Advertising is also regulated in small and large ways. The Supreme Court has developed the **commercial speech doctrine** to determine when and how advertising can be regulated, and, as noted in Ch. 13, the advertising industry has an active self-regulatory system in place to police itself and its participants.

We first turn to areas of First Amendment jurisprudence that affect all forms of mass media, regardless of message or technology.

commercial speech doctrine
a set of Supreme Court mandates giving limited protection to speech that advocates a commercial transaction

Libel

Any media organization, whether news, advertising, public relations, or entertainment, may be sued for **libel**—an untruthful, defamatory statement about someone that is published or broadcast through the media. Organizations are wary of libel suits. According to the Media Law Research Center, the average award for plaintiffs who won libel suits between 1980 and 2006 was $560,092.[4] The highest award against a media organization was $222.7 million, against the *Wall Street Journal* in 1997 (*MMAR Group, Inc. v. Dow Jones & Co.,* 1997). Because of the cost involved, media organizations of all types take libel actions very seriously.

The libel with which Zenger was charged is much different from libel actions of today. Of course, the media have many more protections than they did in Zenger's time, and now the burden rests on the aggrieved party to prove not only

libel
an untruthful, defamatory statement about someone that is published or broadcast through the media

---

[4]Media Law Resource Center, "Annual Study of Media Trials Analyzes 14 Trials In 2006: 9 Wins, 5 Losses," http://www.medialaw.org/Content/NavigationMenu/About_MLRC/News/2007_Bulletin_No_1.htm.

that his or her reputation was harmed (defamation), but also that the publication was false and that the harm resulted in some compensable damage that the court can remedy.

Prior to 1964, libel operated in the common law, and under the common law of libel, a person who believed that he/she had been libeled had only to prove that his/her reputation had been harmed, the information had been published, and he/she had been sufficiently identified in that publication. But in the case of *New York Times v. Sullivan* (1964), arguably one of the most important First Amendment cases in history, the Supreme Court changed the rules.

In that case, L.B. Sullivan, a police commissioner in Montgomery, Ala., argued that he had been identified and defamed in an advertisement taken out by civil rights groups in the *New York Times*. Sullivan was never mentioned by name but said that the text of the ad, which criticized the actions of the police, criticized him as well. The Alabama Supreme Court agreed and awarded Sullivan $500,000 in damages. The *Times* appealed, and the United States Supreme Court reversed the award and developed a new test to determine if public officials like Sullivan have been libeled and are entitled to monetary compensation.

The Court stated that public officials should be open to criticism and that debate on issues of public importance should be "uninhibited, robust, and wide-open" and may contain harsh attacks on public officials. Those public officials may only recover damages for libel under certain limited circumstances. Public officials, in addition to proving defamation, identification, and publication under the common law, must also prove that the media organization acted with **actual malice**—either knew the information it was publishing was false and published it anyway, or acted with **reckless disregard** as to truth or falsity, that is, it didn't care if what it was publishing was true or not. This requirement made it much harder for public officials—and later, public figures like celebrities and professional sports figures—to recover damages for libel. A 1974, *Gertz v. Welch*, set the bar lower for private individuals, who must only prove **negligence** (journalistic sloppiness) rather than actual malice in order to recover for libel.

Libel doesn't just exist on newsprint and over the airwaves. Individuals and companies who libel someone online are subject to the same rules as those who libel in traditional media. However, internet service providers like NetZero or Earthlink are not liable for damages for the distribution of the libelous material, thanks to a law that is part of the Telecommunications Act of 1996. Section 230, as it is often called, exempts internet service providers from liability for libel as long as they do not act as editors of the materials posted. For example, if one individual libels another on a public America Online (AOL) message board, the victim may sue the perpetrator of the libel but not AOL.

Privacy

In the age of identity theft and the omnipresent media, consumers are more concerned than ever about protecting themselves from intrusion into their private lives. Media law considers invasion of privacy to be a **tort**—an injury or wrong inflicted on one person by another person, who is legally responsible for any

---

actual malice
the publication of information with the knowledge that it is false

reckless disregard
the lack of media concern over the truth or falsity of the information they are publishing

negligence
journalistic sloppiness

tort
an injury or wrong inflicted on one person by another person, who is legally responsible for any damages sought

The Food Lion Story

Imagine flipping on your television and watching an investigative program that suggests that your local grocery store, to maximize its profits, was bleaching old meat and reselling it, selling spoiled potato salad, or forcing its employees to work additional hours without paying them. You'd be unlikely to shop at that store again!

In North Carolina in 1996, a jury awarded a $5.5 million verdict against ABC News for a 1992 *PrimeTime Live* investigation on Food Lion, a Southern grocery chain. Food Lion alleged that ABC's journalists had gotten jobs in Food Lion stores by creating fraudulent resumes that lied about grocery work experience and had trespassed with hidden cameras to film behind-the-scenes work at several Food Lion stores. Moreover, Food Lion claimed that the footage had been edited to suggest things that were not true: a clip about an employee telling an ABC reporter disguised as her colleague that a deli product had soured and was cut before the employee instructs the reporter to throw the product away. The verdict was later reduced on appeal.

ABC defended its actions by saying that it was deceiving for a greater good: to reveal dangerous and illegal activities by Food Lion. Food Lion never sued ABC for libel, so the truth or falsity of the broadcast was never considered in court. The case raises issues in both law and ethics. Does the end ultimately justify the means? Should hidden cameras ever be permissible under any circumstances? Should lying to get to the truth be an acceptable ethical approach? Should the law punish truthful information gained by deceptive means?

damages sought. The common law of privacy includes four torts: intrusion upon seclusion, publication of private facts, false light, and misappropriation. Each state may recognize one or more of the privacy torts as causes of action.

> **intrusion upon seclusion**
> a physical invasion of one's personal space or property

Intrusion Upon Seclusion

Intrusion upon seclusion is a physical invasion of one's personal space or property—think of your cranky neighbor's NO TRESPASSING sign. Media professionals are not permitted to trespass on private property to get a story or to use telephoto lenses to peer through a window. As discussed earlier, Jacqueline Kennedy Onassis obtained restraining orders against a photographer who hounded her and her children in search of their images to sell to media publications (*Galella v. Onassis*, 1973).

Publication of Private Facts

As you may have guessed, publication of private facts occurs when the media obtain private facts about a person and publish them. Oliver Sipple experienced this tort when he saved the life of

What is intrusion upon seclusion?
© Vlue/Shutterstock

President Gerald Ford from an assassin's bullet. Sipple was gay and active in the San Francisco gay community, a fact that his family and employer did not know. When the local newspaper found out that he was gay, it hailed him not only as a hero but a gay hero, resulting in his estrangement from his family. Sipple sued the newspaper and lost; the court reasoned that because he was "out" in San Francisco and active in his local gay community, the fact that he was gay was not really private (*Sipple v. Chronicle Publishing,* 1984).

False Light

false light
the effect caused by the media distorting or falsifying information to imply untruths about someone

Similar to libel, **false light** occurs when the media distorts or falsifies information and implies untruths about someone. This tort is perhaps best typified by the story of Linda Duncan, who was filmed walking down the street by a Washington, D.C. news station. A shot of her face accompanied a voiceover for the news story about a possible new cure for genital herpes which said, "For the 20 million Americans who have herpes, it's not a cure." Duncan, who did not have herpes, sued the television station and won because the court said a reasonable person viewing the newscast would assume that the juxtaposition of the voiceover and Duncan's image meant that she had herpes (*Duncan v. WJLA-TV, Inc.,* 1984).

Misappropriation

misappropriation
the use of someone else's name or likeness for commercial gain without consent

Misappropriation occurs when someone uses someone else's name or likeness for commercial gain without consent. Late-night talk show host Johnny Carson successfully sued for misappropriation when a company whose business was to rent and sell portable toilets called its products "Here's Johnny Portable Toilets" without Carson's consent. The defendants admitted they would not have chosen the name without the association to Carson and his famous introduction phrase, "Heeeeeeeeeeeeere's Johnny!" which is strongly associated with him and his nightly program (*Carson v. Here's Johnny Portable Toilets,* 1983).

copyright law
statutes protecting original creations, either published or unpublished, when they are set down in fixed form

Intellectual Property

In the information age, rather than buying and selling wheat and cotton, we trade in information, which has become an important commodity. A large legal practice has arisen around the protection of this kind of property, including written work, music, company product names and logos, and inventions. The Constitution offers protection for intellectual property "to promote the Progress of Science and useful Arts, by securing for limited Times to Authors and Inventors the exclusive Right to their respective Writings and Discoveries."

trademark law
statutes shielding consumers from confusion by protecting words, symbols, or phrases used to identify products and distinguish them from each other

Intellectual property law can be divided into three different areas: copyright, trademark, and patent law. **Copyright law** protects original creations, either published or unpublished, when they are set down in fixed form (like written on paper or saved as a computer file). **Trademark law** shields consumers from confusion by protecting words, symbols, or phrases used to identify products from each other. **Patent law** gives inventors exclusive rights to benefit from their inventions for a limited time; patents can be granted to inventions that are novel, useful, and not obvious.

patent law
statutes giving inventors exclusive rights to benefit from their inventions for a limited time if those inventions are novel, useful, and not obvious

Copyright

Copyright is protected only by federal law. While creators don't have to register their copyrights on their creative works to have protection, doing so gives the creator additional protections and benefits. At the same time, just because a work is copyrighted does not mean that it cannot be used by anyone else for any reason. The **fair use doctrine** provides for some uses of copyrighted materials without the permission of the copyright holder. For example, a newspaper reporter reviewing the latest bestselling novel may quote briefly from the novel to support claims about the book. Courts use the fair use doctrine to assess the nature of the use of the copyrighted work, the nature of the work itself, the amount of the use, and the effect of the use on the market value of the work. The doctrine protects uses like reviews, educational and non-profit endeavors, and research.

fair use doctrine
rules allowing for the use of copyrighted materials without permission of the copyright holder

Sharing music online is not a fair use, and most individuals who engage in file-sharing understand that much of what they are downloading and sharing is in fact copyrighted. The Recording Industry Association of America (RIAA) has been active in pursuing file-sharers. The Supreme Court has also said that services that encourage users to engage in illegal file-sharing can be shut down. In *MGM v. Grokster* (2005), the Court said that "one who distributes a device with the object of promoting its use to infringe copyright, as shown by clear expression or other affirmative steps taken to foster infringement, is liable for the resulting acts of infringement by third parties." In other words, Grokster had encouraged the use of its software to infringe the copyrights on protected songs. Similar lawsuits drove the popular music-sharing software company Napster to bankruptcy in 2002. In October 2007, the RIAA successfully sued a Minnesota woman for $220,000 for copyright infringement of 24 songs through file-sharing, in the first piracy case to go to trial. On retrial, she lost again, and this time the jury awarded the record companies over $1.9 million, a huge award which was later reduced.

Copyright is also protected online by a law called the *Digital Millennium Copyright Act* (DMCA), which was signed into law in 1998. The DMCA did several important things. First, it criminalized any attempt to circumvent copyright protections. Second, it provided protection for online service providers against copyright infringement lawsuits if the online service provider adheres to a set of guidelines and removes allegedly infringing material from its website upon notification.

Trademark

Trademark law, which can be protected at both the state and federal levels, exists primarily to protect the consumer. If, for example, a consumer purchases a brand-name cola product, that consumer expects that cola to taste the way it always has. Trademark law protects symbols, pictures, words, slogans, and even shapes and colors. The owner of a trademark has the exclusive right to use that trademark in whatever manner he/she likes in relation to the products it identifies. The term "trademark" applies to goods, like shoes, computers, or bread; "servicemark" applies to services like banking,

When is it appropriate to use the registered symbol? © fzd.it/Shutterstock

insurance, or airline travel; and the generic "mark" is used to refer to either. If a trademark or servicemark is registered with the U.S. Patent and Trademark Office, it may use the registered symbol, ®. If not, the terms ^{TM} or ^{SM} may be used prior to legal registration.

The strongest marks are "fanciful" or "arbitrary": they bear no obvious connection to the goods or services they identify. The word "Apple" and its corresponding fruit-shaped logo is an arbitrary mark for computer products, as most individuals would not have thought of apples in connection with computers. In fact, legal disputes between Apple Corps Ltd., the commercial guardian of iconic rock legends The Beatles, and Apple Inc., Steve Jobs's computer juggernaut, have persisted for nearly three decades. The original settlement allowed Apple Inc. to use the name and logo with the proviso that the company would not enter the music business. When it began selling iPods and offering digital music downloads on iTunes, Apple Corps filed additional trademark suits, which have led to millions of dollars of settlements and have kept surviving members of The Beatles from allowing their music to be available on iTunes.

Fanciful marks are invented or made up, like Xerox or Kodak. The best marks develop a secondary meaning associated with their use; for example, even though first names are not usually distinctive enough to gain trademark protection, marks like Tiffany for jewelry and Ben & Jerry's for ice cream have enough name recognition to have developed secondary meanings. Most people can easily conjure an image of a Tiffany lamp and will likely think of ice cream when someone says Ben & Jerry's. If you are looking to develop a new trademark, think first of fanciful or arbitrary marks that are easily distinguishable and easy to register.

Patent

Patents protect inventions for a limited amount of time by granting exclusive rights to the inventor. New patents are generally protected for 20 years. The owner gets "the right to exclude others from making, using, offering for sale, or selling" the invention. There are three types of patents. Utility patents may be granted to anyone who invents or discovers new and useful processes or machines. Design patents may be granted to anyone who invents a new, original, and ornamental design for a product. Plant patents can be granted to the inventor or discoverer of any distinct and new variety of plant. An idea or concept may not be patented; only an invention that uses the idea may be patented.

Freedom of Information

As noted earlier, the policy of the United States government is one of openness. To that end, the federal government has two major laws that are meant to ensure open meetings and access to government records. The Government in the Sunshine Act of 1976 provides that all meetings of executive agencies must be open to the public unless they are specifically required to be closed under 10 exemptions (for example, high-level national security or ongoing lawsuits). Minutes of those meetings must also be made available.

The Freedom of Information Act of 1966, as discussed earlier in this chapter, assumes openness for records of those same executive agencies unless the records fall under one of the nine exemptions, which are similar to the Sunshine Act's exemptions. The act was amended in 1996 to encourage the collection and dissemination of electronic records as well as traditional paper records and files. At the end of 2007, President Bush signed an amendment to the FOIA creating a system to track the status of FOIA requests, establishing a hotline for problems faced by federal agencies, and offering ombudsmen as alternatives to litigation in disclosure disputes. President Obama has emphasized openness in his administration. In December 2009 he initiated the Open Government Directive, aimed at increasing government transparency, participation and collaboration.[5]

The FOIA not only allows news organizations access to the information they need to ensure the accuracy of the news they disseminate, but it also, therefore, allows individuals access to the truth. In 2008, the Federal Government approved a $1.5 trillion bailout for financially fledgling banks. Although the Federal Reserve agreed to transparency when doling out the cash, it was sued by the Bloomberg news organization when the Fed refused to disclose the names of the companies set to receive cuts of this chunk of taxpayer money. Bloomberg relied on the FOIA to make its case.

Broadcast Regulation

Over-the-air television and radio broadcasters do not receive the same level of protection as print media. The rationale for this different treatment is that because broadcast media is uniquely accessible. While you can choose whether or not to read a news article, children or anyone else within hearing range of a broadcast may not always be able to avoid hearing it, so broadcasters must be regulated more strongly.

Regulation of the broadcast media can be traced back to the sinking of the ship RMS *Titanic*. In the aftermath of the April 1912 disaster, during which many deaths could have been avoided had all ships been using their wireless systems, Congress passed the Radio Act of 1912, which required all ships to have a 24-hour wireless watch. As more and more individuals and companies began to broadcast, the airwaves became crowded and chaotic. The Radio Act of 1927 created the Federal Radio Commission and gave that commission the power to grant broadcast licenses and assign frequencies to radio stations. This act considered "public interest, convenience and necessity" as it formed the foundation of the dual system of regulation that exists today; no such mandate exists for print media. The Radio Act of 1927 was replaced by the Communications Act of 1934, which created the FCC and gave it broad regulatory powers. The Telecommunications Act of 1996 augmented the Communications Act and will be discussed later. Below are some of the elements of the broadcasting regulatory scheme.

---

[5]http://www.whitehouse.gov/open/documents/open-government-directive.

Political Advertising

As part of their service to the public, broadcasters must provide access to their television and radio stations for political advertising purchased by candidates. The "equal time rule," Section 315 of the Communications Act, says that if a broadcaster permits the purchase of airtime by any candidate for local or state office, that broadcaster must permit all other candidates the option to purchase airtime as well. Broadcasters may deny all candidates for state or local office the ability to buy airtime, but Section 312 of the Communications Act mandates that all candidates for federal office must be permitted to buy airtime if they request it. Moreover, all airtime sold to candidates for political advertising must be sold at the lowest rates the broadcaster charges to any of its regular advertisers.

The V-chip

In response to concerns that broadcast television was becoming more sexual, more violent, and more profane, the Telecommunications Act of 1996 contains a mandate that all new televisions 13 inches or larger manufactured after 1999 have installed V-chip technology. This technology makes it possible for parents to block access to undesirable television content from their children. Broadcasters were offered the chance to voluntarily rate and categorize their programs so that parents could choose to block or receive programming based on these ratings. The ratings appear in Table 13.1. While the V-chip technology has been successfully implemented, a 2007 FCC report focuses on the failure of the V-chip to keep objectionable material away from children. Not only are producers free to set their own ratings, but the report also cites research that suggests that only 15 percent of all parents use the V-chip: many are unaware that their new TVs have the technology, and others are unwilling to navigate the sometimes confusing directions to use it.[6]

Obscenity

obscenity
material not protected by the First Amendment and determined by the *Miller* test

In 1973, the landmark *Miller v. California* case decided that **obscenity** is not protected by the First Amendment and established a test to define obscenity for the purposes of regulating it. Known as the *Miller* test, the following three criteria must be met in order for material to qualify as obscene: (1) an average person, applying contemporary community standards, must find that the material, as a whole, appeals to the prurient interest (i.e., material having a tendency to excite lustful thoughts); (2) the material must depict or describe, in a patently offensive way, sexual conduct specifically defined by applicable law; and (3) the material, taken as a whole, must lack serious literary, artistic, political, or scientific value.[7] The government may ban the creation, distribution, sale, and possession of speech that it finds to be obscene.

Indecency

indecency
material, containing sexual or excretory content that does not rise to the level of obscene, that is protected by the First Amendment but regulated by the FCC

Indecency regulations have been around since the 1920s. In the 1978 *FCC v. Pacifica Foundation* case, the Supreme Court established that indecency could not be broadcast during the hours of 6:00 a.m. to 10:00 p.m., when children are most

---

[6]Federal Communications Commission, "Report: In the Matter of Violent Television Programming and Its Impact on Children," April 25, 2007, http://www.firstamendmentcenter.org/PDF/FCC_TV_violence_2007.pdf.
[7]Federal Communications Commission, "Frequently Asked Questions," http://www.fcc.gov/eb/oip/FAQ.html.

TABLE 13.1	V-CHIP RATINGS

TV-Y (All Children: This program is designed to be appropriate for all children.) Whether animated or live-action, the themes and elements in this program are specifically designed for a very young audience, including children from ages 2–6. This program is not expected to frighten younger children.

TV-Y7 (Directed to Older Children: This program is designed for children age 7 and above.) It may be more appropriate for children who have acquired the developmental skills needed to distinguish between make-believe and reality. Themes and elements in this program may include mild fantasy or comedic violence or may frighten children under the age of 7. Therefore, parents may wish to consider the suitability of this program for their very young children. Note: For those programs where fantasy violence may be more intense or more combative than other programs in this category, such programs will be designated TV-Y7-FV. For programs designed for the entire audience, the general categories are as follows:

TV-G (General Audience: Most parents would find this program suitable for all ages.) Although this rating does not signify a program designed specifically for children, most parents may let younger children watch this program unattended. It contains little or no violence, no strong language, and little or no sexual dialogue or situations.

TV-PG (Parental Guidance Suggested: This program contains material that parents may find unsuitable for younger children.) Many parents may want to watch it with their younger children. The theme itself may call for parental guidance, and/or the program contains one or more of the following: moderate violence (V), some sexual situations (S), infrequent coarse language (L), or some suggestive dialogue (D).

TV-14 (Parents Strongly Cautioned: This program contains some material that many parents would find unsuitable for children under 14 years of age.) Parents are strongly urged to exercise greater care in monitoring this program and are cautioned against letting children under the age of 14 watch unattended. This program contains one or more of the following: intense violence (V), intense sexual situations (S), strong coarse language (L), or intensely suggestive dialogue (D).

TV-MA (Mature Audience Only: This program is specifically designed to be viewed by adults and therefore may be unsuitable for children under 17.) This program contains one or more of the following: graphic violence (V), explicit sexual activity (S), or crude indecent language (L).

Source: Federal Communications Commission website, http://www.fcc.gov/vchip/

likely to be in the audience. The case involved George Carlin's "Filthy Words" monologue, in which the comedian repeats "the seven words you can't say on television" ad nauseum. A radio station broadcast this monologue at 2:00 p.m. on a Tuesday afternoon in October 1973, and a man and his son heard the broadcast, were upset by it, and complained about it to the FCC.

Indecency is legally defined as material that, "in context, depicts or describes in terms patently offensive as measured by contemporary community standards for the broadcast medium, sexual or excretory activities or organs." Indecency is protected by the First Amendment; while it cannot be banned, its broadcast is regulated. An indecent monologue, such as Carlin's, would not be indecent—and certainly not obscene—if it were printed in whole in the daily newspaper or on a website. It would also be permitted to air between the hours of 10:00 p.m. and 6:00 a.m.

Profanity

profanity
material, including words that are so highly offensive that their utterance may be considered a nuisance, protected by the First Amendment but regulated by the FCC

The FCC also regulates the broadcast of **profanity**—words that are so highly offensive that their mere utterance alone may be considered a nuisance. Like indecency, broadcasts containing profanity are also restricted from airing between 6:00 a.m. to 10:00 p.m.

The controversy over indecency and profanity is not over yet: in 2007, the Second Circuit Court of Appeals said that a new FCC policy to punish "fleeting expletives" (one occurrence of the F-word or another profanity) was a change that was not permitted under administrative rules. The FCC appealed to the Supreme

"Bong Hits 4 Jesus"

The case had a graphic hook: a group of high school students holding up a large homemade sign reading "Bong Hits 4 Jesus" on a public street outside their high school. The less exciting *Morse v. Frederick* was the name of the case ultimately decided by the Supreme Court in 2007 that provided more limitations on student free speech rights.

High school senior Joseph Frederick came to school late on the day that his Juneau, Alaska high school was released from normal classes to watch the Olympic torch pass by in a parade in 2002. To get a little attention from television cameras, Frederick unfurled his homemade sign on a public street across from the high school. The high school principal, Deborah Morse, horrified at what she perceived to be a pro-drug message, crossed the street, tore the sign out of Frederick's hands and suspended him. Frederick took the case to court.

The appeals court said that Morse could be held personally liable for damages for abridging Frederick's free speech rights. The Supreme Court disagreed. Chief Justice Roberts wrote that it was reasonable for Morse to think that the banner was supporting drug use, even though Frederick claimed it was nonsense intended to grab television cameras.

Moreover, even though Frederick had not been to school that day and did not display his sign on school property, the fact that the parade took place during school hours and that students were released to watch under administrative supervision meant that the event was "school-sponsored." Therefore, for Morse not to have taken action against the sign would have sent a signal that she was not serious about opposing drug use. The result: a broader interpretation of administrators' abilities to restrict student expression.

The Court was not unanimous. Justice Stevens, one of the more liberal justices on the Court, wrote that an administrator should not be permitted to punish student speech simply because the administrator disagrees with it. As for the idea that the banner would entice students to try drugs, Stevens scoffed, "Admittedly, some high school students (including those who use drugs) are dumb. Most students, however, do not shed their brains at the schoolhouse gate, and most students know dumb advocacy when they see it. The notion that the message on this banner would actually persuade either the average student or even the dumbest one to change his or her behavior is most implausible."

Court, and in 2009 the Court overturned the Second Circuit's ruling and found that the FCC's change in its policy regulating fleeting expletives did not violate administrative rules. The case was remanded (sent back) to the Second Circuit for consideration of the FCC's indecency policy itself.

Children's Television

The Children's Television Act of 1990 was passed for the purpose of increasing the quantity and quality of educational broadcast television programming for children. In particular, broadcasters were mandated to serve the "core" informational programming needs of children by providing weekly educational programs of at least 30 minutes in length and broadcast between 7:00 a.m. and 10:00 p.m. Programs like "VeggieTales" and "Care Bears" fulfill the educational and informational requirements. FCC rules also limit the number of minutes of advertising that may be shown during children's programming to 10.5 minutes per hour on weekends and 12 minutes per hour on weekdays.

Media Ownership Issues

Despite the government's proclivity for regulation, it does seem to agree with the theory that more media voices mean more options and more participation in the marketplace of ideas. Monopolies are considered to be bad for consumers because they limit consumer choices and permit the monopolists to raise prices. The FCC has been inconsistent in promoting diversity in the media marketplace. In December 2007, the commissioners announced rules to promote diversification of broadcast ownership by making it easier to obtain financing and licenses. On the same day, they also announced revisions to the newspaper/broadcast cross-ownership rule, amending a 32-year ban on one entity owning both a daily newspaper and a broadcast station in the same market and permitting cross-ownership in large markets containing what they consider to be sufficient competition.[8]

The Telecommunications Act of 1996, passed with great fanfare and hope, had as one of its major goals the increase of competition between telecommunications organizations in order to bring about reduced costs to consumers as the result of more competition. The act abolishes former restrictions on cross-market competition, letting cable industries compete to offer telephone service, for example. It also lifted broadcast ownership limitations, permitting one owner to own television stations with a maximum service area cap of 35 percent of the U.S. population and eliminating the cap on the numer of radio licenses one owner can own. However, it left in place limits on the number of licenses that can be owned in specific markets.

Critics of the Telecommunications Act suggest that instead of getting lower prices and more competition, as was promised, consumers got more consolidation, higher prices, and less diversity. For example, the removal of ownership caps in the radio industry resulted in an extreme consolidation of radio ownership, as seen in

[8]Federal Communications Commission, "FCC Adopts Revision to Newspaper/Broadcast Cross-Ownership Rule," December 18, 2007, http://hraunfoss.fcc.gov/edocs_public/attachmatch/DOC-278932A1.pdf. Federal Communications Commission, FCC Adopts Rules to Promote Diversification of Broadcast Ownership, December 18, 2007, http://hraunfoss.fcc.gov/edocs_public/attachmatch/DOC-279035A1.pdf.

TABLE 13.2	Number of Radio Stations Owned by Top 10 Broadcasting Companies in 2005		
Rank	Owner	Total # of Stations	# of News Stations
1	Clear Channel	1184	132
2	Cumulus Broadcasting	300	31
3	Citadel Broadcasting	223	19
4	CBS Radio	179	22
5	Educational Media Foundation	161	0
6	American Family Association	128	0
7	Salem Communications	106	23
8	Entercom	103	15
9	Saga Communications	87	12
10	Cox Radio	78	6

Source: Journalism.org, "State of the News Media 2007," http://www .stateofthenewsmedia .com/2007/narrative_radio_ownership.asp?cat=4&media=9.

Table 13.2. The "Big Six" media conglomerates—General Electric, Time Warner, Disney, News Corp., Bertelsmann of Germany, and Viacom—control over 90 percent of the U.S. media industry.

Regulations on Advertising

You might be surprised that the government may regulate even truthful advertising about legal products. Yet even this limited protection is more than advertising got when it was first considered by the Supreme Court in the 1940s. Over time, the commercial speech doctrine developed, giving limited protection to speech that advocates a commercial transaction.

The Supreme Court first considered whether advertising should have First Amendment protection in 1942 in *Valentine v. Chrestensen*. At issue in the case was a flyer that a submarine owner was passing out that advertised paid rides on his submarine on one side and, on the other, complained about the New York commissioner of docks forbidding him to store his submarine at New York piers. The Court dismissed the political speech on the reverse of Chrestensen's flyer, instead focusing on the advertisement and stating that speech of a purely commercial or advertising nature would be outside of the protection of the First Amendment.

Over the years, successive Courts chipped away at the total lack of protection for advertising until the case of *Central Hudson Gas & Electric Corp. v. Public Service Commission* (1980) established a legal test to determine whether a particular regulation on advertising was constitutional. That test looks at the legality of the product or service (illegal goods or services cannot be advertised), the importance of the state interest supported by the regulation, and the "fit" between the regulation and the state interest. Acceptable regulations cannot regulate too much or too little speech, and there must be a direct connection between the regulation and advancement of the state interest.

The current Supreme Court has several justices who would do away with this clumsy test, among them conservative justice Clarence Thomas, who has said that he would get rid of all regulations on advertising that keep consumers "ignorant in order to manipulate their choices in the marketplace." Thomas does not see a reason to protect commercial speech any less than political or other forms of speech. However, his perspective has not yet garnered sufficient support from other justices to be the rule of law. Thus, the *Central Hudson* test, as it is usually called, is usually used to determine whether a regulation on advertising is justified.

The administrative agency responsible for the regulation of advertising by the federal government is the Federal Trade Commission (FTC). The FTC is empowered to prevent unfair competition and enforce truthful advertising laws. It also investigates consumer and company complaints about advertisements. However, because it is a government bureaucracy, it moves much more slowly than the industry itself. As noted earlier in this chapter and in others, the advertising industry has developed a strong self-regulatory regime in which advertisers police each other and generally agree to abide by rulings of its self-regulatory bodies—the National Advertising Division (NAD) and the National Advertising Review Board, both part of the Better Business Bureau. The process of investigation and compliance is much faster and cheaper than that of the FTC, although the rulings of the self-regulatory bodies have no legal force. Although membership in and compliance with the bodies' decisions is voluntary, the Better Business Bureau reports that NAD has resolved more than 3,700 advertising cases and has a 96 percent compliance rate.[9]

Of particular note for public relations specialists is the FCC's 2007 fine against cablecaster Comcast for broadcasting a video news release (VNR) without providing sponsorship information as required by law. The product, "Nelson's Rescue Sleep," was included in a consumer issues segment, and the VNR contained many images and mentions of Rescue Sleep and said that "If you are one of the estimated 70 million Americans who have trouble sleeping, Rescue Sleep may be what you're looking for." Comcast argued that because it had not received any compensation for running the VNR, it should not have to disclose sponsorship, but the FCC disagreed and fined Comcast $4,000.

MEDIA ETHICS

While companies' advertising efforts usually have their own self-interest in mind, most journalists endeavor to provide consumers with an honest account of the stories they cover. They try to get all sides of a story, try to quote their sources accurately and in context, and work hard to get a truthful version of the story published under often-strict deadlines. They seek to eliminate bias and accept criticism from their editors and the public. All of these goals—truth, accuracy, objectivity, accountability, and responsibility—are part of media ethics.

[9]http://www.us.bbb.org/WWWRoot/SitePage.aspx?site=113&id=01a45f12-5b9a-45ab-8d78-49100a077b92.

Most journalists endeavor to provide consumers with an honest account of the stories they cover.
© niderlander/Shutterstock

Media ethics is an example of applied ethics; media organizations often find themselves facing ethical issues, and ethicists attempt to apply moral theories to real-life situations. The ethical imperatives of the law also apply to the media. For example, journalists strive for truth both to avoid libel claims against them and to enlighten the democratic society in which they live.

However, there is much more to ethics than simply "doing the right thing." Ethics refers not to a set of clearly established rules but, rather, involves weighing competing interests and considering moral standards and values as part of a decision-making process. The variables involved in answering an ethical question are rarely clear-cut, and there is almost never a solid right answer to an ethical question.

The Hutchins Report

In 1947, American journalism was dealt a serious blow by the publication of *A Free and Responsible Press,* commonly known as the Hutchins report. The report was a landmark consideration of the role of an ethical press in American society. A searing indictment of the state of American journalism, the report outlined the many ills of the self-serving media and made four recommendations for how journalism could serve democracy: provide a truthful and comprehensive account of the day's events in a meaningful context, offer a forum for the exchange of comment and criticism, project the opinions and attitudes of the groups in a society to one another, and make available the currents of information, thought, and feeling to every member of society.

The Hutchins report was written by a commission of intellectuals without input from members of the media, and the report was met with immediate criticism and strong resistance. Despite this unfavorable reception, the report contained the genesis of what has become the **social responsibility model** of the media, which promotes the idea that the media have responsibilities as well as rights and should work toward fostering positive, informed self-governance. Many would also suggest that today's citizen journalism, public journalism, and participatory Web 2.0 are the progeny of the Hutchins report's call for a more diverse media.

social responsibility model
the idea that the media have responsibilities as well as rights and should work toward fostering positive, informed self-governance

Personal Ethics

While the law aims to reflect the widely accepted standards of society, ethics involves consideration of elements with much more complexity. Individuals are often faced with dilemmas of whether to take an action that is legal but may or may not be ethical. Imagine, for example, that you are a journalist reporting on an alleged rape, and you must decide whether or not to print the names of the alleged perpetrator and victim. Current legal doctrine says that if this information is part of the public record and a reporter accesses it, the reporter may legally publish it. But there may be more for you to consider than just the legal consequences of printing these names. How will the community treat the alleged perpetrator when this story goes public? Is it right to expose him to potential public ridicule before he has even been tried for a crime? What if the police are certain he committed the crime—does that make the decision to publish his name easier? Will you feel responsible if someone decides to take the law into their own hands, and he ends up hurt—or worse? What about the victim—should you expose this personal violation that happened to her? Won't the community look at her differently too? Most reporters would probably choose not to publish this information, and most news organizations even have policies against such publication. In this case, the law permits something that most media professionals would choose not to do.

For situations that are not so clear-cut, Dr. Ralph Potter of Harvard Divinity School developed what has become a classic approach to ethical problem-solving. Dr. Potter's construct, known as the Potter Box, asks individuals to consider several areas and issues within the ethical problem and come to a decision only after balancing the competing interests contained within those issues.

The Potter Box approach requires consideration of issues in four different areas: facts, values, principles, and loyalties. First, determine what facts are important to the final decision. Then, consider the values that are important to you as a person, a professional, a family member—any role that you are playing in this situation. You may come up with terms like "honesty," "integrity," "responsibility," and "open-mindedness." Next, look at guiding principles from moral authorities or ethical theorists; for example, you may take the Kantian perspective that one should always tell the truth or the Aristotelian mandate that the best approach to any problem is to be found in the Golden Mean, not at any extreme. Finally, identify the people or ideas to which you are loyal. They may include family and friends, employers, customers, the public at large. After having considered—and in many cases, reconsidered—these four elements, you can then make your decision.

The Potter Box is one of many approaches to making ethical decisions, but most of them focus on the individual thinking about more than just the self or the obvious answer. Professor Lou Hodges of Washington & Lee University ends his discussions of ethical decision-making with the following question: "How would I feel if the results of my decision were printed on the front page of the *New York Times*?" If the answer is positive, the decision is likely to be morally defensible.

Plagiarism

Unlike other intellectual property violations, **plagiarism**—the presentation of someone else's exact or close words or ideas as one's own original work—is not regulated by the law. However, it is one of the most widely agreed upon ethical misdeeds that students and journalists can commit. Most universities have stringent codes against such academic dishonesty, and journalists whose plagiarizing ways have been discovered rarely keep their jobs for very long.

plagiarism
the presentation of someone else's exact or close words or ideas as one's own original work

In 2003, *New York Times* journalist Jayson Blair resigned after he was accused of plagiarizing and fabricating stories. After his resignation, an investigation found that he had plagiarized or fabricated at least 30 of the stories he had written in less than a year at the paper. In an act of mea culpa, the *Times* printed a front-page story titled "Times Reporter Who Resigned Leaves Long Trail of Deception" that disclosed to the public what the investigation had uncovered. The news of this breach was quite a scandal for a paper with such a well established reputation of reliability that its masthead logo reads "All the news that's fit to print."

Organizational Ethics

It may seem a false division to separate individuals from the organizations they serve, but organizations have resources and power that individuals do not. We focus on three tools that organizations can use to be more socially responsible forces.

Codes of Ethics

One of the first ethics codes, a pledge to do the moral and correct thing, was the Hippocratic Oath traditionally taken by physicians dating from the 4th century B.C. From finance to engineering to real estate, many professions have codes of ethics. These codes are statements of the "best practices" of the industry, instructions to practitioners of that industry, and the values to which the industry adheres. Some ethics codes even have provisions for the loss of membership in the organization or industry if the code is violated.

Of particular importance to media professionals are the codes of the Society of Professional Journalists (SPJ) and the Public Relations Society of America (PRSA). The SPJ code is divided into four sections that exhort journalists to seek and report truth, minimize harm, act independently, and be accountable. Each section of the code provides detailed examples: to act independently, a journalist should avoid conflicts of interest, refuse gifts from sources, and disclose any conflicts that are unavoidable. The SPJ code does not have any legal authority to fine or censure reporters in violation of it, but many news organizations have a copy of the code posted in their newsrooms and consider themselves ethically bound by its recommendations.

The PRSA code of ethics originally had an element of enforcement; a PRSA member who violated an element of the code of ethics faced grievance proceedings that ended with a punitive recommendation. In 2000, the code was revised to focus less on enforcement and punishment and more on encouragement and inspiration. It is a lengthy code with value statements including the importance of advocacy, honesty, expertise, fairness, and loyalty. PRSA members sign a pledge in which they promise "to conduct myself professionally, with truth, accuracy, fairness, and responsibility to the public; to improve my individual competence and advance the knowledge and proficiency of the profession through continuing research and education; and to adhere to the articles of the Member Code of Ethics 2000 for the practice of public relations as adopted by the governing Assembly of the Public Relations Society of America."[10] Members can still have their memberships revoked if they do

---

[10]Public Relations Society of America. "Code of Ethics," http://www.prsa.org/aboutUs/ethics/preamble_en.html.

not adhere to the elements of the code, but the code now focuses more on encouraging positive and ethical behavior rather than promoting fear of enforcement.

News Councils

Only a handful of news councils are in operation in the United States. News councils operate in Minnesota, Washington, Hawaii, and New England, based at the University of Massachusetts at Amherst. Minnesota's news council is the oldest of the four, having heard its first case in 1971. Internationally, there are dozens of news councils, from Canada to Peru to Germany to New Zealand.

When consumers bring grievances against the news media, news councils provide non-legal forums for resolution. Consumers may find this forum preferable to lawsuits, which are expensive and time-consuming—one study estimated that an average case takes four years and costs $250,000. Furthermore, many individuals are more interested in setting the record straight than acquiring financial gain. News councils accomplish several goals: they permit the aggrieved individual to make a case in public in front of the media organization, and they give the media organization a chance to defend the choices it made in the situation. The openness of the hearings provides an opportunity for all parties to learn. Some media organizations do not approve of news councils, which they criticize as an additional layer of bureaucracy or a threat to journalistic freedom. Critics claim that a venue for addressing consumer complaints already exists—in the courts.

Most councils are made up of a combination of media professionals and members of the public. In Minnesota, the staff of the news council works with the media organization and the complainant to resolve the case before a hearing takes place. If the issue cannot be resolved, a hearing is scheduled. No attorneys are permitted. Each side makes its case before the membership of the council, the issues are debated, and a decision is reached the same day.

The newest of the news councils, the New England News Forum, which was formed in 2006, does more than just run hearings for aggrieved individuals. The organization offers seminars and discussions on media ethics, does research on issues of media accountability and responsibility, and examines how the Internet and Web 2.0 are affecting traditional media.

Ombudsmen

Swedish for "representative," the ombudsman is not unique to media organizations. Ombudsmen are employed by companies, governments, and other organizations to serve as intermediaries between the public and the organization.

In the media, an ombudsman may also be called a reader representative or a public editor. The Organization of News Ombudsmen (ONO) is an international group of individuals who serve as ombudsmen for the media. An ombudsman receives complaints or concerns about media coverage or issues of fairness, truth, bias, and taste and investigates those complaints. He or she then responds to the complainant and may publish a column or article about it in the media outlet. Some ombudsmen organize forums for discussion with concerned members of the public or the community, some may supervise corrections, and, in small organizations, they may be called on to perform other news-related duties. They are often senior staff members with a lot of journalistic experience and the ability to relate to the public without being defensive but with sensitivity and concern.

The ombudsman position has yet to catch on in the United States, which has fewer than 40 media ombudsmen. Internationally, however, there are many more news ombudsmen, in India, Colombia, England, South Africa, Sweden, and Turkey. What does the lack of both ombudsmen and news councils in the United States, in comparison to the rest of the world, suggest about the American approach to media accountability and responsibility?

CAREERS IN THE FIELD

If you think you could handle the ethical dilemmas that media professionals face and keep track of all the regulations and restrictions, there are a myriad of jobs you could consider. Reporters, writers, and investigative journalists aim to disseminate truthful information to the public, and their publishers, producers, and editors are first in the line of people ensuring they do so. Advancement opportunities might include administration work for a society of media professionals, where you might establish and write codes of ethics; mediation work for a news council; or attempts to popularize the ombudsman profession in the U.S. If you're more interested in the law, you could consider working for the American Civil Liberties Union (ACLU), which employs staff and volunteer advocates, community organizers, spokespeople, and lawyers to protect the right to free speech, among many other rights. For the most ambitious, you could aim for an appointment as a Supreme Court justice and play a major part in determining the common law.

SUMMARY

- Although laws are intended to reflect and uphold the moral values of society, many issues are not always agreed upon. Organizations may use policies to declare their particular stances on issues, and individuals may find themselves avoiding an action that is legal but which they feel is unethical.
- The First Amendment clearly states the rights of free speech and free press. However, the U.S. has a long and complex history of how these rights have been interpreted, legislated, and enforced. Some forms of speech are more protected than others, and the media are regulated in various ways. These areas of the law continue to change even today.
- Broadcast and print media are regulated differently. Some of the legal and ethical issues these media face include libel, privacy, intellectual property, plagiarism, obscenity, and ownership.
- Individuals and organizations face ethical questions involving competing interests with no clear-cut right answer. Codes of ethics and the Potter Box may help to determine the ethical course of action in a given situation.

- When individuals or organizations feel that their rights to free speech or press have been violated, many venues exist in which they can seek recourse, from media news councils and ombudsmen to appeals courts and the Supreme Court.

DISCUSSION QUESTIONS

1. Can you think of a time when you experienced or observed what may have been a violation of the right to free speech? How might you think about or handle a situation such as this now that you have read this chapter?
2. How do you feel about the extent to which the media are regulated? Would you be in favor or more or less regulations?
3. Have you ever witnessed the broadcast of obscene, indecent, or profane speech that you felt should have been restricted?
4. What ethical questions have you faced? What methods did you use to solve them?
5. Discuss some examples of media actions that are legal but may or may not be ethical. What decisions would you make in these situations, and why?

SUPPLEMENTAL WEB SITES

GLOBAL MEDIA

CHAPTER OBJECTIVES

- Identify and discuss the four theories of the press.
- Discover mass media outlets and their usage in developed and emerging nations.
- Define and discuss Marshall McLuhan's Global Village.

KEY TERMS

Theories of the Press
Authoritarian Theory
Libertarian Theory
Social Responsibility Theory
Soviet Theory
Global Village
Development Theory

INTRODUCTION

So often, Americans, as do citizens of most countries around the world, think in a very ethnocentric way. That is, we put our country's culture at the center of our thoughts and measure all other cultures against it. What we usually surmise is that our culture is superior to all others. While on an intellectual level we know this is not true and is, in fact, the worst type of overgeneralized thinking, we cannot help but turn our patriotism and love for country into something extreme; something not very good.

World map
© kentoh, 2014, Used under license from
Shutterstock, Inc.

Nowhere can this theory of ethnocentrism be more clearly found than on the pages of our newspapers and magazines and as the lead stories on our evening newscasts.

In this chapter, we attempt to discuss the different theological approaches to mass media distribution and control utilized throughout the world and we will also attempt to simply survey the media of different countries without being ethnocentric. So, rather than giving you the author's opinion of how media should work based on his studies and experiences, we will simply report to you the facts as we know them. We will look at what media are used in which countries.

MAJOR THEORIES OF THE PRESS

To being our discussion, we must establish the guidelines by which we will view mass media systems around the world. In the United States, in 1956, Fred Siebert, Theodore Peterson, and Wilbur Schramm outlined what they considered to be the forms the press could take around the world. Their groundbreaking work simply titled *Four Theories of the Press* continues to be the standard by which we view world media systems.[1] The authors argue that the press takes on the political and societal structures of the country or society in which it resides and that structure usually mirrors the government's and/or society's basic ideology.[2]

As we know much has changed in the past 50 years in the political landscape making some or parts of these theories outdated to say the least. In order to fully understand the concepts, let's first take a look at the original *Four Theories of the Press* and then we can update the overall viewpoints with more recent theories that expand the original premise.

The *Four Theories of the Press* as brought forth by Siebert, Peterson, and Schramm are Authoritarian Theory, Soviet Communist Theory, Libertarian Theory, and Social Responsibility Theory. Let's take a closer look at each.

Authoritarian Theory

Authoritarian theory is the oldest theory of the press and has, historically, been the most commonly seen as monarchies, dictatorships, and theocracies have been the chief rulers of societies. The United States, as we know, was founded at least in part as a rebellion against the British monarchy and its suppression of information in the American colonies. Freedom of information is unheard of in an Authoritarian-type government where the press and all information contained in it are strictly controlled by the government. According to the theory, the role

---

[1]Fred S. Siebert, Theodore Peterson, and Wilbur Schramm, *Four Theories of the Press,* University of Illinois Press, Urbana, 1956.

[2]Ibid.

of the press is to be a servant of the government, not a servant of the citizenry. Throughout history, we have seen and continue to see this common practice.[3] In 1529, King Henry VIII of England outlawed imported publications because many presses were producing materials that bordered on sedition and treason. The Soviet Union had its own twist on authoritarianism (we discuss that next). Today, dictatorships and theocracies continue the tradition.[4]

Finally, a chief premise of authoritarian systems is that the government is infallible, which places its policies beyond questioning. As stated earlier, the media's role is subservience to the government. We conclude that **Authoritarian Theory** is top-down governance such as a monarchy or dictatorship.[5]

Soviet Communist Theory

The communist theory first implemented boldly by the now defunct Soviet Union is similar to the authoritarian theory, but its goes even further in its control over information. Instead of overseeing the press and punishing offenders, the communist theory dictates that the government actually runs the media; therefore, its needs are met with no resistance.[6] Thus, the media's main function is to serve as a tool for the government's propaganda. Examples today include China, North Korea, and Cuba. We conclude that **Soviet Communist Theory** says, "the media's main purpose is to act as a tool for government propaganda."

Libertarian

Libertarian philosophy focuses on the ability of the individual to think freely, process information, and apply reason to understand the truth. Therefore, we can say that libertarian theory is the opposite of the authoritarian theory. Instead of the press belonging to and/or being controlled by the government, **Libertarian Theory** says, "the press should be a separate institution that belongs to the people and serves their best interests."[7] Obviously, this is the system or theory that the U.S. media began and operated under for decades. This theory of the press is based on several principles: (1) people want the truth and will use the truth as a guide for thinking and decision making, (2) the only way to achieve this is for ideas to be freely and openly discussed, (3) people have varying opinions of which they must be allowed to develop on their own, and (4) the most rational ideas will then be accepted.[8]

Many believe that this system worked and continued to work while others believe that in a capitalist society, the advertisers or larger corporations who keep the media business alive with their sponsorships and support are as much in

---

[3]Ibid.

[4]John Vivian, *The Media of Mass Communication*, 11th ed., Pearson, Upper Saddle, New Jersey, 2013, p. 391.

[5]Ibid.

[6]Fred S. Siebert, Theodore Peterson, and Wilbur Schramm, *Four Theories of the Press,* University of Illinois Press, Urbana, 1956.

[7]Ibid.

[8]Ibid.

control of media content as governments are in control of their media outlets in an authoritarian system. It is because of this concern, that we develop a newer, updated take on libertarian theory.

Social Responsibility

While the libertarian theory seems to be the theory that most who wish to maintain a separation between the press and the government refer to, it does have a major drawback. A capitalistic society allows for free enterprise. The majority of all media outlets in a libertarian society are owned by private individuals (regardless of the size of the media conglomerate) through either a large group of investors or an individual family and they exist primarily (if not solely as some believe) to make money for those individuals. This idea called **Social Responsibility Theory** says that even though libertarian media are free of government interference, they can still be controlled by corporate interests and, therefore, must be made strong enough to function against outside pressures.[9]

Today, most would agree that media outlets in democratic, capitalistic societies have made the philosophical shift necessary to ensure that the free press remains free. Further, under this theory, the press is obligated to (1) provide the news and information needed to make the political system work, (2) give the public the information they need to effectively self-govern, (3) provide opportunities for diversion, entertainment programming, (4) be a watchdog of the government, (5) provide opportunities for buyers and sellers to communicate, and (6) of course, be profitable enough to avoid outside pressures from advertisers and big business.

Updating the Theories

As we updated the libertarian theory, so did we recognize the need for yet another theory of the press to address those nations in states of change that do not fit into any of our previous categories. Times change, as we know, the Soviet Union has not existed for over 20 years now and we have so many new media platforms today that we didn't even conceive of when the original *Four Theories of the Press* was published. Traditionally, in cultural change, 50 years may or may not be that significant; in fact, throughout history, our civilizations remained constant for hundreds of years with no real changes. But to say societies have changed, world views have changed and the way we disseminate information has changed over the past 50 years, is quite the understatement.

With this is mind, we now look at the 1995 publication *Last Rights: Revisiting the Four Theories of the Press* by John Nerone. Nerone and his colleagues suggested several things about the way we should now view these theories.

---

[9]Fred S. Siebert, Theodore Peterson, and Wilbur Schramm, *Four Theories of the Press,* University of Illinois Press, Urbana, 1956.

[10]John C. Nerone, ed., Last Rights: Revisiting Four Theories of the Press, University of Illinois Press, Urbana and Chicago, 1995.

They believed that we should not view them as a timeless set of categories but instead a critique set that was reflective of the politics and economics of its day.[11] With this in mind, further critics have suggested that we must deal emerging nations that are in the process of building modern economies.[12]

Development Theory

These critics believe that a fifth theory should be added, development theory. Development theory addresses the special needs of the aforementioned emerging nations.[13] **Development Theory** says, "developing nations may need to use temporary controls in order to establish identity as well as interactions with other nations for commerce and

Developing city street dirt
© Creativemarc, 2014, Used under license from Shutterstock, Inc.

good will." Dennis McQuail writes that less-developed societies undergoing the transition from colonial rule to independence have different needs because they lack the money, infrastructure, skills, and audiences to sustain a free market media system.[14]

So we can conclude that whether an established democracy, dictatorship, or monarchy or developing nation, systems, or theories of how to best operate mass media outlets under each of these types of governments have been well documented and are historically well followed. Whether or not you agree or disagree with any or all of these theories is not at question here. What is at the center of the discussion is that mass media is as varied as the nations in which the media outlets do business.

SURVEY OF WORLD MEDIA

Because of the sheer vastness of countries with numerous media outlets that supply countless numbers of media messages daily around the world, we do not have anywhere near the amount of space needed to include a comprehensive survey in this textbook. So, in order to understand the complexities of media systems around the world, we must first simplify our attempt. Instead of offering laundry lists of names of media outlets, this section provides an overview of each country/region's mass media and societal interactions. This section is, by the nature of publishing an introductory course textbook with so many topics, a very brief look at a very complicated and dense topic and cannot, of course, cover all countries.

---

[11] Ibid.

[12] Denis McQuail, *McQuail's Mass Communication Theory,* 5th ed., Sage, London, 2005.

[13] Ibid.

[14] Ibid.

Toronto downtown
© Lissandra Melo, 2014, Used under license from
Shutterstock, Inc.

North America
Canada

From Canadian scholars Rowland Lorimer and Mike Gasher, we hear a nonflinching account of the mass media industry in their country. They state that the majority of Canadian consumption of television, radio, magazine, and books are of American products and not those of Canadian media sources.[15] In a country that is large in geographic area but small in population (with the majority of Canadians living on or near the U.S. border), media outlets must fight to maintain a sense of identity that is separate from that of the United States.

In the broadcasting sector, Canada has a government-funded broadcaster, the Canadian Broadcasting Corporation/Société Radio-Canada, which operates radio and TV networks in English and French. Some provincial governments offer their own public educational TV broadcast services as well, such as Ontario's TVOntario and Quebec's Télé-Québec. Given Canada's small market and its position next to the dominant producer of feature films, the Canadian film industry receives substantial assistance from the government. In the 2000s, about half of the budget of a typical Canadian film came from various federal and provincial government sources.[16]

Brazilian TV soccer flag
© wavebreakmedia, 2014, Used under license from
Shutterstock, Inc.

Central and Latin America

As is the case with Canada, most of Latin American commercial broadcasting is dominated by companies in North America with the addition of Mexican and Brazilian companies. Brazil and Mexico have similar systems to that of the United States and they even export programming to the United States such as sports and soap operas. These systems are as sophisticated and profitable as any media system around the world and they are extensive in scope due in large part to the limit of only two languages, Portuguese and Spanish.

This is not the case in Europe and Africa where many languages create problems in expanding media markets.[17] As economies have stabilized throughout

---

[15]Rowland Lorimer and Mike Gasher, *Mass Communication in Canada*, 5th ed. Oxford University Press, Ontario, 2004.

[16]Steven Globerman; Institute for Research on Public Policy (1983). *Cultural Regulation in Canada*. IRPP. p. 18. ISBN 978-0-920380-81-9.

[17]Donnalyn Pompper, "Latin America and the Caribbean." *In World Broadcasting: A Comparative View*, ed., Alan Wells, Ablex Publishing, Norwood, New Jersey, 1996.

this region, mass media outlets have grown. And unlike the rest of the world, Latin America has actually seen an increase in newspaper publishing with more than 1,000 in the region with daily readership exceeding 100 million.[18]

BBC Web page
© antb, 2014, Used under license from Shutterstock, Inc.

United Kingdom
England

Media of the United Kingdom consist of several different types of communications media: television, radio, newspapers, magazines, and web sites. The country also has a strong music industry. The United Kingdom has a diverse range of providers, the most prominent being the state-owned public service broadcaster, the BBC (British Broadcasting Corporation).

The most well known of perhaps all media around the world is the BBC or the British Broadcasting Corporation. The BBC, developed as a public service during World War I, operates under a public service model in which audience members pay the costs of programming through equipment licensing fees.

The BBC's largest competitors are ITV plc, which operates 11 of the 15 regional television broadcasters that make up the ITV Network, and News Corporation, which holds a large stake in satellite broadcaster British Sky Broadcasting and also operates a number of leading national newspapers. Regional media is covered by local radio, television, and print newspapers. Trinity Mirror operates 240 local and regional newspapers in the United Kingdom as well as national newspapers such as the *Daily Mirror* and the *Sunday Mirror*.[19]

Western Europe
Spain, Portugal, France, Germany, and Scandinavia

According to Broadcast scholar Matthew Rusher, "Each country in Western Europe seeks to preserve its own culture and language and sees the foreign produced programming on the international channels as a threat to its cultural integrity."[20] Cable television is common in the region with satellite programming more prevalent in Scandinavia. Most countries were authoritarian monopolies until 1980s when commercial alternative became commonplace. There are

---

[18]Thomas L. McPhail, *Global Communication: Theories, Stakeholders and Trends*, Blackwell Publishing, Massachuetts, 2006.

[19]Social Trends: Lifestyles and social participation", *Office for National Statistics*, 16 February 2010, archived from the original on 17 June 2011.

[20]Rowland Lorimer and Mike Gasher, *Mass Communication in Canada*, 5th ed. Oxford University Press, Ontario, 2004.

European union map
© koya979, 2014, Used under license from Shutterstock, Inc.

more advertising revenues than ever before but strict government regulations and guidelines remain.[21]

European newspapers tend to take a more obvious political point of view than U.S. newspapers. These newspapers are clearly slanted to one political viewpoint designed to appeal to members of the particular political party they portray. Newspaper readership is higher in Western Europe than in any region of the world, but the area still faces decline in publications as more and more readers are seeking out online sources of information.[22]

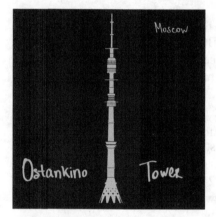

Ostankino tower in moscow
© tanshtyl, 2014, Used under license from Shutterstock, Inc.

Eastern Europe

Russia

The media of Russia is diverse, with a wide range of broadcast and print outlets available to the consumer, offering all kinds of perspectives and catering for all tastes. In total, there are 93,000 media outlets in Russia, including 27,000 newspapers and magazines and 330 television channels. Television is the most popular source of information. There are three television channels with a nationwide outreach and a multitude of regional channels. Local and national newspapers are the second most popular choice, while the Internet comes third. In all media spheres, there is a mixture of private and state ownership. The three nationwide television channels have been criticized for their alleged lack of neutrality. However, there is no lack of independent media in Russia, especially in print media, radio, and the Internet. [23]

Middle East

Perhaps the most volatile of all regions in the world, the Middle East remains a region in flux and in a state of upheaval. Military actions being carried out in the region continue to make the area one of the most dangerous in the history of the world. With this in mind, we look at how most countries including Syria, Sudan, Jordan, and Egypt all remain primarily authoritarian systems but outside influences continue to shake up the balance of information. Along with the official state-controlled media, many Arab nations have Al Hayat, a regional Arabic newspaper published in London, and the Al Jazeera satellite television news channel

---

[21]Ibid.

[22]Kevin Williams, *European Media Studies*, Hodder Arnold, London, 2005.

[23]The Problem with Russia's Free Press Today Is on the Side of Demand, Russia Profile.

(has regular audiences of up to 40 million viewers), which originates in Qatar.[24]

Massive television networks are controlled by the Saudi Arabian government and the Arab League ARABSAT, a network of 21 Arab language channels. Networks such as these provide the majority of citizens with their information and entertainment needs.[25]

Adding to the complexity of the mass media industry in the region is the ongoing conflict between Israel and Palestine. For example, although Israel is a democracy, most reporters there are subjected to government control of stories the government deems sensitive military issues.[26] And so much has been written about the Arab Spring and all the changes taking places in the region. Frankly, it is very difficult to keep up with those changes and to be current in a textbook like this (what an ironic example of how print media is being slowly and steadily replaced by electronic media).

Aljazeera logo
© Gil C, 2014, Used under license from Shutterstock, Inc.

India

Generally, the media of India consist of several different types of Indian communications media: television, radio, cinema, newspapers, magazines, and Internet-based web sites. Many of the media are controlled by large, for-profit corporations that reap revenue from advertising, subscriptions, and sale of copyrighted material. India also has a strong music and film industry. India has more than 70,000 newspapers and over 690 satellite channels (more than 80 are news channels) and is the biggest newspaper market in the world—over 100 million copies sold each day.

The traditional print media, and the television media, are largely family owned and often partake in self-censorship, primarily due to political ties by the owner and the establishment. However, the new media are generally more professional and corporate owned, though these, too, have been acquired or affiliated with established figures. At the same time, the Indian media, viewed as "feisty," have also not reported on issues of the media itself.[27]

Bollywood love story
© Christian Bertrand, 2014, Used under license from Shutterstock, Inc.

[24]Marvin Kalb and Jerome Socolovsky "The Emboldened Arab Press," *Harvard International Journal of Press/Politics* 4, no 3. (1999).

[25]Khalid Marghalani and Philip Palmgreen, "Direct Broadcast Satellite Television—Saudi Arabia," *Journal of Broadcasting & Electronic Media* 42, no. 3, (1998).

[26]Nicole Gaouette, "Mideast's Clash of Images," *Christian Science Monitor*, October 21, 2000.

[27]Why are India's media under fire?". *BBC News*. 12 January 2012.

Japanese manga toy stores
© Sean Pavone, 2014, Used under license from
Shutterstock, Inc.

Japan

The communications media of Japan include numerous television and radio networks as well as newspapers and magazines in Japan. For the most part, television networks were established based on the capital contribution from existing radio networks at that time. Therefore, it is necessary to understand the capital relationship between the media (such as the relationship among newspaper, radio, and TV networks).

Japan is in many ways the technological heart of the modern media world. A great deal of our electronic equipment necessary to create and transmit mass media messages comes from Japan. NHK is Japan's public broadcasting corporation and is financed similarly to the BBC from fees that all television owners pay.

The most popular magazines in Japan are it's manga or comic books that account for over 40% of the books and magazines published in Japan.[28]

Morocco satellite dishes
© Govert Nieuwland, 2014, Used under license from
Shutterstock, Inc.

Africa

An enormous continent with a large number of countries and different languages, Africa faces many issues when it comes to both geographic and language barriers. However, the media in Africa is expanding rapidly due to advances in telecommunications, especially mobile phones and the Internet.

However, Africa is still largely rural, and most of the smaller towns do not have their own newspapers. Newspaper circulation is limited by high levels of poverty and illiteracy.[29] Radio is the most important medium but it is still mainly received through battery-powered sets. Both of these items are very expensive. The programming is designed to teach people how to improve their standard of living but most often is dominated by politicians.[30]

---

[28] HiroshisTokinoya, "Japan," in *World Broadcasting: A Comparative View*, ed. Alan Wells, Ablex Publishing, Norwood, N.J., 1996.

[29] Ibid.

[30] Ibid.

GLOBAL VILLAGE

As we conclude our discussion of global media, we must point out one very basic fact—these systems and countries do not exist in a vacuum. Instead, they are constantly interacting and, therefore, effecting and changing one another. Like no time before in the history of the world have we been able to connect so quickly with people in other parts of the world.

Cell phone world
©Syda Productions, 2014, Used under license from Shutterstock, Inc.

Mass media technology is changing, has changed, and will continue to change the ways citizens of the world interact and view each other.

While this is apparent today, it wasn't always the case. When television first came into existence in the 1940s, broadcasters focused on the local not the global. Most did not see television's vast potential to bring together the people of the world.

Enter Marshall McLuhan. Canadian scholar, who first coined the phrase Global Village in his 1962 book *The Gutenberg Galaxy: The Making of Typographic Man.* Essentially, McLuhan pictured all of us as members of a single **global village** where the electronic media bring us in touch with everyone, everywhere, instantaneously.[31] He said that closed human systems no longer exist.

While he may not be entirely correct in his view that we will all interact with one another because of the new, electronic media, McLuhan is still discussed because his ideas are sound. We now have the information and we hear about kidnapped school girls taken violently from their classrooms and we hear about Russia taking military movement toward Ukraine. So, as McLuhan said, we now know what goes on. Whether or not we care or we do anything about these occurrences in other countries is always debatable. So, we do live in a smaller world thanks to television and the Internet but do we interact as a small world should?

CONCLUSION

Our world truly is an amazingly large, amazingly diverse planet with billions of people who live dramatically different lives. Thanks to mass media outlets we know all have the capability of being informed all major news events happening around the world within seconds of their occurrences. We also have the ability to communicate instantaneously with anyone we choose in mostly any place anywhere in the world. It is actually an amazing time we live in.

---

[31]Marshall McLuhan, *The Gutenberg Galaxy: The Making of Typographic Man,* University of Toronto Press, Toronto, 1962.

SUMMARY

- The four major theories of the press are authoritarian, libertarian, social responsibility, and Soviet theory.
- A fifth theory of the press for developing nations is called development theory.
- Mass media outlets and their usage in developed and emerging nations are quite extensive and diverse.
- Marshall McLuhan exposed that thanks to television and the electronic media we now live a global village where we are in touch with everyone, everywhere, instantaneously.

DISCUSSION QUESTIONS

1. Which theory of the press do you believe to be the most just and ethical? Why?
2. Discuss the key differences in media usage between developed and emerging nations. Use an example of each for your answer (in order to create more awareness of global media structure, please avoid using the United States for this question).
3. What do you believe is the major stumbling block that emerging nations face in the adoption of mass media?
4. How does the development theory update the four theories of the press?
5. Define and discuss McLuhan's global village.

SUPPLEMENTAL WEB SITES

SUPPLEMENTAL READINGS

SUPPLEMENTAL VIDEOS

GLOSSARY

Abolitionists people who believed in getting rid of slavery

Actual malice the publication of information with the knowledge that it is false

Advertising the act of calling the public's attention to a product, service, or need

Aggregator a tool, built into a portal such as My Yahoo! or iGoogle, that shows the subscriber when there has been an update to a Web site or podcast to which the user subscribes

AM radio a broadcasting system using amplitude modulation; 535 kilohertz to 1.7 megahertz

Analog recording recording method that records sound waves directly onto records or cassettes

Antenna a metallic rod or wire that radiates and receives radio waves

Anthology drama high-quality original hour-long and 90-minute plays that aired weekly, often aired live

ARPANet a network that connected computers at government-supported research sites, such as universities and government laboratories and allowed information and computational resources to be shared

Artist & repertoire (A&R) representatives record company talent scouts

Associated Press a cooperative news agency in the United States

Audiometer a device that can record when a radio set or television set is turned on and to which station

Audion a device used to convert radio frequency into audio frequency, so sounds could be transmitted and amplified

Bait and switch a method of fraudulent advertising in which a company advertises a product at an unprofitable price then reveals to a potential customer that the product is unavailable

Band a defined range of radio frequencies

Big band musical form that is a harder, but slower, form of jazz

Block booking the practice in which studios paired popular films with B-list films that the theaters had to accept and screen as part of the deal

Block printing a printing technique that used pieces of paper applied to a block of inked wood

283

Blogs a combination of the words "web" and "log," which can take a number of different forms, from personal diaries to commentaries on current events or any other imaginable topic

Blues style of African-American folk music that expresses emotions rather than telling a story

Broadsheets an early newspaper consisting of single-page impressions made from the full width of the printer's press

Calamity great misfortune or disaster

Catharsis theory a theory that claims media outlets such as television can ease children's urges to participate in violent behavior

Cathode rays beams of electrons used to project images onto a florescent screen inside a vacuum tube

Censorship the process of regulating speech by prohibiting its publication or broadcast

Children's programming television shows that are appropriate and sometimes educational for children under the age of 12

Citizens band (CB) radio 26.96 megahertz to 27.41 megahertz

Citizen journalism the act of citizens taking an active role in the process of researching, collecting, and reporting news and information

Clear and present danger doctrine a doctrine asserting that the government may only punish a speech act if it invokes a clear and present danger of harm

Codex a method of book making in which sheets of papyrus are folded to make pages, and then the pages are covered with waxed wooden tablets and bound together by string

Commercial speech doctrine a set of Supreme Court mandates giving limited protection to speech that advocates a commercial transaction

Common law rulings handed down by judges

Communication process of transmitting and receiving messages between a sender to a receiver

Community antenna television (CATV) a method of broadcasting that uses tall antenna towers to reach remote areas that are cut off from broadcasting centers

Conglomerate an organized group of many smaller businesses that do not all specialize in the same commercial enterprise

Conservative having right-leaning political ideals

Consumerism the theory that an increase in the consumption of goods and services will benefit the economy

Copyright exclusive legal rights to reproduce, publish, sell, or distribute matter

Corporate social responsibility (CSR) the actions or programs adopted by organizations that reflect an interest in and concern for social and environmental issues

Cultivation theory a theory that views television as a main source of storytelling for heavy viewers

Cutlines the line or paragraph of explanation below a photo

Cyberjock sometimes pejorative term for a disk jockey who hosts a radio show from a single locale that is broadcast widely and uses computer software to localize weather, traffic, and advertisements

Daypart a subsection of the day used in radio or television programming

Damage control the first phase of crisis communication in which PR practitioners identify how the crisis has negatively affected the public's perception of the organization and demonstrate that the organization is taking responsibility and has a plan for solving the crisis

Digital recording recording method that breaks down a recording into numerical code using 0s and 1s and records this code onto magnetic tape or discs

Dime novels paperback books which literally sold for 10 cents

Direct mail a type of advertisement sent through the postal service

Documentary a style of photography, film, or writing that looks with a critical eye at social issues such as poverty and injustice

E-commerce the act of buying or selling of goods or services over an electric system such as the Internet

Economies of scale the decreased per-unit cost as output increases; this is because some resources are less expensive in bulk

Electromagnetic waves movements of energy that can travel at the speed of light in a free space detached from wires

Entrepreneurs the person who organizes, manages, and assumes the risks of a business or enterprise

Ethics a set of principles and beliefs intended to guide people to act in a "right" or "correct" way

Ezines magazines that are only published online

Fairness Doctrine a policy created by the FCC that required the coverage of all controversial issues to be fair and balanced

Fair use doctrine rules allowing for the use of copyrighted materials without permission of the copyright holder for educational use or the benefit of the common good and public domain.

False light the effect caused by the media distorting or falsifying information to imply untruths about someone

Feedback new information created in reaction to the original information

Flatbed press a printing press that uses a flat surface for the type against which paper is pressed, either by another flat surface acting against it or by a cylinder rolling over it

FM radio a broadcasting system using frequency modulation; 88 megahertz to 108 megahertz

Focus group interview a research tool in which small groups of selected consumers are interviewed in a formal but open-ended way that allows them to make known to the researchers their interests, preferences, and concerns

Folk music musical style that uses traditional, often acoustic, instruments and has a political agenda

Frequencies the number of complete oscillations per second of energy (e.g., sound) in the form of waves

Gangsta rap form of hip-hop that acts as a window into a lifestyle of poverty and drug use in inner cities; characterized by hyperrealism, thoughts of immortality, and a romanticized image of the outlaw

Gatekeepers individuals or organizations that act as filters for media messages

General programming shows that included a mix of dramas, comedies, sports, news, game shows, variety, talk shows, and other genres aimed at the widest general audience possible

Genre a style

Gramophone early record player that played flat discs

Greenwashing the practice of companies expressing environmental concerns and/or making their products appear to be environmentally sound

Grunge musical form that is a combination of heavy metal/hard rock and punk rock

Guerrilla marketing an unconventional form of advertising that attempts to get the maximum result from minimal resources

Halftone engravings an engraving used to reproduce an illustration, created by a series of dots

Hip-hop musical style that blends rhythmic beats and rhyming lyrics; the background music for rap

Hyperlocal pertaining to a single community, defined ethnically, geographically, or in some other way

Hypertext transfer protocol (HTTP) the "language" computers use to send and receive documents over the Internet

Hypodermic needle model a theory that suggests that media can "inject" the public with whatever thoughts and opinions the media manipulators want inscribed

Imminent lawless action doctrine a revision to the clear and present danger doctrine asserting that the government may only punish speech that directly provokes imminent lawless action

Incunabula printed materials from the fifteenth century

Indecency material, containing sexual or excretory content that does not rise to the level of obscene, that is protected by the First Amendment but regulated by the FCC

Indie or independent record label; record label that is independently funded and not connected to a major label

Indirect-effects model a theory that states people tend to perceive the effect that media messages has on others and then react to their perception

Infotainment a form of programming that combines current news and feature stories

International Standard Book Number (ISBN) an identification number that can be entered into an international book database

Intrusion upon seclusion a physical invasion of one's personal space or property

Inverted pyramid journalistic style of writing where an article begins with the most important information

Investigative journalism a type of reporting in which reporters deeply investigate a topic of interest, often involving crime, political corruption, or some other scandal

Issues management the second phase of crisis communication in which PR practitioners aim to demonstrate to the public that the organization is working to solve or alleviate the problem through cooperation or negotiation with other organizations

Jazz improvisational musical form developed from ragtime and blues

Jazz journalism the journalism style of the roaring twenties, named after its energetic fashion and well illustrated tabloid layout

Joint operating agreements permitting two newspapers, one considered to be "failing," to share business and operating costs

Jukebox coin-operated electric record player that plays selected records

Laws statutes passed by legislative bodies at federal, state, or local levels; administrative mandates from agencies like the Federal Communications Commission; or rulings handed down by judges to implement policy plans or goals

Libel an untruthful, defamatory statement about someone that is published or broadcast through the media

Liberal bias having left-leaning political ideals

Linear model of mass communication a schematic model of a communication system that explains how a message is developed, delivered, and received

Low-power FM stations (LPFM) hyperlocal radio stations, which transmit over only two to four miles

Many-to-many model a model in which information flows in a decentralized way

Marketplace of ideas a theory of free speech and press asserting that all ideas should be permitted to be published and disseminated so that consumers may pick and choose from among them

Mass communication process of sending messages from a source or sender, through mass media to a large and often anonymous audience

Mass media vehicles of communication that allow senders to reach a large, anonymous audience

MBO management by objectives, a technique used by professional managers and borrowed by public relations professionals; it involves laying out specific, quantifiable goals for PR campaigns

Mean world syndrome a condition in which a person interprets the world as a far more dangerous place that it is in reality

Media facilitators industries, such as public relations and advertising, that make the creation and distribution of mass media possible because, directly or indirectly, they underwrite the cost of disseminating information cheaply to large audiences

Media literacy the ability to understand and utilize different forms of mass media

Medium a channel by which a message is delivered

Megahertz one million cycles per second

Misappropriation the use of someone else's name or likeness for commercial gain without consent

Modeling a type of learning that occurs when an individual observes the actions of others to gain information on how to behave

Modem a device that allows computers to "talk" and exchange data by using existing telephone networks

Mosaic a television tube that consists of many tiny photoelectric particles that convert light to an electric charge

Moveable type a printing technique in which individual characters were created and put together to create a full text

Muckraking a term associated with a group of American investigative reporters, novelists, and critics from the late 1800s to early 1900s, who investigated and exposed societal issues such as conditions in slums and prisons, factories, insane asylums, sweatshops, mines, child labor and unsanitary conditions in food processing plants

Musical symbols handwritten accounts of musical notations

Must-carry rule a FCC regulation stating that all local signals had to be carried on cable if it is requested by a local station.

Narrowcasting the act of offering channels for specialized audiences such as children, rock music fans, sports enthusiasts, and hobbyists

Negligence journalistic sloppiness

Network a number of interconnected computers that are able to share data electronically

Newsweekly a magazine dedicated to summarizing the week's news in capsule form

Newsworthiness a news item's level of interest to the general public; determined by characteristics such as timeliness, proximity, and consequence

Nickelodeons parlors that allowed patrons to listen to recordings for a nickel

Niche a smaller subgroup with specific interests

Obscenity material not protected by the First Amendment and determined by the *Miller* test

Oligopoly control of the market by only a few, rather than many, companies

One-to-many model a model in which a centralized cluster of producers tightly controls the content that is created and distributed to consumers

Open architecture networking a process in which networks with fixed standard interfaces would be interconnected by open "gateways"

Outdoor advertising the placement of ads outside in the view of the general public, typically on billboards, signs, or other outdoor objects

Packet switching a form of technology that takes large chunks of computer data and breaks them up into smaller, more manageable pieces, or packets, that can move through any open circuit to a specific destination

Paid search a form of advertising used on a search engine Web site, which allows companies to have a brief advertisement placed on top or next to search results when certain keywords are used

Papyrus a plant that is mashed into a watery pulp and then pressed into long rolls for use as a material on which to be written

Parchment a thin material made from calfskin, goatskin, or sheepskin that is untreated and used as a material on which to be written

Partisan a firm adherent to a party, faction, cause, or person

Patent law statutes giving inventors exclusive rights to benefit from their inventions for a limited time if those inventions are novel, useful, and not obvious

Pass-along rate the frequency at which a publication changes readers

Pay-per-click a form of advertising in which Web page administrators allow outside companies to place advertisements on their Web pages in exchange for a small fee, which is paid to the Web site administrator, when a user clicks on the ad

Payne Fund Studies a series of 13 studies conducted to examine the various aspects of potential effects of motion pictures on individuals, specifically children

Penny press cheap, tabloid-style papers produced in the middle of the 19th century

Phonograph earliest form of the record player

Photoelectricity the act of turning light into an electric signal

Photojournalism the use of photography to document life

Piracy illegal duplication of copyrighted works

Placeshifting consuming live, recorded, or stored music, television shows, or other media on a remote device, either online or over a data network

Plagiarism the presentation of someone else's exact or close words or ideas as one's own original work

Podcast a digital audio or video media file that can be downloaded to a user's computer or MP3 player for listening or viewing at the consumer's leisure

Point of sale advertising the placement of products, promotions, or other offers on or near a checkout counter

Policy an overarching plan or goal of a country or an organization

Political propaganda a widely distributed piece of communication used to harness support for political objectives

Press agent/publicity model a PR model, favored by P.T. Barnum, that emphasizes promotion and publicity with little regard for facts

Print-on-demand a publishing method that prints manuscripts as they are needed

Prior restraint banning the publication or broadcast of material after prior review

Prior review the process of regulating speech by reviewing it in advance of publication

Profanity material, including words that are so highly offensive that their utterance may be considered a nuisance, protected by the First Amendment but regulated by the FCC

Propaganda information deliberately spread to help or hurt the reputation of an individual, organization, or country

Psychographics the process of using research that attempts to measure the values and lifestyles of an audience

Public affairs reporting journalism that informs readers, listeners and viewers about ongoing events and activities

Public information model a PR model, favored by Ivy Lee, that emphasizes one-way (source-receiver, or producer-consumer) dissemination of truthful information

Public opinion poll a research tool in which a large group of randomly selected consumers are surveyed on their opinions on a given topic

Pulp fiction paperback books made out of cheap pulp material

Public relations (PR) the business of bringing about public awareness, understanding, and goodwill toward a person or organization

Punk aggressive form of rock music characterized by confrontational, socially aware lyrics and a sped-up style of music

RACE formula John E. Marston's construct for the implementation of a successful public relations program involving four steps: research, action, communication, and evaluation

Rack jobbers contractors hired by retail stores to stock and order music for the store

Radio telecommunication modulated by electromagnetic waves; may also refer to radio programming, modern music radio, the radio industry, or radio stations in general

Ragtime musical style that displaces regular accents by emphasizing weak beats

Rap vocal style characterized by rhythmic speaking

Ratings statistical measures of listeners or viewers of broadcast programming

Reality TV programs that focus on non-actors that produce unscripted dialog

Rebranding the process through which a product, service, or organization is marketed and associated with new, different, and improved identity

Receiver a component of a mass media message that receives mass media messages from senders

Reckless disregard the lack of media concern over the truth or falsity of the information they are publishing

Records copies of sound recordings that are in the shape of a flat disc

R&B (rhythm and blues) musical form that is a combination of blues and big band and was influential in the formation of rock and roll

Rockabilly musical form that is a combination of rock and roll and hillbilly music

Rotary press a printing press in which the images to be printed are curved around a cylinder

Royalties payments made to the author of a work for sales and live performances

RSS feeds a family of Web feed formats used to publish frequently updated works in a standardized format

Satellite radio radio created from digital signals sent through satellites in space; allows for commercial-free broadcasting over a broad geographical area

Scanning the act of viewing all the elements of a picture successively, rather than all at once, and sending them in a specific order over a single circuit

Scriptoria a room in a monastery used for writing

Sedition criticism of the government or its officials

Selective perception theory a theory that states that individuals respond and perceive media messages differently, based mostly on their own personal needs and interests

Sender Individual, organization or institution involved in the creation and/or transmission of messages to receivers

Share a measurement that is used to express a network's percentage of the viewing audience

Shock-jock a slang term for a disk jockey or talk show host who pushes the boundaries of what is offensive

Shortwave radio 5.9 megahertz to 26.1 megahertz

Sidebar shorter pieces that provide background context or commentary to a main article

Situation comedy a program that typically consists of a group of characters placed in a familiar setting or situation that ultimately generates humorous activity

Sketch comedy shows a program with a series of short comedy scenes

Soap operas serial stories told through a series of characters, usually in installments

Social bookmarking an online place to store URLs to favorite Web sites, share them with others, and see what others are storing

Social learning the process of learning behavior that is controlled by environmental influences rather than by inherent or internal forces

Social networking a trend in which users connect with one another based on shared interests, geography, history, or other factors

Social responsibility model the idea that the media have responsibilities as well as rights and should work toward fostering positive, informed self-governance

Spin PR tactic in which a specific point of view of interpretation of an event is presented with the intention of influencing public opinion

Stereo or stereophonic sound; reproduction of sound using multiple audio channels, such as speakers

Streaming a method of relaying video or audio material over the Internet

Subpublics specialized audiences with specialized information needs and interests that PR professionals must identify before implementing and specifically targeting a program

Superstations broadcast stations that decided to serve the entire country instead of just their local broadcast area by offering themselves to cable operators

Synergy the working together of various entertainment ventures (such as a book, a movie, a theme park exhibit, and retail merchandise) that are all born from a single entertainment property

Tabloids newspapers that tends to emphasize sensational stories and gossip columns

Television stations 54 to 88 megahertz for channels 3 through 6; 174 to 220 megahertz for channels 7 through 13

Third-person effects hypothesis A theory that states that people tend to believe media messages influence others more than themselves

Timeshifting using DVRs or VCRs to recording a show for later consumption

Tin Pan Alley area in New York, near Broadway, that was a popular source for sheet music before the popularity of radio and the record player

Tort an injury or wrong inflicted on one person by another person, who is legally responsible for any damages sought

Trademark law statutes shielding consumers from confusion by protecting words, symbols, or phrases used to identify products and distinguish them from each other

Transmission-control protocol (TCP) an official procedure, which allowed computers to communicate efficiently and consequently be joined in a coherent network of servers

Two-step theory a theory proposed that media messages first influenced economic and political power elites, or opinion leaders, who later propagated them through interpersonal contact or by using the media themselves

Two-way asymmetric model A PR model in which formative research is used to ascertain the attitudes of the target public before a PR plan is implemented; it recognizes that the actions and behaviors of consumer publics affect the actions and behaviors of producers in the competitive business system

Two-way symmetric model A PR model most often applied to businesses subject to heavy government regulation, or where the activist consumer has as much influence as the producer; it recognizes that balanced communication is necessary to adapt the organization to the realities of society

Ubiquity the capability of being everywhere at any time

Underground press independent publications that focus on unpopular themes, or counterculture issues

Uniform resource locator (URL) an address system to store and locate information

Uses and gratifications theory a theory that placed even greater influence on personal needs and individual uses of the media to define how messages affected audiences

Vanity presses printing houses that publish works at the author's expanse

Variety show a live show that features numerous acts such as dancers, musicians, and comedians

Vellum a finer quality of parchment

Vernacular languages non-Latin languages

Vertical integration a process in which one company controls a product from its inception to its final form

Victrola record player with a hand crank designed to look like a piece of furniture

Viral videos videos that are passed on from user to user

Voice-tracking software computer software used in radio programming that allows a DJ to hear the end of one song and the beginning of another so he or she can record the voice tracks so they sound live, though it is played back at a later time. After recording the "break", the song is encoded and can be transmitted anywhere on radio or Internet

Webzines magazines that are only published online

Wire service an organization of journalists established to supply news reports to organizations in the news trade: newspapers, magazines, and radio and television broadcasters

Woodcuts an artistic technique in printmaking in which an image is carved into the surface of a block of wood

Yellow journalism a type of journalism that downplays legitimate news in favor of eye-catching headlines that sell more newspapers

INDEX